WASTE NOT

D1193364

WASTE NOT

A JEWISH ENVIRONMENTAL ETHIC

TANHUM S. YOREH

SUNY
PRESS

Published by State University of New York Press, Albany

© 2019 State University of New York

All rights reserved

Printed in the United States of America

No part of this book may be used or reproduced in any manner whatsoever without written permission. No part of this book may be stored in a retrieval system or transmitted in any form or by any means including electronic, electrostatic, magnetic tape, mechanical, photocopying, recording, or otherwise without the prior permission in writing of the publisher.

For information, contact State University of New York Press, Albany, NY
www.sunypress.edu

Library of Congress Cataloging-in-Publication Data

Names: Yoreh, Tanhum, author.
Title: Waste not : a Jewish environmental ethic / Tanhum S. Yoreh.
Description: Albany : State University of New York Press, [2019] | Includes bibliographical references and index.
Identifiers: LCCN 2018057054 | ISBN 9781438476698 (hardcover : alk. paper) | ISBN 9781438476704 (pbk. : alk. paper) ISBN 9781438476711 (ebook)
Subjects: LCSH: Human ecology—Religious aspects—Judaism. | Bal tashḥit (Jewish law) | Food—Religious aspects—Judaism. | Environmental protection—Religious aspects—Judaism. | Environmental law (Jewish law) | Theological anthropology—Judaism—History of doctrines. | Environmental ethics. | Rabbinical literature—History and criticism.
Classification: LCC BM538.H85 Y67 2019 | DDC 296.3/8—dc23
LC record available at https://lccn.loc.gov/2018057054

10 9 8 7 6 5 4 3 2 1

In honor of my family

Contents

Transliteration and Abbreviations	ix
Preface	xi
Acknowledgments	xiii
Introduction	1
Chapter 1: Classical Rabbinic Texts	39
Chapter 2: Bible and Biblical Commentaries	101
Chapter 3: Codes and Their Cognates	167
Chapter 4: Responsa	203
Conclusions	235
Appendix	259
Bibliography	265
Concept Index	283
Name Index	287
Source Index	289

Transliteration and Abbreviations

Consonants

Ḥet = Ḥ/ḥ
Kaf = K
Khaf = Kh
Kof = Q
Tzadi = Tz

Vowels

Tzeireh maleh = ei.

Sheva na and *Sheva naḥ* are generally not distinguished.

There are variant spellings for certain names and terms. My spellings are consistent throughout, but when they appear in a citation, or in the bibliographical details of a source, I have left them in the form they appear in those texts.

For first names and surnames of individuals, there is some deviation from this system due to the commonly accepted spellings in English. For instance, Yitzḥak is spelled with a k instead of a q, unless the bibliographical details provided in the source indicate a variant spelling.

Words with two or more vowels in a row have the syllables separated with an apostrophe (e.g., *hana'ah*).

Foreign words that have not been adopted by the English language are italicized.

Hebrew words with English suffixes have not been italicized (e.g., *amoraim* is italicized, amoraic is not).

As is standard elsewhere, I have anthropomorphized certain classical rabbinic texts where appropriate. Instead of using the turn of phrase "anonymous voice of the Talmud" or "redactors of the Talmud" (*stam* or *stama* with definite article in Aramaic), I anthropomorphize the text by using terms such as "the Talmud explains" or "the Talmud rejects."

Abbreviations

Rabbinic texts are often presented in their shortened form followed by the name of the specific tractate:

Mishnah = m, Tosefta = t, and Babylonian Talmud = b (e.g., b*Baba Qama*, m*Shevi'it*).

Preface

I could start this book by telling you about the dire consequences of anthropogenic pollution, the resulting climate change, the loss of biodiversity, and the cracks developing in human resilience. People do not want to hear that, though. Chances are, if you are picking up this book, you are already well aware of the perilous condition we find ourselves in and do not require any not-so-subtle reminders. This is a book that explores a hopeful avenue of faith-based wisdom relating to the Jewish prohibition against wastefulness, and explores its journey over the course of history. Faith is one of the greatest arbiters of values and social norms, and although still underdeveloped in terms of environmental values, it has enormous potential to mitigate human impact on the environment. Religion continues to play a strong role in people's lives as they try to cope with the volatility of our times in hopes of finding solace and enlightenment in age-old traditions. Environmentalists have begun to turn their attention to religion, rereading traditional teachings in light of contemporary knowledge. Jewish and Christian wisdom on the environment—or lack thereof—has become a lightning rod in current debate. This book, however, is not an attempt to create an ecotheology. At its core, ecotheology is a constructive theology, and while it is anchored in text and tradition, it reads meaning into the text instead of taking meaning out of the text. This book hopes to avoid reading texts anachronistically, even though ecotheologians often do so knowingly and openly. To the extent possible, this book tries to focus on the *Sitz im Leben* of the texts it analyzes.

The existence of a prohibition against wastefulness in Judaism might lead to expectations that religiously observant communities of Jews would go to great lengths to not be wasteful.[1] There is no indi-

1. Certainly, such communities do exist, especially in liberal Jewish circles.

cation, however, that religious communities are more or less wasteful than society at large. Why is this the case? Is the prohibition against wastefulness not the environmental ethic that it is claimed by some to be? Or, are the parameters of the prohibition as conceptualized throughout history more limiting than many environmentalists expect? The things we throw away, our food waste, the inefficiency of electricity systems, the type of fuel we burn, our (over-)consumption and the associated pollution, many of the environmental choices we make, and those we don't, all come under the purview of wastefulness. Having an existing religious ethic related to avoiding wastefulness, yet a seemingly underwhelming manifestation of the ethic in practice makes for a compelling study. It also gives hope for the future possibility of alignment between the theory and the practice as an environmentalist may envision it.

This book charts the development of the prohibition against wastefulness, and through this narrative it creates a discourse, easily understood by both environmentalists and faith communities, that aims to bridge the gap between theory and practice. Academically it advances our knowledge of the ethical concept of prohibiting wastefulness, while socially it provides a new foundation and framework for dialogue while advancing responsible stewardship of the environment.

Acknowledgments

Writing this book has been one of the most humbling experiences in my life. Coffee, love, and an unwavering commitment to the content found in these pages are what fueled me to the finish line. There is no way I could have accomplished this work without the help and support of many.

First and foremost, I want to thank my teachers Marty Lockshin and Eric Lawee for being with me from the very beginning of my intellectual journey into the Jewish prohibition against wastefulness. They have shaped much of my thinking on this topic, and their helpful insights can be found throughout the pages of this book.

The previously anonymous and now revealed reviewers, Martin Yaffe and Julia Watts Belser, were instrumental in improving the quality and accessibility of the manuscript, and while this book is far from perfect, it is much improved thanks to them.

Thank you to my editor, Rafael Chaiken, who guided me throughout the challenging process of turning my manuscript into a book. Thank you also to the rest of the wonderful team at SUNY Press for helping me get to the finish line, in particular Ryan Morris, Daniel Otis, and Michael Campochiaro.

I would also like to thank SUNY Press for agreeing to print my book in the most ecologically sound manner available to them.

I'd like to thank Nicholas de Lange for the opportunities he gave me to present parts of this research in a variety of forums during the time I spent in Cambridge.

Thank you to Reuven Leigh and Rochel Leigh, for the intellectually stimulating conversations and physical and spiritual sustenance over three years of Shabbat dinners as I worked on this project.

Thank you to Daniel Weiss for the conversations we shared on wastefulness and self-harm.

Thank you to Steven Hermans for encouraging me to prioritize the completion of this book.

Thank you to Stephen Scharper, Kim Strong, and Steve Easterbrook from the School of the Environment at the University of Toronto for their mentorship and for supporting my research.

Thank you to Ben Carniol for his advice on choosing an appropriate title for the book. His gentle thoughtfulness helped shape the part of the book that will be read by the broadest audience.

My deepest gratitude to Oz Aloni for sharpening some of the philological nuances in this book.

Most importantly, I would like to thank my family for the tireless intellectual and moral support over the years that I've engaged in this research. My parents, Harry Fox and Tirzah Meacham, gave generously of their time and acted as sounding boards for my ideas. They encouraged me when I needed it most and always made themselves available to me. One of my earliest memories is going with my parents to a central recycling depot in Toronto, before curbside recycling was available. They instilled in me a passion for caring for the environment and those who dwell in it. This book reflects those values.

I'd like to thank my brother, Tzemah Yoreh, sister, Yoam Yoreh, and brother-in-law, Matthew Iannucci, for their enthusiastic support of me in general and this work specifically, which included looking at sections of this book and helping me improve them.

Thank you to my son, Ḥoni Ben Tzion, who is so often a source of joy and inspiration.

My partner and spouse, Shoshanna Saxe, has been a beacon of light who has lit the path and walks together with me on it. She has often helped me bring some of the esotericism of my work into the practical world. She is a door-opener, a trailblazer, and an inspiration; she is an engineer.

And finally, thank you to you, my reader, for taking interest in this important topic. I hope you will read, learn, enjoy, and share with a friend.

Tanhum S. Yoreh
May 7, 2019
Toronto, Canada

Introduction

Bal tashḥit, the Jewish prohibition against wastefulness and destruction, is considered to be an ecological ethical principle by Jewish environmentalists. This book investigates whether this prohibition has the historical basis to be considered an environmental principle, or whether its interpretation as such is primarily a contemporary development. To this end, the study uses the methodology of tradition histories to produce an intellectual history of the prohibition against wastefulness. This research critically examines the conceptualization of *bal tashḥit* as it develops from its biblical origins. The book traces its evolution through examining relevant passages dealing with wastefulness and destruction in Hebrew Scripture, rabbinic literature, halakhic codes, responsa, the accompanying commentary traditions, as well as the works of scholars in the field of religion and environment. It highlights the important stages in the development of the prohibition, notes the most influential scholars, and uncovers the critical vocabulary that emerges. Perhaps most importantly, it emphasizes the strong connection between self-harm and wastefulness in the conceptualization of the prohibition. This link has been almost completely absent from the contemporary environmental discourse surrounding *bal tashḥit* despite the fact that the connection between harm to humans and the act of wastefulness is fundamental to mainstream environmentalism.

Exploring the Field

Those unfamiliar with the field of religion and environment often ask how the two are related. Roger Gottleib, a scholar of religion and environment and the editor of *The Oxford Handbook on Religion and*

Ecology, has defined the relationship in the following manner: "For as long as human beings have practiced them, the complex and multifaceted beliefs, rituals, and moral teachings known as religion have told us how to think about and relate to everything on earth that we did not make ourselves."[1] Religions in the Abrahamic traditions are accompanied by codes of law and ethical systems about how humans should conduct themselves in society in reference to God, fellow humans, and the natural world. Some argue that these precepts are directly related to the way humans have related to their ecological surroundings over the past millennia.[2]

In "The Historical Roots of Our Ecologic Crisis"—a seminal essay that sparked the development of the entire field of religion and environment—Lynn White Jr. argued that the Judeo-Christian tradition is to blame for the modern environmental crisis.[3] He based this position on the dominion of humans over the rest of the created world found in Genesis 1:28: "God blessed them and God said to them, 'Be fertile and increase, fill the earth and master it; and rule the fish of the sea, the birds of the sky, and all the living things that creep on the earth.' "[4] More specifically, White Jr. argued that "Christianity . . . insisted that it is God's will that man exploit nature for his proper ends,"[5] and that "[b]y destroying pagan animism, Christianity made it possible to exploit nature in a mood of indifference to the feelings of natural objects."[6]

White Jr.'s argument elicited a lively debate, with many agreeing or disagreeing with him to varying degrees. Peter Harrison summarizes the many ways in which White Jr.'s argument has been criticized:

---

1. Roger S. Gottleib, "Introduction: Religion and Ecology—What Is the Connection and Why Does It Matter?," in *The Oxford Handbook of Religion and Ecology*, ed. Roger S. Gottleib (New York: Oxford University Press, 2006), 3.

2. Some argue that ecological realities greatly shaped traditions and their associated values. See Bron Taylor, "Critical Perspectives on 'Religions of the World and Ecology,' " in *The Encyclopedia of Religion, Nature and Culture*, ed. Bron Taylor (New York: Continuum Books, 2008), 1376.

3. Lynn White Jr., "The Historical Roots of Our Ecologic Crisis," *Science* 155, no. 3767 (1967): 1203–7.

4. All quotes in English translation from the Hebrew Bible are taken from the NJPS version unless otherwise stated. *The Jewish Study Bible*, eds. Adele Berlin and Marc Zvi Brettler (New York: Oxford University Press, 2004).

5. White Jr., "Our Ecologic Crisis," 1205. White Jr.'s critique was of Judaism and Christianity, but the major thrust of his argument was directed toward Christianity.

6. Ibid.

"Historians have pointed out that the exploitation of nature is not unique to the West; biblical scholars have maintained that the relevant passages of the Judeo-Christian scriptures do not sustain the interpretation placed on them by White and his followers; social scientists have claimed that no correlation presently obtains between Christian belief and indifference to the fortunes of the environment."[7] A Google search reveals that White Jr.'s article has been cited in academic scholarship over 6,000 times.[8] In the over five decades since the paper was published, religion and environment has been established as an academic field of study. Mary Evelyn Tucker and John Grim made significant headway in expanding the field through the creation of the Harvard series, Religions of the World and Ecology, and the Forum on Religion and Ecology at Yale, which, among many other things, acts as a central academic resource for scholars in the area.[9] A growing number of universities offer courses on the topic from a wide variety of approaches. White Jr.'s essay has remained central to the field over the years, and students in undergraduate university courses dealing with environmental thought from a religious or philosophical approach are often required to write a critique of the paper.

Those critiquing White Jr. make up the earliest wave of scholarship on religion and environment. Due to White Jr.'s attack on the environmental record of the Jewish and Christian traditions, adherents of these religions were the first to respond to his essay. Not surprisingly, given the accusatory nature of White Jr.'s claims, these responses, written by scholars, clergy, and activists, were often theologically and emotionally driven.[10] Like White Jr., religious environmentalists and

7. Peter Harrison, "Subduing the Earth: Genesis 1, Early Modern Science, and the Exploitation of Nature," *Journal of Religion* 79, no. 1 (1999): 86–87.

8. To be exact, 6,168 times as of May 3, 2019.

9. See http://fore.research.yale.edu. Bron Taylor critiqued the Harvard series ("Critical Perspectives" 1375–76) for a number of reasons, including the argument that the series is steeped in what Willis Jenkins categorized as a confessional/ethical approach instead of a historical/social one. (See Willis Jenkins, "After Lynn White: Religious Ethics and Environmental Problems," *Journal of Religious Ethics* 37, no. 2 [2009]: 289.) *The Encyclopedia of Religion, Nature and Culture* comes in part as a response to such criticism.

10. For example, see N. J. Loevinger, "(Mis)reading Genesis: A Response to Environmentalist Critiques of Judaism," in *Ecology and the Jewish Spirit: Where Nature and the Sacred Meet*, ed. Ellen Bernstein (Woodstock, VT: Jewish Lights Publishing, 1998), 32–40; R. C. J. Wybrow, *The Bible, Baconianism, and Mastery over Nature: The Old Testament and Its Modern Misreading* (New York: Peter Lang Publishing, 1991).

scholars of religion and environment used biblical verses in a polemical manner to strengthen their arguments and deliver their messages. They highlighted biblical teachings that lend themselves more readily to demonstrating the environmental concern of the Bible through ideas such as stewardship and sustainability. However, as they generally did not consult the rich, millennia-long interpretive traditions of these sources, their environmental readings of the primary texts often lack an historic basis.

Lynn White Jr.'s claims have been debated widely. Willis Jenkins, for instance, lamented over how White Jr. has shaped the field, drawing attention to the "cosmological roots of environmental problems"[11] instead of other possibly more productive areas. What Jenkins meant by this was that White Jr.'s emphasis on the story of creation as establishing human superiority over the nonhuman world, resulting in the current ecological crisis, was most often rebuffed by creating new cosmologies in which humans were no longer at the top of the hierarchy or the center of attention. Such an approach does not necessarily lead to solving the ecological crisis. The field of religion and environment has started to move on to address other critical areas such as social, legal and historical approaches as well as that of lived religion. The main reason I mention Lynn White Jr. and his legacy is that my own methodology addresses some of his shortcomings.

It is important to understand the extent to which environmental ideas are supported by tradition histories. Reading environmental themes into primary sacred texts allows for a new and important multilayered commentary tradition. Indeed, it is precisely this type of reading that ecotheologians strongly advocate. Roger Gottleib states that "ecotheologians of all types are showing that whatever meaning their texts had *in the past*, for religious environmentalism they must have a different meaning *now*."[12] With regard to the specific edict prohibiting wastefulness he adds, "the warning not to waste . . . [is] *in the scriptures*. In the past, however, such key passages were not used for environmental purposes. Hence the old words must be read anew."[13] The call to reimagine faith-based traditions is shared by Larry Rasmussen, who argues that in a world undergoing "the

11. Willis Jenkins, "After Lynn White," 286.

12. Roger Gottleib, *A Greener Faith: Religious Environmentalism and Our Planet's Future* (New York: Oxford University Press, 2006), 23.

13. Ibid., 24.

death of nature . . . the world's faiths are not up to the present task [of changing course] in most of their present forms."[14] He claims that faiths must take on new expressions to enable them to contend with our degraded environment. Yet he affirms that the reimagining still happens within a faith-based framework: "This is not about beginning, but re-beginning."[15] He evokes Psalms 137, claiming that "we must learn a new song in a strange land."[16]

In a similar vein, Clifford Chalmers Cain offers the essence of ecotheology in a single sentence. He suggests that what we need is "a new consciousness of nature and a new vision of God . . . which see human life as profoundly interrelated with all other forms of life."[17] Jay McDaniel explains the reimagining of tradition through process theology: "Some elements of a path are given to each generation of walkers: the creeds, codes, ritual practices, role models, and memories that they inherit from predecessor generations. These elements help them get their bearings and gain a general sense of direction. Nevertheless, in response to contemporary challenges and opportunities, the actions of the present generation are forever adding new chapters to a religion's history. This means that a world religion, when understood as a social and historical movement in time, is slightly different in every age."[18] According to McDaniel's approach, it is fitting that the changes made in religions during our time should reflect our heightened environmental awareness.

Two of the driving figures behind the emergence of religion and ecology, John Grim and Mary Evelyn Tucker, acknowledge that religions have historically been a source for both positive and negative developments. They advocate for a reimagining of religions in light of environmental urgency. The last century has seen major advances in "equity, fairness and justice,"[19] and they call "to extend this sense

14. Larry L. Rasmussen, *Earth-Honoring Faith: Religious Ethics in a New Key* (New York: Oxford University Press, 2013), 5–6.

15. Ibid., 5.

16. Ibid., 4.

17. Clifford Chalmers Cain, *An Ecological Theology: Reunderstanding Our Relation to Nature*. Toronto Studies in Theology, Vol. 98 (Lewiston, NY: Edwin Mellon Press, 2009) 1.

18. Jay McDaniel, "Ecotheology and World Religions," in *Ecospirit: Religions and Philosophies for the Earth*, eds. Laurel Kearns and Catherine Keller (New York: Fordham University Press, 2007) 37.

19. John Grim and Mary Evelyn Tucker, *Ecology and Religion* (Washington, DC: Island Press, 2014), 15.

of responsibility and inclusivity not only to other humans but also to nature itself."[20]

Arthur Waskow is a strong advocate for engaging in constructive theology in the Jewish context. In support of establishing an eco-Judaism, he writes "Jews have valued the wisdom of the past, without letting it straitjacket them. The practice of midrash, in which an old text was turned in a new direction to afford new meaning, was not just a verbal trick but a deep assertion that the wisdom of previous generations was still important, even when changes needed to be made."[21] David Mevorach Seidenberg builds on Waskow's constructive reimagining of Judaism by claiming that ethics is not enough:

> Generally, Jewish environmental ethics is an area in which both traditional and academic scholars have been content to describe what Judaism already says. But Jewish theology needs to catch up with the urgency of the times. . . . One purpose of theology is to ask, What *should* Judaism say? or, How should we revise what Judaism says in light of what we now know?[22]

While not rejecting *bal tashḥit* as having distinct environmental significance, he rejected the notion that it could be the foundation of a Jewish ecotheology. Seidenberg writes,

> How far have we already come in Jewish ecotheology? *Bal tashchit,* the prohibition against wasting, is a good litmus test. This principle . . . is both far-reaching . . . and extremely limiting. . . . The spiritual importance of *bal tashchit* is not insignificant . . . but the legal framework around *bal tashchit* makes it ineffective for preventing environmental abuses. Any Jewish environmental curriculum or theology that is serious will acknowledge these limitations.[23]

---

20. Ibid.

21. Arthur Waskow, ed., *Torah of the Earth: Exploring 4,000 Years of Ecology in Jewish Thought* (Woodstock, VT: Jewish Lights Publishing, 2000), xiii.

22. David Mevorach Seidenberg, *Kabbalah and Ecology: God's Image in a More-Than-Human World* (New York: Cambridge University Press, 2015), 14.

23. Ibid., 12–13.

Such a position is perhaps somewhat surprising in light of Seidenberg's goal of advancing a Jewish ecotheology. Even if those who adhere to *bal tashḥit* currently practice it within a narrow framework, the basis exists for it to be significantly broadened, depending on how we understand what wastefulness is.

I, too, am a strong advocate of reimagining religion in light of environmentalism. If environmental values are to have any hope of becoming entrenched in our behavior as individuals and as societies, constructive theology is an extremely useful ally. Yet this approach has its limitations. It is not the only way. Ultimately, if the commentary traditions do not sustain environmental readings of the primary texts, it is unlikely that they will be as widely adopted as environmentalists hope. Consulting the tradition histories more widely will bypass some of the academic challenges of anachronistically embedding environmental ideas into primary sources in order to pursue an ideological agenda. Neither approach will speak to everyone, but together they expand the accessibility of faith-based environmental wisdom.

One of the most common critiques of White Jr. was that he neglected to acknowledge the "environmental" content of Genesis 2:15 found in the very next chapter of the Genesis narrative: "The Lord God took the man and placed him in the garden of Eden, to till it and tend it." Within religious environmental discourse, scholars who highlight this passage argue that any dominion granted in Genesis 1:28 was tempered by Genesis 2:15, recasting the role of humanity as stewards, not dominators. Elsewhere I have highlighted the limitations of such conclusions, primarily because until very recently these verses were not read that way.[24] Although Jeremy Cohen has conducted the most thorough study of the tradition histories of Genesis 1:28, he did not extend his study to Genesis 2:15, and therefore his disagreement with White Jr.'s thesis warranted revisiting the topic. In his introduction, Cohen claims, "Although most readers of Genesis casually assumed that God had fashioned the physical world for the benefit of human beings, Gen. 1:28 evoked relatively little concern with the issue of dominion over nature. One might, of course, find that other biblical texts did evince such concern, but in the exegesis of Gen. 1:28 other

24. See Tanhum Yoreh, "Environmental Embarrassment: Genesis 1:26–28 vs. Genesis 2:15," in *Vixens Disturbing Vineyards: Embarrassment and Embracement of Scriptures*, eds. Tzemah Yoreh, Aubrey Glazer, Justin Jaron Lewis, and Miryam Segal (Boston: Academic Studies Press, 2010), 558–91.

issues so eclipsed the matter of dominion that the little attention it receives in this book might appear to be unfair or perhaps altogether unnecessary. Yet the imbalance accurately reflects the data and itself comprises a significant result of this book."[25] In my own review of the Jewish commentaries on Genesis 1:28, I arrived at significantly different conclusions than Cohen concerning White Jr.'s dominion thesis. I argued that the vast majority of the Jewish commentators on this verse take what I termed a "dominionist" approach.[26] While it is true that few had expanded this view with detailed glosses on what this dominion included, they nevertheless saw the dominion of humans over the rest of creation as true mastery, one unmitigated by responsibilities of stewardship, at least in their readings of this specific verse. This does not mean that they necessarily condoned human devastation of the environment. Had they perceived the notion of dominion as limited by environmental responsibility, however, they would probably have mentioned this responsibility specifically in the context of this verse. Moreover, some of the more detailed glosses on the dominion aspect of Genesis 1:28 come from the most influential and important historical Jewish scholars, whose impact on Jewish theory and practice is still felt today. This means that their focus on human mastery over the rest of the created world, and the lack of attention to issues of environmental responsibility, have had a significant effect on the reading of Genesis 1:28 over the centuries.

For instance, one such individual is Saadiah ben Yosef (882–942, Egypt and Babylonia), the head of the important Babylonian academy of Sura and the most important and influential Jewish thinker of his time. As Sarah Stroumsa states: "Saadya's towering figure dominates the emergence of medieval Jewish scholarship in all fields: linguistics and poetics, philosophy and exegesis, polemics and law."[27] Although his gloss on Genesis 1:28 is too lengthy to present here in full, Saadiah Gaon had by far the most detailed account of the ways in which humans hold dominion over the natural world. Some choice excerpts illustrate his approach:

---

25. Jeremy Cohen, *Be Fertile and Increase, Fill the Earth and Master It: The Ancient and Medieval Career of a Biblical Text* (Ithaca, NY: Cornell University Press, 1989), 5.

26. Tanhum Yoreh, "Environmental Embarrassment."

27. Sarah Stroumsa, "Saadya and Jewish *Kalam*," in *The Cambridge Companion to Medieval Jewish Philosophy*, eds. Daniel H. Frank and Oliver Leaman (Cambridge, UK: Cambridge University Press, 2003), 71.

> "Ruling" includes the [use of] equipment by which man may gain dominion over the animals. Over some of them [he has dominion] with mines and hobbles and over others with cords and reins and yet others with pits and collar [and][28] hunting equipment. . . . Others are with cages and towers and the like until God teaches {man} everything [about this]. . . . [Ruling over] "Fish" includes [the use of] tactics in hunting fish from the bowels of the sea and rivers, preparing those permissible [for eating] with cooking utensils so that {one} can eat it, taking pearls from the shell, benefitting from the parts of the skin and bones that one prepares, and whatever applies to this. . . . "[Ruling over] the birds" accords the [various] tactics to hunt birds that fly in the air and to make them work for us until they [actually are used] to hunt each other.[29]

The dominion of humans over the rest of creation in Saadiah Gaon's gloss to Genesis 1:28 is all-encompassing and offers no hint of an accompanying ethic of stewardship to moderate human mastery.

Moses ben Naḥman (Naḥmanides/Ramban) (1194–1270, Spain and Land of Israel), the intellectual and spiritual leader of Iberian Jewry in the thirteenth century is another such figure. Yaakov Elman describes Naḥmanides as "one of the most influential scholars that Spanish Jewry produced, one whose versatility and scope still astonish."[30] Although his gloss to Genesis 1:28 is significantly shorter, its strong dominionist theme is abundantly clear: "He [God] gave them power and governance on the earth to do as they pleased with livestock and insects and all things that crawl in the dust; and to build, to uproot plants, to mine copper from the earth's mountains and the like."[31] A final example (although there are many others) can

---

28. All brackets in this quote, with the exception of these, belong to the translator. Otherwise, {} brackets signify an editorial clarification, and [] signify added words.

29. For the full text see Saadiah Gaon, *Rabbi Saadiah Gaon's Commentary on the Book of Creation*, ed. and trans. Michael Linetzky (Northvale, NJ: Jason Aronson, 2002), 113–15.

30. Yaakov Elman, "Moses ben Nahman/Nahmanides (Ramban)," in *Hebrew Bible/Old Testament: The History of Its Interpretation*, Vol. 1, *From the Beginnings to the Middle Ages (Until 1300)*, Part 2: *The Middle Ages*, ed. Magne Saebo (Gottingen, Germany: Vandenhoek & Ruprecht, 2000), 416.

31. Moses ben Naḥman, *Peirushei HaTorah LeMoshe ben Naḥman*, 9th ed., ed. Ḥaim Dov Chavel (Jerusalem: Mossad HaRav Kook, 1976), 28.

be found in the writings of Ovadiah Seforno, one of the prominent commentators included in publications of *Miqraot Gedolot*.[32] Avraham Grossman describes Seforno as "one of the most important Bible interpreters of Italian Jewry and greatest scholars of the latter part of the Middle Ages and the Renaissance."[33] In his gloss on Genesis 1:28, Seforno wrote: "'And master it:' . . . and prevent the animals from entering your domain, and you will rule them . . . and subdue them with your nets to make them surrender to your work."[34] The gist of his approach rests on his use of the term "surrender" to define the relationship between humans and the rest of creation. Even though the three figures mentioned here are but a few of the many Bible commentators whose works are well known, they are among the most important commentators of all time, whose interpretations cannot be dismissed as marginal. Their dominionist understanding of the verse has set the predominant discourse for the past millennium. Thus, at least as concerns the tradition histories of Genesis 1:28, however much we may want to dismiss such a reading, we cannot easily do so.

Yet, a single verse does not make a complete tradition history, and many environmentalists pointed to another verse, Genesis 2:15. Here, too, Jewish intellectual history does not align with the favorable environmental perspective that contemporary environmentalists argue derives from the verse. As I state elsewhere, "there is . . . little tradition of environmental interpretation for Genesis 2:15."[35] Although a few glossators offer a glimmer of an environmental ideology in their interpretations of Genesis 2:15,[36] these interpretations are rare and often contrived or only implicit. In fact, when looking at the tradition histories of Genesis 2:15, it is even possible to find a commentary trajectory that reads Genesis 2:15 in light of Genesis 1:28 (contrary to contemporary environmentalists, who read 1:28 in light of 2:15). For instance, Baḥya ibn Paquda (c. 1050–c. 1120 Spain) in his philosophical tome *Sefer Ḥovot HaLevavot* (*The Book of Direction to the Duties of the Heart*) wrote:

---

33. Avraham Grossman, "Rabbi Ovadiah Seforno," in *Jewish Bible Exegesis: An Introduction*, 2nd ed., ed. Moshe Greenberg (Jerusalem: Bialik Institute, 1992), 98.

34. Ovadiah Seforno, *Be'ur HaSeforno al HaTorah*, ed. Ze'ev Gotleib (Jerusalem: Mossad HaRav Kook, 1980), 16.

35. Yoreh, "Environmental Embarrassment," 578.

36. For instance, see Isaac Abarbanel's gloss to Genesis 2:15, also found in Yoreh, 2010.

> 4:3 For He has commanded man to work for his livelihood in this world, by tilling the soil, for instance, by ploughing and sowing, as it is said (Gen. 2:15: "And the Lord God took the man, and put him into the garden of Eden to dress it and keep it," by using the animals for his benefit and for his food, by building cities and preparing all kinds of food, by using women and their fertility for the sake of increasing one's offspring—for all these is man rewarded, if he acts for the sake of God also, in his heart and intention, whether his act is completed or not.[37]

In this dominionist (and male chauvinistic) reading, the "keeping" of the garden entails no elements of stewardship. The opposite is the case; man's keeping of Eden is through dominion and subjugation of the rest of creation, including of women.[38]

Using one verse to establish an entire paradigm without properly exploring and exposing its intellectual history is inherently limited. Scripture is quite commonly taken out of context. Hence the interpretation and reception of Scripture vary over generations and geographical locations. One verse can be used to counter another verse, and in such cases weak arguments may be deconstructed through equally weak counterarguments. In my opinion, the way to establish strong arguments that can stand the test of time is through a critical analysis of the intellectual histories of concepts and ideologies. The interpretation of Genesis 2:15 as an environmentally conscious verse is, by and large, an unsupported modern environmental construct. Regrettably, the intellectual history of the verse does not wholeheartedly support its current usage. This is not to say that the environmentally oriented interpretations of Genesis 2:15 are wrong or undesired—actually, the opposite is true—but that they are not supported by any lengthy historical tradition.

---

37. Baḥya ibn Paquda, *The Book of Direction to the Duties of the Heart*, trans. Menahem Mansoor (London: Routledge and Kegan Paul, 1973), 242.

38. It should be noted that David Seidenberg highlights ibn Paquda's writings on wisdom in nature that are often used (uncritically) in Jewish environmental education. Seidenberg, *Kabbalah and Ecology*, 18–19 n60. This, too, highlights the methodological difficulties with taking individual comments out of context and using them to establish entire paradigms.

Other verses and concepts, however, have a more solid historical basis, and hence have the potential to be more useful for environmental ethics. One such concept is *bal tashḥit*, usually translated as "do not destroy," which is the Jewish prohibition against wasteful and destructive behavior.[39] This prohibition is understood to originate from Deuteronomy 20:19–20:

> 19: When in your war against a city you have to besiege it a long time in order to capture it, you must not destroy its trees, wielding the ax against them. You may eat of them, but you must not cut them down. Are trees of the field human to withdraw before you into the besieged city? 20: Only trees that you know do not yield food may be destroyed; you may cut them down for constructing siege-works against the city that is waging war on you, until it has been reduced.

The sages expanded the biblical verse from a highly contextualized circumstance to a general prohibition against wastefulness and wanton destruction. Though unstated in rabbinic literature, it is widely assumed that they used an *a fortiori* argument that if restrictions on the extent of military engagement exist during wartime, how much more so should similar restrictions be applied during times of peace? The sages then took another conceptual leap, expanding the now peacetime prohibition of cutting down fruit trees to all types of waste and wanton destruction through a newly formulated concept, *bal tashḥit*.

Purpose

Bal tashḥit is a concept that arises frequently in Jewish legal scholarship as well as Jewish environmental discourse. Within environmental discourse, scholars often use *bal tashḥit* as proof that Judaism fits well within the teachings of environmentalism, even though not everyone sees it as a silver-bullet solution to all ecological issues. This perspective is similar to the argument that Genesis 2:15 negates White Jr.'s critique

39. I use "wastefulness" and "destruction" interchangeably with a preference for "wastefulness," as wastefulness is a form of destruction and its use is more common in contemporary discourse.

of Genesis 1:28. *Bal tashḥit*, however, is different in an important way. Scholars who build an environmental argument based on *bal tashḥit* often present their position with some accompanying texts, instead of just using the concept as a counterargument to Genesis 1:28 in the manner of verse versus verse. In other words, unlike in the case of the invocation of Genesis 2:15, the historical development of these claims has been evoked in contemporary scholarship. Environmentalists have supported their position by turning to some of the most influential scholars of the Jewish traditional sources, regardless of whether or not such claims are historically accurate.

Yet, the burning question arises: if *bal tashḥit* makes for a sound environmental ideology, as held by many environmentalists, why has the theory not been translated into practice? There is no shortage of wastefulness in Jewish communities.[40] Many Jews are, of course, nonobservant, and as such one (perhaps) would not expect them to observe religious ordinances. Observant Jews, however, only rarely live according to the dictates of the environmental theory. It is not that observant Jews go out of their way to circumvent the prohibition of *bal tashḥit*; rather, there is a marked difference in how many environmentalists and observant Jews conceive of the prohibition.[41]

My research seeks to understand these differences, and to determine whether they can be reconciled or bridged. Specifically, I ask whether *bal tashḥit* has the historical basis to be considered an environmental ethic, or whether its environmental interpretation is mainly a contemporary development. What were the critical stages in the conceptualization of *bal tashḥit*? Were the towering exegetical figures of centuries and millennia past aware of environmental issues that concern us today? How did they interpret biblical passages and rabbinic texts that are used in contemporary environmental discourse? Did specific thinkers strongly influence the development of the concept and, subsequently, environmental thought? If so, from where do they originate and in what period did they live? Studying the evolution of *bal tashḥit* allows us to

40. See, for example, Tanhum Yoreh, "Ultra-Orthodox Recycling Narratives: Implications for Planning and Policy," *Journal of Enterprising Communities: People and Places in the Global Economy* 4, no. 4 (2010): 323–45, and Tanhum Yoreh, "Involuntary Simplicity: A Case Study of Haredi Consumption Patterns in Canada and Israel," in *From Antiquity to the Post-Modern World: Contemporary Jewish Studies in Canada*, eds. Daniel Maoz and Andrea Gondos (Newcastle upon Tyne, UK: Cambridge Scholars Publishing, 2011), 232–49.

41. This is not to claim that the two groups are mutually exclusive.

gain insight into its historical and cultural development, and greatly expands our current understanding of this concept.

It is obvious that the exegetes did not have developed notions of what today can be considered ecophilosophies. In the past, people did not think in the same environmental terms as we do today. These exegetes did not live in a time of rampant overconsumption, global anthropogenically induced climate change, and severe environmental pollution. There are indications, however, that the theologically oriented conception of life of the exegetes made some aware of issues such as sustainability and wastefulness, and made them concerned for the environment—albeit on a much more local scale.

In addition to tracking the critical stages in the development of *bal tashḥit*, in this book I argue that, despite the strongly utilitarian lens through which the prohibition against wastefulness and destruction came to be viewed from late antiquity onward, the earliest conceptualizations of *bal tashḥit* are its strongest manifestations as an environmental ethic. Moreover, I argue that although *bal tashḥit* has predominantly been used throughout history as an economic concept, its ethical and environmental parameters also often factored into its conceptualization.

Methodology

Contemporary Jewish commentary employs the environmental lexicon that informs current environmental thought. To answer the questions mentioned above, it is necessary to analyze critically the vast corpus of Jewish scholarship that deals with the prohibition of *bal tashḥit*. It is with this contemporary environmental lexicon that I will analyze the classic texts and examine whether environmental knowledge can be extracted from the material. Since earlier exegetes may have interpreted the texts similarly, but without employing the critical vocabulary, the task of searching for such readings often becomes more difficult. Biblical Hebrew, for example, lacks the word for nature, even though medieval and later Hebrew possessed more than one such term (e.g., *teva, toledet*). This, of course, does not mean that there are no biblical or rabbinic texts relevant to a discussion about nature, but rather that one must dig deeper to find them. As a result, the language I use is often anachronistic, though I attempt to attribute environmental significance to texts and their interpretations only when justified.

In Hebrew there are a number of different words that could mean waste or destruction (e.g., *bizbuz, heres*). A preliminary analysis of these words in Jewish texts has not proven fruitful. Therefore, this book is limited to the analysis of the root *sh.ḥ.t.* (destroy) as attested in the various strata of the traditions. There is a very rich corpus of traditional Jewish literature that deals with wastefulness using this root. This more limited scope makes sense. *Bal tashḥit* is more than just a prohibition; it is a concept, principle, or ethic. Therefore, most of the literature dealing with the prohibition against wastefulness *qua* concept or ethic will use the root *sh.ḥ.t.* and not other roots that may have similar meaning. Expanding the study of *bal tashḥit* by including the analysis of other roots is one direction for further research.

My use of tradition histories as a research methodology is informed by Jeremy Cohen's masterful study *"Be Fertile and Increase, Fill the Earth and Master It": The Ancient and Medieval Career of a Biblical Text*. I trace the evolution of *bal tashḥit* by looking at relevant passages dealing with wastefulness and destruction in Hebrew Scripture, rabbinic literature, halakhic codes, responsa, and commentary traditions. To access much of this material, I employ the Bar-Ilan Responsa Project, an electronic database. Though this research tries to be as comprehensive as possible, the data is too rich for me to cover it all in one tome. Throughout the various chapters, I mention the limits in my scope for this book.

Chapter Breakdown

In chapter 1, Classical Rabbinic Texts, I examine the early compilations of *Midrash Halakhah*, Mishnah, Tosefta, Talmud, and other rabbinic compositions, together with commentaries on them whenever relevant. These texts form a critical stage in the evolution of the prohibition against wastefulness and destruction, as the concept *bal tashḥit* is named for the first time during this period. I pay particular attention to passages dealing with cutting down trees and wastefulness in general, as well as texts dealing with self-harm.

In chapter 2, the Bible and Biblical Commentaries, I conduct a diachronic analysis of Jewish Bible commentaries on Deuteronomy 20:19–20 and examine and categorize the prohibition against cutting down fruit trees in wartime. I begin with the exegesis of Saadiah and continue all the way to twenty-first-century commentaries. I also conduct an extended analysis of Genesis 9:5 (the prohibition against self-harm/suicide/murder), Leviticus 19:27 (the prohibition against "destroying" facial hair), and 2 Kings 3:19, 25 (a prophetically condoned violation of Deuteronomy 20:19).

Chapter 3, Codes and Their Cognates, addresses how Jewish codifiers understood and applied the legal aspects of *bal tashḥit* in the post-Talmudic era. I also examine the manner in which the concept has evolved over time, especially under Maimonidean influence, to the present. I survey important codes such as the *Mishneh Torah* (authored by Maimonides, 1138–1204, Spain, Morocco, Land of Israel, and Egypt), the *Tur* (authored by Yaakov bar Asher, c. 1270–1343, Germany and Spain), and the *Shulḥan Arukh* (authored by Yosef Karo, 1488–1575, Spain, Portugal, Turkey, Bulgaria, and Land of Israel), as well as commentaries and compositions based on them. I have arranged this chapter by topic, and each topic is ordered chronologically.

Chapter 4, Responsa, discusses some of the major trends in the responsa literature (legal rulings in the form of question/answer) that emerge with regard to *bal tashḥit*. In particular, I highlight the impact of earlier conceptualizations of *bal tashḥit* by Maimonides (*derekh hashḥatah*), Meyuḥas bar Eliyahu (*tzorekh*—need/purpose), the *Midrash Aggadah* (*hana'ah*—benefit/enjoyment), Baḥya bar Asher (*to'elet*—utility), *Sefer HaḤinukh* (*to'elet* and morality).

In the Conclusion, I outline the main stages in the evolution of the concept of *bal tashḥit* and draw conclusions from a critical analysis of the previous chapters. I also discuss the moral and rational dimensions of the prohibition. Finally, I suggest directions for further research.

Synopsis

My research significantly expands the understanding of the concept of *bal tashḥit*. In my critical analysis of the vast corpus of scholarship dealing with the prohibition against wastefulness and destruction, I chart the evolution of *bal tashḥit* throughout its intellectual history, uncovering several important phases in its conceptualization. These include

1. The Tannaitic era (c. 70–c. 220 CE), in which three different teachings connect the prohibition against wastefulness to the prohibition against self-harm:

a. Rabbi Eleazar ben Azariah's *baraita* (b*Baba Qama* 91b).

b. Rabbi Eleazar's student, Rabbi Akiva ben Yosef's mishnah (m*Baba Qama* 8:6).

c. An anonymous teaching from the Tosefta (anonymous, but traditionally attributed to Rabbi Akiva's student, Rabbi Neḥemiah) (t*Baba Qama* 9:31).

2. The Amoraic/Savoraic era (c. 220–c. 630 CE), in which three different teachings significantly alter the understanding of *bal tashḥit*:

 a. The anonymous narrator of the Talmud's (*stam*—probably a redactor) rejection of learning about the prohibition against self-harm from *bal tashḥit* (b*Baba Qama* 91b).

 b. Ravina's economic statement regarding the permissibility of cutting down a fruit tree if it "has greater value" (in a different form) ("*me'uleh bedamim*"), essentially transforming the prohibition into a utilitarian concept (b*Baba Qama* 91b).

 c. Rabbah bar Naḥmani's statement that confirmed a hierarchy between the human body and other material regarding *bal tashḥit* ("the prohibition against wastefulness with regard to my body takes precedence for me over other forms of wastefulness concerning things" [*bal tashḥit de gufai adif li*]) (b*Shabbat* 129a).

3. Maimonides (1138–1204, Spain, Morocco, Land of Israel, and Egypt):

 a. Explicitly turned *bal tashḥit* into a general prohibition against wastefulness (*Sefer HaMitzvot LaRambam, Mitzvat Lo Ta'aseh* 57).

 b. Definitively separated the prohibition against wastefulness and the prohibition against self-harm (*Mishneh Torah, Hilkhot Melakhim*, 6:8–10 and *Hilkhot Ḥovel UMeizik* 5:1).

c. Coined the term *"derekh hashḥatah"* ("destructive/wasteful manner"),[42] introducing an element of subjectivity/intent when it comes to what is included under the prohibition.

4. Meyuḥas bar Eliyahu (twelfth century), *Midrash Aggadah* (twelfth and thirteenth centuries), Baḥya bar Asher (thirteenth and fourteenth centuries), and *Sefer HaḤinukh* (thirteenth century):

   a. In his gloss to Deuteronomy 20:19, Meyuḥas bar Eliyahu asserts that the prohibition of *bal tashḥit* applies to all things for which there is need/purpose (*tzorekh*).

   b. The *Midrash Aggadah* (on Deuteronomy 20:19) claims that the prohibition applies only to things from which one can derive benefit/enjoyment (*"yesh alav hana'ah"*).

   c. Baḥya bar Asher (on Deuteronomy 20:19) and *Sefer HaḤinukh* (529) express essentially the same sentiment as the *Midrash Aggadah,* using the word *"to'elet"* (benefit).

   d. *Sefer HaḤinukh* adds a moral dimension to the prohibition, stating that the righteous do not waste even as little as a mustard seed (*Sefer HaḤinukh* 529).

5. Samson Raphael Hirsch (nineteenth century): Hirsch ushered in the environmental era of the conceptualization of *bal tashḥit,* calling it "the first and most general call of God" (*Ḥorev,* 56).[43]

As part of the process of mapping the most important stages in the development of *bal tashḥit,* I uncovered a conceptual link between Deuteronomy 20:19 and Genesis 9:5. The latter verse constitutes one of the main sources for the prohibition against self-harm, and has never been part of the contemporary Jewish environmental discourse

42. In places I have translated this as "destructive intent."

43. Samson Raphael Hirsch, *Horeb: A Philosophy of Jewish Laws and Observances.* 2nd ed., Vol. 2, trans. I. Grunfeld (London: Soncino Press, 1968), 279.

on wastefulness. Moreover, self-harm has only very rarely been part of the historical discourse on *bal tashḥit*. When linked, however, these two prohibitions can be understood to form an environmental ethic: wastefulness and destruction are harmful to oneself, and in environmental terms, to harm the environment is to harm oneself. The ethic is beautiful in its simplicity, and is relevant both historically and currently. This wisdom can be found in different areas of environmental thought. For instance, Roger Gottleib claims that "we have begun a process of environmental degradation not unlike slow collective suicide."[44] J. Baird Callicott argues that such a perspective is part of the philosophy of Deep Ecology; "Biocide, from a deep ecological point of view, *is* suicide."[45] Historically, the link between *bal tashḥit* and the prohibition against self-harm was first made by the sages Rabbi Eleazar ben Azariah and his student Rabbi Akiva ben Yosef (c. first and second centuries CE, Land of Israel) and anonymously in the Tosefta. The connection was rejected by the sages of the Talmud who asserted that these prohibitions are qualitatively different from each other. Instead they countered with *bal tashḥit degufa adif* (the prohibition against destroying oneself takes precedence), explicitly establishing a hierarchy where human interests take precedence over those of the rest of creation.

Very little extant material on *bal tashḥit* exists from the time of the canonization of the Talmud at the very end of the sixth century CE until the twelfth century. In the twelfth century, Maimonides, one of the most influential figures in all of Jewish history, listed these prohibitions as separate entities in his code of Jewish law, the *Mishneh Torah*. Subsequently, only a handful of scholars until this very day have discussed the connection between them. Nevertheless, though muted, this connection was not entirely forgotten. For instance, Yonah of Gerona (d. 1263, Spain), Menaḥem HaMeiri (1249–1315, Provence), Shlomo Luria (1510–1574, Poland), Abraham de Boton (c. 1560–c. 1605, Greece and Land of Israel), Shneiur Zalman of Liadi (1745–1813, Russia), Israel Lipschutz (1782–1860, Germany), Jacob Ettlinger (1798–1871, Germany), Shlomo Gantzfried (1802–1884, Hungary), Barukh Epstein

44. Roger Gottleib, "Introduction: Religion in an Age of Environmental Crisis," in *This Sacred Earth: Religion, Nature, Environment*, 2nd ed., ed. Roger Gottleib (New York: Routledge, 2004), 8.

45. J. Baird Callicott, "Environmental Ethics: An Overview." www.fore.yale.edu/disciplines/ethics/, 2000.

(1860–1941, Belarus), and Yitzḥak Zilberstein (b. 1934, Poland and Israel), all notable scholars of their periods, understood these prohibitions to be conceptually connected to each other.[46]

Translating the prohibition against wastefulness from theory into practice is, of course, a process fraught with compromise, and it is not surprising that the theory behind the prohibition underwent an evolutionary process. After its expansion into a general prohibition against wastefulness, the major shift in the development of *bal tashḥit* was the separation of the prohibition against self-harm from the prohibition against wastefulness. This conceptual shift resulted in a utilitarian understanding of the prohibition. Rediscovering this link uncovers what is one of the earliest conceptualizations of the prohibition of *bal tashḥit* prior to it being problematized through real-world situations, as will be demonstrated in the book. Connecting self-harm (Genesis 9:5) and wastefulness (Deuteronomy 20:19–20) allows us to move beyond considering *bal tashḥit* as a religio-legal concept that has environmental ramifications, to an environmental ethic with religious origins. These currents exist side by side throughout history, with the utilitarian approach strongly dominating the discourse on *bal tashḥit*, a tendency that continues today. The second approach, the connection between self-harm and wastefulness, has been taken up and developed by several key figures over time. As will be made clear, these approaches do not contradict each other, but with the utilitarian paradigm governing the discourse, what is arguably the environmental approach has not received the attention it deserves. In part, this is due to the absence of an intellectual history of *bal tashḥit*. The impact of the different layers of conceptualization of *bal tashḥit* on our understanding of the prohibition has not been adequately emphasized. As such, the idea that harming the environment is tantamount to harming oneself has not yet entered the environmental discourse on *bal tashḥit*, nor is it prevalent in the contemporary halakhic discourse.

This study sheds light on the prohibition against wastefulness and destruction and advances the field of Jewish environmental thought. Environmentalism has struggled to make inroads into Jewish communities, though there has certainly been more uptake among liberal communities. In part, this has been hindered by the inability to find a common language between environmentalists and religious communities. While it is clear that *bal tashḥit* does indeed

46. This list is by no means exhaustive.

merit being termed an environmental ethic, until a full depiction of its environmental dimensions is brought into mainstream religious discourse—which is one of the goals of this research—it is difficult to imagine that environmentalists will be able to successfully use it to influence behavior and consumption patterns. This study makes progress toward finding this common language, by creating a document that can be understood by both environmentalists and faith communities. This book is relevant to those interested in the legal evolution of the prohibition as well as its moral evolution. Even for those less interested in the legal development of *bal tashḥit*, there is ample room to draw knowledge, inspiration, and guidance from the texts and their synthesis. Moreover, since *bal tashḥit* is one of the first principles that might be construed as an environmental concept in Western thought, understanding the origins and development of this prohibition provides insight into the theoretical framework of environmentalism, the way people conceive of their environment and the obligations they have toward it. Thus far, the fascinating study of evolving textual interpretations has only been conducted in limited areas in general, and the evolution of Jewish environmental thought has scarcely been addressed. It is my intention that this study will encourage others to employ the methodology of tradition histories for historical research in the field of religion and environment.

Contemporary Environmental and Religious Scholarship on the Prohibition Against Wastefulness

Despite the relative dearth of scholarly materials dealing with Judaism and environment, one topic has received significant attention in recent years: *bal tashḥit*. The interest comes both from religious authors dealing with the halakhic (Jewish legal) aspects of the concept and from environmental scholars. In this section, I review scholarly contributions on *bal tashḥit* from both groups. This is the most recent layer in the intellectual history of the prohibition against wastefulness. Although this book attempts to be diachronic, because this book is situated in the scholarship of religion and environment, reviewing this literature first is a natural starting point. I have attempted to be as comprehensive as possible, though undoubtedly some sources will be missed.

Many of the environmentalists dealing with *bal tashḥit* provide brief reviews of traditional literature to demonstrate that one may or may not find a developed environmental ethic within the Jewish tradition. They describe *bal tashḥit* within an environmental framework. Most of the writers of these studies present Deuteronomy 20:19–20, the text that forbids the destruction of fruit-bearing trees in an offensive military siege, and then cite a few Talmudic passages, followed by Maimonides's (1138–1204, Spain, Morocco, Land of Israel, and Egypt) generalization of the prohibition against wastefulness in his code of law, and occasionally commentaries on the biblical verse itself. Some even go further to present material found in the responsa literature. To varying degrees of thoroughness, these scholars include Jeremy Benstein,[47] Ellen Cohn,[48] Eliezer Diamond,[49] Daniel B. Fink,[50] Manfred Gerstenfeld,[51] Ronald H. Isaacs,[52] Walter Jacob,[53] Norman Lamm,[54] Rachel S. Mikva,[55] Israel Rozenson,[56] Hava Tirosh-Samuelson,[57] David

47. Jeremy Benstein, *The Way Into Judaism and the Environment* (Woodstock, VT: Jewish Lights Publishing, 2006), 93–111.

48. Ellen Cohn, "Growing an Environmental Ethic: The Conceptual Roots of *Bal Taschit*," in *Compendium of Sources in Halacha and the Environment*, eds. Ora Sheinson and Shai Spetgang (Jerusalem: Canfei Nesharim Publication, 2005), 38–44.

49. Eliezer Diamond, "Jewish Perspectives on Limiting Consumption," in *Ecology and the Jewish Spirit: Where Nature and the Sacred Meet*, ed. Ellen Bernstein (Woodstock, VT: Jewish Lights Publishing, 1998), 80–87.

50. Daniel B. Fink, "The Environment in *Halakhah*," in *Judaism and Ecology* (New York: Hadassah, The Women's Zionist Organization of America, and Shomrei Adamah, 1993), 34–47.

51. Manfred Gerstenfeld, *The Environment in the Jewish Tradition: A Sustainable World* (Jerusalem: Jerusalem Institute for Israel Studies, Center for Environmental Policy, 2002) and *Judaism, Environmentalism and the Environment: Mapping and Analysis* (Jerusalem: Jerusalem Institute for Israel Studies, Center for Environmental Policy, 1998).

52. Ronald H. Isaacs, *The Jewish Sourcebook on the Environment and Ecology* (Northvale, NJ: Jason Aronson, 1998).

53. Walter Jacob, "Eco-Judaism: Does It Exist? 'The Earth Is the Lord's' versus 'Everything Is Given into Your Hand,'" in *The Environment in Jewish Law: Essays and Responsa*, eds. Walter Jacob and Moshe Zemer (New York: Berghahn Books, 2003), 1–23.

54. Norman Lamm, "Ecology in Jewish Law and Theology," in *Torah of the Earth: Exploring 4,000 Years of Ecology in Jewish Thought*. Vol. 1: *Biblical Israel: One Land, One People*, ed. Arthur Waskow (Woodstock, VT: Jewish Lights Publishing, 2000), 103–26.

55. Rachel S. Mikva, "When Values Collide: Economics, Health and the Environment," in *The Environment in Jewish Law: Essays and Responsa*, eds. Walter Jacob and Moshe Zemer (New York: Berghahn Books, 2003), 34–44.

56. Israel Rozenson, *VeHinei Tov Me'od* (Jerusalem: Yeshivat Beit Orot, 2001), 99–104.

57. Hava Tirosh-Samuelson, "Nature in the Sources of Judaism," *Daedalus* 130, no. 4 (2001): 99–124.

Vogel,[58] Arthur Waskow,[59] Moshe Zemer,[60] and Edward Zipperstein.[61] Surprisingly, except in a few cases, these authors do not indicate that they are aware of each other, which leads to a fairly repetitive discourse. Because of the repetition found in this literature, I will not discuss all of these authors in my review. In contrast to the above-mentioned scholars, David Nir,[62] Eilon Schwartz,[63] and Akiva Wolff[64] stand out for having gone significantly further in their analysis of *bal tashḥit* by looking at a wider range of literature and problematizing the extent of the prohibition as an ethical principle. I present the sources mentioned by these scholars in due course. As will be seen, tension exists between the desire to see *bal tashḥit* as a complete ethic and the practical shortcomings of *bal tashḥit* to date.

Scholars Examining *Bal Tashḥit* as an Environmental Ethic

One of the most common questions concerning scholars writing about the prohibition against wastefulness is whether it is indeed an environmental ethic and whether its existence aligns Judaism with environmentalism. While it is advocated as such by some, others have been more hesitant to confer this standing onto either the concept of *bal tashḥit* or Judaism as a whole. This is not to say that those standing in opposition to viewing Judaism generally and *bal tashḥit*

58. David Vogel, "How Green Is Judaism? Exploring Jewish Environmental Ethics," *Business Ethics Quarterly* 11, no. 2 (April, 2001): 349–63.

59. Arthur Waskow, "Jewish Environmental Ethics: Intertwining *Adam* with *Adamah*," in *The Oxford Handbook of Jewish Ethics and Morality*, eds. Elliot N. Dorff and Jonathan K. Crane (New York: Oxford University Press, 2013), 401–18.

60. Moshe Zemer, "Ecology as a Mitzvah," in *The Environment in Jewish Law: Essays and Responsa*, eds. Walter Jacob and Moshe Zemer (New York: Berghahn Books, 2003), 24–33.

61. Edward Zipperstein, "Waste in the Judaic Tradition," in *Essays in Jewish Thought* (Los Angeles: private printing, 1989), 58–98.

62. David Nir, "A Critical Examination of the Jewish Environmental Law of *Bal Tashchit*," *Georgetown International Environmental Law Review* 18, no. 2 (Winter 2006): 335–53.

63. Eilon Schwartz, "*Bal tashchit*: A Jewish Environmental Precept," in *Judaism and Environmental Ethics: A Reader*, ed. Martin D. Yaffe (New York: Lexington Books, 2001), 230–49.

64. Akiva Wolff, "A Closer Examination of Deuteronomy 20:19–20," *Jewish Bible Quarterly* 39, no. 3 (2011): 143–52; and "Bal Tashchit: The Jewish Prohibition Against Needless Destruction," PhD dissertation, Leiden University, 2009.

specifically in this light are against an alliance between Jewish and environmental values. Rather, for the most part they either see *bal tashḥit* as being limited by a narrow scope, or claim that it offers a good foundation, but requires significant reinterpretation to become relevant in contemporary contexts. Based on the aforementioned gap between theory and practice, it would seem that their dubiousness is justified.

Hava Tirosh-Samuelson, an environmental philosopher, believes that environmental ethics in Judaism are a modern construct. She argues that "it is a prior commitment to environmentalism that dictates [an environmental] interpretation of the traditional sources, not the sources themselves."[65] Yet she sees potential for Jewish wisdom to be part of the solution to contemporary environmental problems. More specifically, she views *bal tashḥit* as the Jewish concept with the most potential for development of environmental policies:

> Above all, the principle of "do not destroy" can provide religious support for a range of environmental policies, such as conservation of natural resources, prevention of water pollution, reforestation, proper disposal of waste products, energy conservation, recycling, and reduction of material consumption.[66]

Norman Lamm, an Orthodox rabbi, is slightly hesitant, yet he, too, sees the potential in considering Judaism in an environmental light. He states that "Judaism—exegetically, halakhically, and theologically—possesses the values on which an ecological morality may be grounded."[67] He states that although the meaning of Deuteronomy 20:19–20 is somewhat unclear, it is still obvious that the Torah prohibits wanton destruction. Lamm argues that:

> [T]he prohibition is not essentially a financial law dealing with property (*mammon*), but religious or ritual law (*issur*), which happens to deal with the avoidance of vandalism against objects of economic worth. As such, *bal tash'hit* is

65. Tirosh-Samuelson, "Nature in the Sources," 117.

66. Ibid., 116.

67. Lamm, "Ecology in Jewish Law," 126.

> based on a religio-moral principle that is far broader than a prudential commercial rule per se, and its wider applications may well be said to include ecological considerations.[68]

Lamm's hesitation lies in the fact that *bal tashḥit* is, in his opinion, not strictly an environmental ethic, nor an economic principle. Instead, he sees *bal tashḥit* as a religious principle with a moral dimension, which also happens to have environmental ramifications.

Manfred Gerstenfeld, an author and policy analyst, discusses the economic and environmental parameters of *bal tashḥit*. He claims that the concept of *bal tashḥit* is very commonly discussed by contemporary Jewish environmental scholars, even though there is not a unified approach:

> Much has been written on the halakhic issue of *bal tashhit*. Even if its exact limits cannot be determined due to lack of a central halakhic authority, there is a substantial core element of prohibitions which are implicitly accepted by all rabbinical authorities.[69]

In his summary of Deuteronomy 20:19–20 he focuses on both the economic and environmental aspects of the verses:

> In this instruction [Deuteronomy 20:19–20] there are "environmental" and economic motifs. The prohibition expresses two sub-categories of the "environmental" ethic: stewardship over elements of nature and also on the natural resources. The fruit of the tree serves as food for humans, and it is forbidden to harm the infrastructure for the livelihood of humanity in times of war. And even though fruit trees are a renewable resource it is fitting for humans to treat them with care, as it takes a long time until they grow and produce fruits. Not harming them denotes they can sustain you for the coming days, meaning that this will secure a food source for those besieging the city.[70]

68. Ibid., 114.

69. Gerstenfeld, *Mapping and Analysis*, 116.

70. Gerstenfeld, *A Sustainable World*, 15.

Gerstenfeld focuses on the human dimension of the prohibition, highlighting the value humans derive from not cutting down the fruit trees. He views *bal tashḥit* primarily as a commandment designed to benefit humanity rather than the natural world, yet he still defines the prohibition as an environmental ethic.

In asking whether eco-Judaism exists, Walter Jacob, a Reform rabbi, claims that the concept of *bal tashḥit* has potential, but needs to be "reinterpreted and expanded"[71] to achieve it. He highlights the problematic that exists in some of the traditional glosses to Deuteronomy 20:19–20, which results in a severely limited utility when it comes to environmental ethics, and he is dubious regarding its contemporary utility. Jacob states,

> Those who commented on the biblical verse interpreted it in its specific wartime setting. Most of the rabbinic literature that dealt with its halakhic setting provides a narrow interpretation by limiting it to fruit trees, by restricting it to times of war, and by stating that virtually any economic benefit, or threat of harm from it, may be sufficient reason for the destruction of the tree or trees.[72]

Jacob concludes that although the concept of *bal tashḥit* is useful, it is not sufficiently developed to suit the environmental circumstances and needs of modern times. He asserts,

> The concept of *bal tash-hit* can become a more valuable tool, but we need to be aware of its limitations. The biblical verse is too narrow and does not lend itself readily to expansion. Those who have done so have largely used it to attack excessive consumption, which is hard to define.[73]

Though his conclusion with regard to the "narrow" extent to which the traditional sources dealt with *bal tashḥit* is open to debate, as will be made apparent in this book, he correctly points out that Jewish law is lagging far behind current scientific knowledge.

---

71. Jacob, "Eco-Judaism," 19.

72. Ibid.

73. Ibid., 20.

In an effort to determine whether Judaism is "green," David Vogel, a professor of business ethics, began with a premise similar to Jacob's, and explored a wide variety of Jewish teachings that Jewish environmentalists perceived to have ecological significance. While discussing many different ideas, his central focus is on *bal tashḥit*, which "is often evoked as a textual basis for Jewish environmental ethics."[74] He concludes that

> While Judaism may be consistent with many contemporary environmental values and doctrines, its teachings are not identical to them. . . . In short, Judaism contains both "green" and "non-green" elements. It is inappropriate to overemphasize either the former, as have some Jewish environmentalists, or the latter, as have some environmental critics of Western religion.[75]

While he does not advocate for a constructive use of *bal tashḥit* as does Jacob, he argues that Judaism has a balanced approach between "the need to protect what God has created and the needs of humans to use nature to sustain life."[76]

Like Vogel and Jacob, Arthur Waskow, a Jewish Renewal rabbi and ecotheologian, also questions the extent to which *bal tashḥit* can be applied as an environmental principle. He claims that the concept was incorrectly used by environmentalists defending Judaism against claims that it supported the unmitigated exploitation of nature:

> Confronted in the twentieth century with the charge that biblical Judaism and Christianity had, through the teaching "Fill the earth and subdue it" (Genesis 1:28), encouraged destruction of nature by human beings, some rabbis responded by citing *Bal tashhit*. But on careful examination, it was realized there was much more apologia than accuracy to this way of exculpating Judaism. Appeals to the biblical traditions cited above [Eden, Sabbath, Sabbaticals, festivals, etc.] were much more accurate.[77]

74. Vogel, "How Green Is Judaism?" 351.

75. Ibid., 350.

76. Ibid., 361.

77. Waskow, "Jewish Environmental Ethics," 415.

It is unclear precisely what "careful examination" Waskow is referring to. It is possible that he bases this claim on the critiques of the limits of *bal tashḥit* made by other scholars presented here. I arrive at different conclusions with regard to *bal tashḥit* as an environmental ethic. Without analyzing the biblical traditions by using tradition histories, there is a limited basis for comparing the efficacy of the ideas mentioned by Waskow. Waskow limits his discussion of the prohibition to the biblical context of fruit trees and the actions of destroying and planting trees in a contemporary framework.

Other voices remain entirely committed to championing Judaism as an ecoreligion and *bal tashḥit* as environmental ethic. For instance, Moshe Zemer, a Reform rabbi, claimed that "this rule of *bal tash-hit* 'do not destroy' is extended to all objects that may have value. This prohibition includes killing animal life and destroying plants and even inanimate objects."[78] He then continued his argument suggesting just how far-reaching the application of *bal tashḥit* should be:

> *Bal tash-hit* sets the outer limits of the enfranchisement given to us to utilize all of the resources of nature for human purposes. When we cross these boundaries and demolish the works of God, we lose our delicate equilibrium with nature. Only by observing the guidelines of the *mitzvot* of ecology may we hope to regain this balance with the world around us.[79]

According to Zemer, *bal tashḥit* is meant to preserve the ecological balance. The laws for sustainability exist within Judaism. It is up to Jews to understand and observe them. Ronald H. Isaacs, a Conservative rabbi, shares this worldview with Zemer and takes it a step further. He claims that "Jewish law requires that its people not merely refrain from polluting the environment. Rather, the Jewish people are obligated to be proactive and take affirmative action to clean up the world and keep it safe for generations to come."[80] In his summary of the parameters of *bal tashḥit* he argues that it not only calls for restricting human behavior, but indeed requires Jews to be proactive in their environmental protection.

---

78. Zemer, "Ecology as a Mitzvah," 26.

79. Ibid., 27.

80. Ronald H. Isaacs, *The Jewish Sourcebook on the Environment and Ecology* (Northvale, NJ: Jason Aronson, 1998), 10.

Over the past few years online resources presenting *bal tashḥit* as an environmental concept have mushroomed, and many of them have an activist bent. It would be impossible to mention them all; suffice it to say that since none of them are more comprehensive in their analysis of *bal tashḥit* than those already presented in this group of environmental scholars, it is unnecessary to do more than mention their existence and encourage their growth.

While the scholars mentioned above do a commendable job in broadly relating to the prohibition, the scholars below have been considerably more engaged.

Eilon Schwartz and David Nir have some of the most encompassing papers on *bal tashḥit* to date. Schwartz states that the meaning of *bal tashḥit* and the translation of that ethic into action and policy remain one of the great conundrums of Jewish environmentalists. At the outset of his article, Schwartz claims

> No single Jewish concept is quoted more often in demonstrating Judaism's environmental credentials than the rabbinic concept of *bal tashchit* ("do not destroy"). It appears in virtually all the literature that discusses Jewish attitudes toward the environmental crisis. Yet, rarely are any more than a few sentences given to actually explain its history and its meaning. Such a superficial approach has been widespread in contemporary environmental ethics with regard to traditional cultures.[81]

After exposing some of the shortfalls of the field, Schwartz analyzes a limited number of the medieval commentaries on Deuteronomy 20:19–20, discusses some of the Talmudic texts dealing with *bal tashḥit*, and then moves on to the responsa literature. He groups the responsa on *bal tashḥit* into two different categories: the "minimalist" and the "maximalist."

> Two positions emerge from the discussion on *bal tashchit*. The first, which is clearly the dominant position, I describe as the minimalist position. It limits *bal tashchit* as much as possible to only those situations that are clearly proscribed by the biblical injunction in Deuteronomy. . . . In contrast,

81. Schwartz, "*Bal Tashchit*," 230.

> the maximalist position does expand *bal tashchit* as a counterweight to human desires. . . . Consumption should be limited to what is necessary, and the inherent value of the creation stands as a countermeasure to human usage.[82]

Thus, he problematizes the literature by stating clearly that not all legists take the same approach to *bal tashḥit*. Schwartz argues that the historical discourse surrounding *bal tashḥit* essentially boils down to whether one espouses a worldview that is concerned primarily with how humans use the natural world, or one that considers more than just human wants. He claims that the minimalist approach "is by far the more dominant within the tradition."[83] I would argue that both these approaches are built into the concept of *bal tashḥit*; one worldview is not rejected in favor of the other. Rather, a moral compass that considers both the human and nonhuman is an essential part of the prohibition. Even if one is prioritized it does not mean the other is inherently ignored, though, of course, in any particular circumstance it might be.

Like Schwartz, David Nir begins by critiquing the existing environmental scholarship on *bal tashḥit*. He states that all too often people have used the concept in an incorrect manner by highlighting the environmentally positive aspects of the prohibition and glossing over the negative ones. He remarks,

> The risk with such selective and highly interpretive understandings of *bal tashchit* is that they threaten to undermine the value that *bal tashchit* does have for those concerned with protecting the environment. . . . An honest appreciation of Jewish law requires an acknowledgement of all relevant source material, both pro and con. Put another way, claims about what *bal tashchit* stands for are too easily punctured if they rest only on hand-picked examples.[84]

Nir analyzes the Talmudic passages dealing with *bal tashḥit* using legal, moral, economic, and environmental frameworks. In his critique, Nir

82. Ibid., 239.

83. Ibid., 244.

84. Nir, "Jewish Environmental Law," 349–50.

argues that *bal tashḥit* does not have a place in determining macro environmental policies, but is still a useful concept for micro applications:

> While it may not be useful for deciding whether American national policy should favor drilling in the Wildlife Refuge, it *does* provide moral guidance on how we, as individuals and businesses, ought to *use* energy. Namely, *bal tashchit* advises conservation—if you are using more energy in your daily life than you have reason to, then you transgress the commandment.[85]

Though he makes many salient points, Nir's claim that *bal tashḥit* cannot be applied on a global or even national scale seems unnecessarily restricting. Just because the framework is enlarged does not mean there cannot be an underlying ethic guiding policies and actions, though he is certainly correct that the legal and moral development of *bal tashḥit* has by and large been focused on the individual. He concludes by stating

> *Bal tashchit* may not function as a broad-based environmental ethic it is often mistakenly thought to be, but, properly understood, it is a more focused—and hence more useful—conservationist principle. As such, it can and should form a strong underpinning for the modern Jewish environmental movement.[86]

In his conclusions, Nir reduces *bal tashḥit* from a broad environmental ethic to a limited conservationist principle. His call for *bal tashḥit* to "form a strong underpinning for the modern Jewish environmental movement" is well taken, but limits the utility of the concept to a relatively small demographic. By focusing on the relationship between self-harm and wastefulness, this study reaches different conclusions.

Among the environmental scholars to date, Akiva Wolff stands out as one of the most comprehensive in his analysis of *bal tashḥit*, though not as comprehensive as the works undertaken by contemporary scholars of classical Jewish sources listed in the next section. His stated

85. Ibid., 351.

86. Ibid., 353.

purpose was to understand what *bal tashḥit* is, how it can be applied, and what it can contribute to environmental management. Interestingly, he argues that *bal tashḥit* can be broken down into two distinct categories, one being a principle and the other a legal prohibition:

> The *principle* of *bal tashchit* prohibits the *needless* destruction of any created object—since the natural world was ultimately created for the benefit of man. Nevertheless, a *legal prohibition* can only operate within clear delineations. If there is not likely to be any tangible benefit to humans from a specific object, such as a wild animal in a distant forest, then the object is not protected under the legal prohibition.[87]

While making this division may help simplify the complexities of *bal tashḥit*, it is not an entirely compelling distinction to make. First, it should be noted that the opinion that *bal tashḥit* does not apply to ownerless objects is not universally held among the legal authorities. Moreover, while it is true that certain legists have discussed the difference between what we might call the letter of the law and the spirit of the law,[88] it is impossible to fully divorce these two categories from one another, as they constantly inform each other.

Wolff asserts that the three most influential scholars on the conceptualization of *bal tashḥit* are Maimonides, the author of *Sefer HaḤinukh*, and Samson Raphael Hirsch.[89] Our current study corroborates this finding, though the list of the most influential scholars presented here is more comprehensive. As my focus in this book is to analyze the prohibition in light of its intellectual history, I emphasize the important shifts in conceptualization that may initially seem subtle, but throughout the generations prove to be monumental.

Wolff stands out from most other environmental scholars in that on a number of occasions he mentions that harm of the body is a significant part of *bal tashḥit*. He uses the hierarchy found in the later layers of the Talmud to confirm that human interests rest on top of the pyramid. He did not, however, highlight the paramount significance of the connection between bodily harm and wastefulness

87. Wolff, *Bal Tashchit*, 57.

88. For example, see Yeḥezkel Landau, *Noda BiYehudah, Mahadurah Tinyana, Yoreh De'ah* 10.

89. Wolff, *Bal Tashchit*, 72.

that is fundamental to environmentalism. Harming the environment eventually equates to harming oneself by compromising the integrity of the resources and natural systems on which human life depends.

Scholars Examining *Bal Tashḥit* as Religious Law

As a well-developed religious concept, *bal tashḥit* is not written about only by environmental scholars. Scholars of Jewish law differ in one significant aspect from their environmental counterparts. While a prohibition against wastefulness clearly has environmental ramifications regardless of how one perceives Judaism's approach to the environment, these scholars by and large do not indicate any awareness or interest in this prohibition as an environmental concept. They simply do not conceive of the prohibition in this manner. The scholars of rabbinics dealing with *bal tashḥit* can be broken down into four categories. Because I analyze large sections of the material they cover later in this book, I only nominally mention the four categories here.

Trees

The first group consists of scholars who have written about the prohibition specifically within the framework of fruit trees. These scholars include Meir Ayali,[90] Meir Bransdorfer,[91] She'ar Yashuv Cohen,[92] Moshe Gartenberg and Shmuel Gluck,[93] Avraham Hillel Goldberg,[94] and Yisrael Meir Lau.[95] While it is clear that they are well aware that *bal tashḥit* extends beyond fruit trees, these scholars do not address the prohibition in broader terms. While most environmentalist writ-

---

90. Meir Ayali, "*HaḤaradah Bifnei Keritat Etz-Ma'akhal BeSafrut HaShu"t*," in *Tura: Studies in Jewish Thought, Simon Greenberg Jubilee Volume* (Tel-Aviv, Israel: Hakibbutz Hameuchad Publishing House, 1989), 135–40.

91. Meir Bransdorfer, "*BeInyan Qetzitzat Ilanei Peirot*," *Or Yisrael* 18 (2000): 58–64.

92. Shaar Yeshuv Cohen, "*Keritat Ilanot BiShe'at Milḥamah UViShe'at Shalom*," *Teḥumin* 4 (1983): 44–53.

93. Moshe Gartenberg and Shmuel Gluck, "Destruction of Fruit-Bearing Trees," *Journal of Halacha and Contemporary Society* 38 (Fall 1999): 86–99.

94. Avraham Hillel Goldberg, "*Akirat Atzei Pri*," *Noam* 13 (1972): 203–21.

95. Yisrael Meir Lau, "*Issur Bal Tashḥit BiMeqom Mitzvah*," *Teḥumin* 22 (2002): 293–300.

ings on *bal tashḥit* use the biblical context of fruit trees as a launching pad for their discussion of wastefulness, these scholars limited their discussion to fruit trees, even if they did occasionally mention that *bal tashḥit* applies more broadly. Within this framework, the scholars in this group by and large have a much more comprehensive analysis than any scholar in the environmentalist category.

General Wastefulness

The second group consists of scholars who address *bal tashḥit* as a general prohibition, beyond its biblical context of fruit trees. These scholars include Yaakov Bazak[96] and Yosef Gavriel Bechhofer.[97] Yaakov Bazak bemoaned the increase in acts of vandalism against property. While not mentioning the word "environment," he nevertheless made a strong argument for *bal tashḥit* as a guiding principle in daily life. His argument was that "the universe should be treated as a precious resource that was given to humans and should not be wasted or destroyed . . . as one day that very person or other people will need what was wasted."[98]

Yosef Gavriel Bechhofer wrote about recycling and the prohibition against wastefulness. In his work he asks whether it is a transgression to not recycle when the option presents itself. He analyzed some of the critical texts dealing with *bal tashḥit* and ultimately focused on whether the prohibition applies when there is a prevention of gain or only in cases where a person physically engages in wastefulness. His approach is discussed in the responsa chapter. Ultimately, he does not mention the environment at all in his writing even though we may consider recycling to be an inherently environmental topic.

This group also includes the *Encyclopedia Talmudit,* one of the best starting places for research on *bal tashḥit,* as it lists and sources many of the key halakhic components of the concept.[99] Importantly, the encyclopedia mentions bodily harm as one component of *bal tashḥit,* something most other sources address insufficiently, if at all.

96. Yaakov Bazak, "*Ma'asei Vandalism VeIssur 'Bal Tashḥit,'*" *Teḥumin* 1 (1980): 329–39.

97. Yosef Gavriel Bechhofer, "*HaMiḥzur BaHalakhah,*" *Teḥumin* 16 (1996): 296–302.

98. Yaakov Bazak, "*Ma'asei Vandalism,*" 339.

99. Shlomo Yosef Zevin (ed.), *Encyclopedia Talmudit LeInyanei Halakhah,* Vol. 3, s.v. בל תשחית (Jerusalem: *Hotza'at Encyclopedia Talmudit,* 1951), 335–37.

Book-Length Works

The scholars who wrote books on *bal tashḥit* are by far the most thorough and comprehensive in the depth of their halakhic analyses. Even within this group, however, one must differentiate between Siman Tov David,[100] whose work is broad, but it is not nearly as comprehensive as the works of Yitzḥak Eliyahu Shtasman[101] and Moshe Yitzḥak Vorhand.[102] All three of these scholars present the concept both as a prohibition against cutting down fruit trees and as a general prohibition against wastefulness. While their scope is comprehensive within the religious framework, and covers a wide variety of classical, medieval, and modern Jewish scholarship, their focus is inevitably narrowed as a consequence of limiting their analyses to the religious context alone. These scholars do an excellent job dividing the extensive material on the prohibition by topic, and present numerous references to legal codes, commentaries, and responsa for a long list of specific cases. They make little effort, however, to advance the halakhic discourse on *bal tashḥit*. Instead they read more like anthologies. This is, perhaps, not surprising, as one of Shtasman's stated goals when writing his book was to collect the scattered teachings on *bal tashḥit*, not to create a treatise on practical applications of the law. Another shortfall of their work is that they are somewhat limited in their coverage of Bible commentaries, a gap filled by the present work. It is also important to mention that all three of these scholars discuss *bal tashḥit* in reference to self-harm. Shtasman and Vorhand, in particular, relate to the dissenting opinions from the Talmud onward regarding whether to include the prohibition against self-harm in the concept of *bal tashḥit*.

Between Environment and *Halakhah*

The final category is made up of scholars whose work is grounded in Jewish law but who have written on environmental themes within

100. Siman Tov David, *Sefer al Pakkim Qetanim: Hilkhot Bal Tashḥit* (Jaffa, Israel: S. M. Publishers, 2000).

101. Yitzḥak Eliyahu Shtasman, *Sefer Etz HaSadeh: BeDinei Bal Tashḥit, Qetzitzat Ilanot UVizui Okhalin* (Jerusalem: Foundation for the Advancement of Torah Study, 1999).

102. Moshe Yitzḥak Vorhand, *Sefer Birkat HaShem: Leqet Dinei Issur Qetzitzat Ilanei Ma'akhal, Bal Tashḥit BiShe'ar Devarim, VeIssur Hefsed UVizui Okhalim* (Jerusalem: private printing, 2000).

Judaism.[103] This group includes Nahum Rakover[104] and a group of scholars headed by Meir Zikhel in conjunction with the Bar-Ilan Responsa Project. They are arguably the group of scholars of classical Jewish sources who write most seriously about *bal tashḥit* as an environmental concept. Grounded by rigorous training in classical Jewish texts, they have produced a very high level analysis. They do not go into nearly as much depth as the scholars of classical Jewish sources from the previous category who wrote book length tomes, but again, this was not their objective as their publications deal with a number of environmental topics beyond just *bal tashḥit*. A case could be made to list Akiva Wolff among these scholars as well, but a significant portion of his work focuses on turning *bal tashḥit* into a legal and economic concept divorced from its religious origins, and in turn relating it to major environmental issues such as water management.

Nahum Rakover provided one of the best early compilations of Jewish sources on the environment. He highlights *bal tashḥit* as one of many concepts for the protection of nature found in the Jewish tradition. He states that "The subject of the commandment is to not destroy objects that give benefit/enjoyment to humans. This prohibition includes the destruction of animals, plants and even inanimate objects."[105] Even at the outset of his book he declared that although there is a rich variety of sources in Jewish writings that call for the protection of the environment, they do not account for situations where there are competing interests. He writes, "'Environmental protection' [in the Jewish tradition] does not provide solutions for conflicts of interests, but it does contain elements which can enrich the decision-making process. . . . Decisions must eventually be made based on economic, social and ethical principles."[106] This raises the interesting question that if the prohibition against wastefulness comes first and

103. David Salomon, Yaakov Weinberger, Meir Batiste, Meir Zikhel, Menaḥem Slae, and Tzvi Ilani, *Eikhut HaSvivah (Ecologia) BiMeqorot HaYahadut* (Ramat-Gan, Israel: Bar-Ilan Responsa Project, 1990), 7–36.

104. Nahum Rakover, *Eikhut HaSvivah: Heibetim Ra'ayoniyim UMishpatiyim BaMeqorot HaYehudiyim* (Jerusalem: *Moreshet HaMishpat BeYisrael*, 1993), 32–41; and *Environmental Protection: A Jewish Perspective*, Policy Study No. 4 (Jerusalem: Institute of the World Jewish Congress, 1996).

105. Nahum Rakover, *Eikhut HaSvivah*, 32.

106. Ibid., 18.

foremost to prevent the needless waste of things that benefit humans, is it permissible to waste in order to benefit humans? He discusses this problematic in the context of *bal tashḥit*: "One of the greatest challenges in the area of the environment is finding a balance between protecting nature and the benefit that arises from damaging nature."[107] Rakover provides a number of examples from the responsa literature that demonstrate competing interests at play. He reminds the reader that despite the fact that there are multiple considerations to take into account, the prohibition itself is unique insofar as even indirect harm is considered a transgression.[108]

Zikhel's group analyzes the concept of *bal tashḥit* using a broad range of sources, including commentaries and responsa. In their introduction they claim that "the problems that concern us today were already discussed at length by the sages of antiquity; there is nothing new under the sun."[109] Their collection of sources is excellent, and they explicitly declare that their "intention was to demonstrate the negative attitude that the *halakhah* has to the waste/destruction of anything that could have human utility."[110] They conclude their work on *bal tashḥit* by stating, "One demand is common to all the sages of Israel—a strict preservation of nature and the environment and an attitude of respect for God's world."[111] Schwartz and Nir are critical of such scholarship for its lack of objectivity.

Very few of the scholars presented here demonstrate an awareness of the connection between the prohibition against wastefulness and self-harm and the implications this has for *bal tashḥit* as an environmental ethic. Those who do mention this link have not highlighted its monumental significance. Many of the scholars mentioned here have made significant progress in bridging the worlds of environment and religion with regard to the prohibition against wastefulness. I acknowledge my indebtedness to their pioneering efforts, while the limitations of their work provide the impetus for the present study.

---

107. Ibid., 38.

108. Ibid., 41.

109. David Salomon et al., *Eikhut HaSvivah BiMeqorot HaYahadut*, 6.

110. Ibid., 35.

111. Ibid.

Chapter 1

Classical Rabbinic Texts

Having presented some of the perspectives expressed by environmental scholars on the prohibition against wastefulness, our journey into the evolution of *bal tashḥit* continues with the earliest stages of its conceptualization. The rabbis became known as such in the wake of the destruction of the Second Temple in 70 CE. The prohibition against wastefulness undergoes considerable evolution in the thought and writings of the rabbinic sages. Within the corpora of various canonical rabbinic literatures we observe the transition from an unnamed prohibition to a highly developed concept. This shift is indicative of what we might call a conceptual change or the development of an idea. Classical rabbinic literature spans several centuries, from c. 200 to 550 CE. This chapter will engage materials from the Mishnah, Tosefta, Midrash, Minor Tractates, Babylonian Talmud, and the commentaries on them. The earliest mention of the concept of *bal tashḥit* is in the Babylonian Talmud (c. 220–550 CE). There are a number of statements attributed to *tannaim* (the sages of the Mishnah [c. 70–200 CE]) in the Talmud that use the term *bal tashḥit* (see below b*Baba Qama* 91b, b*Ḥullin* 7b, *Semaḥot* 9:23); however, these named tannaitic authorities do not appear in tannaitic sources. Part of what this chapter does is analyze the early texts (tannaitic) relative to the later ones (amoraic—[*amoraim* are the sages of the Talmud]) and make inferences based on the differences. Through this analysis I demonstrate the following:

1. It was tannaitic rabbis who understood the prohibition against wastefulness/destruction to be integrally connected with the prohibition against harming oneself. Through these connections one might infer the existence of a simple yet straightforward environmental ethic that harming the environment is harmful to oneself.

2. The Midrash confirms the established position of hierarchical value between humans and nonhumans (save the Divine), and within the nonhuman world (fruit trees in relation to non-fruit-bearing trees).

3. There is a marked shift in the development of the prohibition against wastefulness/destruction from the tannaitic to the amoraic periods. In particular, it was amoraic rabbis who introduced a conceptualization of *bal tashḥit* that can be categorized as utilitarian and market based. Amoraic rabbis also redefined the relationship between the prohibition against harming oneself and the prohibition against wastefulness as hierarchical through the development of the concept of *bal tashḥit degufa adif* (favoring self-interest in avoiding personal harm).

4. Though the redactors of the Talmud directly reject both the connection between Genesis 9:5 and the prohibition against self-harm, and the connection between the prohibition against self-harm and *bal tashḥit*, there is a tradition of scholars who accept the validity of these connections and kept this association alive in their teachings.

5. Through its position on wastefulness and ownerless items, the Talmud becomes an important source for a Jewish notion of the commons (public land).

6. The tannaitic period highlighted the inherent connections between wastefulness and destruction, idol worship, and emulation of foreign cultural practices already extant during the biblical era. These connections were integral to the development of *bal tashḥit* insofar as the prohibition was in part designed to distance Jews/Israelites from such behavior.

This chapter is not an exhaustive list of all the instances of wasteful behavior discussed in classic rabbinic texts. Moreover, not all the texts that use the term *bal tashḥit* in reference to wastefulness are mentioned. While their number is not considerable, some have not elicited a lengthy discussion in the commentary tradition and have little to contribute to the conceptualization of *bal tashḥit*. Listing every single example would take too much time and space, and in any case those who wish to study these references even more thoroughly may easily do so with modern search engines. In particular, passages dealing with wasting food are excluded. The texts connected with semen wastage and the flood story using the root *sh.ḥ.t.* are mentioned but not dealt with in any depth.

It should be noted that in this chapter I attribute teachings to specific rabbinic figures, either because the texts mention them by name, or because the texts have been traditionally attributed to them. Modern textual analysis has called into question the historicity of specific attributions. It is not my goal in this book to enter this debate. While I do highlight certain chains of transmission, my arguments are not dependent on the historicity of the connection between a specific text and a specific legal authority. Rather, when I mention a tradent it is due to the rationale of argumentation. In other words, I use tradents to reinforce an argument that already stands on its own merit, but does not depend on any specific chain of transmission.

Scripture

Deuteronomy 20:19–20

New Jewish Publication Society:

> 19: When in your war against a city you have to besiege it a long time in order to capture it, you must not destroy [*lo tashḥit*] its trees, wielding the ax against them. You may eat of them, but you must not cut them down. Are trees of the field human [*ki ha'adam etz hasadeh*] to withdraw before you into the besieged city? 20: Only trees that you know do not yield food may be destroyed; you may cut them down for constructing siege-works against the city that is waging war on you, until it has been reduced.[1]

1. *The Jewish Study Bible*, eds. Adele Berlin and Marc Zvi Brettler (New York: Oxford University Press, 2004).

King James:

> 19: When thou shalt besiege a city a long time, in making war against it to take it, thou shalt not destroy [*lo tashḥit*] the trees thereof by forcing an axe against them: for thou mayest eat of them, and thou shalt not cut them down (for the tree of the field is man's life) [*ki ha'adam etz hasadeh*] to employ them in the siege: 20: Only the trees which thou knowest that they be not trees for meat, thou shalt destroy and cut them down; and thou shalt build bulwarks against the city that maketh war with thee, until it be subdued.[2]

As will be seen below, these translations reflect different possible interpretations offered in the Midrash.

Midrash Halakhah

Classical rabbinic legal exegesis of the Bible is called *Midrash Halakhah*.[3] Richard Kalmin describes "midrash" as "A rabbinic interpretation, virtually always of a scriptural word, phrase, or verse, which searches, or ferrets out a meaning which is not immediately obvious upon first encounter with the text."[4] The *midrashim* found in this chapter were probably extant in an oral form well before they were redacted around the third to fifth centuries CE. The most important and influential legal compilations that use Midrash are the Jerusalem Talmud, Babylonian Talmud, and to a much lesser extent Mishnah and Tosefta. These genres are the foundational texts of Jewish law, and are broadly arranged by legal topic. The texts relevant to *bal tashḥit* in these genres will be presented in this chapter.

---

2. *The New Cambridge Paragraph Bible, with the Apocrypha*, King James Version, ed. David Norton (Cambridge, UK: Cambridge University Press, 2005).

3. For an introduction to the genre of midrash see H. L. Strack and G. Stemberger, "Part Three: *Midrashim*," in *Introduction to the Talmud and Midrash*, trans. Markus Bockmuehl (Edinburgh: T & T Clark, 1991), 254–393.

4. Richard Kalmin, "Patterns and Developments in Rabbinic *Midrash* of Late Antiquity," in *Hebrew Bible/Old Testament: The History of Its Interpretation*, Vol. 1, *From the Beginnings to the Middle Ages (Until 1300)*, Part 1: *Antiquity*, ed. Magne Saebo (Gottingen, Germany: Vandenhoeck & Ruprecht, 1996), 287.

Sifre (late third century, Land of Israel) (Finkelstein Edition) Book of Deuteronomy, *Shofetim pisqa* 203–204.[5] The midrash asked that if the text specifies the prohibition of cutting down fruit trees with an axe, how do we know that the Torah also prohibits killing off the trees by preventing water from reaching them? The answer provided is that since Scripture uses the term *"lo tashḥit"* ("do not destroy"), it implies all forms of destroying the tree.

Eating from the tree is considered to be a positive commandment, a commandment that must be performed through an action.[6] The prohibition of cutting it down is a negative commandment, one that requires abstention from a particular action. *Ki ha'adam etz hasadeh* also teaches that human life is sustained by fruit trees. Rabbi Yishmael (first and second centuries CE, Land of Israel) taught that if God has compassion for the fruit tree, how much more is his compassion for the fruit itself? The sages determined, however, that if the fruit trees are preventing the city from coming under effective siege, it is permissible to cut them down.

The midrash clarifies that "only trees which you know" in verse 20 refers to fruit trees and "do not yield food" refers to non-fruit-bearing trees. The midrash then asked, if we ultimately allow even fruit trees to be cut down, why bother differentiating between the trees? The answer was, to create a hierarchy between fruit trees and non-fruit-bearing trees. Since fruit trees are more important, the non-fruit trees should be cut down first, so if possible, the fruit trees are spared. Finally, the midrash asked whether this is the case even where the non-fruit-bearing tree is of greater value than the fruit tree, to which it replied that Scripture teaches us that "you shall destroy them and cut them down." The enigmatic response does not indicate a clear course of action. This very same midrash is brought in b*Baba Qama* 91b–92a, but as will be seen later in this chapter, the text is slightly different, making it clear (though perhaps reinterpreting the text) that a fruit tree can be cut down before a non-fruit-bearing tree if the economics of doing so are more beneficial.

---

5. *Sifre Devarim*, ed. L. Finkelstein (New York: Beit HaMidrash LeRabanim BeAmerica, 1969).

6. In this case the commandment is derived from the section of the verse that states "you may eat of them" (*ki mimenu tokhel*). This phrase could also be translated as "for you will eat of them."

***Midrash Tannaim*,**[7] Deuteronomy 20:19–20.[8] The midrash stated that the word "destroy" is a prohibition on cutting off the branches of the tree, while the words "putting an axe to them" indicate a prohibition on chopping down a tree with an axe. The words "do not cut them down" refer to uprooting the tree, which is a transgression of all three. The midrash continued by asking how we know that the prohibition includes actions such as preventing water from reaching the tree, to which the answer is that "destroy" includes all forms of destruction. The midrash then asked what the meaning of *ki ha'adam etz hasadeh* is, to which it answered that humans see their enemy coming to kill them and run away. In other words, the statement is seen as rhetorical—the tree, of course, cannot escape from those wishing to cut it down.

Another interpretation offered by the midrash is that the text includes within it two separate commandments, one positive and one negative. One should eat from the fruit tree (positive), while at the same time abstain from cutting it down (negative). *Ki ha'adam etz hasadeh* is also a statement indicating that human life is sustained by fruit from trees. Nevertheless, if a given tree is an obstacle in carrying out the siege, it should be cut down. It is then asked, if in the end it is permissible to cut down both fruit-bearing and non-fruit-bearing trees, why bother differentiating them? Like *Sifre*, the explanation is that the differentiation creates a hierarchy as to which tree should be cut down first. The text then asks what happens in cases where the lumber of a non-fruit-bearing tree is more valuable than a fruit tree. In such cases fruit trees may be cut down before non-fruit-bearing trees. Finally, a homiletic interpretation of the verses is offered that compares trees to humans. Fruit trees are compared to the righteous. If God holds fruit trees dear because of the fruits they produce despite the fact that they do not see, hear, or speak, how much more does God hold dear the righteous who can do the will of God? Non-fruit-bearing trees, which in addition to not being able to see, hear, or speak do not bear fruit and as such are not held dear by God, how much more so are the wicked not pitied by God?

---

7. *Midrash Tannaim* was compiled by David Tzvi Hoffmann (1843–1921) from other midrashic anthologies, illustrating that there existed a full *Midrash Halakhah* compilation on Deuteronomy.

8. *Midrash Tannaim al Sefer Devarim*, ed. David Tzvi Hoffmann (Tel-Aviv: Offset Israel-America, 1963).

Sifra (third century, Land of Israel) Leviticus, *Qedoshim, parashah* 10, 10:6–7.[9] Similar to what we see in *Sifre Devarim/Midrash Tannaim* 20:19, here there is the same comparison of trees to humans. Fruit trees are equated to the righteous, while non-fruit-bearing trees are compared to the wicked. Contextually, this homily is more at home in *Sifra*. Leading up to the tree–human being analogy, the text offers a list of comparisons between humans and objects and creatures without rational faculties. The text starts off with dealing with the ethical conundrum of why the animal should be put to death (along with the transgressing human) when a human commits bestiality with that animal. The transgressor is clearly the human and not the animal. *Sifra*, however, explains that the animal is guilty of tempting the human and must be put to death. Whether or not we accept this logic, *Sifra* draws an *a fortiori* conclusion about humans. If an animal without rational faculties is put to death for tempting a human to transgress, then a human who does have rational faculties and tempts another human to transgress in such a grievous manner is even more culpable. This sets a hierarchy between humans and the rest of creation that exists in many other places and here helps shape the narrative with regard to wastefulness. The text eventually deals with the case of trees. If God holds fruit trees dear because of the fruit they produce despite the fact that they do not see, hear, or speak, how much more does God hold dear the righteous who can do the will of God? Alternatively, non-fruit-bearing trees, which in addition to not being able to see, hear, or speak do not bear fruit and as such are not held dear by God, how much more so are the wicked not entitled to God's pity?

Midrash and Environmental Ethics

Multiple layers of meaning can be found in the above midrashic sources. First and foremost, it is important to point out that *Midrash Halakhah* treats the legal boundaries of the prohibition to cut down fruit trees more broadly than the wartime context of Deuteronomy 20:19. While not yet relating to the edict as a blanket prohibition against wastefulness, it does extend the prohibition to nonwar situations. This appears to be a first step in expanding the prohibition to include all forms of wastefulness and destruction.

9. *Sifra*, ed. I. Weiss (Vienna: Jacob Schlosberg Publishing, 1862).

Two central themes arise in these three *midrashim*. The first is the notion that there is a hierarchy between humans and nonhumans, and also within the nonhuman world through the preferential status given to fruit trees over their non-fruit-bearing counterparts. This preferential status within the nonhuman world appears to be a spillover from the superiority of humans over the nonhuman world because of the sustenance fruit trees provide. The second theme, which is intricately connected to the first, is that the two interpretations offered for *ki ha'adam etz hasadeh* seemingly represent different worldviews with regard to the value of the natural world. One is that the fruit trees are a future source of food, and long-term sustainability should not be compromised unnecessarily, even in the heat of battle. This worldview gives the fruit trees status because of their instrumental value. It protects them because of their utility. The other worldview suggests that the natural world might have inherent value. Fruit trees are defenseless, unable to escape a marauding army; no benefit is gained through their needless destruction and as such it is prohibited to destroy them.[10]

The problems posed by hierarchical worldviews and the intrinsic vs. instrumental value of anything nonhuman have been some of the central debates within environmental discourse, and there is no consensus on a "winning" approach. Both can offer environmental protection under different premises. Peter Hay summarizes the positions quite comprehensively, and there is little to be gained in repetition.[11] Nevertheless, it is relevant to our subject matter to understand which worldviews in the field of environmental ethics are most similar to the worldviews represented in these particular *midrashim*. The varying interpretations of the midrash for *ki ha'adam etz hasadeh* will be taken up in the chapter on Biblical interpretation, mainly because the different positions have been championed by different schools of Biblical exegetes.

Scholars of religion and environment, especially from within the monotheistic traditions, have found it challenging to abandon

10. The reason we cannot determine with certainty that the midrash espouses this view is because here, too, it is possible that protecting the defenseless trees may ultimately be just a way to inculcate humans with moral values, ultimately making both approaches resonate as anthropocentric.

11. Peter Hay, *Main Currents in Western Environmental Thought* (Bloomington: Indiana University Press, 2002), 26–71.

the notion that humans are morally superior to nonhumans. For instance, even though environmental philosopher Holmes Rolston III argues that there is no fundamental conflict between human and nonhuman interests, where conflict does exist, human interests take precedence.[12] This view appears to be consonant with the midrash, insofar as it protects both the fruit trees and human interests. Within environmental thought, the main conflict with this position would be with deep ecologists such as Arne Naess and George Sessions, who base some of their philosophy on Baruch Spinoza's (1632–1677, Netherlands) notion that there is no hierarchy in nature.[13] While the midrash itself appears to establish legal parameters through which fruit trees are protected, deep ecologists and ecofeminists would argue that the very notion of hierarchies allows for humans (or, for ecofeminists, men) to dominate the natural world (and women), ultimately resulting in ecological crisis.

It could, of course, be argued that the fruit trees have no inherent value and that they are only protected by virtue of their instrumental value. The fact that human life can be sustained (at least in part) by fruit does not necessarily attribute any value to the tree; it only confirms that humans have inherent value and that sustaining human life is paramount. This view is consistent with that of environmental philosophers such as Bryan Norton, who argue that there is no inherent value in nature, yet this does not prevent humans from protecting the environment. Instead, Norton champions the idea of "weak" anthropocentrism, an ethic through which humans do not have the license to unreservedly exploit the environment. In fact, according to Norton, when viewed holistically, it becomes apparent that long-term human sustainability depends on environmental protection.[14] For Norton, the two interpretations presented in the midrash might ultimately just be versions of "weak" anthropocentrism.

A point that deserves further consideration from an environmental perspective is the idea in *Sifre* (and in later commentaries) that the prohibition against destroying fruit trees includes taking action to

12. Holmes Rolston III, *Environmental Ethics: Duties and Values in the Natural World* (Philadelphia: Temple University Press, 1988), 62–71.

13. Peter Hay, *Main Currents*, 42.

14. Bryan Norton, *Toward Unity Among Environmentalists* (New York: Oxford University Press, 1994), 240.

prevent water from reaching the tree. The environmental cost of human activities is often neglected due to its indirect nature. In addition to the direct, obvious, and immediate consequences of human actions, one could derive from this midrash the importance of understanding the indirect consequences of human actions. This will be discussed further in the concluding chapter.

Mishnah and Talmud

It would be unnecessarily confusing to present the Mishnah and then the entire Talmudic discourse surrounding it on the relevant passages. Instead, certain sections from the Talmud are quoted and their context explained. In this manner, the reader can appreciate the context in which the relevant material arises and still benefit from the partial citation. Only the central Talmudic passages will be presented in a more comprehensive format.

Trees

The biblical verses introducing the term *lo tashḥit* do so in the context of trees, making this topic an obvious starting point.

bBaba Qama 91b–92a[15]

This is part of the central passage in rabbinic literature concerning the prohibition against wastefulness in reference to fruit trees. To appreciate the transformation the concept has undergone over the course of history, it is essential to focus special attention on the literature that has had the most impact on the tradition of *bal tashḥit*. This passage stands on its own, and for the time being will be analyzed as such, but the context from which it emerged is of vital importance to the arguments advanced in this book and will be revisited in the final analysis of this section. This is the latter part of a much more elaborate narrative dealing with *bal tashḥit* as a general prohibition and the

15. Unless otherwise stated, all the English translations are from the Soncino edition of the Talmud. Most citations have been slightly modified to provide the most straightforward reading possible.

prohibition against self-harm. This passage much more closely relates to the scriptural origins of the prohibition against wastefulness. The context is discussed in considerable depth in the next section.

> Rav said: A palm tree producing even one *qab*[16] of fruit may not be cut down. An objection was raised [from the following]: What quantity [of fruit] should be on an olive tree so that it should not be permitted to cut it down? A quarter of a *qab*.[17] Olives are different as they are more important. Rabbi Ḥanina said: Shiveḥat[18] my son did not pass away except for having cut down a fig tree before its time. Ravina, however, said: If its value [for other purposes] exceeds [the value] for fruit, it is permitted [to cut it down]. It was also taught to the same effect: [Deuteronomy 20:20] *Only the trees of which you know* implies even fruit-bearing trees; that they be not trees for food, means a non-fruit-bearing tree. But since we ultimately include all things, why then was it stated, [Deuteronomy 20:20] "*that they are not trees for food*?" To give priority [for the cutting down of] a non-fruit-bearing tree over one bearing edible fruit. As you might say that this is so even where the value [of the non-fruit-bearing tree] exceeds [the value of] fruit, it says [Deuteronomy 20:20] "*only*." Samuel's field labourer brought him some dates. As he partook of them he tasted wine in them. When he asked the labourer how that came about, he told him that the date trees were placed between vines. He said to him: Since they are weakening the vines so much, bring me their roots tomorrow. When Rav Ḥisda saw certain palms among the vines he said to his field labourers: Remove them with their roots. [The produce of] vines can easily buy palms but [the produce of] palms cannot buy vines.

---

16. A *qab* or *qav* is a measure of volume equivalent to two dozen eggs (Yitzḥak Frank, *The Practical Talmud Dictionary* [Jerusalem: Ariel, United Israel Institutes], 1991), 300.

17. The original context for this statement can be found in m*Shevi'it* 4:10, discussing the felling of fruit trees in a Sabbatical year.

18. The *baraita* regarding Rabbi Ḥanina's son also appeared above in the section on b*Baba Batra* 26a with a variant spelling.

The first thing to notice in this passage is that the prohibition against cutting down fruit trees has been removed from its context of war found in Deuteronomy 20:19 and viewed as a general ban on cutting down fruit trees during all times. On the face of it, it appears that this passage deals with the protection of fruit trees. After all, the Talmud explains that even fruit trees that produce very little fruit still receive protected status. It would be more accurate, however, to view this passage not as a discussion of the protected status of fruit trees, but as dealing with the terms under which fruit trees can be cut down. Even according to the opening statements in this passage, it is permissible to cut down fruit trees that produce less than the amount of fruit listed. These unproductive fruit trees could be old or diseased, or barren for some other reason. Moreover, while the initial statement of the Talmud in this passage relates to quantity (one *qab* of dates for palm trees), the next sentence affirms that we are in fact dealing with relative quantities based on economic value. Olive trees have greater market value than palm trees, and in the economic realities of the time when and place where these laws were promulgated, olives were considered four times as valuable as dates. Perhaps if this comparison were being made today or at any other time or place, the ratio might have been different. The idea that market value is highly contextualized and perhaps even culturally specific is evident from the demands made by Samuel and Rav Ḥisda to uproot palm trees due to their harm to grapevines. Jacob L. Wright explains, for example, that in other Near Eastern cultures, grapevines were considered inferior to date palms (and olive trees) due to the relative lack of nutrients in their fruit and the short time they needed to reach maturity and bear fruit.[19]

Left unanswered is the chronological framework of this equation. Is the value of the fruit based on only one season's worth of production, or the entire projected life span of the tree? This information is of vital importance for making such a determination. The Talmud's silence on this matter is surprising, and with no official final decree the door is, at least in theory, left open for leniency on the subject. Regardless, Ravina made this claim somewhat irrelevant by asserting that even fruit trees producing much larger quantities of fruit can be

19. Jacob L. Wright, "Warfare and Wanton Destruction: A Reexamination of Deuteronomy 20:19–20 in Relation to Ancient Siegecraft," *Journal of Biblical Literature* 27, no. 3 (2008): 434.

cut down if it is justified economically. Any discussion of the possibility of trees having intrinsic value is marginalized and replaced by monetary considerations. If the land is of greater value than the fruit tree, or if the fruit tree is worth more as lumber, it becomes entirely permissible to cut it down. So much do the considerations become monetary that the sages imagined a scenario in which non-fruit-bearing trees have greater economic value than fruit trees, making it permissible to cut down the fruit trees while the non-fruit-bearing trees are left standing. The Talmud clarified that even though there always exist theoretical situations in which fruit trees can be cut down, in cases where a fruit tree and a non-fruit-bearing tree are of equal value, the non-fruit-bearing tree should be cut down first if one of these must be cut down. This might in theory strengthen the position viewing fruit-bearing trees as having inherent value, though not nearly enough to overcome the damage done to the intrinsic worth of fruit trees by the utilitarian approach in which the value of a tree is based primarily on the monetary value placed on it by the market. It would, of course, be very difficult for a society to function without the ability to make certain emendations to the prohibition against cutting down fruit trees. Yet to understand the ramifications of this approach it is useful to imagine an extreme circumstance. If the market is the only tool through which to value a fruit tree, it is possible to imagine a scenario in which even the last fruit tree in the world could be cut down if justified monetarily.[20]

Not to be forgotten is Rabbi Ḥanina's statement (also seen below in b*Baba Batra* 26a) in which he claimed that his son died for cutting down a fig tree prematurely. To add to the points made above, it is important to consider the context in which Rabbi Ḥanina's statement is presented. Here, permission is granted to cut down poorly producing fruit trees, but directly after this comes the warning of Rabbi Ḥanina urging the one taking such an action to think twice and proceed with caution. Throughout the legal responsa literature (seen in the responsa chapter), it becomes clear that when someone asks a rabbi whether it is permissible to cut down a fruit tree (in whichever one of many different contexts), the answer is almost always affirmative. Some rabbis added a warning with their response that cutting down fruit trees is dangerous due to Rabbi Ḥanina's sorrowful hortatory tale, and if

20. This would, of course, imply that other sources of food were available and sufficient for the population.

there is any possibility the act can be avoided, steps should be taken in that direction, even though one may make an argument in favor of cutting such trees down.[21] This may be understood as a quasilegal ethical framework that informs the reader/practitioner that even though a certain action is permitted according to the law, it should still be avoided, or at least seriously deliberated before undertaken.

bBaba Batra 26a

Context: The Mishnah preceding this passage dealt with the distance one must keep between one's own trees and one's neighbor's trees. The Mishnah presented a case in which two neighbors have a fence between them and both have planted trees adjacent to the fence and the roots of one person's trees grow into the property of the other. If the neighbor who has been invaded by the roots decides to dig a trench or pit adjacent to the fence, it is permissible to destroy these roots during the process. The following emerged in the Talmud from a discourse on the Mishnah:

> Rabbah, son of Rav Ḥanan, had some date trees adjoining a vineyard of Rav Joseph, and birds used to roost on the date trees and fly down and damage the vines. So, Rav Joseph told Rabbah, son of Rav Ḥanan, to cut down his date trees. The latter said: But I have kept them [four cubits] away! This, replied the other, applies only to other trees, but for vines we require more. But does not our Mishnah say that THIS APPLIES BOTH TO VINES AND TO ALL OTHER TREES?[22] He said: This is so where there are other trees or vines on both sides, but where there are other trees on one side and vines on the other a greater space is required. Rabbah, son of Rav Ḥanan said: I will not cut them down, because Rav

21. Meir Ayali demonstrates how this became a serious consideration among the *aḥaronim* (legal decisors after the medieval era), and in fact some prohibited or limited the circumstances under which it was permissible to cut down a fruit tree. See Meir Ayali, "*HaḤaradah Bifnei Keritat Etz-Ma'akhal BeSafrut HaShu"t*," in *Tura: Studies in Jewish Thought, Simon Greenberg Jubilee Volume* (Tel-Aviv: Hakibbutz Hameuchad Publishing House, 1989), 135–40.

22. All fully capitalized words here and subsequently are direct excerpts from the Mishnah and are used to differentiate the text of the Mishnah from that of the Talmud.

> has said that it is forbidden to cut down a date tree which bears a *qab* of dates, and Rabbi Ḥanina has said, "My son Shikheḥat only died because he cut down a fig tree before its time." You, Sir, can cut them down if you like.

There are three noteworthy elements in this passage. The first is that the rabbis were dealing with the prohibition against cutting down fruit trees. This particular case emerged as part of a discussion on property rights and damages. The second issue is that the term *bal tashḥit* is not mentioned. This observation is important, but must be put aside at this time until the remaining material is presented. Finally, the example brought by Rabbah of Rabbi Ḥanina's son indicates a belief in the connection between the welfare of humans and the integrity of fruit trees, as evidenced by Rabbi Ḥanina's understanding that the sin of cutting a fig tree outside of these parameters was the cause of the premature demise of his son. Had his son not transgressed by cutting down the fruit tree, then presumably he would not have died before his father.

Like the previous text from *Baba Qama*, it is important to see that the rabbis took the prohibition in Deuteronomy 20:19, which specifically deals with cutting down fruit trees during wartime, and *applied the prohibition to everyday conduct*. In other words, they understood the example from the Torah as being an extreme circumstance from which one must derive an understanding of acceptable legal behavior in general. If it is prohibited to cut down fruit trees during wartime, then *a fortiori* it is prohibited to cut them down in times of peace. The rabbis, of course, understood that it is at times necessary to bypass this prohibition for reasons such as the one found in the above passage. They, therefore, attempted to create a legal framework in which this could be done.

The third and most interesting observation is the most important for understanding the connections between self-harm and wastefulness. The belief promoted here, that cutting down a fruit tree can result in a human death, has significant implications for the concept of *bal tashḥit*. First and foremost this is indicative of a hyperliteral reading of the phrase *"ki ha'adam etz hasadeh"* found in Deuteronomy 20:19. If the human is indeed coequal to a tree of the field, then destroying the fruit tree is equivalent to destroying a human. This is precisely the claim made by Rabbi Ḥanina and accepted by Rabbah. Moreover, such an act would be a transgression of the prohibition against suicide/

self-inflicted harm (Genesis 9:5). While there are alternative ways to understand these verses and Talmudic passages, there appears to be an integral, though still implicit, connection in the rabbinic sources between the two aforementioned verses and the concept of *bal tashḥit*. The explanation of this connection is further enhanced in the conclusion of this chapter.

bTa'anit 7a

Context: The Mishnah preceding this Talmudic discourse dealt with the time of the year when one ceases to pray for rain. This particular passage stands on its own and is not obviously connected to what precedes and follows it.

> Rabbi Jeremiah said to Rabbi Zera: Pray, Master, come and teach. The latter replied: I do not feel well enough and am not able to do so. [Then Rabbi Jeremiah said] Pray, Master, expound something of an aggadic character, and he replied: Thus Rabbi Yoḥanan said: What is the meaning of the verse, [Deuteronomy 20:19] *"For is the tree of the field human?"* Is then a human the tree of the field? [This can only be explained if we connect the verse with the words immediately before it] where it is written, [Deuteronomy 20:19] *"For you may eat of them, but you shall not cut them down"*; but then again it is written, [Deuteronomy 20:20] *"It* [the non-fruit-bearing tree] *you shall destroy and cut down."* How is this to be explained?—If the scholar is a worthy person learn [eat] from him and do not shun [cut] him, but if he is not, destroy him and cut him down.

What is particularly important with regard to these passages is the fact that they attribute the specific prohibition to cut down fruit trees in Deuteronomy 20:19 to the words *"lo tikhrot"* (do not cut down) as opposed to the words *"lo tashḥit"* (do not destroy).[23] It seems that the "cutting down" is the manner in which the "destruc-

23. Yitzhak Eliyahu Shtasman, in his book *Sefer Etz HaSadeh: BeDinei Bal Tashhit, Qetzitzat Ilanot UVizui Okhalin* (Jerusalem: Foundation for the Advancement of Torah Study, 1999), summarized the various approaches throughout Jewish literature with regard to the relationship of *lo tashḥit* to *lo tikhrot* found in Deuteronomy 20:19.

tion" is carried out. This possibility becomes more likely when we take into account the midrashic text on this verse from *Sifra,* which asks if chopping down the fruit tree with an axe is the only way the prohibition is transgressed. To this the midrash replies no, because the text *"lo tashḥit"* would include all forms of destruction. Based on the rabbinic principle that there is no redundancy in Scripture, it becomes necessary to explain why the verse uses both *"lo tikhrot"* and *"lo tashḥit."* One explanation is that the former applies to the specific context of the verse, while the latter expands the prohibition beyond the verse. This helps explain the absence of the term *bal tashḥit* in the Talmudic passages dealing with the cutting down of fruit trees and its use when the discussion is of wastefulness in general. Regardless, the midrash appears to be the first point where we begin to see a methodological analysis of the verse enabling the development of a general ethic beyond fruit trees and war.

bPesaḥim 50b

Context: The Mishnah dealt with the issue of laboring before noon on the eve of the festival of *Pesaḥ* (Passover). Though the prohibition on work only comes into effect after noon, towns had varying traditions on when they actually ceased their labors; some stopped prior to noon and others at noon. The rabbis of the Talmud asked why this issue was raised in the context of *Pesaḥ*. After all, ceasing work prior to the Sabbath and to other festivals is also applicable. The Talmud explained that the difference is that on the Sabbath and other festivals labor is prohibited only after the afternoon prayer, whereas on *Pesaḥ* the prohibition begins precisely at noon. In all cases, the Talmud claimed, the transgressors will never see a blessing in their lifetime from any labor done after the deadline, but if labor is done on the eve of *Pesaḥ* the transgressors are also ostracized from the community. The Talmud then discussed other instances where it is determined that those engaging in certain behaviors will also never be graced with blessings.

> Our Rabbis taught: Traders in the market-stands and those who breed small cattle, and those who cut down beautiful trees, and those who cast their eyes at the better portion, will never see a sign of blessing. What is the reason? Because people gaze at them.

It is most likely that the beautiful trees in question in this passage are in fact fruit-bearing trees. This would be consistent with the approach of the commentaries on 2 Kings 3:19, where very similar language was used (*etz tov* in 2 Kings 3:19 vs. *ilanot tovin* here).[24] What makes this passage of interest is the social stigma associated with cutting down these trees. The fact that people stare at people cutting down these trees is an indication that such behavior is socially suspect. Consequently, those engaging in the described behaviors are condemned to an unblessed life, probably as a way to discourage such actions.

General *Bal Tashḥit*

bYevamot 11b–12a

Context: Jewish law stipulates that if a married man dies childless, his paternal brother has an obligation to continue his lineage by marrying his widow. This act is called Levirate marriage. The brother can refuse, in which case the woman performs a ceremony called *ḥalitzah*. A woman who performs this ceremony is now eligible to remarry, but is prohibited from marrying a priest (because she is now like a divorcée). The Talmud dealt with cases of polygamous marriages that terminated with the death of the man. The discussion of interest revolved around a hypothetical case in which the deceased had two widows. One of the widows had been married to the deceased, then divorced, and then remarried him. Such a marriage is prohibited by Jewish law if the man was a priest or if she were married to another in the interim. While this woman, who had previously been divorced, is prohibited from marrying a priest, the other widow is not. The brother is only required to marry or release by *ḥalitzah* one of the women. The relevant passage in the Talmud stated that if the brother is uninterested in either woman, he must perform the *ḥalitzah* ceremony with the woman who is prohibited to a priest due to the illicit nature of her marriage, instead of the one who would be permitted. Since the permitted woman never undergoes the ceremony of *ḥalitzah*, she is permitted even to marry a priest. The reason for performing the *ḥalitzah* on the forbidden woman is explained in the Talmud:

---

24. See the chapter on Bible for an in-depth analysis of this verse.

> One must take into account the moral lesson of Rav Joseph. For Rav Joseph said: Here, Rabbi taught that a man shall not pour the water out of his cistern so long as others may require it.

Though the prohibition against wastefulness is not mentioned explicitly, it is nonetheless clear that this is the concept that Rav Joseph in the name of Rabbi is evoking. This concept lends itself, in my opinion, to an unnamed but existing environmental ethic. Contextually, the application of the moral lesson is that since the brother is not planning on marrying either of his deceased brother's wives, why prevent the widow who could in theory still marry a priest from doing so? As such, the Talmud advised that the *ḥalitzah* ceremony should be performed by the woman who was in any case ineligible to marry a priest. The context for the original moral lesson brought by Rabbi in the second century is unknown, and speculation in this regard is futile. What is relevant to the discourse on wastefulness is the statement "so long as others may require it." In other words, the focus of the moral lesson is not on the intrinsic worth of water, but only on its worth relative to the utility it provides to humans. In a globalized world, the question becomes more complex because somewhere there is always an "other" who needs water. Applying the principle more broadly, Susan Strasser highlights the social stratification of consumption: "What is rubbish to some is useful or valuable to others, and the ones who perceive value are nearly always the ones with less money."[25]

mBaba Qama 8:6 (bBaba Qama90b)

Without a doubt, the greatest motivation for environmental concern is self-concern. There are, of course, many other reasons to protect the environment, but primary among them is our own well-being. This Mishnah and the ensuing Talmudic text based on it are the central texts in which the sages made firm connections between the acts of wastefulness and self-harm. These texts are paramount to understand-

25. Susan Strasser, *Waste and Want: A Social History of Trash* (New York: Henry Holt and Company, 1999), 9.

ing how the rabbis conceptualized the act of wastefulness in terms of self-harm, initially through the destruction of trees. When the concepts of self-harm and wastefulness are integrated, they create a foundation for an environmental ethic. We will see that this link is strongest in the tannaitic literature, but when problematized by the rabbis of the Talmud, the link is fragmented and wastefulness and self-harm each begin to develop new conceptual trajectories.
Mishnah:

> If a man boxes another man's ear, he has to pay him a *sela*. Rabbi Judah in the name of Rabbi Jose the Galilean says that [he has to pay him] a *maneh*. If he slapped him [on the face] he has to pay him two hundred *zuz*; [if he did it] with the back of his hand he has to pay him four hundred *zuz*. If he pulled his ear, plucked his hair, spat so that the spittle reached him, removed his garment from upon him, uncovered the head of a woman in the market place, he must pay four hundred *zuz*. This is the general rule: all depends upon the dignity [of the insulted person]. Rabbi Akiva said that even the poor in Israel have to be considered as if they are freemen reduced in circumstances, for in fact they all are the descendants of Abraham, Isaac and Jacob. It once happened that a certain person uncovered the head of a woman in the market place and when she came before Rabbi Akiva, he ordered the offender to pay her four hundred *zuz*. The latter said to him, rabbi, allow me time [in which to carry out the judgment]; Rabbi Akiva assented and fixed a time for him. He watched her until he saw her standing outside the door of her courtyard, he then broke in her presence a pitcher in which there was oil of the value of an *isar*, and she uncovered her head and collected the oil with her palms and put her hands upon her head [to anoint it]. He set up witnesses against her and came to Rabbi Akiva and said to him: Have I to give such a woman four hundred *zuz*? **But Rabbi Akiva said to him: Your argument is of no legal effect, for where one injures oneself, though forbidden, he is exempt, yet, were others to injure him, they would be liable: so also he who cuts down his own plants, though not acting law-**

fully, is exempt, yet were others to [do it], they would be liable.[26]

The above passage is the Mishnah on which the central Talmudic discourse dealing with *bal tashḥit* is based. As can be seen, the Mishnah covered instances in which a person inflicted damage on another individual. The damage inflicted falls into a special category of damage in the form of embarrassment through physical contact. In other words, the damage inflicted is not just physical and not just embarrassing, but a combination of the two. The Mishnah then related a particular case in which a man removed the head-covering of a woman in the marketplace. The man tried to get out of paying his fine by demonstrating through subterfuge that the woman would remove her head-covering in the public domain of her own volition. Rabbi Akiva, who issued the fine, asserted that the man's argument was not valid due to the fact that even though there is a prohibition against the infliction of self-injury, one is still exempt from punishment. Others inflicting exactly the same injury, however, are liable and held accountable for their actions. Rabbi Akiva then drew a comparison between the infliction of injury and the cutting down of plants. One is prohibited from cutting down one's own seedlings, but is exempt from punishment. If anyone else were to cut down that person's seedlings, however, they would be liable. Contextually, Rabbi Akiva rejected the man's argument, because the woman was exempt from liability for taking off her own head-covering, whereas the man was liable. The exemption from punishment to people harming themselves is intuitive; such a punishment would entail a fine, but owing oneself a fine is a meaningless concept.

The Mishnah is discussed in more depth in the Talmudic discourse that ensues, but a number of important things should be noted from this passage before engaging the Talmud. The first is that this specific chapter in the Talmud is titled "*HaḤovel,*" literally translated as "the one who harms." The root *ḥ.b.l.* is used throughout the Aramaic translations of the Bible when translating the root *sh.ḥ.t.*, which is the root on which the term *bal tashḥit* is based. This creates a semantic connection between them. It is our contention, however,

26. The boldface is my emphasis.

that *the prohibition against self-harm was once integrally connected to the prohibition against wastefulness/destruction*, at least in the minds of some important thinkers.

Much stronger than the semantic connection, though still not definitive proof of an inherent connection, is the parallel drawn by Rabbi Akiva between self-harm and the cutting down of trees, and ultimately wastefulness. In my estimation the connection is not random, and the association being made between self-harm and trees is deliberate. It is far more than an exercise comparing similar forms of exegesis. If the point was hermeneutic similarity, Rabbi Akiva could have chosen any number of different examples to emphasize the point being made regarding self-harm. The comparison he chose to make was with the prohibition against cutting down seedlings. This fits so well into the argument I make regarding a connection between these ideas and the ethic that they form, that it seems implausible to me that the association made by Rabbi Akiva could be random. These are just a few points in a long list of many that establish and reinforce the coherence of the paradigm presented in this book.

bBaba Qama 91a–91b

> HE WATCHED UNTIL HE SAW HER STANDING OUTSIDE THE DOOR OF HER COURTYARD [. . . FOR IF ONE INJURES ONESELF, THOUGH IT IS FORBIDDEN TO DO SO . . .] But was it not taught: Rabbi Akiva said to him, You have dived into the depths and have brought up a potsherd in your hand, for a man may injure himself. Rabbah said: There is no difficulty, as the Mishnaic statement deals with actual injury, whereas the other text referred to degradation. But surely the Mishnah deals with degradation, and it nevertheless says: If one injures oneself, though it is forbidden to do so, he is exempt? It was this which he said to him: There could be no question regarding degradation, as a man may put himself to shame, but even in the case of injury where a man may not injure himself [he is still exempt], if others injured him they would be liable.

The Talmud questioned Rabbi Akiva's statement from the Mishnah declaring that one is prohibited from harming oneself because there exists a *baraita* in which Rabbi Akiva declares the exact opposite.[27] Nevertheless, the rabbis of the Talmud made an attempt to reconcile the two statements. The rabbis ended up drawing a distinction between shaming someone and physically injuring them. The rabbis of the Talmud claimed that Rabbi Akiva indeed stood by the approach that one is permitted to shame oneself while others who shame an individual are liable. Even in the case of physical injury, where a person is prohibited from engaging in self-harm and nevertheless is not liable, however, were someone else to harm this person, he/she would be liable. The Talmud then deliberated further on the question of whether a person was in fact permitted to engage in self-harm:

> But may a man not injure himself? Was it not taught: You might perhaps think that if a man takes an oath to do harm to himself and did not do so he should be exempt. It is therefore stated [Leviticus 5:4]: "*To do evil or to do good,*" [implying that] just as to do good is permitted, so also to do evil [to oneself] is permitted; I have accordingly to apply [the same law in] the case where a man had sworn to do harm to himself and did not do harm? Samuel said: The oath referred to was to keep a fast. It would accordingly follow that regarding doing harm to others it would similarly mean to make them keep a fast. But how can one make others keep a fast? By keeping them locked up in a room.

An attempt was made to prove that it actually is permissible to harm oneself. Leviticus 5:4 was used as a proof-text illustrating that someone who makes an oath, whether to do good or to do harm, and then does not follow through is liable. The fact that someone can make an oath to do a harmful act and then be liable for it is learned

27. It is important to understand the basic way in which rabbinic methodology works. A *baraita* (plural *baraitot*) is a statement made by a *tanna* that was not included in the Mishnah. *Baraitot* are often brought as proof-texts to drive home an argument made by the rabbis of the Talmud. On the whole, however, they are considered less authoritative than the Mishnah, but still of greater authority than an *amoraic* statement. In this case there is a contradiction between the Mishnah and the *baraita*. It is, of course, possible that the transmission of the *baraita* was fragmented, and that the statement as found in the Mishnah is the correct one.

by analogy to benefitting oneself; since an oath is to be taken with the utmost seriousness, this is considered an indication that it is indeed permissible to harm oneself. After all, the verse would not assert that one was liable for breaking an oath to do harm if doing harm was a transgression. Samuel, an *amora*, claimed that the harm referred to in the verse was not actually direct physical harm, but indirect harm such as fasting. Thus, the harm to others in this context refers to forcing someone to fast against their will. The Talmud continued its analysis by dealing with actual instances of physical harm:

> But was it not taught: What is meant by doing harm to others? [If one says], I will smite a certain person and will split his skull. It must therefore be said that *tannaim* differed on this point, for there is one view maintaining that a man may not injure himself and there is another maintaining that a man may injure himself.

Our text in *Baba Qama* quotes a different Talmudic teaching found in b*Shavu'ot* 27a, which indicates that doing harm or evil to others specifically means physical harm. After this matter is clarified it becomes clear that attempts to reconcile both of Rabbi Akiva's statements have not yet satisfied the rabbis of the Talmud. Though both *tannaim* being referred to in this instance happen to be Rabbi Akiva, the Talmud assumes that they come from different traditions. The *tosafot*[28] explained that in fact the argument was not between Rabbi Akiva and himself but rather between *tannaim* who were conflicted on how to understand Rabbi Akiva. This makes it easier to understand the trajectory of the argument that follows in the Talmud:

> But who is the *tanna* maintaining that a man may not injure himself? If you say that he was the *tanna* of the teaching [Genesis 9:5], "*And surely your blood of your lives will I require,*" [upon which] Rabbi Eleazar remarked [that] it meant I will require your blood if shed by the hands of yourselves, [I would answer that that is not necessarily the case, for] perhaps killing [oneself] is different [from other forms of self-harm].

28. The *tosafot*, literally translated as 'addenda," were a large group of commentators on the Talmud and Bible that emerged in France and Germany during the twelfth and thirteenth centuries.

In the process of trying to deduce from which tradition the approach that a person may not injure himself derives, we enter the part of the deliberations that is of great significance to the theme of this book. An effort is made to narrow down the possible source of the position that self-harm is prohibited based on an undisputed teaching. Genesis 9:5 is quoted as a possible source. The primary argument by the Talmud[29] that self-harm is prohibited is found in Rabbi Eleazar's exegesis on this verse, which claimed that a reckoning will be had for anyone spilling their own blood. The Talmud then rejected this approach due to the possibility that suicide might be qualitatively different than other forms of self-harm.

The Talmud continued the deliberations with other possibilities. For the purposes of our arguments, we are not able to move on to the next option quite as quickly. As we will see in the chapter on biblical interpretation, the sources mostly understood Genesis 9:5 as a prohibition against either murder or suicide, with the majority favoring the understanding that it is a prohibition against suicide.[30] There is, however, no indication that Rabbi Eleazar understood Genesis 9:5 as including only a prohibition against suicide. Rather, one may argue that he favored a more inclusive interpretation of the verse as a prohibition against self-harm in general. Due to the possibility that Rabbi Eleazar did in fact view injury and suicide as substantively different from one another, the Talmud asserted that this teaching must not be the source of the prohibition against self-harm.

---

29. As mentioned in the preface, instead of using the turn of phrase "anonymous voice of the Talmud" or "redactors of the Talmud" (*stam* or *stama* with the definite article in Aramaic), I anthropomorphize the text by using terms such as "the Talmud explains" or "the Talmud rejects."

30. Different midrashic compilations offer both possible readings. *Sifre Zuta* (third century, Land of Israel) 35:27—in the context of the "blood avenger" found in Deuteronomy 19, the words "But for your own life-blood" from Genesis 9:5 are understood to mean that a reckoning will be required from anyone who murders (*Sifre DeVei Rav, Sifre Zuta*, ed. Ḥaim Shaul Horowitz [Jerusalem: Wahrmann, 1966]). *Bereishit Rabbah* (fifth century, Land of Israel) *Noaḥ* 34, 9:5—"But for your own life-blood" is seen by the midrash as a prohibition against committing suicide. The text mentions that the prohibition includes those who strangle themselves, in order to cover methods of suicide that do not actually shed blood. The text goes on to give examples of various people who seemingly transgressed this prohibition, but are absolved by the midrash. These include Saul, who fell on his sword during his final battle with the Philistines, and Ḥananiah, Mishael, and Azariah who entered a burning furnace (in the book of Daniel) as martyrs (*Midrash Bereishit Rabbah*, eds. J. Theodor and Ch. Albeck [Jerusalem: Wahrmann Books, 1965]).

It is important to note that it was the Talmud that first offered the possibility that the source of the prohibition against injuring oneself could be Genesis 9:5. Regardless of how the Talmud went on to build its argument, the fact that the Talmud offered it confirmed the possibility of the existence of a tradition that viewed Genesis 9:5 as the source of the prohibition against harming oneself. As will be seen in the biblical chapter, Yaakov bar Asher and Barukh HaLevi Epstein both asserted that Genesis 9:5 is in fact a prohibition against self-harm (and not simply suicide). This is of great importance to building the case that Genesis 9:5 was instrumental in developing the concept of *bal tashḥit*. This allows for an understanding that the prohibition against injuring oneself is, in fact, an integral part of *bal tashḥit*. At this point, however, it is still somewhat premature to continue the analysis of the parallels between self-harm and wastefulness, because this particular Talmudic passage rejected such a connection.

Ultimately, the Talmud in this specific instance looks for a solution elsewhere. The Talmud continued to search for a teaching that would allow them to attribute the position that a person is prohibited from causing self-harm to a specific tradition:

> He might therefore be the *tanna* of the following teaching: Garments may be rent for a dead person as this is not necessarily done to imitate the ways of the Amorites. But Rabbi Eleazar said: I heard that he who rends [his garments] too much for a dead person transgresses the command, "Thou shalt not destroy (*bal tashḥit*)," and it seems that this should be the more so in the case of injuring his own body. But garments might perhaps be different, as the loss is irretrievable, for Rabbi Yoḥanan used to call garments my honorers, and Rav Ḥisda whenever he had to walk between thorns and thistles used to lift up his garments [s]aying that whereas for the body [if injured] nature will produce a healing, for garments [if torn] nature could produce no cure.

This is one of the *most critical passages* with regard to the development of *bal tashḥit*. It starts by mentioning a practice that has become part of Jewish law: tearing garments as a sign of mourning. The Talmud is quick to mention that this practice is not considered an emulation of the Amorite tradition. This stipulation is important and will be discussed in greater depth in the section dealing with foreign practices and idolatry.

Rabbi Eleazar reflected on the practice of tearing clothes as part of the process of mourning the dead. He stated that he was familiar with a teaching that placed limits on this tradition, and that tearing clothes as part of mourning had to be done within reasonable parameters, otherwise the person tearing would be liable for transgressing *bal tashḥit*.[31] This could mean one of two things: either the limits in question are with regard to a single garment (i.e., the tear should not be too extreme) or to many garments (i.e., one should limit the tearing to a single garment so as not to damage multiple articles of clothing). Both of these options receive attention throughout Jewish scholarship. Regardless of which of these options Rabbi Eleazar is referring to, our concern is with the *a fortiori* deduction made with regard to self-harm: if someone transgresses the prohibition of *bal tashḥit* by destroying something material, how much greater is the transgression with reference to destroying or harming one's own body?

It must be noted that there is no clear consensus regarding the author of the *a fortiori* deduction mentioned above. I contend that it was Rabbi Eleazar himself who made the deduction, whereas others (for instance the Artscroll edition of the Talmud)[32] claim that this deduction belongs to the anonymous voice of the Talmud. This difference is ultimately minor in light of the entire tradition history of *bal tashḥit*, but because this is a critical stage in the development of the concept, it is important to be as accurate as possible. As such, I will list the arguments supporting each position.

Let us begin with the claim that Rabbi Eleazar is the one who makes the *a fortiori* argument from clothing to self-harm.[33] The first indicator that the words "and it seems that this should be the more so in the case of injuring his own body" (*vekhol sheken gufo*) in the Middle

31. It should be noted that the *tosafot* ask why Rabbi Eleazar bothered mentioning such an obvious example. They concluded that it was to emphasize that *bal tashḥit* still applies even in cases where destroying or wasting something is proscribed by a commandment. Even in such cases one should still fulfill the commandment within the parameters of the law; exceeding these parameters would be a transgression of *bal tashḥit*.

32. Abba Zvi Naiman, *The Schottenstein Edition Talmud Bavli: Tractate Bava Kamma*, Vol. 3, ed. Yisroel Simcha Schorr (New York: Mesorah Publications, 2001).

33. Unfortunately, there are no parallel sources in other rabbinic texts for this specific *baraita* by Rabbi Eleazar, which means that our analysis is limited to the text in the Babylonian Talmud.

Hebrew of the *tannaim* belong to Rabbi Eleazar and not the Talmud is the overall structure of the passage (*sugya*). The Talmud was concerned with finding the *tanna* who held the position that it is prohibited to engage in self-harm. The Talmud provided three options, rejected the first two (which we will now deliberate at length), and (as we will see) accepted the third.[34] Just as the voice of the Talmud began with the word "perhaps" (*dilma*) in the first case, it is reasonable to also assume that the Talmud begins with the word "perhaps" (*dilma*) in the second case. The words "and it seems that this should be the more so in the case of injuring his own body" (*vekhol sheken gufo*) directly precede the "perhaps" (*dilma*) of the second case. As such, it is reasonable to assume that they belong to the *baraita* of Rabbi Eleazar, and not to the Talmud. This reading is reinforced by various translations of the Talmud. For instance, the Soncino translation into English and the Steinsaltz translation into Hebrew simply have a comma separating "is liable for transgressing *bal tashḥit*" (*loqeh mishum bal tashḥit*) and "and it seems that this should be the more so in the case of injuring his own body" (*vekhol sheken gufo*).[35]

Louis Jacobs, a prominent Jewish thinker from the past century and a Talmudist, clearly understood the words "and it seems that this should be the more so in the case of injuring his own body" (*vekhol sheken gufo*) to belong to the *baraita*. He wrote, "If a man, according to this tanna, must not even destroy his clothes it must surely follow that he is not allowed to engage in such destructive practices as self-injury."[36]

---

34. The language used in the rejection of the first option was "perhaps killing is different" (*dilma qetala shani*) is Aramaic, the language of the Babylonian Talmud. The same formula was used in rejecting the second option, "perhaps garments might be different" (*dilma begadim shani*), again in Aramaic.

35. The same sentence division can be found in the vocalized Yemenite edition of the Talmud (Yosef bar Aharon Amar HaLevi, *Masekhet Baba Qama, Talmud Bavli: Menukad al pi Masoret Yehudei Teiman*, ed. Yosef bar Aharon Amar HaLevi [Jerusalem: HaMenaked Publishing, 1980]). This would suggest that the *baraita* ends after the word(s) "his own body" (*gufo*) and not after the word *tashḥit*. Ezra Tzion Melamed's translation of the text into Hebrew could go either way, as he uses a dash to separate the words "is liable for transgressing *bal tashḥit*" (*loqeh mishum bal tashḥit*) and "and it seems that this should be the more so in the case of injuring his own body" (*vekhol sheken gufo*). *Talmud Bavli: Masekhet Baba Qama*, trans. Ezra Tzion Melamed (Jerusalem: Dvir and Mesada Publishing, 1952).

36. Louis Jacobs, *Religion and the Individual: A Jewish Perspective* (Cambridge, UK: Cambridge University Press, 1992), 60.

As indicated above, there is also a linguistic argument to be made, insofar as the voice of the Talmud usually changes between Hebrew and Aramaic. Here this Hebrew would belong to the *baraita* and the Aramaic to the anonymous narrator.

The counterargument can be approached from two different angles. The most obvious one is, if the words "and it seems that this should be the more so in the case of injuring his own body" (*vekhol sheken gufo*) in fact belonged to Rabbi Eleazar, the Talmud would have had to accept this *baraita* as the source of the prohibition against self-harm, which it clearly does not. This, however, is not necessarily the case. In the Talmud, legal positions are held either by a majority (*rov*) or by an individual (*da'at yaḥid*), as in our case. In cases where an opinion is held by an individual, his position is not necessarily authoritative. The two cases used by the Talmud to refute the *baraita* as the source of the prohibition both belong to *amoraim* (Rabbi Yoḥanan and Rav Ḥisda). As such, they do not carry with them the necessary clout to undermine the teaching of a *tanna*. Another tannaitic source, however, does have such authority. There is a *baraita* with multiple parallels that stated the following:

> Rabbi Eliezer said [Deuteronomy 6:5]: "And you shall love the Lord thy God with all your heart and with all your soul, and with all your might." Since "with all your soul" is stated, why is "with all your might" stated? And, if "with all your might" is written, why also write "with all your soul?" For the man to whom life is more precious than wealth, it is written "with all your soul"; while he to whom wealth is more precious than life is bidden, "with all your might" [i.e., substance].[37]

In other words, some people hold their bodies more dearly than their possessions and some people their possessions more dearly than their bodies. At least when the *baraita* was being formulated, there was no definitive legal stance on the matter. The *tanna* of this *baraita* is Rabbi Eliezer, perhaps Rabbi Eliezer ben Hyrcanus. He was senior to Rabbi Eleazar and one of Rabbi Akiva's teachers. It is entirely reasonable to assume that while Rabbi Eliezer himself did not hold

37. b*Sanhedrin* 74a with parallels in b*Berakhot* 61b, b*Pesaḥim* 25a, b*Sotah* 12a, and b*Yoma* 82a.

an opinion on the matter, Rabbi Eleazar did.[38] The fact is that Rabbi Yoḥanan and Rav Ḥisda did have a tannaitic source which would have allowed them to hold a different opinion than Rabbi Eleazar.[39]

If this is the case, it can justifiably be asked why the Talmud bothered continuing this trajectory. The Talmud was looking for a *tannaitic* source for the prohibition against self-harm. Even if Rabbi Eleazar holds an individual opinion (*da'at yaḥid*), he could still be such a source. In fact, we would not expect to find any consensus on this matter. After all, the Talmud clearly states that there is a *tannaitic* debate on whether it is permissible or prohibited to harm oneself, and Rav Ḥisda falls in the camp of those who permit self-harm. The Talmud would not cast aside the *baraita* of Rabbi Eleazar just because there are examples of individuals who hold opposing views. This opens the possibility that the reason the Talmud cast aside this particular *baraita* was not because Rabbi Eleazar does not hold the position that one cannot engage in self-harm. Menachem Fisch argues that the Babylonian Talmud has two layers of meaning. The first layer is meant to convey the tools of pedagogy and the legal system at its face value. The second and less-obvious layer, however, advances an antitraditionalist agenda.[40] Thus, in our case, the reason the two *baraitot* of Rabbi Eleazar may have been cast aside by the Talmud, even though they appear to be more solid sources than the one that the Talmud eventually rests his case on, could very well be that the Talmud's agenda is to advance a different idea altogether. The most likely reason was that the Talmud

38. The vast majority of Talmud manuscripts available through the Lieberman Database attribute this *baraita* to Rabbi Eliezer. A few manuscripts, however, have the author of the *baraita* as Rabbi Eleazar (for instance, Munich 95 for b*Pesaḥim* 25a and Oxford Opp. Add. fol 23 for b*Pesaḥim* 25a and b*Yoma* 82a). The Vilna edition of b*Sotah* also lists the author as Rabbi Eleazar. The conflation of such similar names is not uncommon in rabbinic literature, and can be attributed to copyist errors or issues with oral transmission. Even if the author of this particular *baraita* is Rabbi Eleazar, the point made above still holds. In one *baraita* he could maintain that there are people who have different approaches to the importance of material and the self, while in a separate *baraita* he could indicate where he himself falls on that spectrum.

39. All this comes to demonstrate that the "and it seems that this should be the more so in the case of injuring his own body" (*vekhol sheken gufo*) could belong to Rabbi Eleazar as an individual opinion (*da'at yaḥid*), even though the anonymous narrator still rejected the *baraita* as the source of the prohibition against self-harm.

40. Menachem Fisch, *Rational Rabbis: Science and Talmudic Culture* (Bloomington: Indiana University Press, 1997), 185–86.

wanted to assert that there is a qualitative difference between the human body and material possessions.

The second possibility is that the words "and it seems that this should be the more so in the case of injuring his own body" (*vekhol sheken gufo*) are superfluous and not actually needed to make the argument work. This would mean that the passage (*sugya*) flows in a logical way that makes sense independent of this phrase. In fact, at least one manuscript of this text omits these words.[41] Ḥananel bar Ḥushiel (c. 980–c. 1057, Tunisia), one of the earliest and most important commentators on the Talmud, did not appear to have the words "and it seems that this should be the more so in the case of injuring his own body" (*vekhol sheken gufo*) as part of the Talmudic text. For him, the rejection of this *baraita* as the source for the prohibition against self-harm was based on the word "perhaps" (*dilma*).[42] The absence of the words "and it seems that this should be the more so in the case of injuring his own body" (*vekhol sheken gufo*) indicates that it is an essential component neither of the *baraita* nor of the anonymous narrator. Nevertheless, the majority of extant Talmudic manuscripts from various geographical locations do contain this phrase.[43]

In my opinion, understanding the words "and it seems that this should be the more so in the case of injuring his own body" (*vekhol sheken gufo*) both as part of the text and not a scribal addition, and as part of the *baraita* of Rabbi Eleazar is the more compelling option. In addition to the arguments advanced above, the approach that *bal tashḥit* includes both the prohibition against self-harm and the prohibition against wastefulness belongs to a tradent. The progenitor of this approach appears to have been Rabbi Eleazar ben Azariah.[44] If the words "and it seems that this should be the more so in the case of injuring his own body" (*vekhol sheken gufo*) belong to Rabbi Eleazar, then his position was that one can learn about the prohibition

41. See Hamburg 165 manuscript.

42. Ḥananel bar Ḥushiel, *Perushei Rabbeinu Ḥananel bar Ḥushiel LaTalmud*, ed. Yosef Mordekhai Dubowik (Jerusalem: Makhon Lev Sameaḥ Publishing, 2011).

43. There is the possibility that both are authentic versions coming from varying ancient traditions in Babylonia. Further analysis on this topic is beyond the scope of this work.

44. See Florence II-I-8 and Hamburg 165 manuscripts. Hamburg 165 does not contain the words "and it seems that this should be the more so in the case of injuring his own body" (*vekhol sheken gufo*), but it does attribute the *baraita* to Rabbi Eleazar ben Azariah.

against self-harm from the prohibition against wastefulness. He was a senior colleague of Rabbi Akiva. We saw Rabbi Akiva's position in the Mishnah, that just as a person may not engage in self-injury, so, too, may a person not engage in the waste of material. These teachings reach the same conclusion from different angles; Rabbi Eleazar learns about the body from material and Rabbi Akiva learns about material from the body. The continuation of this tradent can be found in the Tosefta text, which will be discussed shortly.

Ultimately, the Talmud ended up rejecting the *a fortiori* argument because there are clearly exceptions to the rule, even if they are somewhat forced. For instance, just because Rabbi Yoḥanan called his clothes "my honorers," does not mean that he considered them to be of greater import than his physical well-being, though the Talmud does not challenge the assertion. The example given with Rav Ḥisda is more substantive since he actually sacrifices his well-being for the sake of his clothes. A number of things can be said in this regard. Most importantly, Rav Ḥisda, who takes a stance on this issue, does not yet make his opinion acceptable to others. In the case of this particular Talmudic deliberation, however, it seems to be sufficient to motivate the rabbis to continue in their search, even if his actions were subjective and based on his own convictions or life circumstances. His biography indicates that in his early years Rav Ḥisda was poor and might not have had a spare garment. Also, Rav Ḥisda took a stance with regard to scratches on his legs from thorns. Such injuries would easily heal, as opposed to torn clothing that would be difficult or impossible to mend. Thus, the loss of property was considered to be greater than a minor injury to oneself. Rav Ḥisda clearly fell on the side of Rabbi Eliezer ben Hyrcanus's teaching that some hold their possessions more dearly than they do their bodies. There is a statement made by Rabbi Eleazar in this regard, namely that the righteous hold their possessions more dearly than their bodies, because they consider all things that come into their possession, even the most minor, to be Divinely bequeathed.[45] Nevertheless, this leaves us to question whether he would have held the same position if the injury was more severe or if it occurred on a different part of his body, perhaps a visible part.[46] Indeed, we do know that he assumed his legs would heal from the

45. b*Ḥullin* 91a.

46. See the responsum of Yitzḥak Zilberstein in the responsa chapter.

scratches; perhaps his approach would have been different in a case where he was less certain regarding the outcome.

The Talmud, through the rejection of the first two possibilities, may have played a significant role in distancing the association of the prohibition against self-harm from the prohibition against wastefulness, thus impacting the further development of these connections.

The text in b*Baba Qama* continues:

> He must therefore be the *tanna* of the following teaching: Rabbi Eleazar HaQappar BeRabbi said: "What is the point of the words [Numbers 6:11]: '*And make an atonement for him, for that he sinned regarding the soul.*'" Regarding what soul did this [Nazirite] sin unless by having deprived himself of wine? Now can we not base on this an argument *a fortiori*: If a Nazirite who deprived himself only of wine is already called a sinner, how much more so one who deprives oneself of all matters?

With the argument of Rabbi Eleazar HaQappar regarding the Nazirite, the Talmud is finally satisfied that it has found a *tanna* who holds that self-harm is forbidden. A Nazirite is considered a person who deprives himself of wine, does not cut his hair, and does not defile himself by coming into contact with the dead. Upon accidentally coming into contact with a corpse, the Nazirite is required to bring a sacrifice, a sin offering, to the Temple (Numbers 6:11). The plain sense of this verse as offered by Rashi and many others is that the sin offering is made due to the fact that the Nazirite came into contact with a corpse. There is a midrash given by Rabbi Eleazar HaQappar originating in *Sifre BeMidbar* (*Parashat Naso, Piska* 30) and reappearing in this Talmudic passage, however, which claimed that the reason the Nazirite required a sin offering is because of depriving himself of wine.[47] He then made an *a fortiori* deduction with regard to self-harm: if depriving oneself from the consumption of wine, which is a luxury, is considered sinful, how much more so is any type of action that actually harms the body? The Talmud accepted that we

47. *Sifre im Peirush Toledot Adam: Sefer BeMidbar*, ed. Moshe David Avraham Troyes Ashkenazi (Jerusalem: Mossad HaRav Kook, 1972). Here, however, the midrash is presented without mention of Rabbi Eleazar HaQappar.

have now succeeded in finding one *tanna* who says that self-harm is prohibited and pursued the matter no further. One may argue, perhaps, that this argument also has its weak points.[48] These are not pursued, however, since all the Talmud was trying to do was find one *tanna* who said that self-harm is forbidden, and it successfully did so. Nevertheless, this part of the discussion is beyond the scope of this book because pursuing this critique does not contribute to expounding the prohibition against wastefulness.

Tosefta

The Tosefta is a compilation of laws recorded at approximately the same time (or a generation later) as the Mishnah, in the early third century. While there are differing approaches in the scholarship regarding the exact date of its redaction, suffice it to say that its teachings, if not the final redaction, were the product of *tannaim*. It is divided in a similar manner to the Mishnah, but differs somewhat in the way it presents the material. While the Mishnah is considered the more authoritative of the two, the Talmud often uses the teachings of the Tosefta as proof-texts in its argumentation. The passage of interest in the Tosefta is thematically very similar in content to the above Mishnah and Talmud; it deals with humiliation, self-harm, and wastefulness/destruction:

tBaba Qama 9:31

> [If] he hit him with the back of his hand, with paper, a notebook, untanned hides, a volume of documents which he had in his hands, he pays him four hundred *zuz*. Now this is not because it is a painful blow, but because it is a humiliating one, as it is said, [Psalms 3:8]: *Rise, O Lord! Deliver me, O my God! For You slap all my enemies in the face; You break the teeth of the wicked.* And it says [Micah 4:14]: *Now you gash yourself in grief. They have laid siege to us; They strike the ruler of Israel on the cheek with a staff.* And it says, [Isaiah 50:6]: *I offered my back to the floggers, And my cheeks*

48. For instance, abstention and self-harm could be viewed as entirely different categories. Also, the idea that the sin offering be made due to abstention from wine is not something about which there is consensus, nor is it the plain sense of the verse.

> *to those who tore out my [beard]; I did not hide my face from insult and spittle.* And just as one is liable for injury done to his fellow, so he is liable for injury done to him by himself. For if he spit into his [own] face in the presence of his fellow, pulled out his [own] beard, tore his [own] clothing, broke his [own] utensils, scattered his [own] money in a fit of wrath, he is exempt from punishment by the laws of man, and his case is handed over to Heaven, as it is said, [Genesis 9:5]: *But for your own life-blood I will require a reckoning.* Rabbi Simeon ben Eleazar says in the name of Rabbi Ḥilpai ben Agra who said in the name of Rabbi Yoḥanan ben Nuri, "[If] a person pulled out his [own] hair, tore his [own] clothing, broke his [own] utensils, scattered his [own] coins in a fit of anger, he should be in your eyes as if he did an act of idolatry. For if his impulse should say to him, 'Go, commit idolatry,' he would go and do it."[49]

It is important to note that just as in the Mishnah there is no specific mention of the concept *bal tashḥit,* so too in the Tosefta there is no mention thereof. This is not to suggest that a prohibition against wastefulness did not exist, but rather that perhaps the nomenclature/terminology was not fully developed. This argument will be elaborated on later. Let us first understand the content of this passage. To begin with, we observe that the *tannaim* of the Tosefta issued an edict levying a fine for physical acts that cause humiliation. This much is also clearly stated in the Talmudic discourse. The rabbis brought three different passages from Scripture as proof-texts for their claim (Psalms 3:8, Micah 4:14, and Isaiah 50:6). All the passages deal with humiliation that has a degree of physicality to it. The narrative continues by asserting that one is liable not only for harming a fellow person, but for harming oneself. While it appears that the central topic of this passage deals with physical forms of humiliation, it would be difficult to argue that this is the prevailing theme throughout the entire passage. Once the assertion is made regarding the prohibition to engage in self-harm, it would appear that there is a thematic shift away from humiliation toward other aspects of self-harm.

---

49. This is a modified version of Jacob Neusner's *The Tosefta: Translated from the Hebrew, Fourth Division—Neziqin (The Order of Damages)* (New York: Ktav Publishing House, 1981), 58.

The text seems to suggest that the person engaging in self-harm only has an audience for the first example, that in which he spits in his own face. To humiliate oneself, having an audience is essential, otherwise there is no foundation for embarrassment. With the latter examples damage still occurs whether someone else is present or not, whereas if one spits in one's own face in private, the act cannot be considered damaging either physically or emotionally. In other words, the list of examples used by the Tosefta to illustrate self-harm appears to include a wide variety of different types of damage in addition to humiliation, specifically, physical harm and financial damage.

Most importantly for our argument, the verse used by the Tosefta as a proof-text to illustrate that engaging in self-harm is prohibited is Genesis 9:5. The significance of this has multiple layers. This passage from the Tosefta combines the themes of self-harm and wastefulness. First the Tosefta connects the prohibition of self-harm to Genesis 9:5 and then creates a conceptual link between harm of the body and of material by putting them both under the umbrella of the "self." In other words, the notion of the "self" not only includes the physical body, but extends to material possessions. Understood in this light, wasting or destroying one's property is de facto wasting or destroying oneself.

The connection between all the different types of damage listed in the Tosefta is that they all fit under the category of self-inflicted harm. While it is possible that the list of examples of different types of self-harm is random, it seems more likely that they were purposefully chosen. To start, the examples that are mentioned in the Tosefta reappear on an individual basis in the Talmud. The example of tearing clothing can be found in b*Baba Qama* 91b and b*Qiddushin* 32a, and breaking utensils in b*Shabbat* 129a, whereas b*Ḥullin* 7b, b*Shabbat* 67b, and *Semaḥot* 9:23 deal with further examples of the waste of material. The Talmud and the minor tractate of *Semaḥot* categorically refer to the destruction of said materials as a transgression of the prohibition of *bal tashḥit*.

According to Talmudic tradition, any anonymous statement made in the Tosefta belongs to Rabbi Neḥemiah (c. 150 CE).[50] Rabbi Neḥemiah was one of Rabbi Akiva's students. The connection made in the Tosefta between the prohibition against self-harm and the prohibition against wastefulness can thus be viewed as a part of a series

50. See b*Sanhedrin* 86a.

of tradents starting with Rabbi Eleazar ben Azariah, continuing with Rabbi Akiva and then with Rabbi Neḥemiah in the following generation. The fact that these teachings are consistent over the course of three (or two and a half) generations of *tannaim* makes it possible to argue that understanding the two prohibitions as inherently linked to each other was a dominant position during this era.

The Tosefta also sheds light on the conceptual connection between the *lo tashḥit* of Deuteronomy 20:19 and that of Leveticus 19:27. The examples in the Tosefta make a strong case for the interrelatedness of self-harm (which includes the destruction of beards from Leviticus 19:27) and wastefulness in general. I expand on this elsewhere.[51]

Self-Harm and Wastefulness

In spite of the rejection by the Talmud of the *baraitot* of Rabbi Eleazar, there were still a handful of post-Talmudic scholars who explicitly accepted one or both of these *baraitot* as the source of the prohibition against self-harm. Through their writings they kept the association between *bal tashḥit* and self-harm alive, and thus the link between Deuteronomy 20:19 and Genesis 9:5.

Yonah of Gerona (d. 1263, Spain)

Yonah of Gerona, in his ethical treatise *Sha'arei Teshuvah, Sha'ar* 3:82, dealt with the prohibition against wastefulness systematically. He began with the prohibition against cutting down fruit trees, and continued by stating, "And so we were warned to not waste possessions without purpose, even those of the least legally significant value (*shaveh perutah*)." He then cited the rabbis from b*Baba Qama* 91b regarding the prohibition against the excessive tearing of clothing over the dead, claiming that anyone breaking utensils in anger is liable *a fortiori* because he both transgresses *bal tashḥit* and is governed by anger. With regard to being governed by anger, he brought as a proof-text the *baraita* from the Tosefta, which also appears in the Talmud. This text, b*Shabbat* 105b, stated that a person who destroys utensils in

51. Tanhum Yoreh, "Rethinking Jewish Approaches to Wastefulness," in *Review of Rabbinic Judaism* 22, no. 1 (2019): 31–45.

a fit of anger should be perceived as an idol-worshipper. He then continued by saying that those who engage in self-harm transgress the prohibition found in Genesis 9:5, clearly relating the prohibition against wastefulness to self-harm.[52]

A number of important insights can be taken from Yonah of Gerona's writings. The process through which he arrived at this conclusion demonstrates a holistic and systematic understanding of *bal tashḥit*. He started with the prohibition against destroying fruit trees and expanded the prohibition to include the destruction of all things. Most important, however, is the fact that he then related the prohibition against wastefulness to self-harm and connected all of the above to idol worship. It would appear that he understood the links between these ideas to be organic.

Menaḥem ben Shlomo HaMeiri (1249–1315, Provence)

Menaḥem HaMeiri in his commentary on the Talmud, *Beit HaBeḥirah*, b*Baba Qama* 91b, also understood the prohibition against self-harm to originate from Genesis 9:5. The connection he made between the prohibition against self-harm and the prohibition against wastefulness was somewhat different from what Rabbi Eleazar brought in the Talmud. Instead of claiming that we learn about the prohibition against self-harm as an *a fortiori* derivation from the prohibition against wastefulness, he viewed the relationship as an analogy (similar to the Tosefta and Rabbi Akiva): just as one is prohibited from engaging in self-harm, one is prohibited from engaging in wastefulness of material.[53]

Shlomo ben Yeḥiel Luria (1510–1574, Poland)

Shlomo Luria, in his Talmudic commentary *Yam shel Shlomo*, b*Baba Qama* 8:59, asserted that one is specifically prohibited from engaging in self-harm as part of the general prohibition of *bal tashḥit*.[54] He then cited the opinion of Yaakov bar Asher (c. 1270–1343, Germany and Spain), the author of the legal code the *Tur*, who presented another great legal authority, Meir HaLevi Abulafia (c. 1170–1244, Spain).

52. Yonah of Gerona, *Sha'arei Teshuvah* (Venice: 1544).

53. Menaḥem HaMeiri, *Beth HaBehira on the Talmudical Treatise Baba Kamma*, 2nd rev. ed., ed. Kalman Schlesinger (Jerusalem: private printing, 1961).

54. Shlomo Luria, *Sefer Yam shel Shlomo al Masekhet Baba Qama* (Prague: 1616–1618).

Abulafia accepted the first argument presented in the Talmud that one is indeed permitted to harm oneself. Even Abulafia, however, acknowledged that such behavior is only permitted when harming oneself is necessary. This, Luria argued, was a unanimous opinion. Everyone agrees that any type of destruction, whether of the self or of material for no purpose, is prohibited under the law of *bal tashḥit*. According to Abulafia, however, there are instances in which one is permitted to engage in wastefulness and destruction, and just as this applies to material, so too does it apply to the self.

Luria himself accepted Rabbi Akiva's ruling in the Mishnah that one is not permitted to engage in self-harm, even for monetary purposes. In other words, even when there is a hypothetical need to engage in self-harm, it is prohibited. To this end he brought Genesis 9:5 as a proof-text that one is prohibited from taking one's own life even if one is subjected to torture.[55] He then presented a number of sources (he refers to as the elders of France) that make an exception to the prohibition, specifically when one fears that one will be coerced into engaging in blasphemous activities. This approach was rejected by Luria, who countered with the tosafist Isaac ben Samuel's assertion that even when people fear they will be forced to abjure Judaism, they are not permitted to engage in self-harm. One can allow oneself to be killed, or can even indirectly cause oneself to die (for instance, by setting on fire the building one is in), but one is not permitted to directly harm oneself, and certainly not others.[56] Ultimately, Luria also conceded that there are exceptions to this rule, but they concern more extreme circumstances where the lives of others are at stake, or for the sake of doing the king's bidding or honoring the king.

Abraham de Boton (c. 1560–c. 1605, Greece and Land of Israel)

Abraham de Boton in his commentary on Maimonides's *Mishneh Torah*, *Leḥem Mishneh* (Laws of Ethical Behavior 3:1), discussed the Talmudic

55. Although he initially brought this verse in the context of suicide, he later cited the midrash of Genesis (*Bereishit*) *Rabbah* for this verse claiming that the midrash prohibited engaging in self-harm. This is of interest, because the text in the midrash specifically mentions suicide, but not lesser extents of self-harm.

56. Luria had in mind those who kill their children so that they not be brought up in a foreign religion. He claimed that children who are coerced to live in a different faith (one can assume that he had Christianity in mind) often come back to the Jewish fold after a number of years, and if not them then their children.

deliberations of b*Baba Qama* 91b. Among his assertions were that the prohibition against self-harm originates either from the prohibition of *bal tashḥit* or from Genesis 9:5. As is evident, de Boton did not accept the Talmud's rejections of both of the *baraitot* brought in the name of Rabbi Eleazar as the source of the prohibition against self-harm. Although de Boton used the word "or" with regard to sourcing the prohibition against self-harm, the fact is that he considered both to be equally appropriate.[57]

Israel Lipschutz (1782–1860, Germany)

Israel Lipschutz in his commentary on the Mishnah, *Tiferet Yisrael* (*Yakhin*, m*Baba Qama* 8:6:39), asserted that the prohibition against self-harm falls under the prohibition of *bal tashḥit*. More specifically, he claimed that there is no distinction between the body and garments with regard to the prohibition of *bal tashḥit*.[58]

Jacob Ettlinger (1798–1871, Germany)

Jacob Ettlinger, the author of the commentary on the Talmud *Arukh LaNer*, added an interesting comment on this topic in his commentary on b*Niddah* 13a. The Talmudic discussion revolved around the prohibition against men handling their penis due to the fact that they are easily aroused. The Talmud presented a *baraita* by Rabbi Eleazar, who claimed that someone who touches their member while urinating is said to be as one who has brought a flood to the world. Ettlinger cited Naḥmanides, Shlomo ben Aderet, and Nissim of Gerona as understanding this *baraita* as a proof-text that like men, women are also prohibited from wasting male ejaculate. This is understood from the fact that both men and women perished in the flood. Ettlinger eventually came around to mentioning the Talmudic discussion from b*Baba Qama* 91b. He argued that the text does not clarify what the exact transgression is from Numbers 6:11 (regarding the Nazirite). Hence, we still need to learn about the prohibition against self-harm from the prohibition of *bal tashḥit*. Likewise, we learn in part about

57. Abraham de Boton, "*Leḥem Mishneh*," in Moshe ben Maimon, *Mishneh Torah hu HaYad HaḤazaqah: Sefer HaMada* (Warsaw: Kalinberg and Partners, 1881).

58. Israel Lipschutz, *Mishnayot Tiferet Yisrael, Yakhin veBoaz* (New York: Pardes, 1953).

the prohibition against wasting semen from the prohibition of *bal tashḥit*.[59]

Barukh Epstein (1860–1941, Belarus)

Barukh Epstein, author of the *Torah Temimah,* in his commentary on Genesis 9:5 rejected the Talmud's position that the verse only relates to suicide and not self-harm in general. He claimed that this approach is only a nonsubstantive rejection (*diḥui be'alma*), and that in fact Genesis 9:5 included the prohibition against self-harm.[60] This would make Rabbi Eleazar's connection between *bal tashḥit* in general and self-harm still relevant even after being cast aside by the Talmud.

Bal Tashḥit DeGufa Adif

Just as there are circumstances in which a fruit tree can be cut down despite the prohibition, there are instances when the general prohibition against wastefulness is overruled because of exceptional circumstances. The exceptional circumstances in the Talmud relate to instances in which wastefulness is directly pitted against well-being. These examples strengthen the distancing of the prohibition against wastefulness from the prohibition against self-harm.

bShabbat 129a

Context: The Mishnah dealt with the ways in which one may assist an animal and a woman who give birth on the Sabbath. Though there are limits to the degree to which an animal may be helped, the Sabbath can be violated for a woman giving birth, because human life is more sacred than the Sabbath. The Talmudic discussion continued by relating to other circumstances in which one can violate various laws to mitigate the inherent risk to human life. The case of interest

59. In two other places Ettlinger asserted that the source of the prohibition against self-harm is indeed *bal tashḥit*. These two sources are *Arukh LaNer* (b*Yevamot* 13b) and his Responsa *Sefer Binyan Tzion* (Altona: Gebruder Bonn, 1867), 137.

60. Barukh HaLevi Epstein, *Ḥamishah Ḥumshei Torah im Ḥamesh Megilot, Torah Temimah: Sefer Bereishit* (New York: Avraham Yitzḥak Friedman, 1962).

to us deals with rabbis who had just undergone bloodletting and were now destroying expensive furniture to kindle a fire to warm their bodies:

> A teak chair was broken up for Samuel; a table [made] of juniper wood was broken for Rav Judah. A footstool was broken for Rabbah, whereupon Abaye said to Rabbah, But you are infringing, *you shall not destroy* (*bal tashḥit*)? "You shall not destroy" in respect of my own body is more important to me (*bal tashḥit degufai adif li*), he retorted. Rav Judah said in Rav's name: One should always sell [even] the beams of his house and buy shoes for his feet. If one has let blood and has nothing to eat, let him sell the shoes from off his feet and provide the requirements of a meal therewith.

"The prohibition against destroying my body is more dear to me" (*bal tashḥit degufa adif li*) is not a specific circumstance in which an exception to the prohibition of *bal tashḥit* is made but a general rule; the welfare of the individual always trumps consideration for the nonhuman world. It is possible to claim that Rabbah's argument was a conviction held by him alone. After all, his statement was subjective; he was speaking about the esteem in which he held his own body, and did not make a general statement with regard to the consideration all people should have regarding their personal health. Rav Judah, however, following the tradition of Rav, gave credence to Rabbah's position through his statement that the well-being of the body should always take precedence over material considerations. In the next passage (*sugya*) we observe a shift from the subjectivity of Rabbah to his position becoming the norm.

bShabbat 140b

Context: The Mishnah listed certain activities that are prohibited on the Sabbath, while at the same time delineating a manner in which such activities could be performed that did not violate the Sabbath. The Talmudic discussion eventually came around to rabbis sharing their worldly wisdom through snippets of savvy advice. One such saying relates to *bal tashḥit*:

> Rav Ḥisda also said: When one can eat barley bread but eats wheaten bread he violates, you shall not destroy (*bal tashḥit*). Rav Papa said: When one can drink beer but drinks wine, he violates, you shall not destroy (*bal tashḥit*). But this is incorrect: You shall not destroy, as applied to one's own person, stands higher (*bal tashḥit degufa adif*).

The Talmud shared the opinions of two rabbis, Rav Ḥisda and Rav Papa, with regard to abstention from luxurious foods. They claimed that if one has recourse to both high-quality food and low-quality food, one should consume the lower-quality option. The reasoning, they claimed, was that consuming the higher-quality food would be a transgression of *bal tashḥit*, because of the waste of money. The Talmud, however, rejected their opinions by claiming that not harming one's body takes precedence over wastefulness and destruction of material goods (*bal tashḥit degufa adif*). It is important to understand the prevailing ideas present in this passage that elicited the varying opinions. Rav Ḥisda and Rav Papa viewed the issue from a utilitarian lens. Wheat bread and wine are more expensive than barley bread and beer, and if all options satiate an individual to the same degree, it is a waste of money to opt for the more-expensive options. The Talmud rejected this approach through the understanding that while more expensive, wheat and wine have better nutritional qualities than barley and beer. The more expensive foods in this case are more nutritious (i.e., healthier).[61] The ethic that prohibits wastefulness and destruction is overruled by the ethic that holds human welfare to be of greater importance. Another possibility is that wheat and wine are simply more enjoyable than beer and barley, and the psychological benefits that they offer are enough to overrule the prohibition. If this is indeed the case, this is yet another significant weakening of the prohibition against wastefulness, because it is a de facto removal of all limits on wastefulness when it conflicts with human desire. We will

61. See David E. Sulomm Stein, "*Halakhah*: The Law of *Bal Tashchit* (Do Not Destroy)," in *Torah of the Earth: Exploring 4,000 Years of Ecology in Jewish Thought*, ed. Arthur Waskow (Woodstock, VT: Jewish Lights Publishing, 2000), 100. Stein also argues that the concerns regarding wastefulness were that barley did not deplete the soil as much as wheat, and that brewing beer instead of wine was a more effective use of resources.

see this approach taken to its extreme in the responsum of Alexander Sender Schorr.

The significant difference between b*Shabbat* 129 and b*Shabbat* 140b is that the subjective element used by Rabbah to convey his position in the first text is not present in the second text. The voice that rejected Rav Ḥisda and Rav Papa's positions belonged to the anonymous narrator and came at least a century later. By the time the text was being redacted, Rabbah's position had become authoritative and no longer needed the subjective "for me" (*li*).

bTa'anit 20b

Context: The Mishnah dealt with harrowing instances in which an alarm is raised calling people to fast and pray. Such instances could include drought, plague, and infestations, among other things. One occurrence that would elicit fasting and prayer was the collapse of buildings in a particular city. The Talmud then went on to discuss meritorious individuals whose presence could prevent a building from collapsing. Eventually the Talmud came around to discussing the merits of a particular *amora*, Rav Huna:

> Rabbah said to Rifram bar Papa: Tell me some of the good deeds which Rav Huna had done. He replied: Of his childhood I do not recollect anything, but of his old age I do. On cloudy [stormy] days they used to drive him about in a golden carriage and he would survey every part of the city and he would order the demolition of any wall that was unsafe; if the owner was in a position to do so he had to rebuild it himself, but if not, then [Rav Huna] would have it rebuilt at his own expense. On the eve of every Sabbath [Friday] he would send a messenger to the market and any vegetables that the [market] gardeners had left over he bought up and had them thrown into the river. Should he not rather have had these distributed among the poor? [He was afraid] lest they would then at times be led to rely upon him and would not trouble to buy any for themselves. Why did he not give the vegetables to the domestic animals? He was of the opinion that food fit for human consumption may not be given to animals. Then why did he purchase them at all? This would result in [the gardeners providing an] inadequate [supply] in the future.

While this particular passage does not mention *bal tashḥit* by name, one of the issues that arises in it is the waste of produce. One must keep in mind that the central theme of this passage is the good deeds of Rav Huna. Since Rav Huna engages in the wastage of food, we must consider why that act is justified. On the one hand, he wanted to ensure that the poor did not become reliant on charity, presumably so that if charity did not arrive they would not starve. On the other hand, he felt like he needed to balance that concern by ensuring that there would always be an adequate supply of food. Feeding animals with this surplus was abhorrent to Rav Huna. We must also consider the fact that the Talmud asserted that "he was of the opinion," opening the possibility that there may not have been consensus on this matter. When considering these justifications and their implied acceptance we see scenarios in which there are exceptions to the prohibition of *bal tashḥit*. In this particular instance the exceptions (save the approach to animal consumption of food fit for humans) are primarily existential. In no way should a prohibition compromise human welfare, on both the micro and macro levels. Again, while there is no specific mention of *bal tashḥit*, the principle at play in this context, which deals with famine and starvation, appears to be "the prohibition against destroying the body is more dear" (*bal tashḥit degufa adif*). If indeed our analysis is correct, what makes this passage so important is that the concept of "the prohibition against destroying the body is more dear" is shown to take precedence even in hypothetical situations. Rav Huna could not have known the outcome of noninterference in the market (though he seems to possess the attribute of clairvoyance), yet he engaged in wastefulness due to the theoretical possibility that nonaction could have resulted in practical concerns. While the scenario is similar to b*Shabbat* 129a, the difference lies in the fact that Samuel and Rabbah after their bloodletting were in scenarios in which the consequences of not wasting at those given moments were actual rather than theoretically possible.

The Commons

Garrett Hardin brought light to the issue of the environmental degradation of the commons in his seminal essay from 1968, "The Tragedy of the Commons."[62] The general theory he advanced was that ratio-

62. Garrett Hardin, "The Tragedy of the Commons," *Science* 162, no. 3859 (1968): 1243–48.

nal beings acting in their own self-interest would overexploit and undiscernibly pollute common resources, that is, resources owned by no one in particular but belonging to the public in general. His conclusions that humanity should limit its reproduction aside, the question of whether the prohibition against wastefulness applies to the commons is an important one, and at least from a legal standpoint the answer is not clear.

Responsibility for the commons is a frequent trope in texts emphasized by Jewish environmentalists, but not in the literature on *bal tashḥit*. The wisdom is as follows: (a) God is the master of all of creation, (b) human ownership is always a temporary state, and (c) ultimately all ownership reverts to God (and should thus be respected and protected). As mentioned in the introduction to this book, some argue that Genesis 2:15 advances the notion of human stewardship (and not ownership). Yet for better or worse, this is a modern environmental construct. The concept of temporary human ownership is more historically grounded within the framework of sabbaticals and jubilees.[63] Nevertheless, even if human ownership is viewed as temporary, the fleeting nature of ownership can still have the impact of a permanent nature.

The connection between the commons and the prohibition against wastefulness emerge through the following text.

bḤullin 7b

Context: The Mishnah dealt with the issue of who is permitted to conduct ritual slaughter of animals for consumption. The Talmudic text dealing with the topic of *bal tashḥit*, however, is part of a digression from the original topic.

> When Rabbi heard of the arrival of Rabbi Pinḥas, he went out to meet him. Will you please dine with me? asked Rabbi. Certainly, he answered. Rabbi's face at once brightened with joy; whereupon Rabbi Pinḥas said: You imagine that I am forbidden by vow from deriving any benefit from an Israelite. Oh, no. The people of Israel are holy. Yet there are some who desire [to benefit others] but have not the means; whilst others have the means but have not the desire, and

63. See Leviticus 25:23.

> it is written: [Proverbs 23:6–7] "*Do not eat of a stingy man's food; Do not crave for his dainties; He is like one keeping accounts; 'Eat and drink,' he says to you, But he does not really mean it.*" But you have the desire and also the means. At present, however, I am in a hurry for I am engaged in a religious duty; but on my return. I will come and visit you. When he arrived, he happened to enter by a gate near which were some white mules. At this he exclaimed: "The angel of death is in this house! Shall I then dine here?" When Rabbi heard of this, he went out to meet him. "I shall sell the mules," said Rabbi. Rabbi Pinḥas replied: [Leviticus 19:14]: "*You shall not place a stumbling block before the blind.*" "I shall abandon them." "You would be spreading danger." "I shall hamstring them." "You would be causing suffering to the animals." "I shall kill them." "There is the prohibition against wanton destruction (*bal tashḥit*)." Rabbi was thus pressing him persistently, when there rose up a mountain between them. Then Rabbi wept and said, "If this is [the power of the righteous] in their lifetime, how great must it be after their death!"

Rabbi (Rabbi Yehudah the Patriarch), in trying to overcome Rabbi Pinḥas's refusal to enter his home due to the presence of two white mules, suggests a number of solutions to the predicament, including killing the mules. Rabbi Pinḥas remains steadfast in his refusal and ultimately does not dine with Rabbi. This exchange is instrumental in much later reflections on whether the prohibition against wastefulness applies to the commons. As some of the discourse surrounding this issue emerges in the chapter on responsa, I will only partially elaborate.

Yeḥezkel Landau (1713–1793, Poland and Bohemia) was asked whether it is legally permissible to engage in hunting for sport.[64] While he ultimately prohibited hunting unless done in pursuit of a livelihood, at first he could find no reason to prohibit such activities. His first deliberation on the matter concerned *bal tashḥit*, but he concluded that hunting could not be prohibited on such grounds because wild animals are ownerless and the commons do not fall under the

64. Yeḥezkel Landau, *Sefer Noda BiYehudah, Mahadurah Tinyana, Yoreh De'ah* 10, Part 1, ed. David Aharon Freundlich (Jerusalem: Makhon Yerushalayim, 2004).

prohibition against wastefulness. His position on the commons is not the consensus approach. For instance, Shneiur Zalman of Liadi (1745–1813, Russia) rejected the notion that the commons can be needlessly destroyed and explicitly stated that *bal tashḥit* applies to ownerless items.[65]

What do these approaches have to do with b*Ḥullin* 7b cited above? This comes to light through a much more recent text found in the responsa of Menasheh Klein (1923–2011, Ukraine, USA, and Israel), who claimed that the way we know that *bal tashḥit* applies to the commons is precisely through the exchange between Rabbi and Rabbi Pinḥas.[66] The first option Rabbi presents to Rabbi Pinḥas is to relinquish his ownership of the mules. Rabbi Pinḥas rejects this solution by claiming that releasing the mules into the commons would endanger others. After his suggestion of hamstringing the animals, which Rabbi Pinḥas rejects as a transgression of the prohibition against causing animals to suffer needlessly (*tza'ar ba'alei ḥayim*), Rabbi finally offers to kill the animals. Here Rabbi Pinḥas evokes the prohibition against wastefulness as the reason why this was no option at all. Klein explains that the combination of the first and third suggestions and rejections are how we know that the commons is protected by *bal tashḥit*. If destroying the commons were permitted, Rabbi could have relinquished ownership over the mules and then killed them. Because this was not raised as a possibility, Klein deduces that the commons is in fact offered a measure of protection through the prohibition against wastefulness. Even though it appears that the more common approach is that *bal tashḥit* does apply to ownerless items, whether that measure is sufficient to translate into actual environmental protection remains an open question.

Jeremy Benstein writes that Jewish wisdom dictates that the commons belongs to everyone as opposed to no one.[67] He bases this on b*Baba Qama* 50b, which presents an exchange between an individual who is in the process of removing stones from his private property to the public domain and is reprimanded by a bystander for placing

---

65. Shneiur Zalman, *Shulḥan Arukh HaRav*: Part 6, *Ḥoshen Mishpat, Laws of Protecting the Body* (Jerusalem: Even Yisroel Publishing, 2011), 14.

66. Menasheh Klein, *Sefer Mishneh Halakhot—Mahadurah Tinyana*, Part 12 (New York: Makhon Mishneh Halakhot Gedolot, 2000), 12:432.

67. Jeremy Benstein, *The Way into Judaism and the Environment* (Woodstock, VT: Jewish Lights Publishing, 2006), 130–31.

obstacles from his own property to property that was not his. The culprit dismisses the claims as absurd, yet later in life he loses his property and trips over the stones he placed in the public realm, ultimately realizing that the commons does indeed belong to everyone. The text highlights that private ownership is temporary yet the commons belongs to everyone, and should be cared for by all. Interestingly, we observe yet another connection between wastefulness and self-harm. The individual described in this text engages in destruction of the commons, and ultimately is found to be damaging himself.

Idol Worship and Foreign Cultural Practices

Eilon Schwartz argues that the development of a Jewish environmental ethic has been stifled by the strong antipagan trope in Judaism.[68] Even from the evidence in this chapter, one can see the complexity in the conceptualization of *bal tashḥit* as a concept, let alone an environmental ethic. I have argued elsewhere,[69] in contrast to Schwartz, that while *a priori* it might appear that taking a stance against the beliefs of nature worshipers is also a conceptual assault on nature, this is not the case in relation to Jewish stances on wastefulness. In fact, the opposite can be argued; by associating wasteful/destructive behavior with idolatry and foreign cultural practices, the rabbinic sages in fact aim to distance Jews from both. Here, I will reiterate some of the central arguments from my article.

The only instance in Scripture where wastefulness is permitted outright is with regard to eliminating idolatry (Exodus 34:13 and Deuteronomy 7:5). I argue that "By justifying wastefulness in the context of idolatry, the text essentially does two things. It strengthens the polemic against idolatry, but by doing so it also suggests that the norm is that other forms of wastefulness are essentially prohibited."[70]

In multiple places in rabbinic literature associations are drawn between idolatry, foreign cultural practices, and wastefulness/destruc-

68. Eilon Schwartz, "Judaism and Nature: Theological and Moral Issues to Consider While Renegotiating a Jewish Relationship to the Natural World," in *Judaism and Environmental Ethics: A Reader*, ed. Martin Yaffe (New York: Lexington Books, 2001), 301.

69. Tanhum Yoreh, "Rethinking Jewish Approaches to Wastefulness," 35.

70. Ibid.

tion. These do not always appear expressly using the term *bal tashḥit*, yet they remain inherently connected, from a philological perspective, through the triliteral root *sh.ḥ.t.* (b*Avodah Zarah* 23b, b*Baba Qama* 91b, *Semaḥot Baraitot MiEvel Rabbati* 4:11).

While a number of texts relevant to the topic appear in this chapter, I will elaborate only on the two instances where the expression *bal tashḥit* is used explicitly and one other closely associated text.

This passage is found in the midst of a list of prohibited behaviors considered to be either idolatrous or an emulation of foreign cultural practices. The specific reference to *bal tashḥit* is in the context of inefficient (and thus wasteful) use of resources, a common theme within contemporary environmental discourse.

bShabbat 67a–67b

> A *tanna* recited the chapter of Amorite practices before Rabbi Ḥiyya ben Abin. . . . Rav Zutra said: He who covers an oil lamp or uncovers a *naphtha* [a type of lamp] infringes on the prohibition of wasteful destruction (*bal tashḥit*).

This example is relatively clear; anyone who uses a fuel source inefficiently is considered to be transgressing *bal tashḥit*. The fact that there is no obvious reason as to why this would be considered idolatrous or an emulation of foreign cultural practices suggests that it is the act of wastefulness itself that is considered to fall under one of these subversive categories.

Semaḥot 9:23[71]

> Whosoever retrieves effects from the dead robs the dead. There is a time to retrieve and a time not to retrieve. So long as the effects cast before the dead have not come in contact with the coffin, they may be retrieved. Once they have come in contact with the coffin, they may not be retrieved. **Even so, a man must be taught not to be wasteful, for has it not been said that whosoever heaps effects upon the dead transgresses the injunction against wanton**

71. *The Tractate "Mourning" (Semaḥot)*, Yale Judaica Series, Vol. 17, trans. Dov Zlotnick (New Haven, CT: Yale University Press, 1966), 72.

> **destruction (*bal tashḥit*)?** So [said] Rabbi Meir. Rabbi Eleazar bar Tzaddok says: "He disgraces him." Rabban Simeon ben Gamaliel says: "It is more worms that he is inviting." Rabbi Nathan says: "In the same clothes in which a man descends to Sheol will he appear in the age to come, for it is written [Job 38:14]: *It is changed as clay under the seal; and they stand as a garment.*"

Semaḥot, Baraitot MiEvel Rabbati 4:11[72]

> It is prohibited to bury [the dead] in shrouds of silk and clothing embroidered in gold, even if they are a leader. Such an act is disgraceful, and wasteful, and idolatrous.

Traditions of burying the dead with a variety of material goods were well developed in the Near East, with well-documented cases among the Greeks and Egyptians.[73] *Semaḥot* 9:23 demonstrates the rabbinic concern with emulating such practices, particularly with regard to the notion of such customs being wasteful. Though the text does not mention foreign cultural practices specifically, it is not unlikely that this is yet another measure to separate the Jews from the traditions of the surrounding cultures. The later text, *Baraitot MiEvel Rabbati* (4:11), goes so far as to declare such wasteful practices idolatrous.

New Testament

Although the New Testament is not a Jewish text per se, it contains valuable information regarding Jewish life in the early part of the Common Era. Analysis of Christian commentary is beyond the scope of this book, however, and the narratives presented here are for illustrative purposes only. The narratives that follow are accounts from Jesus's life as told by the Gospels. The two narratives, which exist in

---

72. This text is not in the canonized version of *Semaḥot*, yet in the Higger edition is a group of *baraitot* considered to be part of tractate *Semaḥot* by the *geonim*. *Treatise Semaḥot and Treatise Semaḥot of R. Ḥiyya and Sefer Ḥibbut ha-Keber and Additions to the Seven Minor Treatises and to Treatise Soferim II*, ed. Michael Higger (Jerusalem: Makor Publishing, 1969), 246.

73. See Grajetski, *Burial Customs*, and Rohde, *Psyche*.

parallel renditions in the Gospels, deal with accounts of wastefulness. These texts are another strong indicator that a prohibition against wastefulness already exists as a concept, or at least as a social norm, albeit only as part of a Jewish oral tradition.

John 6:1–12 (Miracle of the Loaves)

In this narrative Jesus shows concern for leftover food procured in a miraculous manner. Even though the food came by way of miracle, Jesus is concerned that none of it should be wasted. This narrative indicates the possibility of a Jewish oral tradition that predates the rabbinic era yet postdates the Hebrew Bible. In chapter 6 of John, Jesus delivered a sermon to a crowd of 5,000 people on a mountainside in the Galilee. There were only five loaves of bread and two fish to feed the large number of people. Through a miracle, Jesus was able to distribute this food among all those present so that they ate their fill and even had leftovers. Jesus then directed his disciples to collect all the leftovers so that no food be wasted.

Jesus Feeds the 5,000 (New International Version)

> 6:1 Some time after this, Jesus crossed to the far shore of the Sea of Galilee (that is, the Sea of Tiberias), 2 and a great crowd of people followed him because they saw the signs he had performed by healing the sick. 3 Then Jesus went up on a mountainside and sat down with his disciples. 4 The Jewish Passover Festival was near. 5 When Jesus looked up and saw a great crowd coming toward him, he said to Philip, "Where shall we buy bread for these people to eat?" 6 He asked this only to test him, for he already had in mind what he was going to do. 7 Philip answered him, "It would take more than half a year's wages to buy enough bread for each one to have a bite!" 8 Another of his disciples, Andrew, Simon Peter's brother, spoke up, 9 "Here is a boy with five small barley loaves and two small fish, but how far will they go among so many?" 10 Jesus said, "Have the people sit down." There was plenty of grass in that place, and they sat down (about five thousand men were there). 11 Jesus then took the loaves, gave thanks, and distributed to those who were seated as much as they

> wanted. He did the same with the fish. 12 When they had all had enough to eat, he said to his disciples, "Gather the pieces that are left over. **Let nothing be wasted**." 13 So they gathered them and filled twelve baskets with the pieces of the five barley loaves left over by those who had eaten.

Jesus's concern with wastefulness is highlighted through the fact that he requested that even the smallest morsel of food not be wasted.

Mark 14:1–9; Matthew 26:6–13; John 12:1–8 (Anointing of Jesus)

Context: Though it is possible that more than one anointing of Jesus occurs in the narratives presented, thereby resolving their contradictions, it is more likely that these texts refer to one incident. Both Mark and John have the incident occurring just prior to Passover and Jesus's death. A woman anoints Jesus with very expensive perfume, and there is an outcry among those present regarding the supposed waste of the perfume. Jesus in return rebukes the critics by claiming that the woman was anointing his body in preparation for burial. The purported betrayal of Jesus by Judas and his subsequent crucifixion at this stage is imminent.

Mark 14:1–9 (New International Version)

> 1 Now the Passover and the Feast of Unleavened Bread were only two days away, and the chief priests and the teachers of the law were looking for some sly way to arrest Jesus and kill him. 2 "But not during the Feast," they said, "or the people may riot." 3 While he was in Bethany, reclining at the table in the home of a man known as Simon the Leper, a woman came with an alabaster jar of very expensive perfume, made of pure nard. She broke the jar and poured the perfume on his head. 4 Some of those present were saying indignantly to one another, "Why this waste of perfume? 5 It could have been sold for more than a year's wages and the money given to the poor." And they rebuked her harshly. 6 "Leave her alone," said Jesus. "Why are you bothering her? She has done a beautiful thing to me. 7 The poor you will always have with you, and you

can help them any time you want. But you will not always have me. 8 She did what she could. She poured perfume on my body beforehand to prepare for my burial. 9 I tell you the truth, wherever the gospel is preached throughout the world, what she has done will also be told, in memory of her."

Matthew 26:6–13 (New International Version)

6 While Jesus was in Bethany in the home of a man known as Simon the Leper, 7 a woman came to him with an alabaster jar of very expensive perfume, which she poured on his head as he was reclining at the table. 8 When the disciples saw this, they were indignant. "Why this waste?" they asked. 9 "This perfume could have been sold at a high price and the money given to the poor." 10 Aware of this, Jesus said to them, "Why are you bothering this woman? She has done a beautiful thing to me. 11The poor you will always have with you, but you will not always have me. 12 When she poured this perfume on my body, she did it to prepare me for burial. 13 I tell you the truth, wherever this gospel is preached throughout the world, what she has done will also be told, in memory of her."

John 12:1–8 (New International Version)

1 Six days before the Passover, Jesus arrived at Bethany, where Lazarus lived, whom Jesus had raised from the dead. 2 Here a dinner was given in Jesus' honor. Martha served, while Lazarus was among those reclining at the table with him. 3 Then Mary took about a pint of pure nard, an expensive perfume; she poured it on Jesus' feet and wiped his feet with her hair. And the house was filled with the fragrance of the perfume. 4 But one of his disciples, Judas Iscariot, who was later to betray him, objected, 5 "Why wasn't this perfume sold and the money given to the poor? It was worth a year's wages." 6 He did not say this because he cared about the poor but because he was a thief; as keeper of the money bag, he used to help himself to what was put into it. 7 "Leave her alone," Jesus replied.

> "It was intended that she should save this perfume for the day of my burial. 8 You will always have the poor among you, but you will not always have me."

These parallel narratives each present a slightly different account of the anointing of Jesus. Scholars have been uncertain as to whether the above accounts are actually describing the same events, or whether events with a wide number of similarities occurred a number of times.[74] While this is an interesting question, it takes us beyond the scope of the reason these narratives were presented in this chapter. Our concern is to demonstrate that Jesus's disciples are taken aback by his supposed waste of perfume. Jesus and his disciples are mainly Jewish, and as such followed Jewish law. The disciples are alarmed when they perceive their teacher to be transgressing the law, indicating a high likelihood of the existence of a prohibition against wastefulness at this point in Jewish history.

Though the focus of this book is the development of the concept of *bal tashḥit* in the Jewish intellectual histories, the narratives in the New Testament concerning Jesus are of interest because the Jesus movement at this point is still largely a Jewish movement. The Gospels contain narratives that specifically deal with the topic of wastefulness. Although a number of narratives in the Gospels deal with the destruction of fruit trees, they have been by and large interpreted metaphorically and therefore are not presented here. In addition, the Christian commentary tradition is beyond the scope of the present research endeavor. Nevertheless, the presentation of the bare narratives themselves allows some special insights. Most importantly, the "Miracle of the Loaves" narrative indicates Jesus's concern with the waste of food. Even though the food was procured by miraculous means, Jesus nonetheless was concerned with wasting even a morsel. This concern indicates a well-established ethic concerning the wasting of food. It seems clear that this ethic extends beyond food when Jesus's disciples question his supposed contradictory waste of perfume. The implication of their outcry is that the established ethic concerning the wastage of food is, in fact, an ethic that clearly extends to all things of worth. The connection between the food and

74. See J. H. Bernard, The International Critical Commentary: A Critical and Exegetical Commentary on the Gospel According to St. John, Vol. 2, ed. A. H. McNeile (Edinburgh: T & T Clark, 1942), 409.

the perfume is that both have material value. Regardless of what the implications are for Jesus's approach to wastefulness, or for that matter the Christian approach to wastefulness, one thing is abundantly clear. At the beginning of the first millennium CE the notion that wastefulness was abhorrent was well established. From a rational perspective, the idea that wastefulness was repugnant at this time in history makes complete sense. This was not the throw-away society we currently live in. This was not a time of mass-produced goods. Rather, most people lived on a subsistence diet from hand to mouth. People did not necessarily need a law prohibiting wastefulness; the mere thought of wasteful behavior would have seemed reprehensible. Nevertheless, it is important to consider the socioreligious context in which Jesus and his companions lived. From the miraculous story mentioned above, it is apparent that they did not live during a time of great abundance. They lived in Judaea during the period of the Second Temple, when Jewish customs (though difficult to determine) must have been the norm. As such, there is extremely good reason to suggest that the views of Jesus and his disciples were directly related to their antecedent status in Jewish custom and law. What makes these narratives so compelling for the Jewish context is that these are the earliest examples of Jews putting the prohibition on wastefulness into practice. Moreover, it is quite clear that Jesus and his disciples take the prohibition seriously. This lends credence to the nonanachronistic nature of the attributions regarding *bal tashḥit* made to early *tannaim* in the Babylonian Talmud, where tannaitic sources, apparently well known to them but not us, are cited.

Conclusion

The prohibition against wastefulness was significantly conceptualized in the tannaitic and amoraic periods. We begin by making some general observations. First, the passages in the Babylonian Talmud dealing with the cutting down of trees do not mention the term *bal tashḥit* even once. Moreover, the passages that do mention the concept *bal tashḥit* by name do not do so in the context of destroying trees. This is of great significance with regard to the evolution of the concept. After all, it is largely in the Talmudic literature that the prohibition against wastefulness is developed. Since the sources we have analyzed appear to be silent in this regard, it is necessary to offer a possible explanation.

A wide variety of texts concerning either specific examples of the prohibition against wastefulness or the destruction of fruit trees were presented in this chapter. These texts were not presented in chronological order, but arranged in a narrative that exposes the reader to certain nuances with regard to the development of the concept of *bal tashḥit*. The first texts presented were those concerning the cutting down of fruit trees. As mentioned above, the concept of *bal tashḥit* is not mentioned by name in these passages. To a degree, this was clarified above in b*Ta'anit* 7a, where it was elucidated that a rabbinic approach exists that the specific prohibition of cutting down fruit trees found in Deuteronomy 20:19 emerged from the words "*lo tikhrot*," translated as "do not cut down."

The next set of texts specifically mentions the term *bal tashḥit*. Although the term is used with regard to particular situations, it is still implicit that *bal tashḥit* is concerned with wastefulness/destruction in a general sense. Moreover, the texts that use the term make it clear that *bal tashḥit* is a general prohibition against wastefulness/destruction. Although none of the six passages that use the term *bal tashḥit* presented in this chapter appear in the Mishnah or Tosefta, three are presented in the name of *tannaim* (b*Baba Qama* 91b, b*Ḥullin* 7b, and *Semaḥot* 9:23). While it initially may have appeared that the term itself was an amoraic formulation, the fact that three separate texts attributed to three different *tannaim* makes a very solid case that the term *bal tashḥit* is pre-amoraic. The three texts attributed to the *tannaim* all deal with specific examples of wastefulness to which the prohibition of *bal tashḥit* is applied. The one attributed to Rabbi Eleazar is of particular interest. Recall that we argue that he is the *tanna* who inferred that just as one is prohibited from wasting/destroying material that has value, so too *a fortiori* one is prohibited from harming oneself. In the Tosefta we observed a similar line of reasoning, but from the other direction: just as one is prohibited from harming oneself, so too is it prohibited to waste/destroy material that has value. The relationship between human value and material is not purported to be on the same level, nor would we imagine it to be. The *a fortiori* argument is only offered in one direction. Nevertheless, the two texts lead to the same place, but from different points of origin: we learn about self-harm from wastefulness and about wastefulness from self-harm. This relationship can be defined in terms of an environmental ethic: being wasteful and destructive is harmful to oneself, and harming oneself is wasteful and destructive. Or to simplify further and put it in environmental terms: harming the environment is harmful to oneself. The ethic is profound in its simplicity, and is relevant both historically and today. This ethic is not stated explicitly in the texts, but the relationships noted here make a compelling case for this wisdom to have been self-evident.

This ethic appears to be in its simplest form in the tannaitic era. At this point in its development, the *amoraim* have not yet problematized the concept. The relationship between self-harm and wastefulness is at its clearest point in the evolutionary history of the ethic of *bal tashḥit*. This is especially the case in the Tosefta, but also strongly reinforced through the two *baraitot* in b*Baba Qama* 91b brought in the name of Rabbi Eleazar. The Tosefta (t*Baba Qama* 9:31) and Rabbi Eleazar's *baraita* on Genesis 9:5 illustrate a firm connection between the verse and the prohibition against self-harm. At the same time, the Tosefta and Rabbi Eleazar's *baraita* on *bal tashḥit* indicate an integral connection between Genesis 9:5 and the prohibition against wastefulness/destruction.

These connections are muted by the *amoraim* in the Talmud. It would seem to me that one of the tasks the *amoraim* took upon themselves was to problematize the legal statements presented in the Mishnah. This they accomplish by bringing the abstract nature of the *tannaitic* discourse back into the real world, where pure legal precepts no longer operate in a vacuum. Let us begin by analyzing the amoraic approach to fruit trees. We observed above that the *amoraim* established parameters through which fruit trees could be cut down. At first we encounter the opinion of Rav, a first-generation *amora*, who based the decision of whether a fruit tree could be cut down on the productivity of the tree. Ravina, a fifth- or sixth-generation *amora*, expanded these parameters to include any instance in which the value of a fruit tree as a producer of fruit was less than that of the same tree used for other purposes (for instance as lumber or for the land on which the tree is growing). Ultimately, these modifications to the *halakhah* in its simplest form are essential. After all, realistically it would be very difficult to function as a society if there was no flexibility within this law. From the perspective of the environment, however, neglecting to consider fruit trees as having intrinsic value beyond their instrumental value, which is one possible interpretation of the rationale behind the biblical prohibition, severely weakens any original ethical considerations. As mentioned above, through this understanding it is possible to imagine a scenario in which even the last tree in the world is cut down. The removal of intrinsic value from the equation and replacing it with an economic, utilitarian parameter that emphasizes relative worth results in a significantly weakened principle, from an environmental perspective.

Wastefulness and Self-Harm

Finally, the connection between wastefulness and self-harm must be addressed. This relationship was also transformed during the amoraic period. Let us first consider that Genesis 9:5 and *bal tashḥit* as possible sources for the prohibition against self-harm were rejected by the Talmud. These rejections weakened the connection between self-harm and wastefulness. Moreover, we are introduced to the amoraic construct, "the prohibition against destroying the body is more dear" (*bal tashḥit degufa adif*) (b*Shabbat* 129a and 140b). This nuanced version of *bal tashḥit* takes the relationship between the prohibition against self-harm and the prohibition against wastefulness and turns it on its head. I argue that these prohibitions were on relatively equal footing during the tannaitic period, with material considered to be an extension of the self. Hierarchically speaking, of course the self was considered to be of higher standing (we see that quite clearly in the midrash from the beginning of the chapter), but from the texts presented here there is reason to assume an awareness that harming material is in fact an indirect way of harming oneself. "The prohibition against destroying the body is more dear" (*bal tashḥit degufa adif*) was an amoraic way through which the hierarchical element of the relationship between material and the self is highlighted and translated into a legal norm from which various ethical postulates might be inferred. It is used in the Talmud to create a paradigm in which the value of the self always trumps the value of material. In other words, whereas the nuance between direct and indirect harm to one's own body is not strongly differentiated by the *tannaim*, it is differentiated to a great extent by the *amoraim*. This is not to say that the *tannaim* would have considered material to be on par with the self. If they were faced with the scenarios presented in b*Shabbat* 129a of destroying furniture to provide a fire for individuals who had just undergone bloodletting, it is safe to assume that they would also have allowed the furniture to be burned. The difference then rests in the fact that the *amoraim* legislated that preventing direct harm to the body always takes precedence over preventing indirect harm, even if the indirect harm has the potential to cause greater damage.

From an environmental perspective of long-term sustainability, this approach can be critiqued as somewhat shortsighted. It allows for short-term gratification but disregards the potential impact that such actions may cause. This is not to say that this nuanced approach condones unsustainable practices. Instead, it shifts the focus from long-term sustainability to immediate preservation. The biggest problem with this modified ethic is that its boundaries were not legislated. For instance, whereas there would be little disagreement regarding the actions taken in the example of b*Shabbat* 129a, the discourse of b*Shabbat* 140b, the only other example we have where this nuanced version of *bal tashḥit* is presented is not as clear. We are presented with two individuals who claim that when one has the choice of consuming inferior or superior products, choosing the superior products is a transgression of *bal tashḥit*. Their approach is rejected by the Talmud because of the principle of "the prohibition against destroying the body is more dear" (*bal tashḥit degufa adif*). It certainly is possible that the superior products mentioned in b*Shabbat* 140b do indeed have greater health benefits than the inferior products. Nevertheless, used in this context, "the prohibition against destroying the body is more dear" (*bal tashḥit degufa adif*) demonstrates the potential for a slippery slope that would tolerate unsustainable practices for the purpose of self-gratification. Again, this is not to say that the rabbis of the Talmud had such practices in mind when this principle was created. Still, since parameters were not established, the door is opened for this possibility. This may point to a bigger issue of a law-based approach to environmental challenges, which may require more contextual flexibility rather than added layers of rigid law.[75] As Garrett Hardin put it: "The laws of our society follow the pattern of ancient ethics, and therefore are poorly suited to governing a complex, crowded, changeable world."[76]

As can be seen, the transition from the tannaitic to the amoraic approach to *bal tashḥit* is fraught with compromises. The impact of the parameter of self-harm on the development of *bal tashḥit* established by the *tannaim* was subsequently muted by the *amoraim*. The

75. My thanks to Eric Lawee for raising this possibility.

76. Garrett Hardin, "The Tragedy of the Commons," *Science* 162, no. 3859 (1968): 1245.

commoditization of material further distanced the amoraic approach to *bal tashḥit* from its place in tannaitic thought. As will be seen in the legal literature that arose in the wake of the Talmud, the stage set by the *amoraim* of Babylon endures over the course of history, especially as seen from the Maimonidean lens through which it was summarized. The relationship between self-harm and wastefulness was all but forgotten in the literature. Nevertheless, these connections lived on in a series of voices throughout Jewish history, including those of Yonah of Gerona, Menaḥem HaMeiri, Shlomo Luria, Abraham de Boton, Israel Lipschutz, Jacob Ettlinger, and Barukh Epstein, all among the greatest scholars of their times.[77]

The question remains, however, of why these specific scholars stand out in this regard. Did something about their times and places contribute to their making a connection between *bal tashḥit* and self-harm? It is interesting to consider their circumstances, even though ultimately they shed little light on the matter. Both Yonah of Gerona and Menaḥem HaMeiri hailed from the same Spanish region of Catalonia (HaMeiri moved there from Provence). Their lives overlapped by a few years, but probably did not overlap there long enough for any direct transmission of knowledge. Ta-Shma and Derovan claimed that even though HaMeiri referred to Yonah of Gerona as his teacher, this could just be because he studied his teachings rather than directly learning from him.[78] At any rate, in his later years Yonah of Gerona lived in Toledo while HaMeiri spent his life in Perpignan.

Jacob Ettlinger was the only one in this group who received a university education.[79] Aside from being a renowned *halakhist*, he clearly was immersed in secular knowledge as well. Most important is the fact that one of his most prominent students was Samson Raphael Hirsch.[80] Hirsch, as we will see in the chapter on the Bible, was one of the harbingers of the Jewish environmental movement and undoubtedly had the most environmentally mature understanding of

77. Other scholars belong to this group, but they will only be presented in the next chapters.

78. Israel Moses Ta-Shma and David Derovan, *Encyclopaedia Judaica*, 2nd ed., s.v. Meiri, Menaḥem ben Solomon, eds. Michael Berenbaum and Fred Skolnik (Detroit: Macmillan Reference USA, 2007).

79. Shlomo Eidelberg, *Encyclopaedia Judaica*, 2nd ed., s.v. Ettlinger, Jacob, eds. Michael Berenbaum and Fred Skolnik (Detroit: Macmillan Reference USA, 2007).

80. Ibid.

bal tashḥit up to the rise of contemporary Jewish environmentalism. While it is true that Hirsch does not directly associate the prohibition against self-harm and the prohibition against wastefulness/destruction as does his teacher, he was still the only Bible commentator who drew an implicit connection between Genesis 9:5 and *bal tashḥit*.

In the end, however, it is probably beyond our capacity to understand why these scholars kept this voice alive. Though they were clearly prominent in their immediate communities and beyond, their approaches to *bal tashḥit* are not the basis of their fame. In fact, expounding *bal tashḥit* was probably no more than a marginal note to the prolific careers of these scholars, nor should we expect it to have been otherwise. It is only with Ettlinger's student Samson Raphael Hirsch where we see a shift that put *bal tashḥit* into the spotlight. Hirsch called *bal tashḥit* "the first and most general call of God."[81] It is possible that Hirsch understood the ethical implications of Ettlinger's position and greatly expanded them. One should note, however, that he does not reproduce Ettlinger's approach in his own writings. Nevertheless, Ettlinger's propagation of the approach that the prohibition against self-harm and the prohibition against wastefulness/destruction are one and the same seems to have influenced Hirsch.

---

81. Samson Raphael Hirsch, *Horeb*, 279.

Chapter 2

Bible and Biblical Commentaries

The Bible is a foundational document of Western culture. It gave birth to Judaism and later on Christianity, while also strongly influencing Islam. It has given the world the first recorded concept of monotheism. In its many books one can find the story of the creation of the world, the covenant between God and Abraham and his descendants the Israelites, their enslavement in Egypt, and their subsequent exodus and settlement in the Land of Israel. It speaks of the monarchy and prophets, the building of the First Temple, its later destruction, and the exile of the Israelites. Perhaps most importantly, it provides a legal and ethical framework with universal laws applicable to all of humanity, as well as a lengthy set of laws that apply only to Israelites. Over the course of history these laws have been expounded and expanded. There has been and remains a drive to interpret the requirements of the laws, to live life according to the dictates of the Bible. The stories and laws of the Bible, however, are not always written in a straightforward manner that can be easily understood. Sometimes the language employed is esoteric or ambiguous. Sometimes the language is simply outdated and as such no longer understood. Sometimes the text contradicts itself, and sometimes the heroes of the Bible act in ways that many would consider to be morally repugnant. For all these reasons, the Bible requires interpretation. Interpretation is not a static endeavor, however; it is highly influenced by factors external to the text being interpreted. As Michael Fishbane puts it, "As interpretations succeeded or complemented one another, a massive texture of texts and techniques formed the warp and woof of rabbinic culture, setting its patterns and forms for the ages. Each new period saw successive developments along these lines, even as radically new expressions emerged."[1]

1. Michael Fishbane, "Introduction," *The Midrashic Imagination*, ed. Michael Fishbane (Albany: State University of New York Press, 1993), 1.

The prohibition against wastefulness and destruction in the Jewish tradition is almost universally seen to have originated from Deuteronomy 20:19–20, despite the fact that we already saw in the previous chapter that other biblical texts have also influenced the conceptualization of *bal tashḥit*. There is no doubt that the verses from Deuteronomy have shaped the legal discourse surrounding the prohibition of *bal tashḥit* even though contextually they deal with trees and war. As this prohibition has its foundations in Scripture, to fully understand its scope it is necessary to conduct a comprehensive study of the key verses that form its basis.

Goals

The goals of this chapter are as follows:

1. To collect, analyze, and synthesize the comments of as many glossators as possible.
2. To assess whether these verses have elicited comments on *bal tashḥit* as a general prohibition against wastefulness.
3. To note the commentators who have had a significant impact on the conceptualization of *bal tashḥit*.
4. To see whether there are exegetes who connect the prohibition against wastefulness and the prohibition against self-harm.
5. To analyze whether any of the commentators have what might be considered profound environmental insights in their comments.

When deciding how the chapters in this book should be arranged, the placement of the chapter on biblical commentary caused the greatest predicament. Ultimately, it made the most sense to approach the analysis of *bal tashḥit* chronologically. After all, a study of the evolution of a concept should be traced in a linear manner. This is especially the case here, since the vast majority of biblical commentators are grounded in the rabbinic tradition and base their interpretations on it. Moreover, since Jewish biblical commentaries in their familiar style did not begin to appear until the tenth century CE with Saadiah, close to eight centuries of written rabbinic material needed to be taken into account prior to analyzing the contributions of Bible interpreters. This is not to suggest that biblical commentaries did not exist prior to Saadiah; certainly they did, as we saw in the previous chapter with the *Midrash Halakhah* and *Midrash Aggadah*. Robert Brody, referring to Saadiah and a number of the *geonim* who succeeded him, describes the main difference between rabbinic and geonic exegesis:

> Geonic exegesis in general may be characterized as more disciplined and less fanciful than earlier rabbinic exegesis, and more concerned with a close, systematic reading of the biblical text, in which attention is devoted both to the smallest textual units and to the integrity of larger narratives.[2]

In terms of the influence of this type of exegesis on subsequent generations, Brody writes,

> In a broader sense, the work of the *Geonim* provided a precedent for the writing of systematic biblical commentaries in a form essentially different from that of classical rabbinic *midrash*, and doubtless provided inspiration and a sense of legitimacy to numerous commentators who had no direct access to their works.[3]

From Saadiah onward, Bible commentators became more concerned (though not always) with the plain or simple meaning of the text (*peshat*).[4] Exegetes who are dedicated to *peshat* offer glosses to the text that take into consideration grammar, syntax, and context,[5] and usually offer an alternative interpretation to the midrash of the rabbis.

2. Robert Brody, "The Geonim of Babylonia as Biblical Exegetes," in *Hebrew Bible/Old Testament: The History of Its Interpretation*, Vol. 1, *From the Beginnings to the Middle Ages (Until 1300)*, Part 2: *The Middle Ages*, ed. Magne Saebo (Gottingen, Germany: Vandenhoeck & Ruprecht, 2000), 87.

3. Ibid., 88.

4. For more on *peshat* see Martin Lockshin, "Introductory Essay: *Peshat* and *Derash* in Northern France," in *Rashbam's Commentary on Deuteronomy: An Annotated Translation*, ed. and trans. Martin Lockshin (Providence, RI: Brown Judaic Studies, 2004), 24.

5. Ibid., 2.

This chapter follows an historical sequence, and the biblical exegetes consulted are listed according to a linear timeline. It is worthwhile acknowledging that many different methods could have been used to divide the glosses offered by the commentators. Groups could have been made based on geography, schools of thought (e.g. *peshat, derash,* etc.), historical eras (medieval vs. modern), or culture (Ashkenazi vs. Sephardi). It was decided to present the commentaries chronologically and only then to divide them into groups based on the actual comments. Each method of division has merits. The goal of this chapter is to uncover the manner in which the verses fundamental to the concept of *bal tashḥit* are interpreted. As such, although the commentators have significantly different spheres of influence, the primary concern of this chapter is the commentary and not the commentators. Only after the glosses have been analyzed do the commentators themselves become a focus. Due to this distinction, and the fact that the commentators are later broken down into groups based on their comments, it made sense to first present them chronologically.

The format of this chapter is as follows: each relevant verse is presented along with a paragraph explaining the biblical context in which the verse or verses emerged. Next, the medieval compilations of midrash are presented, followed by a diachronic arrangement of all the biblical commentators and a synthesis of their comments. After all the glosses for a given verse are presented, an analysis of the commentaries is given, followed by an overall conclusion to the chapter. The verses covered in this chapter, Genesis 9:5, Leviticus 19:27, Deuteronomy 20:19–20, and 2 Kings 3:19, 25, are pertinent to the development of the concept of *bal tashḥit*. Almost all contemporary environmental commentary on *bal tashḥit* has focused on the verses from Deuteronomy. This research exposes readers to additional verses that were critical in influencing Jewish attitudes to wastefulness.

This chapter makes no claim to have covered the entire gamut of Jewish biblical glossators, though an attempt was made to be as comprehensive as possible. One issue that arises is how to distinguish between the quality of one specific commentator and another. After all, as mentioned in the introduction, this was one of my major critiques of Jeremy Cohen. If I do not make this distinction, perhaps the same critique could be made of this work. It is therefore pertinent to open this chapter with a number of important statements that address this issue. This book is primarily interested in the quality of the gloss and only secondarily in the quality of the glossator. The quality of a gloss is measured by two parameters. The first is through its environmental insight. Having situated itself in the field of religion and environment, this book is interested in the environmental concern demonstrated by particular individuals through their comments.[6] Accordingly, certain scholars might stand out even though they are less acclaimed as biblical exegetes than others. The second area of interest is in the impact a gloss has on the conceptualization of *bal tashḥit*. By going beyond the historical time frame that Jeremy Cohen prescribed to his work and taking the study of *bal tashḥit* into the current era, this book can observe if scholars from earlier times had a profound impact on the development of the concept and duly note it.

Bible commentaries from Saadiah onward are not always presented in the format that he popularized. Some of the individuals in this chapter are better known for scholarship in fields other than Bible. Nevertheless, they appear here because they wrote a commentary on a part of the Bible, because someone extracted a commentary from the works of scholars who did not themselves write one, or because they wrote a work that is not a biblical commentary per se, but still comments on the Bible and fits better into this chapter than anywhere else in this book. Due to the difficulties of collecting relevant material from this last group of writings, such literature is by and large (though not entirely) beyond the scope of this chapter. It must also be noted that for many commentators we have no extant comments available to share with the reader. At times this is because, even though we possess their complete commentary, the exegete sometimes apparently thought it unnecessary to write a gloss on the passage in question. At other times, there were commentators who only wrote comments on one book and not on another—for example, on Genesis and not on Kings. In many cases, however, the commentary is missing due to incomplete, lost, or missing manuscripts. Only exegetes who make relevant comments on the passages in question are included in the body of this chapter. Commentators who had little new to add and mostly repeat earlier material are mentioned either in footnotes or in the synthetic analysis of each verse.[7] The writings of the Bible

6. Again, as argued in the introduction, this is a very different enterprise than claiming that any of these historical figures was an environmentalist in the contemporary sense.

7. The first time I mention a commentator I provide details on the time and place he lived, and a bibliographical reference. I repeat these details for each new verse, and for commentators whom I present under their own heading.

interpreters that were analyzed but were devoid of comments on the relevant verses are listed in the appendix to acknowledge that their writings have been taken into consideration.

Deuteronomy 20:19–20

Context

Chapter 20 of Deuteronomy instructs the Israelites on their obligations in a time of war. For the most part, the commandments in this chapter are of an ethical nature.[8] The chapter starts by encouraging the Israelite army to put their faith in God, who will ensure their victory. Those who have recently built a house but not lived in it, planted a vineyard but have not yet enjoyed it, were betrothed but have not consummated their marriage, or were simply afraid, are prohibited from participating in the battle. In the battle itself, the Israelites are commanded to negotiate a peaceful surrender of their enemies. The inhabitants of the cities that surrender are not to be killed, but instead are to be subservient to the Israelites. The adult male inhabitants of the cities that do not surrender are to be put to death, but everyone and everything else can be taken as spoils of war. This is the procedure in cities that are distant from the Land of Israel. The text, however, does not provide the same leniencies to the seven nations of Canaan that were in close proximity to the Israelites. They were to be completely destroyed, men, women, and children, even down to the last animal.[9] The reasoning behind this was so that the Israelites would not be influenced by their idolatrous practices. Finally, the chapter concludes with the two verses that are of interest to us.
New Jewish Publication Society (NJPS)

> 19: When in your war against a city you have to besiege it a long time in order to capture it, you must not destroy its trees, wielding the ax against them. You may eat of them, but you must not cut them down. Are trees of the field human

8. It should be noted that at times biblical ethics and contemporary ethics differ greatly.

9. The Jewish Bible commentary tradition by and large understood this edict to include men, women, and children but not animals. As some grammarians have pointed out, and as the plain sense of the text indicates, the edict in Deuteronomy 20:16 includes animals.

> to withdraw before you into the besieged city? 20: Only trees that you know do not yield food may be destroyed; you may cut them down for constructing siege-works against the city that is waging war on you, until it has been reduced.[10]

King James

> 19: When thou shalt besiege a city a long time, in making war against it to take it, thou shalt not destroy the trees thereof by forcing an axe against them: for thou mayest eat of them, and thou shalt not cut them down (for the tree of the field is man's life) to employ them in the siege: 20: Only the trees which thou knowest that they be not trees for meat, thou shalt destroy and cut them down; and thou shalt build bulwarks against the city that maketh war with thee, until it be subdued.[11]

The reason two different translations are presented is because they highlight the major divide in the tradition histories of the verses. The NJPS translates the words *"ki ha'adam etz hasadeh"* as a rhetorical question: "Are trees of the field human . . . ?" The King James Bible, however, translates these words as a statement: "For the tree of the field is man's life . . ." This will be expanded on in depth in the analysis of this section.

Medieval Midrash

Midrash Aggadah (twelfth and thirteenth centuries, anonymous) (Buber) *Devarim* 20:19.[12] The prohibition of destroying fruit trees is an indicator that anyone who destroys something from which someone can derive benefit/enjoyment (*yesh alav hana'ah*) transgresses the prohibition of *lo tashḥit*. He is the first to use this critical terminology. The midrash added that a non-fruit-bearing tree may be cut down.

10. *The Jewish Study Bible*, eds. Adele Berlin and Marc Zvi Brettler (New York: Oxford University Press, 2004).

11. *The New Cambridge Paragraph Bible, with the Apocrypha*, King James Version, ed. David Norton (Cambridge, UK: Cambridge University Press, 2005).

12. *Sefer Midrash Aggadah al Ḥamishah Ḥumshei Torah*, ed. Solomon Buber (Jerusalem: M. D. Bloom, 1961).

Yalqut Shimoni (Shimon HaDarshan, thirteenth century, Germany) *Shofetim* 923.[13] Though very similar to early *midrashim* on Deuteronomy 20:19–20 seen in the previous chapter, *Yalqut Shimoni* offers one very significant addition. The *Yalqut* mentions the text from b*Shabbat* 67b, which states, "Rav Zutra said: He who covers an oil lamp or uncovers a *naphtha* [lamp] infringes on the prohibition against wastefulness (*bal tashḥit*)." As I elucidated in the previous chapter, the indication is that anyone who causes a lamp to burn inefficiently is transgressing the prohibition against wastefulness. The *Yalqut Shimoni* is one of the earliest instances in which a connection is made between the prohibition on cutting down trees, and wastefulness in general. The exact date and author of the compilation of Midrash is unknown, but it includes midrashic material from the span of over a millennium. It is currently thought that the author lived in early-thirteenth-century Germany.[14] Due to the relatively late date of the compilation, it does not come as a surprise that the *Yalqut* contains a large quantity of material for each verse of the Torah on which it is commenting. The *Yalqut* is still one of the only sources to connect the verse in Deuteronomy and an example of wastefulness that is not associated with trees. Nevertheless, in spite of the early association of Deuteronomy 20:19 with the general prohibition against wastefulness, the *Yalqut* did not add any particular terminology that impacted the conceptualization of the prohibition against wastefulness.

Geonic Commentary

Saadiah Gaon (*Rasag*) (882–942, Egypt and Babylonia).[15] The earliest postmidrashic source that dealt with the rationale behind not cutting down fruit trees was Saadiah Gaon. As Robert Brody argues, the methodology of interpretation used by Saadiah and the other *geonim* was to interpret the text literally unless it contradicted a different text, in which case it was to be understood metaphorically.[16] Saadiah

13. Shimon HaDarshan, *Yalqut Shimoni LeRabbeinu Shimon HaDarshan: Sefer Devarim*, Vol. 1, *Devarim—Shofetim*, eds. Aharon Heiman and Yitzḥak Shiloni (Jerusalem: Mossad HaRav Kook, 1991).

14. Jacob Elbaum, *Encyclopedia Judaica*, 2nd ed., s.v. Yalkut Shimoni, eds. Michael Berenbaum and Fred Skolnik (Detroit: Macmillan Reference USA, 2007).

15. Saadiah Gaon, "*Targum HaTafsir shel Rav Saadiah Gaon*," in *Torat Ḥaim—Devarim*, ed. Yosef Kapaḥ (Jerusalem: Mossad HaRav Kook, 1993).

16. Brody, "The Geonim of Babylonia," 80–81.

Gaon also emphasized linguistic points as important in a biblical commentary. Saadiah wrote that fruit trees should not be cut down under the mistaken premise that they are like humans who can hide during a siege. In other words, Saadiah interpreted the statement of *ki ha'adam etz hasadeh* as a rhetorical question.

Post-Geonic Commentary

Shlomo Yitzḥaki (*Rashi*) (eleventh century, northern France).[17] Rashi saw the words *ki ha'adam etz hasadeh* as rhetorical; trees cannot escape the battlefield in the manner that humans can. Accordingly, why destroy them? Eliyahu Mizraḥi (*HaRe'em*) (c. 1450–1526, Turkey),[18] a Rashi supercommentator, dealt with Rashi's gloss on *ki ha'adam etz hasadeh*, repeating his rhetorical statement that indeed trees cannot escape from war as humans can by running away, so why destroy them? He finished his own gloss by questioning Rashi's: if Rashi's gloss were indeed correct, the definite article "*ha*" of "*ha'adam*" becomes superfluous.

Samuel ben Meir (*Rashbam*) (c. 1080–1174, northern France).[19] Rashbam indicated that part of the process of laying siege to a city requires cutting down trees. For Rashbam, the initial reason to not cut down fruit trees in this context is because after a successful siege, the trees will provide sustenance to its new inhabitants. He was aware, however, that the trees themselves could be used to aid the enemy by impeding the advance of the troops, or by providing cover for the enemy. As such, the prohibition on cutting down fruit trees applies first and foremost to the fruit trees that belong to the city but are far enough from it so as not to shield the enemy. The status of the fruit trees close to the city will be elucidated in the continuation. Regarding *ki ha'adam etz hasadeh*, Rashbam used the linguistic rule that any time the word *ki* (for, because) appears after the word *lo* (no/negation), it should be read as "rather." Martin Lockshin, the editor of the Rashbam

17. Shlomo Yitzḥaki, *Peirushei Rashi al HaTorah*, ed. Ḥaim Dov Chavel (Jerusalem: Mossad HaRav Kook, 1982).

18. Eliyahu Mizraḥi, *Ḥumash HaRe'em: Sefer Devarim*, ed. Moshe Filip (Petaḥ Tiqva, Israel: private printing, 1992).

19. Samuel ben Meir, *Peirush HaTorah LeRabbeinu Shmuel ben Meir*, Vol. 2, *VaYiqra, BeMidbar, Devarim*, ed. Martin I. Lockshin (Jerusalem: Chorev Publishing House, 2009).

edition used here, states that while Rashbam's gloss on these verses is difficult to understand in certain places, what is clear is that Rashbam was offering an alternative interpretation to the midrashic glosses that draw parallels between humans and fruit trees, and at the same time disagrees with the interpretations that viewed *ki ha'adam etz hasadeh* as a rhetorical question. Lockshin suggests that it is likely that the version of Rashbam we have is somewhat corrupted, but offers the possibility that Rashbam's gloss either meant that the enemy used the trees close to the city as a way of entering and exiting, or that the act of cutting down the trees close to the city will itself put the city under siege. Ultimately, this aspect of Rashbam's gloss is of less interest for our purposes. Rashbam interpreted verse 20 as meaning that any non-fruit-bearing trees, regardless of their location in reference to the city, can be cut down and used in the siege works. Fruit trees, however, are only to be cut down when they are close to the city, and only when they fit the criteria listed above.

Rashbam was one of the few to offer a nonmidrashic interpretation of *ki ha'adam etz hasadeh*. For him these words were not the rationale behind not cutting down the fruit trees, but an elucidation of exactly which trees could or could not be cut down. In other words, only the fruit trees belonging to the city but still far enough away from it to not assist the enemy or act as a hindrance to the army laying siege were not to be cut down. This same logic is echoed later on by *Ba'alei HaTosafot* (anonymous authors, c. twelfth to fourteenth centuries, France and Germany),[20] a group to which Rashbam belonged. Meir Leibush Weiser (1809–1879, Ukraine, Poland, Romania, and Prussia)[21] also presented Rashbam's view in his gloss, but this did not preclude him from accepting the midrash as a valid interpretation of the verse.

Like Rashbam, the midrash of *Sifre*, Hoffmann's *Midrash Tannaim*, Tuvia bar Eliezer's *Pesikta Zutarta* (late eleventh century, Byzantium),[22] along with a large group of later commentaries including Meyuḥas bar Eliyahu (1150–1200, Byzantium),[23] *Ba'alei HaTosafot*, Naḥmanides

20. Ba'alei HaTosafot, *Da'at Zeqenim MiBa'alei HaTosafot* (Jerusalem: HaMeir LeYisrael, 2008).

21. Meir Leibush Weiser, *Otzar HaPeirushim al Tanakh, Miqraot Gedolot, Sidra 2, HaTorah VeHaMitzvah* (Tel-Aviv: Mefarshei HaTanakh, n.d.).

22. Tuvia bar Eliezer, *Midrash Leqaḥ Tov HaMekhuneh Pesiqta Zutarta al Ḥamishah Ḥumshei Torah—Devarim*, Vol. 2, ed. Shlomo Buber (Israel: Books Export Enterprises, 1960).

23. Meyuḥas bar Eliyahu, *Peirush al Sefer Devarim*, ed. Yeḥiel Mikhel Katz (Jerusalem: Mossad HaRav Kook, 1968).

(1194–1270, Spain and Land of Israel),[24] Asher ben Yeḥiel (*Rosh*) (1250 or 1259–1327, Germany, France, and Spain),[25] Ḥizqiyah bar Manoaḥ (*Ḥizquni*) (thirteenth century, France),[26] Ḥaim Paltiel (c. thirteenth century, Germany),[27] and others, claimed that the trees that hinder the siege in any way should be cut down. This distinction demonstrates a rational approach to warfare. The initial idea is to be as careful as possible and not to destroy needlessly. If and when the fruit trees prove to be a hindrance, however, they may be cut down. Destroying fruit trees under such circumstances cannot be viewed as wanton destruction, because their removal serves a military function. In fact, it could even be argued that cutting down the trees in this case would be considered avoidance of self-harm.

Abraham ibn Ezra (1089–1164, born in Spain, but lived and traveled all over the Mediterranean basin, northern France, and England).[28] Ibn Ezra analyzed the term *ki ha'adam etz hasadeh* from a linguistic perspective. He mentioned that a great Sephardic scholar claimed that the text is shortened, and actually should be read as *hakhi ha'adam etz hasadeh*. This distinction would turn the text into a rhetorical question instead of a statement. The rhetorical question is, can a tree of the field truly run away from you in battle as a human would? Ibn Ezra rejected this interpretation by claiming that the text has no reason to ask this type of question. Instead, ibn Ezra offered an alternative interpretation, stating that because the life of the human is derived from the sustenance given by the tree of the field, the tree is equated to the human, a "you are what you eat" approach.

Ibn Ezra was the first to reject reading the text as a rhetorical question, on both linguistic and logical grounds. He claimed that linguistically, the text has no interrogatory elements, and further, has absolutely no reason to engage in rhetorical questions. Accordingly,

24. Moshe ben Naḥman, *Peirushei HaTorah LeRabbeinu Moshe ben Naḥman*, 9th ed.,Vol. 2, ed. Ḥaim Dov Chavel (Jerusalem: Mossad HaRav Kook, 1976).

25. Ba'alei HaTosafot, *Sefer Hadar Zeqenim: al HaTorah*, ed. Avraham Forianti (Jerusalem: Herbert Zarkin Offset Institute, 1963).

26. Ḥizqiyah bar Manoaḥ, *Ḥizquni: Peirushei HaTorah LeRabbeinu Ḥizqiyah bar Manoaḥ*, ed. Ḥaim Dov Chavel (Jerusalem: Mossad HaRav Kook, 1981).

27. Ḥaim Paltiel, *Peirushei HaTorah LeRabbeinu Ḥaim Paltiel*, ed. Isaak Shimshon Lange (Jerusalem: private printing, 1981).

28. Abraham ibn Ezra, *Peirushei HaTorah LeRabbeinu Avraham ibn Ezra*, Vol. 3, 2nd ed., ed. Asher Weiser (Jerusalem: Mossad HaRav Kook, 1977).

it would be erroneous to think that it does. Instead, ibn Ezra offered a reading of the text that equates humans with fruit trees as the rationale for not cutting them down, even during a time of war and even if the act of cutting down the fruit trees puts the city under siege. Fruit trees are an important source of human sustenance and should be viewed as necessary to human life. This approach could be criticized insofar as, if this parallel is taken literally, destroying the fruit trees would be equivalent to killing the enemy. Yet clearly, the assumption is that victory will be achieved. Thus, cutting down the trees is tantamount to self-harm.

Commentators such as Naḥmanides, Yaakov bar Asher (*Ba'al HaTurim*) (c. 1270–1343, Germany and Spain),[29] Isaac Abarbanel (1437–1508, Portugal, Spain, and Italy),[30] and Ovadiah Seforno (c. 1480–c. 1550, Italy)[31] approach this from a different angle, asserting that if the people of Israel put their faith in God, they will end up winning the war and colonizing the city. As such, destroying the fruit trees would harm the besieging army and not the besieged populace. Others following ibn Ezra's plain-sense exegetical approach include Menaḥem Recanati (c. 1250–c. 1310, Italy),[32] Ḥaim Paltiel (c. thirteenth century, Germany),[33] Yaakov bar Asher, Nissim of Marseille (thirteenth and fourteenth centuries, southern France),[34] and Samson Raphael Hirsch (1808–1888, Germany and Moravia).[35] Some commentators, such as Ḥizqiyah bar Manoaḥ (*Ḥizquni*) (thirteenth century, France),[36] Avraham Saba (*Tzeror HaMor*) (1440–1508, Spain, Portugal, Morocco,

---

29. Yaakov bar Asher, *Peirush HaTur al HaTorah LeHaRabbi Yaakov ben HaRosh*. Vol. 2: *VaYiqra—Devarim*, ed. Yaakov Kapel Reinitz (Jerusalem: Feldheim Publishers, 2006).

30. Isaac Abarbanel, *Peirush al HaTorah—BeMidbar, Devarim* (Jerusalem: Bnei Arbael Publishing, 1964).

31. Ovadiah Seforno, *Be'ur al HaTorah LeRabbi Ovadiah Seforno*, ed. Ze'ev Gottleib (Jerusalem: Mossad HaRav Kook, 1980).

32. Menaḥem Recanati, *Sefer Levushei Or Yaqar*, ed. Ḥaim Yaakov HaCohen (Jerusalem: private printing, 1960).

33. Ḥaim Paltiel, *Peirushei HaTorah*.

34. Nissim ben Moshe, *Ma'aseh Nissim: Peirush LaTorah LeRabbi Nissim ben Rabbi Moshe MiMarseille*, ed. Howard Kriesel (Jerusalem: Mekitzei Nirdamim, 2000).

35. Samson Raphael Hirsch, *Ḥamishah Ḥumshei Torah im Peirush Rashar Hirsch: Sefer Devarim*, 4th ed., ed. and trans. Mordekhai Breuer (Jerusalem: Mossad Yitzḥak Breuer, 1989).

36. Ḥizqiyah bar Manoaḥ, *Ḥizquni: Peirushei HaTorah*.

and Turkey),[37] David Tzvi Hoffmann (1843–1921, Slovakia, Austria, and Germany),[38] Gunther Plaut (1912–2012, Germany, USA, and Canada),[39] and ArtScroll (2009, USA)[40] offered both Rashi's rhetorical reasoning and ibn Ezra's assertion as two possible nonconflicting readings of the verse.

Meyuḥas bar Eliyahu (1150–1200, Byzantium).[41] Meyuḥas bar Eliyahu began by claiming that the straightforward meaning of the text is that the trees are designated to become a food source and should not be cut down. He then presented the *a fortiori* interpretation offered in the midrash, which claimed that if the fruit tree is prohibited from destruction, how much more so is the fruit itself prohibited from destruction? This, he claimed, is the source that indicates that the Torah is concerned with the waste of food. From this the rabbis derived both that one is prohibited from throwing out food and that one is prohibited from destroying anything that has utility (*"davar shehu tzorekh"*—a thing that has usefulness/utility), such as utensils and animals. This is also seen as an indicator that God is concerned with the welfare of the world. It is here that the editor of this commentary, Yeḥiel Mikhel Katz, refers the reader to t*Baba Qama* 9, b*Shabbat* 105b, and Maimonides's Laws of Kings, all of which are discussed in depth in other chapters. Meyuḥas then commented that *ki ha'adam etz hasadeh* is a *"miqra mesoras,"* meaning that the order of the words in the verse needs to be changed for it to be properly understood. The new arrangement indicates that humans, and in this particular case, enemies, are liable to end up besieged. Trees of the field, however, remain in the field at all times and should not be cut down. If, however, the trees impede the siege in some way, they should be cut down. The following verse is understood as establishing a hierarchy in terms of which trees are to be used in building siege works. Non-fruit-bearing trees are to be cut

37. Avraham bar Yaakov Saba, *Sefer Tzeror HaMor al Ḥamishah Ḥumshei Torah* (Tel-Aviv: Offset Brody-Katz, 1975).

38. David Tzvi Hoffmann, *Sefer Devarim* (Tel-Aviv: Netzaḥ Publishing, 1961).

39. Gunther Plaut, *The Torah: A Modern Commentary*, ed. Gunther Plaut (New York: Union of American Hebrew Congregations, 1981).

40. *The Schottenstein Edition Interlinear Chumash: Deuteronomy*, ed. Menachem Davis (New York: Mesorah Publications, 2009).

41. Meyuḥas bar Eliyahu, *Peirush al Sefer Devarim*.

down before fruit trees, with two utilitarian caveats. The first is that if the non-fruit-bearing tree is of greater value than the fruit-bearing tree, then the fruit tree is to be cut down first. The second is that if the value of the lumber of a fruit bearing tree is greater than that of the fruit it produces, then it too may be cut down.

Meyuḥas bar Eliyahu was the earliest post-Talmudic-era exegete to relate this verse to the general prohibition on wastefulness/destruction in his gloss. He stands out in this regard, because no other medieval commentators make this attribution after him, save the *Midrash Aggadah, Yalqut Shimoni,* and Baḥya bar Asher (1255–1340, Spain).[42] The *Midrash Aggadah* made this connection at around the same time period as Meyuḥas bar Eliyahu. The language used by the *Midrash Aggadah* (*hana'ah*—benefit/enjoyment) is used in later materials discussing the prohibition, and thus clearly influenced the conceptualization of *bal tashḥit*. The actual commentary, however, is much terser than Meyuḥas bar Eliyahu's gloss. Meyuḥas was also the first medieval commentator to discuss the utilitarian-driven exceptions to the prohibition of cutting fruit trees found in the Talmud. Others include Menaḥem Recanati, Baḥya bar Asher, Samson Raphael Hirsch, Meir Leibush Weiser, David Tzvi Hoffmann, and Barukh HaLevi Epstein (*Torah Temimah*) (1860–1942, Belarus).[43]

Moshe ben Naḥman (*Ramban,* Naḥmanides) (1194–1270, Spain and Land of Israel).[44] Naḥmanides appreciated ibn Ezra's comment regarding the life of the human as being dependent upon fruit trees. Nevertheless, he took issue with it, because ibn Ezra's conclusion was contrary to the rabbinic position found in the Talmud. There, the rabbis permitted the cutting down of fruit trees to build siege works, and the only reason the matter is mentioned by the Torah is so that non-fruit-bearing trees are cut down before fruit-bearing trees. The text was seen by the rabbis as prohibiting cutting down trees needlessly (i.e., for a purpose other than building siege works), that is, prohibiting a scorched-earth policy. When Israelites embark on a siege, they need

---

42. Baḥya bar Asher, *Rabbeinu Baḥya: Be'ur al HaTorah,* Vol. 3, *BeMidbar, Devarim,* ed. Ḥaim Dov Chavel (Jerusalem: Mossad HaRav Kook, 1974).

43. Barukh HaLevi Epstein, *Ḥamishah Ḥumshei Torah im Ḥamesh Megilot, Torah Temimah: Sefer Devarim* (New York: Avraham Yitzḥak Friedman, 1962).

44. Moshe ben Naḥman, *Peirushei HaTorah LeRabbeinu Moshe ben Naḥman,* Vol. 2.

to put their faith in God that the siege will succeed and that the fruit trees will be a source of sustenance for the future inhabitants of the city. There are, however, situations in which cutting down fruit trees is permitted, such as if the enemy city's inhabitants use the trees to gather lumber, or use the trees to hide in for an ambush, or use them as a shield against projectiles.

Menaḥem Recanati (c. 1250–c. 1310, Italy).[45] Recanati presented the rabbinic statement that there is no creation on earth that is not connected to heaven. Destroying a creation on earth also affects its connection to heaven. He claimed that *ki ha'adam etz hasadeh* is to be understood in its plain sense. To this end he used the Talmud (b*Baba Qama* 91b) as evidence. There Rabbi Ḥanina claimed that his son died for cutting down a fig tree before its time. The implication here is that cutting down the fruit tree is commensurate with committing murder. He also cited *Pirqei deRabbi Eliezer* 33, which claimed that when a fruit tree is cut down its voice is heard from one end of the world to the other.

Baḥya bar Asher (1255–1340, Spain).[46] Baḥya stated that earlier commentaries viewed the term *ki ha'adam etz hasadeh* in a manner similar to ibn Ezra; the life of the human is dependent on sustenance from trees. Baḥya, however, offered his own interpretation of the verse, similar to that of Rashi. Unlike humans, trees cannot escape during war. Wise people do not needlessly destroy things that have utility (*to'elet*). As such, the fruit tree should be used for the utility it provides and not be destroyed. Destroying the tree would destroy its utility. The main difference between his view and Rashi's is that Rashi's rhetorical approach is replaced with a rhetorical utilitarianism. In this nuanced approach, trees should not be destroyed because they cannot escape the battlefield, but moral considerations are not a reason to avoid destroying them. Rather, the trees should not be needlessly destroyed due to their value or utility. Baḥya bar Asher introduced the term *to'elet* (benefit/utility) in his description of the prohibition against cutting down fruit trees, implying that the prohibition extends to all things from which humans derive utility. Gersonides (directly below), who died just four years after Baḥya, also used the term *to'elet*, but

45. Menaḥem Recanati, *Sefer Levushei Or Yaqar*.

46. Baḥya bar Asher, *Rabbeinu Baḥya: Be'ur al HaTorah*, Vol. 3, *BeMidbar, Devarim*.

his gloss was phrased in a way that does not readily extend beyond fruit trees.[47] Like the *Midrash Aggadah*'s *hana'ah*, the term *to'elet* also influenced the conceptualization of the general prohibition against wastefulness. It is only in the modern era that some exegetes, albeit few in number, made these associations. They include Samson Raphael Hirsch, David Tzvi Hoffmann, Barukh HaLevi Epstein, Gunther Plaut, and the ArtScroll commentary.

Levi ben Gershom (*Ralbag*, Gersonides) (1288–1344, France).[48] Gersonides claimed that the text indicates that destroying a fruit tree is prohibited even when it belongs to the enemy. This edict is *a fortiori* with regard to fruit trees belonging to Israel. The text, however, only prohibits cutting down fruit trees in a destructive manner. It is permissible to cut down fruit trees for beneficial/utilitarian purposes (*to'elet*). It is also prohibited to destroy fruit trees in ways other than cutting them down, for instance by preventing water from reaching their roots. The words *ki ha'adam etz hasadeh* for Gersonides pose a rhetorical question: "Is the tree like a person who can escape from you on the battlefield?" For Gersonides, the prefix "*ha*" on the word "*ha'adam*" is indicative of a question rather than a definite article. Non-fruit-bearing trees and fruit-bearing trees that no longer produce fruit, for instance if they are dried out, can be cut down for the purposes of building the siege works.

Isaac Abarbanel (1437–1508, Portugal, Spain, and Italy).[49] Abarbanel asserted that Israelites should not act as others do during a time of war and should avoid following a scorched-earth policy. There are two reasons why fruit trees should not be cut down unnecessarily during a siege. The first is that the trees are to act as a source of food. This reason is also seen as a promise from God that the siege will succeed and the fruit trees will be a future source of sustenance. Accordingly, it is not fitting to waste or destroy something from which one can derive benefit (*mah sheyo'ileihu*). The second reason is that trees are unable to protect themselves and it is not fitting for the strong to subjugate

47. Compare Baḥya's "Wise and intelligent people do not destroy things of value without purpose" (*davar hara'u'i lelo to'elet*) with Gersonides's "If there is no destruction, only utility (*to'elet*), it is permissible to cut it [the fruit tree] down."

48. Levi ben Gershom, *Peirushei HaTorah LeRabbeinu Levi ben Gershom (Ralbag)*, Vol. 5, *Devarim*, ed. Yaakov Leib Levi (Jerusalem: Mossad HaRav Kook, 2000).

49. Isaac Abarbanel, *Peirush al HaTorah—BeMidbar, Devarim*.

the weak. Trees have no arms with which to engage in battle and are unable to escape a siege. In other words, it appears that Abarbanel agreed with Rashi's reading of *ki ha'adam etz hasadeh* as a rhetorical statement. The following verse then allows the cutting down of non-fruit-bearing trees, and as Naḥmanides stated, fruit trees themselves may be used for the purpose of the siege.

Avraham bar Yaakov Saba (*Tzeror HaMor*) (1440–1508, Spain, Portugal, Morocco, and Turkey).[50] Saba first related to the words *ki ha'adam etz hasadeh* by claiming that the statement is an indication that human life is sustained by fruit trees. He saw two reasons for the prohibition of cutting down fruit trees. The first is that humans eat the fruit of these trees and are sustained by it. This reason relates to the words "you may eat of them." The second reason is that just like humans, trees have souls and should not be needlessly destroyed. This reason relates to the words "you must not cut them down." To this end, Saba presented a homiletic midrash (*Pirqei deRabbi Eliezer* 33) stating that when a tree is cut down, its cry can be heard from one end of the world to the other. This reasoning can also be argued *a fortiori*: if one is prohibited from cutting down the branches to preserve the fruit, how much more is one prohibited from cutting down the entire tree? Saba also drew a parallel between humans who produce fruit and trees that produce fruit. The difference between them, he argued, is that humans have the intuition to escape during a battle, but trees do not. As such it is not fitting (*ein ra'u'i*) to destroy them. Trees that do not bear fruit, however, do not fall into this category and may be cut down and used in the siege. For this reason this text is adjacent to the text that deals with finding a dead body in the field (Deuteronomy 21). Just as the voice of the tree is heard from one end of the world to the other when it is cut down, so too is the voice of a human heard when killed. Finally, Saba also mentioned the midrash that compared a fruit tree to a scholar who is worthy of respect, and a non-fruit-bearing tree to an uneducated person who is unworthy of respect.

Ovadiah Seforno (c. 1480–c. 1550, Italy).[51] Seforno contended that the text stipulated that cutting down fruit trees for no purpose but to harm the people of the besieged city is prohibited. He rationalized

---

50. Avraham bar Yaakov Saba, *Sefer Tzeror HaMor*.

51. Ovadiah Seforno, *Be'ur al HaTorah*.

this by claiming that only armies that are uncertain of victory engage in scorched-earth tactics, but an army that is guaranteed victory, such as the army of the Israelites, need not take such a drastic approach. While it is fitting to harm the enemy with tools of war, it is not fitting (*ein ra'u'i*) to destroy the fruit trees, because their destruction will not bring about victory. According to Seforno, fruit trees that are damaged or are old and no longer produce fruit are considered non-fruit-bearing trees and can be cut down. Seforno presumably maintains a similar approach to Rashi. His gloss is only implicit in this regard, claiming that it is not appropriate to cut down fruit trees since it will not bring about victory. The words "not fitting" (*ein ra'u'i*) are precisely the ones used by Saba and seem to imply that such behavior would be morally reprehensible and not a matter of mere utility. After all, the question of what is "fitting" and "not fitting" human behavior goes beyond the legal dimensions of the issue. While it is possible that Seforno did not see the prohibition to cut down fruit trees as a question of morality, I argue that outside the sphere of utilitarianism the most likely way to view this prohibition is from an ethical perspective.

Moshe Alsheikh (1507–c. 1600, Turkey, Land of Israel, and elsewhere).[52] Moshe Alsheikh offered a unique nonmidrashic interpretation of *ki ha'adam etz hasadeh*. He started off by claiming that Deuteronomy 20:19 demonstrates that God has compassion not only for humans, but for all His creations. In Alsheikh's research into Scripture he found that the terms "tree of the field" (*etz hasadeh*) and "tree of the land" (*etz ha'aretz*) are used differently. "Tree of the field" is used to describe only non-fruit-bearing trees, while "tree of the land" can be used to describe both fruit-bearing and non-fruit-bearing trees. He then claimed that the prohibition against cutting down a fruit tree after eating from it and deriving benefit/enjoyment (*hana'ah*) from it is similar to the prohibition against blocking up a well with earth after drinking from it (b*Baba Qama* 92b). Destroying something from which one derives utility (*to'elet*) would indicate ingratitude. Nevertheless, Alsheikh then questions why God would show mercy for trees while at the same time allowing humans to be killed in the siege. It is here that the linguistic distinction comes into play; the phrase *ki ha'adam etz hasadeh* is used to describe humans as non-fruit-bearing trees. This allowed Alsheikh

52. Moshe Alsheikh, *Torat Moshe: Derushim, Peirushim UVe'urim LeḤamishah Ḥumshei Torah—Sefer Devarim*, ed. Makhon Lev Sameaḥ (Jerusalem: H. Vagshel, 1990).

to explain why it appeared that God took mercy on trees and not on the humans who were actually engaging in the battle. Drawing a parallel between humans and non-fruit-bearing trees allowed for the necessity of killing during war. If humans were equated with fruit trees, it would be prohibited to kill them even during a time of war. Alsheikh, however, understood humans to be equated with non-fruit-bearing trees, which may be cut down. He also interpreted *ki ha'adam etz hasadeh* as an assertion, which viewed humans as trees. Unlike ibn Ezra, however, Alsheikh equated humans with non-fruit-bearing trees, whereas ibn Ezra viewed humans as fruit trees.

Herz Homberg (*HaKorem*) (1749–1841, Bohemia, Austria, and Germany).[53] Homberg cited Rashi's rhetorical reading of *ki ha'adam etz hasadeh*, which also influenced Moses Mendelssohn's (1729–1786, Germany) German translation of the Torah. He critiqued this interpretation, however, claiming that if this truly were the meaning of the text, then the question would have the tree as subject and the human as subject completion, whereas the verse reads the other way around. For this reason he considered as more likely the interpretation offered by ibn Ezra, which did not see the text as a question, but rather as a statement equating human life to the fruit tree that provides sustenance.

Samuel David Luzzatto (*Shadal*) (1800–1865, Italy).[54] Luzzatto started off by presenting various glosses on Deuteronomy 20:19. He began by listing a Christian interpretation of the verse, that of Clericus (probably Johannes Clericus, 1657–1736, Switzerland and Holland). He also cited Herz Homberg, the *Korem*. They contended that the fruit trees should not be cut down, because as the siege lengthens in days the army might require an additional food source. He then cited Abarbanel, Seforno, and Abraham Menaḥem Rappaport (1520–c. 1594, Italy), who claimed that the fruit trees should not be cut down because the conquering army would need a food source after the city was subdued.

Luzzatto, however, was not satisfied with such interpretations, stating that the Torah does not deal with the minutiae of humans finding different ways to benefit. Rather, the Torah is meant to increase human compassion even in ways that are not beneficial to humans.

53. Herz Homberg, *Sefer Netivot HaShalom: Sefer Devarim* (Jerusalem, 1974).

54. Samuel David Luzzatto, *Peirush Shadal—Rabbi Shmuel David Luzzatto al Ḥamishah Ḥumshei Torah* (Tel-Aviv: Dvir Publishing, 1971).

He was not alone in this approach, asserting that Philo and Josephus Flavius also viewed this commandment as being a decree calling for compassion and the avoidance of cruelty. For Luzzatto the main aspect of the commandment was to distance people from ungratefulness and teach them to love the things they benefit from (*sheyohav et hameitiv lo*), so that they do not cast them away after their utility (*to'elet*) ceases. The case in point is that the fruit trees provided sustenance, and it would be ungrateful to then destroy them. A parallel example, Luzzatto pointed out, can be found in b*Baba Qama* 92b, which states that people should not fill with earth a well from which they have drunk. Regarding the prophet Elisha's directive to cut down every good tree during a war with the Moabites (analyzed later in this chapter), Luzzatto explained that the prohibition only concerns fruit trees from which one has benefited. If the fruit trees were not used as a food source, then according to him they may be cut down, even wantonly.

Luzzatto then offered a gloss for the next part of the verse, *ki ha'adam etz hasadeh*. He mentioned a supercommentator on Rashi, presumably Eliyahu Mizraḥi, who explained that the text should have been arranged differently so that the question asked is about the tree and not the person. Luzzatto rejected this position, stating that in Hebrew it is common to have the predicate precede the subject, whereas philosophers tend to have it the other way around. Luzzatto then went into a lengthy analysis of ibn Ezra, claiming that his interpretation of the verse was grammatically incorrect on several points. Most importantly, Luzzatto rejects ibn Ezra's interpretation that human life is derived from the fruit trees that should therefore not be cut down. According to Luzzatto, in time of war human life is hanging in the balance, and building siege works could make the difference between life and death. It is, therefore, highly implausible that the Torah would be concerned with the fate of fruit trees over the fate of humans. In fact, Luzzatto claims the exact opposite of ibn Ezra. It is precisely the cutting down of the trees that sustains those laying siege, and protecting them for concerns of sustenance in the future is irrelevant. But according to Luzzatto's interpretation of the verse, which states that the reason not to cut down the trees is to reinforce good qualities and teach gratefulness, such grammatical problems are solved. In other words, Luzzatto's interpretation allows for the cutting down of the fruit trees should it be necessary, but the reasoning behind trying to avoid such actions are not utilitarian. Rather, it is designed to encourage people to act with good character and be concerned with the general welfare of creation and not just their own.

As one of the later Bible commentaries, Luzzatto had the benefit of access to a rich selection of glosses. Luzzatto was also part of a milieu of scholars who approached the study of biblical exegesis in a scientific manner.[55] As such, Luzzatto presented an anthology of glosses on the verses that included exegetes from antiquity to the modern era, both Jewish and Christian. Luzzatto rejected ibn Ezra's reading of the verse outright, by claiming that when human life is in the balance, the fate of a fruit tree is of little consequence. Implicitly, he was a proponent of Rashi's rhetorical reading of Deuteronomy 20:19 and even criticized one of Rashi's supercommentators, probably Eliyahu Mizrahi, for what he considered an incorrect critique of Rashi. For Luzzatto, however, the true reason that one should avoid cutting down fruit trees is because such behavior is ungrateful (to the tree, and through the tree to God). Something from which a person derives benefit should not then be wasted or destroyed. Luzzatto's approach is that the prohibition is meant to inculcate good character in people. This approach is environmentally oriented, but strongly tempered by the fact that it does not extend to things from which humans do not derive benefit. An example of this is when the prophet Elisha allows the wanton destruction of the Moabites' trees, fields, and springs. It is difficult to imagine that Luzzatto believed one can indulge in wanton destruction and wastefulness and still develop a good character. Rather, it should be assumed that he understood there to be certain very limited circumstances in which such behavior was considered necessary.

Samson Raphael Hirsch (1808–1888, Germany and Moravia).[56] Hirsch claimed that it is forbidden to cut down fruit trees for the sole purpose of destroying them. Their fruit is to be eaten, which is an affirmative commandment, and they are not to be cut down, which is a negative

55. For a fuller account of this phenomenon see Edward Breuer, "Jewish Study of the Bible Before and During the Jewish Enlightenment," in *Hebrew Bible/Old Testament: The History of Its Interpretation*, Vol. II, *From Renaissance to the Enlightenment*, ed. Magne Saebo (Gottingen, Germany: Vandenhoeck & Ruprecht, 2008), 1006–23.

56. Samson Raphael Hirsch, *Ḥamishah Ḥumshei Torah im Peirush Rashar Hirsch: Sefer Devarim*.

commandment. Destroying a fruit-bearing tree is a transgression of both of these commandments. The tree of the field is like a human insofar as it provides humans with sustenance. As such, securing the trees themselves is part of the objective of the siege and should be seen as part of securing the city. Only trees that are known to be fruit trees are prohibited from being cut down. This implies that it is permissible to cut down fruit trees if they are not recognized as such. Hirsch also provided a synopsis of some of the material found in the Babylonian Talmud and Maimonides. The discussion in the Babylonian Talmud (*Baba Qama* 91b) indicated that fruit trees that produce only a very small quantity of fruit are also excluded from the prohibition. The Talmud explicitly mentions that both date trees that yield a *qav/qab* of fruit, and olive trees, which are considered more valuable, that produce a quarter *qav/qab* are prohibited from being cut down. The Talmud also adds that if the value of the lumber (for purposes such as building) is greater than the value of the fruit, the tree may be cut down. Maimonides, in the Laws of Kings 6:8, stated that the Torah only prohibited the cutting-down of fruit trees in a destructive manner. In circumstances where it would make no difference what kind of lumber is used, non-fruit-bearing trees should take precedence over fruit-bearing trees.

According to Hirsch, the prohibition to cut down fruit trees during a siege should be viewed as an example of a prohibition against general wastefulness and destruction. The concept of *bal tashḥit* indicates that purposeless destruction of anything is forbidden. The warning issued in the Torah should be seen as a comprehensive warning issued to humans not to abuse the position of having dominion over the world granted to them by God. God only granted humans dominion over the rest of creation for wise uses. Accordingly, the text regarding the prohibition against destroying trees should be understood as including non-fruit-bearing trees when the only thing achieved is destruction. Nevertheless, the cutting down of trees for constructive purposes is permissible. Hirsch writes that Maimonides asserted that the extension of *bal tashḥit* to a general prohibition against wastefulness is a rabbinic prohibition derived from the Torah, but not from the Torah itself.

Hirsch was the first Bible commentator since Baḥya bar Asher nearly 500 years earlier to associate the prohibition of cutting down fruit trees with the general prohibition of *bal tashḥit*. He went into the greatest detail regarding the transformation of the specific prohibition found in the verse to the general prohibition of *bal tashḥit*. His approach was strongly influenced by Maimonides, who claimed that the prohibition included only actions done in a destructive/wasteful manner. Hirsch referred to this as purposeless destruction. In addition, Hirsch related this prohibition to Genesis 1:28 and viewed the prohibition of *bal tashḥit* as the ethic through which dominion over the rest of creation is to be executed.

Meir Leibush bar Yeḥiel Mikhel Weiser (*Malbim*) (1809–1879, Ukraine, Poland, Romania, and Prussia).[57] Weiser started his gloss by asking why the issue of cutting down trees is only brought up after the siege is a few days old. Logic would have it that the trees are cut down immediately in order for the siege works to be built. This, he claimed, was answered by the rabbis who stated that even during a siege an opportunity is given for a peaceful resolution of the conflict. If, however, the enemy does not surrender peacefully, then siege works are undertaken. He continued by stating that the reason the text indicates that the intention is to capture the city is because if the intention was to destroy the city, destroying the trees would be acceptable, as was the case in 2 Kings 3. Moreover, he reasoned that the text did not specify the manner in which the trees could be destroyed in order to include any form of destruction, such as diverting the trees' water source. Weiser also asserted that even where it is permissible to cut down fruit trees, the activity should be avoided when possible. He mentioned that Tuvia bar Eliezer and Naḥmanides presented a somewhat different version, which contended that it is permitted to cut down fruit trees to distress the besieged city. Weiser then added that the *Sifre* interpreted the difficult text of *ki ha'adam etz hasadeh* as meaning that the life of humans is dependent on fruit trees, and that was ultimately the position of Weiser himself. He then presented Rashbam's gloss, who claimed that instead of being destroyed, they should be used as a food source after the city is conquered. This interpretation is based on the linguistic rule that any time the word *ki* (for/because) appears after the word *lo* (no), it should be read as *ela* (rather). As such, the verse should be read as fruit trees should not be cut down unless they are being used by the enemy to hide. Fruit trees sufficiently distant from the city, however, should not be cut down.

Weiser also drew a distinction between fruit trees that are currently producing fruit and fruit trees that are either not in season or

57. Meir Leibush Weiser, *Otzar HaPeirushim al Tanakh, Miqraot Gedolot, Sidra 2.*

no longer produce fruit. Making this distinction would mean that the text would make more sense if it stated that "trees from which you will not eat can be cut down." Of course, this is not what the text states, and as such Weiser claimed that if this was all the text said then indeed it would be referring to trees that never bear fruit. The text, however, contains the words "which you know." Weiser made the assumption that everyone is able to distinguish between a fruit-bearing tree and a non-fruit-bearing tree. So what do these words come to elucidate? That only fruit trees that are known to no longer produce a sufficient amount of fruit (explained in b*Baba Qama* 91b) can be cut down. The text then makes it clear that there is a hierarchy between the trees that are to be cut down. First, one should cut down trees that never produce fruit. Once non-fruit-bearing trees can no longer be found, one may cut down fruit trees, but only those that are known to no longer be producing food. In this manner Weiser claimed to have solved a disagreement between a number of legists (whose side he takes) and Maimonides. Maimonides's approach was to claim that things that are in doubt are permitted according to the Torah, whereas here it is clear that trees of a dubious nature cannot be cut down. Rather, only trees that one is certain no longer produce fruit in sufficient quantity may be cut down.

Finally, Weiser asked why verse 20 uses the word "destroy" instead of "cut down." The use of the word "destroy" implies that this is not a simple cutting-down, but rather that there is destruction involved in the process. The destruction implied by the text is that the tree loses value as it is transformed into lumber. Trees that appreciate in value after being cut down, however, are not considered to have been destroyed, and there is no prohibition against cutting down a fruit tree in such an instance.

David Tzvi Hoffmann (1843–1921, Slovakia, Austria, and Germany).[58] Hoffmann asserted that Deuteronomy 20:19 charged humans with assuming benevolence not only toward humans, but to trees as well. This is both because trees provide sustenance for humans and because they cannot protect themselves as enemy soldiers can. He then went through the various ways in which it is prohibited to destroy a tree, such as cutting off its branches, cutting it down with an axe, and uprooting it. All these methods are specifically mentioned through-

58. David Tzvi Hoffmann, *Sefer Devarim*.

out various rabbinic texts. He cited Luzzatto, who claimed that one should not cut down a tree whose fruit one has consumed, because such behavior is considered ungrateful. Hoffmann also mentioned that the interpretations of *ki ha'adam etz hasadeh* have historically tended to fall into two categories. The first category viewed the text as being rhetorical in nature, from which it can be deduced that indeed the tree is not like a human and cannot escape the dangers of the battlefield and therefore should not be cut down. This interpretation is shared by Onkelos, the Septuagint, the *Mekhilta* of Rabbi Yishmael, and Josephus, among many others mentioned in this chapter but not listed by Hoffmann. Hoffmann claimed that this prohibition includes a general lesson: if one is not to harm a defenseless tree, how much more so is one not to harm a defenseless human?

The second position with regard to this text is that the trees should not be destroyed because human life is sustained by their fruit. This position is stated by Rabbeinu Hillel, *Sifre*, *Midrash Tannaim*, and ibn Ezra, among others mentioned in this chapter but again not listed by Hoffmann. In his gloss on verse 20, Hoffmann claimed that the *Sifre* and b*Baba Qama* 91a derive their utilitarian exceptions to the prohibition of *bal tashḥit* of allowing non-fruit-bearing trees and fruit trees that are relatively unproductive to be cut down from the words "trees which you know." In other words, this exception is based on human knowledge and judgment. Nevertheless, if trees must be cut down, non-fruit-bearing trees should be cut down before fruit-bearing trees. Finally, Hoffmann asserted that these verses are the source of the prohibition of *bal tashḥit*, which forbids the destruction of anything of value (*Sefer Mitzvot Gadol*, prohibition 229). Hoffmann added that according to Maimonides the prohibition is rabbinic.

Barukh HaLevi Epstein (*Torah Temimah*) (1860–1942, Belarus).[59] In his gloss to the words *lo tashḥit*, Epstein presented the rabbinic opinion of "the prohibition against destroying the body is more dear" (*bal tashḥit degufa adif*), which states that it is preferable to waste/destroy nonhuman things for the sake of human welfare. Epstein illustrated how the rabbis reached this edict. The first step was establishing that destroying fruit trees in a destructive/wasteful manner at any time is prohibited. The exceptions to this edict are if the trees are damaging

59. Barukh HaLevi Epstein, *Ḥamishah Ḥumshei Torah im Ḥamesh Megilot, Torah Temimah: Sefer Devarim*.

other trees or a neighbor's field, or if the lumber is more valuable than the fruit. He went on to explain that *"ki ha'adam etz hasadeh"* demonstrates that human life depends on fruit trees, and one should not destroy that which is necessary for human life. From this the rabbis established that it is not fruit trees alone whose destruction is prohibited, but also dishes, clothing, buildings, fresh water resources, and food. It is, however, permissible to destroy all these things if it is a question of human welfare, because even though destroying them is transgression of *bal tashḥit,* it is a greater transgression to destroy one's own body. This, Epstein claimed, was because the foundation of the prohibition is mainly to prevent the destruction/waste of things that have utility to humans. Epstein questioned why Maimonides did not bother mentioning "the prohibition against destroying the body is more dear" (*bal tashḥit degufa adif*), and was even more perplexed as to why the legal compendium *Shulḥan Arukh* neglected to include the prohibition of *bal tashḥit* altogether. Epstein, similar to Hirsch, went into detail regarding how the prohibition from the context of the verse was eventually expanded to a general prohibition against wastefulness/destruction. Where they diverged was in their reasoning behind the prohibition. Hirsch viewed the prohibition as putting limits on human dominion over the rest of creation, whereas Epstein understood the prohibition to apply only to things that are useful to humans.

Gunther Plaut (1912–2012, Germany, USA, and Canada).[60] Plaut mentioned that scorched-earth policies were prohibited, save the one instance in 2 Kings 3:19 where God retracted the prohibition during the war against the Moabites. Plaut presented the words *"ki ha'adam etz hasadeh"* as both a rhetorical question and an assertion. He specified that the text only prohibited the cutting down of fruit trees, whereas the other trees could be used for building siege works. Plaut went on to assert that this principle places a limit on the dominion that humans were granted over the rest of creation in Genesis 1:28. He then explained that the rabbis expanded the prohibition found in this verse into the general prohibition on wastefulness, *bal tashḥit*. Finally, he gave examples of this generalization from the midrash, Talmud, and Maimonides.

60. Gunther Plaut, *A Modern Commentary*.

ArtScroll (2009, USA).[61] ArtScroll presented *Sefer HaḤinukh,* a thirteenth-century composition elucidating the rationale behind the various commandments. *Sefer HaḤinukh* stated that good behavior should be adhered to even in the most trying times, to the degree that not even a mustard seed is wasted. This refers to the fact that all types of wastefulness are prohibited. The ArtScroll then offered the reading of *ki ha'adam etz hasadeh* as both an assertion and a rhetorical question.

Synthetic Analysis

The first thing that strikes one studying the commentary tradition on Deuteronomy 20:19–20 is the absence of references to the general prohibition of *bal tashḥit*. Except by a few individuals, this connection is simply not drawn. While there is ample discussion of the prohibition on destroying fruit trees, the commentaries have by and large neglected to draw a connection between these verses and the prohibition on wastefulness/destruction. This is in spite of the fact that it is beyond doubt that they were fully aware of the existence of the prohibition. The fact that the same "silence" exists in the earlier rabbinic literature makes this deficiency less of a surprise. After all, the vast majority of Bible commentators were immersed in Talmudic learning, and if the term *bal tashḥit* did not appear in reference to trees in the Talmud, then why would it appear in the exegesis of the Torah? Instead, the commentary tradition focused its attention on the immediate context of the verses, and not beyond. Though the commentaries deal with almost every aspect of the verses, their major focus was on the words "*ki ha'adam etz hasadeh,*" the only part of these verses that is truly shrouded in mystery. The difference in approaches is reflected by the variant translations of the text (e.g., King James vs. NJPS), and of course in the commentaries themselves.

Unlike many edicts in the Torah that come with no reasoning behind them and that many have tried to rationalize over the course of history, the directive to not cut down fruit trees comes with an explanation. The problem, of course, is that the rationalization, the words "*ki ha'adam etz hasadeh,*" is not so simple to understand. Their meaning has split the long list of commentaries presented here, with most interpreting the phrase either as a rhetorical question or as an

61. *The Schottenstein Edition Interlinear Chumash: Deuteronomy.*

assertion. Although both approaches can be found in the midrash as we saw in the previous chapter,[62] the tradition histories view each to be championed by a different towering exegete. The rhetorical approach was adopted by Rashi, while the approach of the phrase as an assertion was taken up by ibn Ezra. The stature of these commentators was such that many who came after them and fell on one side or other of the debate attributed these positions to them. The rhetorical approach, which was adopted by the NJPS translation of the Bible, views the words "*ki ha'adam etz hasadeh*" as a question. Since a tree cannot escape the battlefield and protect itself, why should it be cut down in a war between humans? The other approach, adopted by the King James translation of the Bible, views the same text as an assertion. Trees should not be cut down because they are the source of human sustenance. Destroying them would be a pyrrhic victory—even if the city is vanquished, its new inhabitants would not be able to survive without a food source. Thus, according to this approach, the tree of the field truly is like a human, because human life depends on it. Interestingly, this approach can be understood as a metaphor viewing humans both as trees and as those whose lives are dependent on trees. As discussed in the previous chapter, both positions have significant implications for environmental ethics.

Certainly, it is possible to understand the various interpretations of this verse outside of an ethical framework. Whether it is an assertion or a rhetorical question, the directive could simply be advice issued under the rubric of common sense. This, however, is unlikely. Deuteronomy 20:19–20 relates to human behavior during war. More specifically, the verses relate to how humans should treat the nonhuman world in the most trying of times. Consequently, a reasonable assumption is that most of those belonging to the Jewish interpretive tradition have understood these verses within what might today be considered an ethical structure. This understanding is reinforced by the prohibition being taken well beyond its context of fruit trees and war and turned into a general principle, something that we saw in the previous chapter. The rhetorical reading can be viewed as implying that fruit trees have some degree of ethical standing. They are not solely bound to the needs and wants of humans, but must be considered in their own right. As such, it would be wrong to destroy them during

62. See *Midrash Tannaim* (*Devarim* 20:19–20) and *Midrash Leqaḥ Tov* (*Devarim—Shofetim* 34a).

a time of war as a means of causing the enemy grief. If only human needs and wants were taken into consideration, it would seem reasonable in certain contexts to cut down these trees. After all, during wartime intimidating the enemy and causing them grief are fitting, something that Naḥmanides believed to be a legitimate endeavor, at least in foreign lands.[63]

Even though, as Nili Wazana cogently points out, reading *ki ha'adam etz hasadeh* as a rhetorical question is linguistically problematic, it does not change the evidence that such a reading exists and has been part of the tradition histories of the verse from the earliest translations, including the Septuagint, Vulgate, Syriac, and various Aramaic *targumim*.[64] It is pointed out by many commentators over the course of the tradition histories of this verse that the rhetorical reading of *ki ha'adam etz hasadeh* is inconsistent with the rest of the text. Tuvia bar Eliezer (*Midrash Leqaḥ Tov, Pesiqta Zutarta*) (late eleventh century, Byzantium), who essentially provided his readers with a summary of the midrash, primarily offered the "phrase-as-an-assertion" reading of the text, but also presented the rhetorical possibility.[65] Certainly aware of both possibilities of interpreting *ki ha'adam etz hasadeh* found in the midrash, Rashi nevertheless chose to present the rhetorical reading. Others who shared the rhetorical reading include Ephraim bar Shimshon (c. late twelfth and thirteenth centuries, France),[66] Gersonides, and Judah Loew (*Maharal*) (c. 1520–1609, Bohemia).[67]

The question that remains unanswered, as pointed out by scholars such as Nili Wazana and Eilon Schwartz, is this: if indeed this is the preferred reading of the verse in such a large number of commen-

---

63. Moshe ben Naḥman, "*Hasagot HaRamban LeSefer HaMitzvot LaRambam*," in Moshe ben Maimon, *Sefer HaMitzvot*, ed. Yitzḥak Simḥah Horowitz (Jerusalem: 1927), *Shikheḥat HaAsin, Mitzvah Vav*.

64. Nili Wazana, "Are Trees of the Field Human? A Biblical War Law (Deuteronomy 20:19–20) and Neo-Assyrian Propaganda," in *Treasures on Camels' Humps: Historical and Literary Studies from the Ancient Near East Presented to Israel Eph'al*, eds. Mordechai Cogan and Dan'el Kahn (Jerusalem: Hebrew University Magnes Press, 2008), 276.

65. Tuvia bar Eliezer, *Midrash Leqaḥ Tov HaMekhuneh Pesiqta Zutarta al Ḥamishah Ḥumshei Torah—Devarim*.

66. Ephraim bar Shimshon, *Peirush Rabbeinu Ephraim bar Shimshon UGedolei Ashkenaz HaQadmonim al HaTorah*, Part 2: *VaYiqra—BeMidbar—Devarim*, eds. Tzvi Yehoshua Leitner and Ezra Koraḥ (Jerusalem: Orthodox Publications Co., 1992).

67. Judah Loew ben Bezalel, *Ḥumash Gur Aryeh HaShalem*, Vol. 8, *Devarim—Zot HaBerakha*, ed. Yehoshua David Hartman (Jerusalem: Makhon Yerushalayim, 1989).

taries, how can we reconcile with this that only fruit trees are given this status, whereas non-fruit-bearing trees are not?[68] From the sources covered in this section, only Hirsch explicitly stated that non-fruit-bearing trees also merit protection under the prohibition of *bal tashḥit*. Nevertheless, seen outside of the context of (fruit) trees during war, this approach solidly resonates as a concern for the nonhuman world and subsequently as an environmental ethic. It states that the natural world must be taken into consideration even in the most extreme and trying circumstances. This is precisely the *a fortiori* line of thinking adopted by the rabbis who turned this wartime directive into a general prohibition on wastefulness/destruction operational at all times. If even in the most perilous of times the nonhuman world must be taken into consideration, how much more so during peaceful times?

The "phrase-as-an-assertion" reading can be viewed as anthropocentric, because it appears to value the fruit trees only insofar as they are useful to humans. If fruit trees were not an important source of food, their status might have been similar to that of non-fruit-bearing trees. It is their utility that gives them protection, not their intrinsic worth. Such an approach does not necessarily view the fruit trees as having any inherent value whatsoever. Fruit trees provide humans with sustenance and contextually can benefit the army during a siege by providing a food source, or they can be an important source of food during postvictory colonization. This approach still has environmental merit because, regardless of the reasoning, fruit trees are still given protected status. This is consistent with some studies in environmental psychology, which have demonstrated that egoism can be a driver for pro-environmental behavior.[69] Yet, from here it is possible to see how the prohibition could evolve into a utilitarian concept, as we saw in the rabbinic chapter. Once the protection of a tree rests on its value to humans, its ability to provide fruit is pitted against its other characteristics (lumber, space) that also have value. Only very recently have benefits such as carbon storage been taken into consideration when valuing trees.

A number of commentators explicitly commented on other major moral components of the verse that have been highlighted by environ-

68. Ibid., 277–78, and Schwartz, "*Bal Tashchit*," 232–33.

69. Paul C. Stern, "New Environmental Theories: Toward a Coherent Theory of Environmentally Significant Behavior," *Journal of Social Issues* 56, no. 3 (2000): 407–24.

mental scholars. For instance, Meyuḥas bar Eliyahu asserted that God has compassion for all his creations. This compassion comes despite his understanding that the prohibition against wastefulness includes all things for which humans have need (*tzorekh*). In other words, God's compassion is independent of human utility and goes beyond things that have utility to humans. Isaac Abarbanel also viewed the prohibition as encompassing a moral dimension. He claimed that the verse taught that one should not prey on the weak and helpless—in this case, fruit trees. The main point of interest is that the weak and helpless do not have to be human, leaving significant room to develop an environmental ethic. Avraham Saba understood trees as having souls (*nefesh*), and cutting them down needlessly would be inappropriate behavior (*ein ra'u'i*), though it is unclear if this understanding included all nonsentient beings.

Environmentalists and traditional scholars alike see Deuteronomy 20:19–20 as the source of the general prohibition against wastefulness/destructiveness. While it is relatively simple to understand how such a prohibition applies to material goods, it takes a somewhat deeper though certainly not illogical analysis to see the prohibition as extending to human life as well. This connection, however, is the direction toward which many of the commentators on Deuteronomy 20:19 angled their glosses. If human life depended on the tree of the field, then destroying the tree is commensurate with destroying human life. It is through this understanding that one can begin to see an association between this verse and Genesis 9:5, which is understood to deal either with suicide or murder. The relationship between *bal tashḥit* and self-harm was discussed at length in the rabbinic chapter. In presenting the glosses on Genesis 9:5, it should be clarified again that not every element of the commentators' glosses is summarized. Rather, the comments most relevant to the topics of interest in this book are presented.

Genesis 9:5 (9:4–6)

Context

The events of chapter 9 of Genesis take place following the Great Deluge. At this point the waters have subsided and Noah, his family, and all the animals aboard his ark are now safely on dry land. The chapter begins with God establishing a new world order. As part of this new order, Noah is explicitly given permission to consume the flesh of animals, something that the majority of commentators have understood to mean that flesh consumption was prohibited in the antediluvian world. Jewish exegetes understand this chapter to explicitly contain two of the seven Noahide Laws (ethical laws pertaining to all of humanity)—the prohibition against eating the flesh of a living animal (Genesis 9:4), and the prohibition against murder (9:5–6). God establishes a covenant with all of creation promising to never bring such a devastating flood upon the earth again. The sign God sets as symbolizing the new covenant with the rest of creation is a rainbow. While Genesis 9:6 is an explicit prohibition against murder, the message of Genesis 9:5 is much less clear and has been debated throughout the commentary traditions. Is this esoteric verse a prohibition against murder, or a prohibition against suicide? Does the prohibition concern humans, or does it concern animals?

> 4. You must not, however, eat flesh with its lifeblood in it. **5 But for your own life-blood I will require a reckoning: I will require it of every beast; of man, too, will I require a reckoning for human life, of every man for that of his fellow man!** 6 Whoever sheds the blood of man, by man shall his blood be shed; for in His image did God make man. [emphasis added]

Medieval Midrash

Tuvia bar Eliezer (*Midrash Leqaḥ Tov, Pesikta Zutarta*) (late eleventh century, Byzantium).[70] Tuvia bar Eliezer claimed that the verse is a prohibition against suicide, and includes death caused by means that do not draw blood. All have the responsibility to mete out justice—animals, Jews, and Gentiles.

Geonic Commentary

Saadiah Gaon (*Rasag*) (882–942, Egypt and Babylonia).[71] Saadiah Gaon interpreted this verse as a prohibition against committing suicide. He

70. Tuvia bar Eliezer, *Midrash Leqaḥ Tov HaMekhuneh Pesiqta Zutarta al Ḥamishah Ḥumshei Torah—Bereishit*, Vol. 1, ed. Shlomo Buber (Israel: Books Export Enterprises, 1960).

71. Saadiah Gaon, *Peirushei Rav Saadiah Gaon LiVereishit*, ed. Moshe Tzuker (New York: Beit HaMidrash LeRabanim BeAmerica, 1984).

then discussed King Saul, who is called "God's chosen" (2 Samuel 21:6) and who is later glorified by the rabbis (b*Sukkah* 52b), but appeared to commit suicide on the battlefield (1 Samuel 31:4–5). Finally, he claimed that while he did indeed fall on his sword intentionally, it was an Amalekite who dealt him the death blow (2 Samuel 1:6–9).

Post-Geonic Commentary

Shlomo Yitzḥaki (*Rashi*) (eleventh century, northern France).[72] Rashi explained that this verse clarifies that even though the taking of animal life is permitted, one is still prohibited from killing oneself. He understood the word *nafshoteikhem* (your souls) as implying that even killing oneself in a manner that does not spill blood is prohibited. He claimed that the verse also warns both animals against killing humans and humans against committing murder.

Abraham ibn Ezra (1089–1164, born in Spain, but lived and traveled all over the Mediterranean basin, northern France, and England).[73] Ibn Ezra claimed that even though humans are permitted to kill all other beings, they are still prohibited from killing one another. He rejected the opinion that the verse is a prohibition against committing suicide. As a *peshat* commentator, he would have less concern with rabbinic rules of exegesis and would not necessarily see it as problematic that two adjacent verses say the same thing.

Yosef Bekhor Shor (twelfth century, France).[74] Bekhor Shor viewed this verse as a prohibition against committing suicide. He explained that the verse clarifies that one should not assume human blood can be shed just because animals are now permitted for consumption. The assumption is that animals are permitted for consumption due to their being saved by humans (Noah). As such, the purpose of the verse is to prevent humans from assuming that they could take their own lives because they govern themselves. Not only are humans prohibited from shedding their own blood, but even animals that kill humans are also judged, and to this end Bekhor Shor cited the example of an ox that gores a human (see Exodus 21:28).

72. Shlomo Yitzḥaki, *Peirushei Rashi*.

73. Abraham ibn Ezra, *Peirushei HaTorah LeRabbeinu Avraham ibn Ezra*, 2nd ed., Vol. 1, ed. Asher Weiser (Jerusalem: Mossad HaRav Kook, 1977).

74. Joseph Bechor Shor, *Commentary on the Pentateuch* (Jerusalem: Makor Publishing, 1978).

Yosef Bekhor Shor was the first to offer a contextual explanation of the text, by demonstrating that the verse needs to be read in light of the verse that comes before it (Genesis 9:4). Now that animals have been permitted for human consumption, Bekhor Shor claimed that it was necessary to elucidate that this permission did not also include human flesh. The rationale presented by Bekhor Shor, while possibly redundant, is still rational. The postdiluvian existence of animals is on account of humans (i.e., Noah), who saved them from the Deluge by sheltering them aboard the ark. Through this act the relationship between animals and humans was understood to have changed, and consumption of animals came to be permitted.[75] Like animals, humans are made of flesh. There is the possibility that some would have understood this new injunction as meaning that human life can be taken. Bekhor Shor understood this to mean suicide, possibly because murder was prohibited separately in the very next verse. The gloss from the compilation of *Ba'alei HaTosafot* (*Otzar Peirushei Ba'alei HaTosafot*) (c. twelfth century, France)[76] echoes Bekhor Shor's comments, and may in fact have been his own words as he himself was a member of this group. Ḥizqiyah bar Manoaḥ (*Ḥizquni*) (thirteenth century, France),[77] who also interpreted the verse within its own context, had a different approach to the rationale behind the verse. He, too, viewed the verse as a prohibition against suicide, but from a contextual perspective he understood it as forbidding cannibalism.[78]

Meyuḥas bar Eliyahu (1150–1200, Byzantium).[79] Meyuḥas bar Eliyahu saw this verse as a continuation of the previous verse, which permitted the eating of animal flesh. He stated that even though spilling

75. The sages understood the antediluvian humans to be vegetarians. See b*Sanhedrin* 59b.

76. Ba'alei HaTosafot, *Sefer Tosafot HaShalem: Otzar Peirushei Ba'alei HaTosafot*, Part 1: *Bereishit—Noaḥ*, ed. Yaakov Gliss (Jerusalem: Mifal Tosafot HaShalem, 1982).

77. Ḥizqiyah bar Manoaḥ, *Ḥizquni: Peirushei HaTorah*.

78. Ḥaim Paltiel (c. thirteenth century, Germany) (*Peirushei HaTorah*); Eliyahu Mizraḥi (HaRe'em) (c. 1450–1526, Turkey) (*Ḥumash HaRe'em: Sefer Bereishit*, ed. Moshe Filip [Petaḥ Tiqva, Israel: private printing, 1992]); and David Tzvi Hoffmann (1843–1921, Slovakia, Austria, and Germany) (*Sefer Bereishit* [Tel-Aviv: Netzaḥ Publishing, 1969]) also held that the verse was relating to suicide.

79. Meyuḥas bar Eliyahu, *Peirush Rabbi Meyuḥas al Bereishit*, eds. A. W. Greenup and C. H. Titterton (Jerusalem: private printing, 1967).

the blood of animals is acceptable, spilling the blood of humans is not. He then stated that while the verse specifically mentions blood, there is still a prohibition against suicide through means that do not literally spill blood, such as strangulation. In other words, he viewed this verse as a prohibition against both murder and suicide. Justice will be demanded from animals and humans alike.

Moshe ben Naḥman (*Ramban,* Naḥmanides) (1194–1270, Spain and Land of Israel).[80] Naḥmanides offered a number of different interpretations of this verse. The first was that the words *"dimkhem lenafshoteikhem,"* literally "your blood for your souls," should be understood as "the blood which is your soul." This reading is nicely reflected in the NJPS translation of "lifeblood." He then suggested that another possibility was that *"lenafshoteikhem"* (for your souls) means *"benafshoteikhem"* (in your souls). He claimed that the most correct interpretation is that the verse is referring to the spilling of not just any blood (such as blood that flows from a paper cut), but specifically the spilling of blood that results in death. He then mentioned that the sages viewed this as a prohibition against suicide, though he himself does not appear to take a stance on the matter. Naḥmanides had difficulty understanding the phrase "I will require it of every beast," because according to him animals do not have the mental capacity to understand being punished or rewarded for their actions. He suggested that perhaps the reference to animals means that should an animal kill a human, in return it too would be killed, whether it can be considered morally culpable or not.

Baḥya bar Asher (1255–1340, Spain).[81] Bar Asher saw one of the lessons derived from this verse as a prohibition against suicide. This he derived from the word *lenafshoteikhem* (for your souls), which he claimed should be read as *menafshoteikhem* (from your souls), meaning the blood of the individual himself. For those who commit murder, justice will either be carried out by animals in cases where there are

80. Moshe ben Naḥman, *Peirushei HaTorah LeRabbeinu Moshe ben Naḥman (Ramban),* Vol. 1, *Bereishit Shemot,* ed. Ḥaim Dov Chavel (Jerusalem: Mossad HaRav Kook, 1959).

81. Baḥya bar Asher, *Rabbeinu Baḥya: Be'ur al HaTorah,* Vol. 1, *Bereishit,* ed. Ḥaim Dov Chavel (Jerusalem: Mossad HaRav Kook, 1974).

no witnesses to testify in court, and by the courts for cases in which there are witnesses.

Yaakov bar Asher (*Ba'al HaTurim*) (c. 1270–1343, Germany and Spain).[82] Like Naḥmanides, Yaakov bar Asher clarified that the words should be understood as "in your souls" (*benafshoteikhem*) and not "for your souls" (*lenafshoteikhem*). The implication of this reading is that the reckoning for murder is capital punishment, which is not the case for the spilling of blood that does not take life. Some manuscripts have bar Asher presenting the rabbis' opinion that the verse is a prohibition against suicide. He then cited Naḥmanides's deliberation regarding the reckoning required of animals that do not have a rational capacity. Naḥmanides concluded that any animal causing the death of a human would in due course be killed, as in the example of the goring ox (Exodus 21:28). In other words, anyone who spills human blood will require a reckoning, whether the perpetrator is human or animal. Another possible interpretation suggested by Yaakov bar Asher is that animals, like humans, have the responsibility to mete out justice to murderers. He then claimed that the deeper meaning of the verse (*sod ha'inyan*) is that the nature of humans was to be vegetarian, but this changed after the Flood, when flesh was permitted to both humans and animals. It was necessary, therefore, for God to instill fear of humans into the animals. This clarification became necessary to limit the consumption of flesh only to animal flesh; the prohibition to consume human flesh needed to be reinforced. Finally, Yaakov bar Asher presented the midrash that gave examples of characters from the Bible who killed themselves or were willing to martyr themselves. The implication suggested by him is that it is prohibited for humans to harm themselves.

Levi ben Gershom (*Ralbag*, Gersonides) (1288–1344, France).[83] Gersonides claimed that those who interpreted the verse as indicating that God would punish animals for harming humans were wrong, because animals do not have the mental faculties that make punishment relevant. He

82. Yaakov bar Asher, *Peirush HaTur al HaTorah LeHaRabbi Yaakov ben HaRosh*, Vol. 1, *Bereishit—Shemot*, ed. Yaakov Kapel Reinitz (Jerusalem: Feldheim Publishers, 2006).

83. Levi ben Gershom, *Peirushei HaTorah LeRabbeinu Levi ben Gershom (Ralbag)*, Vol. 1, *Bereishit*, ed. Yaakov Leib Levi (Jerusalem: Mossad HaRav Kook, 1992).

preferred the interpretation offered by some commentators that humans were culpable even if they used animals to kill other humans instead of committing the act themselves. Nevertheless, Gersonides rejected this interpretation as unsuitable linguistically. Grammatically speaking, the animals are the ones carrying out the action, not the humans. As such, the proper interpretation of the verse is that these animals are those who are to deliver justice. Why animals and not the legal system? In cases where the courts are unable to carry out a verdict or the case never reaches the courts but the individual is guilty, God continues to deliver justice through a variety of agents, and in this case the agents are animals. Gersonides expanded on this, explaining that the prohibition against murder was necessary at this point, because by permitting humans to consume animal flesh in the postdiluvian era, confusion may have arisen regarding whether killing humans was also permitted.

An avid rationalist, Gersonides contextualized the verse, and understood that the establishment of the new postdiluvian world order necessitated clarifying that permission to kill animals for consumption did not include the killing of humans. He, however, understood the prohibition as being against murder and not suicide. Similarly, Nissim ben Reuven Gerondi (*Ran*) (early fourteenth century–1380, Spain),[84] Avraham bar Yaakov Saba (*Tzeror HaMor*) (1440–1508, Spain, Portugal, Morocco, and Turkey),[85] Judah Loew ben Bezalel (*Maharal*) (c. 1520–1609, Bohemia),[86] and Solomon Dubno (1738–1813, Russia, Galicia, Holland, and Germany)[87] all contextualize the verse, but view it as a prohibition against murder.[88]

Moshe Alsheikh (1508–c. 1600, Turkey, Land of Israel, and Syria).[89] From the previous verses Alsheikh understood that the righteous individual casts his fear on the animals and through this elevated status is

84. Nissim ben Reuven Gerondi, *Rabbeinu Nissim ben Reuven Gerondi (HaRan): Peirush al HaTorah*, ed. Leon Aryeh Feldman (Jerusalem: Makhon Shalem, 1968).

85. Avraham bar Yaakov Saba, *Sefer Tzeror HaMor*.

86. Judah Loew ben Bezalel, *Ḥumash Gur Aryeh HaShalem*, Vol. 1, *Bereishit—Ḥayei Sarah*, ed. Yehoshua David Hartman (Jerusalem: Makhon Yerushalayim, 1989).

87. Solomon Dubno, *Sefer Netivot HaShalom: Sefer Bereishit* (Jerusalem, 1974).

88. Ovadiah Seforno (c.1480–c. 1550, Italy) also viewed the verse as a prohibition against murder. See his *Be'ur al HaTorah*.

89. Moshe Alsheikh, *Torat Moshe: Derushim, Peirushim UVe'urim LeḤamishah Ḥumshei Torah—Sefer Bereishit*, ed. Makhon Lev Sameaḥ (Jerusalem: H. Vagshel, 1990).

permitted to eat them. Humans are inherently above animals insofar as they were created in God's image. Anyone who "*ḥata al hanefesh,*" literally translated as "sinned on the soul," presumably meaning a person who committed murder, however, is no longer above the level of animals and can be put to death even by animals. Nevertheless, someone who murders a person who has sinned will still be held accountable for diminishing the image of God.

Samuel David Luzzatto (*Shadal*) (1800–1865, Italy).[90] Luzzatto claimed that an animal that kills a human would eventually fall into human hands and justice would be served. He held that it should be an *a fortiori* understanding that if an animal will be brought to justice for its transgressions, how much more will humans be judged? He also claimed that the understanding of the rabbis of the verse as a prohibition against suicide is incorrect linguistically, as instead of "*lenafshoteikhem*" (to your soul) it would have had to have been written "*menafshoteikhem*" (from your soul).

Samson Raphael Hirsch (1808–1888, Germany and Moravia).[91] Hirsch differentiated the flesh and souls of animals, which were both created from the earth, and the flesh and souls of humans, of which the former was created from the earth, but the soul was given directly from God. Animal flesh can transform into human flesh through consumption, but animal souls will never be permitted to become human souls. Animal blood, that is, the right to slaughter animals for food, and animal flesh belong to humans, but human life-blood belongs to God. God is considered to have deposited human blood in the individual, and as such, human blood will always need to be accounted for. For Hirsch this is first and foremost a prohibition against suicide. Additionally, animals need to provide a reckoning for any human blood they spill, and humans need to provide a reckoning for human souls. Humans are considered to be God's representatives and must protect all the creations of this world according to the will of God. Recognition of the godly soul present in oneself will result in the recognition that it is also present in all humans. All humans are responsible for the

90. Samuel David Luzzatto, *Peirush Shadal*.

91. Samson Raphael Hirsch, *Ḥamishah Ḥumshei Torah im Peirush Rashar Hirsch: Sefer Bereishit*, 4th ed., ed. and trans. Mordekhai Breuer (Jerusalem: Mossad Yitzḥak Breuer, 1989).

soul of each human. Should even a moment of life be taken away from oneself or from another, judgment of the one responsible is in the hands of God.

Hirsch offered the most environmentally nuanced interpretation of Genesis 9:5. Aside from his positions on whether the verse deals with a prohibition against murder or suicide (in his opinion, both), Hirsch took a stance on animals and humans with regard to creation. He considered humans to be superior to animals, and as such humans were permitted to consume them. Animals were not granted reciprocal rights. Nevertheless, humans are held accountable for their treatment of both animals and humans. According to Hirsch, human life is sacrosanct and causing its diminishment for even a moment is a transgression, covered by the prohibition against both murder and suicide. This is with regard to humans. With regard to animals, humans are responsible as God's representatives on earth to protect all of creation. Such an approach implies a prohibition against wastefulness/destruction. While this is still not an explicit affirmation that Genesis 9:5 is viewed as connected to *bal tashḥit*, the implication seems clear enough. Interestingly, the notion of human responsibility for the protection of the rest of creation is something we might have expected to see in the debate regarding the (non)environmental reading of Genesis 1:28 ("God blessed them and God said to them, 'Be fertile and increase, fill the earth and master it; and rule the fish of the sea, the birds of the sky, and all the living things that creep on earth.'"). The fact that Hirsch's gloss is much more closely associated with the concept of *bal tashḥit* than with Genesis 2:15 (*le'ovdah uleshomerah*—"to till it and tend it") is further proof that there are more suitable biblical passages that can be used to argue for an environmental ethic in Judaism rather than Genesis 1:28 vs. Genesis 2:15, as I argue elsewhere.[92]

In addition to Hirsch's implicit connection between Genesis 9:5 and *bal tashḥit*, other commentators stand out in this regard. Yaakov bar Asher specifically stated that Genesis 9:5 is a prohibition against self-harm. Distinguishing this from the prohibition against suicide is important, because it is in this form that an association is made with the prohibition against wastefulness/destruction in t*Baba Qama* 9:31. By differentiating the two, Yaakov bar Asher can be added to

92. See Tanhum Yoreh, "Environmental Embarrassment: Genesis 1:26–28 vs. Genesis 2:15," in *Vixens Disturbing Vineyards: Embarrassment and Embracement of Scriptures*, eds. Tzemah Yoreh et al. (Boston: Academic Studies Press, 2010), 558–91.

an exclusive list of scholars who form a tradent contributing to this narrative. No claim can be made that Yaakov bar Asher connected the prohibition against self-harm and *bal tashḥit*, but viewing Genesis 9:5 as the source of the prohibition against self-harm contributes to the ranks of scholars who held this view in spite of the arguments advanced by the *amoraim* in b*Baba Qama* 91b seen in the previous chapter.

Meir Leibush bar Yeḥiel Mikhel Weiser (*Malbim*) (1809–1879, Ukraine, Poland, Romania, and Prussia).[93] Weiser began his gloss by stating that although God permitted the killing of animals, the killing of fellow humans was still prohibited and there will be a reckoning for the murderer. He interpreted this verse as having two meanings. The first is that the eternal soul of those who take their own lives (whether through the literal shedding of blood [*dimkhem*] or through other means [*nafshoteikhem*]) will be held accountable. The second meaning is with regard to the responsibility of testifying in court after witnessing a murder. The sages interpreted this verse as indicating that a Noahide (a universal term for a Gentile) can be held accountable even by only one judge, with no warning, with only one witness, by a man but not a woman, and even by a relative.

Barukh HaLevi Epstein (*Torah Temimah*) (1860–1942, Belarus).[94] For Epstein this verse indicated that Noahides who are accused of murder may be judged by one judge, and even through the testimony of only one witness; the witness, however, must be a man, though he could be a relative. He also presented the *baraita* quoting Rabbi Eleazar found in b*Baba Qama* 91b interpreting the verse as a prohibition against harming oneself. He then claimed that the *amoraim* of the Talmud accepted this as a source for the prohibition against suicide, but rejected it as a source for the prohibition against self-harm because they are qualitatively different from each other. Epstein, however, understood this rejection by the Talmud as a nonsubstantive casting-aside of a proof (*diḥui be'alma*). In other words, while it is indeed the case that the Talmud did not accept this proof, Weiser nonetheless holds that this is the simple meaning.

93. Meir Leibush Weiser, *Otzar HaPeirushim al Tanakh, Miqraot Gedolot, Sidra 1, HaTorah VeHaMitzvah* (Tel-Aviv: Mefarshei HaTanakh, n.d.).

94. Barukh HaLevi Epstein, *Ḥamishah Ḥumshei Torah im Ḥamesh Megilot, Torah Temimah: Sefer Bereishit* (New York: Avraham Yitzḥak Friedman, 1962).

Menaḥem Mendel Kasher (*Torah Shlemah*) (1895–1983, Poland and Israel).[95] Kasher weighed in on the debate in the Talmud (b*Baba Qama* 91b) as to whether Genesis 9:5 is in fact a proof-text for the prohibition against self-harm or only a prohibition against suicide. He mentioned that t*Baba Qama* 9:31 presented a number of examples that clearly deal with self-harm and not suicide and use Genesis 9:5 as a proof-text. He, however, accepted the Talmud's rejection of this verse as the source for the prohibition against self-harm. He surmised that perhaps the Tosefta just uses Genesis 9:5 as a scriptural support (*asmakhta*), for the prohibition against self-harm without it actually being the source.

Synthetic Analysis

Although a large number of exegetes commented on this verse, the variation in the content of their glosses is quite small. The majority considered the verse to be a prohibition against suicide or a prohibition against murder. In considering whether Genesis 9:5 is a prohibition against murder or suicide, a number of factors reinforce the notion that the verse is indeed a prohibition against suicide. First, the prohibition against murder found in Genesis 9:6 is presented in a very straightforward manner: "Whoever sheds the blood of man, [b]y man shall his blood be shed; [f]or in His image [d]id God make man." In the opinion of traditional exegetes, the fact that Genesis 9:6 is an explicit prohibition against murder leaves Genesis 9:5 open to mean something else. After all, why would two prohibitions on murder be juxtaposed? Moreover, t*Baba Qama* 9:31 uses Genesis 9:5 as a proof-text for the prohibition against self-harm, while b*Baba Qama* 91a–b discusses the culpability of the individual in cases of self-inflicted harm and suggests the possibility that Genesis 9:5 is the source of this prohibition. Although the Talmud goes on to reject this verse as the source of the prohibition against self-harm, it does so by accepting it as a source for the prohibition against suicide. In spite of this, both Yaakov bar Asher and Barukh HaLevi Epstein connected this verse to the prohibition against self-inflicted harm.

As we saw in the rabbinic chapter, this Talmudic discussion comes in precisely the same place as the discussion of the limits to the prohibition against cutting down fruit trees. Although we see

95. Menaḥem Mendel Kasher, *Ḥumash Torah Shlemah*, Vol. 2 (Jerusalem: Levin-Epstein Bros. and Partners Press, 1936).

interpretations of both murder and suicide emerge from the midrash (murder in *Sifre Zuta* and suicide in *Bereishit Rabbah*),[96] something that is quite common, it is clear from the discussion in the Talmud (b*Baba Qama* 91b) that the sages favored the understanding that the verse is a prohibition against suicide. This does not preclude the possibility that the verse is also a prohibition against murder; after all, suicide is a form of (self-)murder.

In spite of the rabbinic leaning toward the verse as a prohibition against suicide, there is a relatively even division among the commentators as to whether Genesis 9:5 deals with suicide or murder. While some of the exegetes who asserted that the verse is a prohibition against murder explicitly rejected the notion that the verse is a prohibition against suicide (Abraham ibn Ezra, Judah Loew ben Bezalel, and Samuel David Luzzatto), none of those claiming that the verse was a prohibition against suicide explicitly rejected the notion that the prohibition was against murder. This is possible since suicide is a form of (self-)murder, as mentioned above.

Beyond the debate over whether the verse is a prohibition against murder or suicide, there is also the issue of the animals in the verse. Where do they fit into the narrative? This is a component that is not dealt with by the midrash, opening the door to a wider variety of interpretations by the exegetes who chose to incorporate this aspect of the verse into their glosses. Bekhor Shor, Ḥizqiyah bar Manoaḥ, *Ba'alei HaTosafot*, and Gunther Plaut (1912–2012, Germany, USA, and Canada),[97] explained that animals would be held accountable for killing humans, as in the case of the "goring ox." David Qimḥi (*Radaq*) (1160–1235, southern France)[98] and Solomon Dubno also held this view, but without referencing the goring ox. The much earlier pseudo-epigraphal Aramaic translation of Scripture of Pseudo-Jonathan (known also as *Targum Yonatan*) also held this view.[99] While Yaakov bar Asher took a similar approach to the above exegetes in claiming that animals are held accountable for killing humans, he added that animals were also prohibited from eating humans. Although this might be implied

96. Both positions are later on also offered by Meyuḥas bar Eliyahu, Baḥya bar Asher, Yaakov bar Asher, Samson Raphael Hirsch, and the ArtScroll (*The Schottenstein Edition Interlinear Chumash: Genesis*, ed. Menachem Davis [New York: Mesorah Publications, 2006]).

97. Gunther Plaut, *A Modern Commentary*.

98. David Qimḥi, *Peirushei Rabbi David Qimḥi al HaTorah*, 2nd ed., ed. Moshe Kamlher (Jerusalem: Mossad HaRav Kook, 1975).

99. *Targum Yonatan*, ed. S. Wertheimer (Jerusalem: 1997).

by the other commentators, Yaakov bar Asher stated so explicitly. To this Nissim ben Reuven Gerondi added that the way in which the transgressing animal in the wild receives justice is through a divinely delivered weakening of the animal that results in that animal being killed by other animals. Samuel David Luzzatto also believed that animals would be punished for their transgressions against humans.

Tuvia bar Eliezer and Meyuḥas bar Eliyahu insisted that animals, like humans, have the responsibility to carry out justice. Such an approach was shared by Baḥya bar Asher. For him, animals could be divine messengers who carry out God's justice in cases where humans are unable to do so. For example, if a murder has no witnesses, the murderer is still punished, but through nonhuman means. Bar Asher viewed the animals not as those on which justice is delivered, but rather as agents through which justice is delivered. The role of agency through animals was shared by Gersonides and Isaac Abarbanel (1437–1508, Portugal, Spain, and Italy).[100] Moshe Alsheikh had a nuanced approach stating that those who transgress by committing murder are no longer superior to animals and therefore can be killed by them.

As mentioned above, Naḥmanides believed that animals lack the mental capacity to understand punishment or reward. He nevertheless accepted the possibility of animals being punished for their actions. Gersonides, too, took issue with animals being considered to have rational faculties. He held that God would not punish animals, for whom punishment was irrelevant. Gersonides believed that the only logical interpretation of the verse was that animals were used as God's agents to carry out justice when humans were unable to do so.

In conclusion, the commentary tradition on Genesis 9:5 does not explicitly connect the verse and the prohibition against wastefulness/destruction. Because the link between Deuteronomy 20:19 and the general prohibition of *bal tashḥit* is hardly apparent in the commentaries, this comes as little surprise. Nevertheless, through his claim that humans have the responsibility to protect God's creations, Hirsch made this connection implicitly. Together with Yaakov bar Asher and Barukh HaLevi Epstein, who asserted that Genesis 9:5 is the source for the prohibition against self-harm, there is a basis on which the ideas that arise in the following chapters can rest. If a general prohibition against wastefulness is all-encompassing, what could have more value than human life? Whether the prohibition in Genesis 9:5 is of murder or suicide, both approaches view human life as sacrosanct.

100. Isaac Abarbanel, *Peirush al HaTorah—Bereishit* (Jerusalem: Bnei Arbael Publishing, 1964).

Both murder and suicide could be interpreted as the most extreme example of wastefulness/destruction. In utilitarian terms, human life is so precious, monetary value cannot be placed on it. Indeed, there is little that humanity values more. Jewish law indicates that all laws are forfeit when it comes to preserving a human life, save the prohibition against murder, idolatry, and sexual immorality.[101]

A number of verses in the Torah specifically deal with the prohibition against murder (for example, Genesis 9:6, Exodus 20:12 and 21:12, and Deuteronomy 5:16). Genesis 9:5 is much more vague in this regard, which is why it is compelling to view it as a prohibition against suicide and not murder. Needless to say, it is not our goal here to choose which interpretation is most suitable. Rather, we are interested in understanding the role of Genesis 9:5 in the conceptualization of *bal tashḥit*. Conceptually, it makes sense to think of wastefulness as something applicable not only to material goods, but to the body. In the Jewish tradition, one is prohibited not only from wasting and destroying material goods but also human life. Objectively, human life is the most valuable thing in the world. Subjectively, however, it is not just any human life that is considered to be of greatest value, but one's own life. Certainly this assertion has its limitations, such as valuing members of one's family more than one's own life, or a person's willingness to die for a particular cause. These, however, should be seen as exceptions to the rule. The directive of Genesis 9:5 asserts that even the thing that humans might assume belongs most to them, their own body, is not theirs to destroy. From this perspective, one can detect a theocentric guiding principle behind the ethic of *bal tashḥit*. From a Jewish perspective, ownership, like life, is a transient condition. Neither one's own life nor one's material possessions are under exclusive human ownership. Never having complete ownership over anything makes any act of wastefulness/destruction of person or property a transgression.

Leviticus 19:27

Context

Chapter 19 of Leviticus is replete with what can be considered social and ethical laws, and includes a number of commandments found in the Decalogue. In addition, some of the laws relate to sacrificial

101. b*Sanhedrin* 74a.

practices. The specific commandment of not "destroying" one's facial hair comes with no rationalization, and as such left ample room for rationalists and others to offer an explanation for this commandment.

27: You shall not round off the side-growth on your head, or destroy the side-growth of your beard.

The reason this verse is included in the analysis of *bal tashḥit* is because it is the first of the only two times the term *lo tashḥit* appears in the Torah (the second, of course, being Deuteronomy 20:19).[102] In contemporary environmental literature dealing with the concept of *bal tashḥit* this verse has been entirely overlooked. Seemingly, there is at most very little connection between the two verses in which these words appear. Contextually, the verse in Deuteronomy deals with obligations during war, while the verse in Leviticus is one of a long list of commandments that appear to have very little rationale. The only reasoning behind the commandment to not "destroy" one's facial hair is provided in Leviticus 19:37, the final verse in the chapter: "You shall faithfully observe all My laws and all My rules: I am the Lord." "I am the Lord" might be a good reason to fulfill the edict, and present sufficient motivation to do so, but it fundamentally lacks a rationale as to why one should fulfill it. Nevertheless, due to the fact that the very same language is used (*lo tashḥit*) and the rarity of its use, analyzing this verse is an essential component of the tradition histories of *bal tashḥit*.

Medieval Midrash

The midrash is presented to give context regarding the rabbinic understanding of the prohibition against "destroying" one's facial hair.[103]
Yalqut Shimoni (Shimon HaDarshan, thirteenth century, Germany)—

102. *Lo* and *bal* are synonymous.

103. The *Sifra*, though considerably earlier, offers less detail than Shimon HaDarshan. *Sifra* (c. third century, Land of Israel)—*Qedoshim*, *Parashah* 3, 6:4–6. The midrash started by stating the prohibition on "destroying" one's facial hair. The midrash then asked if scissors were included in the prohibition, and concluded that they are not since they do not "destroy." The midrash then asked whether one is culpable if he used a plane (a blade used by carpenters) or tweezers, to which the answer again is no, because these are not instruments that shave. Rabbi Eliezer, however, had a different approach and claimed that the use of a plane or tweezers was still a transgression of the prohibition. He also claimed that even if one removes the hair from all five different parts of the face he is still only liable to be punished once (*Sifra*, ed. I. Weiss [Vienna: 1862]).

Qedoshim 19:690.[104] The midrash began by defining exactly what is included in the side growth of one's beard, and concluded that it includes five different sections of the face. Rabbi Eliezer stated that if someone removes all of them at once he is still only liable for one punishment. The rabbis claimed that he is only liable if he removes his facial hair with a razor. Rabbi Eliezer claimed that one is also liable if he uses tools such as a plane or tweezers to remove one's beard. What was the rabbis' reasoning? They drew a parallel between the prohibition in Leviticus 19:27 and that in Leviticus 21:5, which states that priests should not shave their beards but does not use the word "destroy." The rabbis understood these prohibitions as synonymous, meaning that the prohibition on shaving one's beard entailed destruction. Therefore, trimming one's beard with scissors is permissible because it is a tool that does not destroy, while using a plane or tweezers is not a transgression of this particular prohibition (though it possibly is a transgression of the prohibition on harming oneself), because a plane does not shave and tweezers do not destroy. According to Rabbi Eliezer, who did not use the exegetical rule to learn from one verse to the other and did not see them as equivalent, even the use of scissors would be prohibited.

Post-Geonic Commentary

Abraham ibn Ezra (1089–1164, born in Spain, but lived and traveled all over the Mediterranean basin, northern France, and England).[105] Ibn Ezra asserted that the beard should not be cut because it emulates Gentiles. Moreover, head and facial hair were created for purposes of splendor and as such should not be destroyed.

Menaḥem Recanati (c. 1250–c. 1310, Italy).[106] Recanati claimed that destroying one's facial hair results in the destruction of special elements of righteousness. These powers are missing from pagan priests who shave their faces.

---

104. Shimon HaDarshan, *Midrash Yalqut Shimoni: VaYiqra*, ed. Daniel Bitton (Jerusalem: HaMaor Institute, 2001).

105. Abraham ibn Ezra, *Peirushei HaTorah LeRabbeinu Avraham ibn Ezra*, 2nd ed., Vol. 2, ed. Asher Weiser (Jerusalem: Mossad HaRav Kook, 1977).

106. Menaḥem Recanati, *Sefer Levushei Or Yaqar*.

Baḥya bar Asher (1255–1340, Spain).[107] Baḥya bar Asher discussed the prohibition in terms of not eliminating a characteristic given by God to differentiate men and women. He drew a parallel between engaging in such activity and *kilayim* (mixtures and creating hybrid species), by claiming that they are both opposed to God's intention. He continued by offering a rational explanation (*al derekh hasekhel*), claiming that the five corners of one's head from which hair may not be cut with a razor represent the five senses. The reason for the prohibition is that destroying the five corners is equivalent to destroying the five senses, which can be considered the same as destroying oneself. He, however, did consider trimming one's beard with scissors to be permissible.

Moshav Zeqenim (c. thirteenth to fourteenth centuries, anonymous).[108] This compilation of glosses from the *tosafists* claimed that the prohibition includes razors, but the use of scissors is permissible. They then presented ibn Ezra's opinion that the prohibition is to distinguish Jews from Gentiles, as well as his gloss regarding the splendor of the beard, and that it was wrong to destroy something splendid. They also cited Elazar of Worms's gloss regarding God's knowledge of the future and the fact that Christian priests and monks would shave their heads, and the prohibition stems from not emulating them.

Ovadiah Seforno (c. 1480–c. 1550, Italy).[109] Seforno claimed that the reason behind the prohibition is that such behavior is the domain of fools, drunkards, and Gentile priests. Also, the beard is considered a thing of splendor.

Pinḥas bar Tzvi Hirsch HaLevi Horowitz (*Panim Yafot*) (1730–1805, Poland).[110] Horowitz stated that using scissors is not considered a transgression of the prohibition. He also offered an allegorical interpretation stating that the various corners of one's head represented

---

107. Baḥya bar Asher, *Rabbeinu Baḥya: Be'ur al HaTorah*, Vol. 2, *Shemot, VaYiqra*, ed. Ḥaim Dov Chavel (Jerusalem: Mossad HaRav Kook, 1974).

108. *Sefer Moshav Zeqenim al HaTorah*, ed. Saliman D. Sassoon (London: L. Honig and Sons, 1959).

109. Ovadiah Seforno, *Be'ur al HaTorah*.

110. Pinḥas HaLevi Horowitz, *Sefer Panim Yafot HaShalem al HaTorah*. Part 1, *Sefer Bereishit* (Jerusalem: private printing, 1998).

the Thirteen Principles of Faith, which connected to the heavens and could either sustain the world or destroy it.

Bernard J. Bamberger (1904–1980, USA).[111] Bamberger viewed the destruction of one's beard a forbidden pagan practice.

ArtScroll (2008, USA).[112] ArtScroll claimed that it is prohibited to cut one's sideburns even with scissors, though the prohibition on one's beard is limited to razors because they destroy the beard.

Synthetic Analysis

After a thorough analysis of commentaries, it is clear that none of them makes any explicit connections between the two instances in which the term *bal tashḥit* appears. The entire gamut of commentaries analyzed for Deuteronomy 20:19–20 and Genesis 9:5 were also analyzed for this verse. The vast majority of the commentators who did comment on this verse focused on explaining what the word *"pe'at"* means and what part of the head it includes. These glosses were of little interest insofar as they pertain to the subject of this book. As such, these glosses and their authors were not included in the analysis of this verse and have not been included in the appendix. The exegetes who do appear in this section are those that offered a rationalization of the prohibition found in the verse, as well as those who dealt with the issue of destruction in a manner that implicitly connects Leviticus 19:27 to the greater theme of wastefulness/destruction. At this point, readers may be asking themselves: why bother dealing with the rationalization behind the prohibition, if it is not associated with wastefulness/destruction per se? The answer to this is that it is possible, through the rationalization of the prohibition found in the verse at hand, that light can be shed on how the issue of wastefulness/destruction is understood by the commentators over time.

Those whose glosses included a rationalization of the prohibition fall into two groups with some overlap between them. The first group rationalized not "destroying" one's facial hair because such

111. Bernard J. Bamberger, *The Torah: A Modern Commentary*, ed. Gunther Plaut (New York: Union of American Hebrew Congregations, 1981).

112. *The Schottenstein Edition Interlinear Chumash: Leviticus*, ed. Menachem Davis (New York: Mesorah Publications, 2008).

practices emulate Gentiles. Those who rationalized the prohibition in these terms were essentially engaging in anti-Gentile polemics. For some, the polemic was explicitly against Christians (Elazar of Worms [1160–1237, Germany][113] and *Moshav Zeqenim*), for some against the Amorites (Avraham Saba [*Tzeror HaMor*] [1440–1508, Spain, Portugal, Morocco, and Turkey]),[114] for some against idol worshipers or idol-worshiping priests (Yosef Bekhor Shor [twelfth century, France],[115] Menaḥem Recanati, Levi ben Gershom [*Ralbag*, Gersonides][1288–1344, France],[116] Ovadiah Seforno, Moshe Alsheikh [1508–c. 1600, Turkey, Israel, and Syria],[117] and Bernard J. Bamberger), and for some against Gentiles in general (Abraham ibn Ezra, Meyuḥas bar Eliyahu [1150–1200, Byzantium],[118] Yaakov bar Asher [*Ba'al HaTurim*] [c. 1270–1343, Germany and Spain],[119] Nissim ben Moshe of Marseille [thirteenth to fourteenth centuries, southern France],[120] and *Moshav Zeqenim*). Ephraim bar Shimshon (c. late twelfth to thirteenth centuries, France),[121] who did not elaborate beyond his statement that such practices separate the pure and impure, can be assumed to also have been alluding to some form of the above. Regardless of who the polemic's target is, this line of argument was the most common manner of rationalizing the prohibition. Initially, these glosses appear to be unrelated to the general prohibition against wastefulness/destruction. Nevertheless, after encountering the rabbinic material in the previous chapter we can see that distancing Jews from emulating Gentiles is a core aspect of the conceptualization of *bal tashḥit*.

The rationalization offered by the second group is more obviously connected to the prohibition of *bal tashḥit*. This group can be divided

113. Elazar of Worms, *Peirush Rabbeinu Elazar MiGermaiza Zal Ba'al Sefer HaRoqe'aḥ al HaTorah ve'al Megilat Ester*, ed. Yosef Gad (London: private printing, 1959).

114. Avraham bar Yaakov Saba, *Sefer Tzeror HaMor*.

115. Joseph Bechor Shor, *Commentary on the Pentateuch*.

116. Levi ben Gershom, *Peirushei HaTorah LeRabbeinu Levi ben Gershom (Ralbag)*, Vol. 3, *VaYiqra*, ed. Yaakov Leib Levi (Jerusalem: Mossad HaRav Kook, 1997).

117. Moshe Alsheikh, *Torat Moshe: Derushim, Peirushim UVe'urim LeḤamishah Ḥumshei Torah—Sefer VaYiqra*, ed. Makhon Lev Sameaḥ (Jerusalem: H. Vagshel, 1990).

118. Meyuḥas bar Eliyahu, *Peirush Rabbeinu Meyuḥas al Sefer VaYiqra*, ed. Yitzḥak Yaakov Har Shoshanim Weinberg (Bnei Braq: private printing, 2005).

119. Yaakov bar Asher, *VaYiqra—Devarim*.

120. Nissim ben Moshe, *Ma'aseh Nissim*.

121. Ephraim bar Shimshon, *VaYiqra—BeMidbar—Devarim*.

into two subgroups. The first is headed by Abraham ibn Ezra, who claimed that the beard was created for purposes of splendor, and splendid things should not be destroyed. This group includes Yaakov bar Asher, the tosafist compilation of *Moshav Zeqenim*, and Ovadiah Seforno. The statement asserting that splendid things should not be destroyed can be understood as a generalization beyond its contextual application to facial hair. Thus, there is a distinct possibility that the prohibition to destroy splendid things includes all splendid things, and not just facial hair. As we have seen above in the glosses of Meyuḥas bar Eliyahu, the *Midrash Aggadah* and Baḥya bar Asher (and others) on Deuteronomy 20:19, the general prohibition against wastefulness/destruction is understood to apply to the nonhuman world relative to human need (*tzorekh*), benefit/enjoyment (*hana'ah*), and utility (*to'elet*). It is possible that one might include splendid things in the category of benefit/enjoyment, but the categories are by and large economic. Ibn Ezra and the rest of those in this group, however, show no indication that their pronouncement depends on utilitarianism. Facial hair has no discernible market value. Its value, then, might be considered to be intrinsic, which is an essential category of environmental ethics.[122]

The other group consists of Menaḥem Recanati, Baḥya bar Asher, and Pinḥas bar Tzvi Hirsch HaLevi Horowitz. Recanati claimed that the rationale behind not cutting one's facial hair is based on special mystical elements that connect humans to God through their hair. Destroying the hair would also destroy this connection. In other words, the absence of these connections harms the individual, which goes against the prohibition of self-inflicted harm (Genesis 9:5). Baḥya's allegorical gloss implicitly connects Genesis 9:5 with Leviticus 19:27. Though he did not mention the verse from Genesis specifically, he drew a parallel between "destroying" one's facial hair and destroying one's self. For him, each of the five corners of the head represented one of the five senses, and "destroying" the facial hair was like destroying one's senses. As we saw in the analysis of Genesis 9:5, many commentators understood the verse to be a prohibition against suicide, with a few asserting that the prohibition includes even nonlethal forms of self-harm. As mentioned in the introduction, what makes *bal tashḥit* stand out as an environmental ethic is the dual understanding that

122. See Holmes Rolston III, "Value of Nature and the Nature of Value," in *Philosophy and the Natural Environment*, eds. Robin Attfield and Andrew Belsey (Cambridge, UK: Cambridge University Press, 1994), 13–30.

wastefulness is destructive not just to the environment but also to oneself. The understanding materializing through this is that even the "self," the entity that humans might assume most securely belongs to them, is not theirs to damage or destroy, but rather belongs to God. By focusing on self-harm, Baḥya may be said to have implicitly connected the *bal tashḥit* of Leviticus 19:27 to the *bal tashḥit* that eventually emerges from Deuteronomy 20:19. Horowitz took this one step further by suggesting that the corners of one's head represented the thirteen principles of faith, which if destroyed could destroy the entire world. In other words, while Baḥya understood the issue at hand to be self-destruction, Horowitz viewed the act of "destroying" one's facial hair cosmically to have the potential to destroy everything. In a general sense, these two exegetes are conceptually similar, but Baḥya's gloss is much closer in terms of actual content to Genesis 9:5. This is important from the perspective of finding links between the verses foundational to the concept of *bal tashḥit*. The notion that the prohibition against "destroying" one's facial hair is associated with self-harm can also be found in contemporary scholarship. For instance, in his discussion of human dignity, Amnon Shapira included in the category of the prohibition against self-harm the commandment in Leviticus 19:27 regarding the "destroying" of the beard.[123]

The main topic of debate among the commentators included in this section, however, was whether the prohibition against destroying one's facial hair de facto only includes the use of a razor, or whether scissors are also prohibited. On its surface, this debate appears to have little to do with the topic of wastefulness. The debate is focused on understanding what is encompassed by the prohibition and whether the prohibition is transgressed based on the tool used. The majority opinion was that the actions of shaving the face and "destroying" the beard must happen simultaneously for the transgression to occur. Trimming one's facial hair with scissors, while "destroying" the beard, does not shave one's face. In fact, during a careful trim, the scissors may not even come in contact with one's face. Using a razor, however, has a completely different outcome. This is where the theoretical connection to the self-harm dimension of *bal tashḥit* comes into play. When using even the most sophisticated razors available today, and even if one is careful, one is frequently left with nicks and scratches

123. Amnon Shapira, "'Human Dignity' [K'vod HaAdam] in the Hebrew Bible," *Mo'ed: Annual for Jewish Studies* 19 (2009): 20.

or in-grown hairs. The tools of antiquity were not nearly as sophisticated, and one can assume that the process was somewhat bloodier.

These abrasions, which like any break in the skin may become infected, are a form of self-harm. Shaving with a razor is relatively benign compared with some other forms of self-inflicted harm. Nevertheless, any degree of self-harm can be considered a transgression. As Samson Raphael Hirsch wrote (though not in his gloss to Leviticus 19:27), "Every smallest weakening is partial murder."[124] It is not obvious from the rabbinic tradition and legal sources that the prohibition against using a razor to shave is because of the prohibition against self-harm, but the fact that a razor is prohibited and scissors are permitted raises this possibility.[125] Moreover, the fact that the terminology of destruction *"lo tashḥit"* is used and the fact that some commentators understood this as a form of self-harm reinforces this connection. While this evidence is still not definitive, it still creates a plausible-enough narrative to merit further research into the matter.

2 Kings 3:19, 25

Context

In chapter 3 of 2 Kings, the king of Moab, who was at this point a tributary of the kingdom of Israel, rebelled against Israel by not paying his tribute. Yoram the king of Israel called on Jehoshaphat the king of Judah and the king of Edom to join him in attacking the Moabites. These three kings departed through the desert to face Moab, and eventually were left without water. The kings eventually called on the prophet Elisha, who happened to be with the army. Elisha prophesied that God would make water appear in the desert and that their army would vanquish the Moabites. In his directive from God, in addition to conquering all the Moabite cities and towns, the kings

124. Samson Raphael Hirsch, *Horeb: A Philosophy of Jewish Laws and Observances*—Vol. 2, 2nd ed., trans. I. Grunfeld (London: Soncino Press, 1968), 300.

125. This sits well according to the position of Rabbi Eliezer in the midrash, who prohibits the use of any tool. For the sages who do permit the use of scissors, one would assume that the use of tools such as a carpenter's plane to shave, which according to them would not be a transgression of *lo tashḥit*, would still be transgressing the prohibition against self-harm due to the damage caused to one's face.

are commanded to cut down every good tree, block up every spring, and ruin every good field. In other words, the kings are commanded to carry out a scorched-earth policy, contrary to the commandment of Deuteronomy 20:19–20 in which this policy is specifically prohibited. The kings then destroyed the Moabites and carried out the scorched-earth policy.

19. "You shall conquer every fortified town and every splendid city; you shall fell every good tree and stop up all wells of water; and every fertile field you shall ruin with stones."

25. "[A]nd they destroyed the towns. Every man threw a stone into each fertile field, so that it was covered over; and they stopped up every spring and felled every good tree.[126] Only the walls of Kir Hareseth were left, and then the slingers surrounded it and attacked it."

Medieval Midrash

BeMidbar Rabbah (Moshe HaDarshan, eleventh century, Narbonne) *Pinḥas* 21:6.[127] The biblical text sets the scene for the prophet Elisha's directive in 2 Kings 3 to destroy the trees of the Moabites. In Numbers 25, the Israelites are involved in idol worship and sexual immorality with the Moabites. After a brazen act of sexual transgression by an Israelite man with a Midianite woman and the priest Pinḥas's (Phineas's) killing of them, God commanded the Israelites to kill the Midianites. Though they are two separate peoples, *BeMidbar Rabbah* drew a parallel between the Midianites and the Moabites, in terms of the directive to seek their destruction as opposed to living peacefully with them. As such, even though with other nations the prohibition of destroying fruit trees during a siege found in Deuteronomy 20:19–20 holds, with the Moabites the directive is to destroy them utterly, including pursuing a scorched-earth policy.[128]

126. The NJPS translates this as "fruit tree," but *etz tov* is more appropriately translated as "every good tree."

127. Moshe HaDarshan, *BeMidbar Rabbah*, Vilna ed., 1878, reprinted in Jerusalem.

128. This text can also be found in *Midrash Tanḥuma al Ḥamishah Ḥumshei Torah*, Vol. 2, ed. Shlomo Buber (Jerusalem: Ortsel Ltd., 1964), *Pinḥas* 5.

Post-Geonic Commentaries

Shlomo Yitzḥaki (*Rashi*) (eleventh century, northern France).[129] Rashi stated that in spite of the prohibition of *lo tashḥit* from Deuteronomy 20:19, cutting down the fruit trees in this instance was permissible because Moab is a despised nation. Deuteronomy 23:7 states that Israel should not seek out their (the Moabites') peace (*shlomam*) and well-being (*tovatam*), which in this context means trees.

David Qimḥi (*Radaq*) (1160–1235, southern France).[130] Qimḥi stated that even though there is the prohibition of *lo tashḥit*, it is only applicable in the context of a siege, and in this context there is no siege. Even though the rabbis understood the prohibition to include all fruit bearing trees at all times, the plain sense of the text is that it is only relevant to siege situations. The midrashic meaning, however, is that Moab is despised more than other nations, and when it says that Israel should not seek their peace or well-being, the reference here is to good trees (fruit-bearing trees).

Aharon ben Yosef HaRishon (Karaite)—(*Mivḥar Yesharim*) (c. 1260–c. 1320, Byzantium).[131] Aharon ben Yosef HaRishon claimed that the trees they were instructed to cut down were all sorts of good trees, such as cedars, cypresses, or other non-fruit-bearing trees (though not fruit-bearing trees) because of the prohibition of *lo tashḥit*.

Moshav Zeqenim (c. thirteenth to fourteenth centuries, anonymous) (On Deuteronomy 20:19).[132] The tosafists interpreted Deuteronomy 20:19 in light of the difficulties raised by 2 Kings 3:19, where a directive is given by the prophet Elisha to destroy all the fruit trees of Moab. They concluded that Moab was the one exception to the prohibition of *bal tashḥit* because of the specific directive to not seek peace with them.

---

129. Shlomo Yitzḥaki, *Nevi'im UKhetuvim HaMefo'ar Miqraot Gedolot: Melakhim*, Vol. 3 (Jerusalem: HaḤumash HaMefo'ar, 1996).

130. David Qimḥi, *Nevi'im UKhetuvim HaMefo'ar Miqraot Gedolot: Melakhim*, Vol. 3 (Jerusalem: HaḤumash HaMefo'ar, 1996).

131. Aharon ben Yosef, *Mivḥar Yesharim*, ed. Avraham ben Shmuel (Yevpatoria, Crimea: 1835).

132. Ba'alei HaTosafot, *Sefer Moshav Zeqenim al HaTorah*.

Levi ben Gershom (*Ralbag*) (1288–1344, France).[133] Gersonides claimed that despite the prohibition of *lo tashḥit* found in the Torah, in this case it was God's specific commandment to strike Moab in this way, which included springs and fields.

Isaac Abarbanel (1437–1508, Portugal, Spain, and Italy).[134] Abarbanel claimed that even though there is the commandment of *lo tashḥit*, in this case it is contradicted by a short–term edict (*hora'at sha'ah*). He also cited *Midrash Tanḥuma*, which taught that the kings themselves were concerned about the prohibition of *lo tashḥit*, but the prophet told them that for all other nations this holds, but not for Moab, which is a despised nation.

Synthetic Analysis

The number of commentaries on 2 Kings is quite limited.[135] As might be expected, due to the problematic content of this passage, the commentaries were preoccupied with the issue of a prophet issuing a directive contradicting a specific commandment found in the Torah. The burning question that arises from this passage is, Why did the prophet Elisha (and ultimately God) issue an edict that transgresses *bal tashḥit*? Since no explanation is offered in the text itself, the commentators needed to reconcile the edict with the prohibition.

The assumption that must be made is that the words of the prophet Elisha are considered to be divinely sanctioned, something that is reinforced through the positive outcome of the war. The exegetes came up with a variety of interesting responses, all of which can be seen as apologetic resulting from embarrassment about the text.[136] Due

133. Levi ben Gershom, *Nevi'im UKhetuvim HaMefo'ar Miqraot Gedolot: Melakhim*—Vol. 3 (Jerusalem: HaḤumash HaMefo'ar, 1996).

134. Isaac Abarbanel, *Peirush al Nevi'im Rishonim* (Jerusalem: Torah VeDa'at, 1976).

135. To this short list we may add the exegetes who referenced this narrative in their glosses on Deuteronomy 20:19: Ba'alei HaTosafot in *Moshav Zeqenim*, Shmuel David Luzzatto, Meir Leibush Weiser, and Gunther Plaut.

136. For more on the topic of embarrassment with Scripture, see Harry Fox, "The Embarrassment of Embarrassment," in *Vixens Disturbing Vineyards: Embarrassment and Embracement of Scriptures*, eds. Tzemah Yoreh et al. (Boston: Academic Studies Press, 2010), 5–18.

to the divinely sanctioned transgression, an excuse must be found for the edict. The majority of glossators found the answer in the nature of the particular foe. This was not just any enemy that Judah and Israel were warring against, but the nation of Moab. The special status of this enemy is evident from a different directive found in Deuteronomy 23:7 that prohibits seeking a peace treaty with Moab. As such, the standard requirements of behavior during wartime are suspended. This approach was shared by Moshe HaDarshan in *BeMidbar Rabbah*, Rashi, David Qimḥi, and Isaac Abarbanel. Qimḥi, however, considered this to be the midrashic understanding of the text. The *peshat* or simple meaning is that the directive of Deuteronomy 20:19–20 is only applicable in the context of a siege. Since in this particular war there was no siege, there was no reason not to engage in scorched-earth tactics. Qimḥi admitted, though, that the rabbinic tradition viewed this as a prohibition against destroying fruit trees at any time. Gersonides, always the avid rationalist, claimed that Deuteronomy 20:19 is a commandment given by God, but then so is 2 Kings 3:19. One should understand Gersonides as meaning that Deuteronomy 20:19 is the rule, but sometimes there are exceptions to the rule, such as 2 Kings 3:19. In such cases the new directive should be followed, but in general the initial edict stands. Abarbanel also suggested that the edict in 2 Kings 3:19 should be considered a directive in a time of need, a legal status that allows certain transgressions to fill a need dictated by a particular circumstance. Aharon ben Yosef HaRishon, the only Karaite (a breakaway sect from rabbinic Judaism) commentator presented in this book, had a unique approach. He clearly rejected the idea that a "good tree" must imply a fruit-bearing tree. For him there could be many kinds of good trees that did not produce fruit. As a Karaite, ben Yosef HaRishon was not bound by the rabbinic tradition like the other exegetes. The important thing for him was that there not be contradictory directives in the Bible. Making a distinction between "good trees" and fruit-bearing trees was a simple way to deal with a problem that needed to be reconciled in other ways by those beholden to the Oral Law. The rabbinic law of *bal tashḥit* that generalizes the prohibition on wastefulness and destruction would find all three types of destruction (trees, springs, and fields) problematic. For a Karaite a general law of *bal tashḥit* would not necessarily exist, and the only problem would be with the trees, something which is resolved by interpreting them as non-fruit-bearing trees.

Conclusions

After a thorough analysis of the material it is possible to arrive at a number of conclusions. The simplest and most obvious will be dealt with first. A number of commentators made implicit connections between the prohibition against self-harm in Genesis 9:5 and the prohibition against "destroying" one's beard originating in Leviticus 19:27. None, however, explicitly connects these verses with Deuteronomy 20:19–20. In fact, none of the exegetes mentioned any explicit relationship between any of the verses. If Deuteronomy 20:19 and Genesis 9:5 are indeed the source of the general prohibition against wastefulness, one would expect the commentators to mention this and illustrate a thematic connection between the verses. While this was surprising, it was not altogether unexpected. If the connection between these verses was obvious, it would have received a prominent place in the abundant literature on the topic. The fact is that these connections are rather obscure in the literature, and a main purpose in this book is to expose these connections to enable a fuller understanding of the concept of *bal tashḥit*.

What is more surprising, however, is that among the commentators analyzed, even the commentary on Deuteronomy 20:19–20, the verse considered to be the progenitor of the general prohibition against wastefulness, there are almost no references to the general prohibition. Prior to the modern era, only Meyuḥas bar Eliyahu, the *Midrash Aggadah*, and Shimon HaDarshan and Baḥya bar Asher (implicitly) mention this connection. From the beginning of the modern era until the present, the handful of commentators who highlight this connection includes Samson Raphael Hirsch, David Tzvi Hoffmann, Barukh HaLevi Epstein, Gunther Plaut, and the ArtScroll commentary. In fact, even the Talmudic discourse on the prohibition of cutting down fruit trees, without reference to the general prohibition against wastefulness, is hardly mentioned. Clearly, a plethora of issues can be discussed in the interpretation of the verses in question, but the outright absence of this line of commentary is very difficult to understand.

The reason for the dearth of commentators making this connection remains an enigma, but I offer a theory as to why this might be the case. The connection between Genesis 9:5 and Deuteronomy 20:19–20 was established during the rabbinic era. As we saw in the rabbinic chapter, in the Talmudic discussions surrounding the destruction of trees there is also no mention of *bal tashḥit*. Only with regard to wastefulness/destruction of things other than fruit trees is there reference to the concept of *bal tashḥit*. One possible reason for this, which was discussed in the introduction to this chapter, can be derived from what the Bible commentator understood his role as an exegete to be. Many Bible commentators were focused on presenting the reader with the *peshat*, which would not necessarily include any aspect of *bal tashḥit* as a general concept. This, however, is not an altogether satisfying answer, as many of the exegetes did engage the classic rabbinic material in their glosses.

The proliferation of commentaries dealing with a generalized and decontextualized form of *bal tashḥit* from the age of Enlightenment onward is to be expected. The Enlightenment brought with it new methods of biblical interpretation and began to view the endeavor as a science instead of religiously motivated.[137] It gave rise to what became known as *Wissenschaft des Judentums*, or Jewish Studies as an area of scientific and critical study. Understandings of the text not offered in the medieval era and early modern period were now being brought to life. In fact, all those who made the connection between Deuteronomy 20:19–20 and the general prohibition of *bal tashḥit* in the modern era received a university education as well as their classical Jewish education, save Barukh HaLevi Epstein. In spite of the more critical approach to the biblical text, the number of commentaries dealing with the concept from the early modern period onward is hardly abundant.

Two exegetes emerge as sui generis with regard to *bal tashḥit*: Meyuḥas bar Eliyahu in the medieval era, and Samson Raphael Hirsch in the modern era. Meyuḥas's commentary was in part concerned with connecting the text of the Torah with rabbinic law. According to Katz, the editor of his commentary, Meyuḥas is unique among Bible commentators for his approach that Torah and *halakhah* are actually one cohesive unit, around which he constructed his commentary.[138] He

137. For instance, see Breuer, "Jewish Study of the Bible," 1006–1023, and Edward Beuer and Chanan Gafni, "Jewish Biblical Scholarship Between Tradition and Innovation," in *Hebrew Bible/Old Testament: The History of Its Interpretation*, Vol. 3: *From Modernism to Post-Modernism (The Nineteenth and Twentieth Centuries)*. Part I: *The Nineteenth Century—A Century of Modernism and Historicism*, ed. Magne Saebo (Gottingen, Germany: Vandenhoeck & Ruprecht, 2013), 262–306.

138. Yeḥiel Mikhel Katz, "Introduction," in *Peirush Rabbeinu Meyuḥas al Sefer Devarim*, ed. Yeḥiel Mikhel Katz (Jerusalem: Mossad HaRav Kook, 1968), 12. It can, however, be argued that many Bible commentators had a similar approach.

posited that this was probably the result of a growing conflict between Jews following rabbinic law and the Karaites.[139] If this assertion is correct, then it goes a long way to explain the absence of reference to the general prohibition against *bal tashḥit* in other commentaries. Regardless of the accuracy of Katz's claim, Meyuḥas bar Eliyahu had a novel understanding of *bal tashḥit*. Aside from touching on the connection between Deuteronomy 20:19 and the general prohibition against wastefulness, which on its own makes him stand out, he also discussed the prohibition as an indication that God has compassion for all his creations. Though centered on God, such a moral rationalization carries with it a strong environmental cadence. Additionally, he defined the prohibition as encompassing all things for which humans have need (*tzorekh*), a term used in abundance by later scholars. Taken on its own, it already furthers the conceptualization of *bal tashḥit*, which had stagnated since the amoraic/savoraic eras. Taken together with his comment regarding God's compassion, however, we encounter a developed moral rationalization of the prohibition that goes well beyond human utility. God's compassion for all His creations is independent of human need. While this rationalization resonates as "*Imitatio Dei*," it does not preclude it from containing moral instruction for humans. As Moshe Sokol argues, ethics can be derived from theology, and the notion that the earth belongs to God is a good reason to protect it.[140]

The *Midrash Aggadah* and Baḥya bar Asher also stand out in terms of the language they use to describe the prohibition (benefit/enjoyment, *hana'ah*, and utility, *to'elet*, respectively). Gersonides also used the term *to'elet*, but limited his description to fruit trees, whereas Baḥya used the term as a generalization. This language clearly influenced the tradition, as will be seen in subsequent chapters. Each of the words used has its own nuances and contributes independently to the conceptualization of *bal tashḥit*, but they are still similar enough to Meyuḥas bar Eliyahu's need (*tzorekh*) to be considered derivatives of the same idea. This is not to say that the *Midrash Aggadah* and Baḥya bar Asher were aware of Meyuḥas bar Eliyahu's gloss and were rewording it. Rather, because they emerge after Meyuḥas bar Eliyahu and are not as expressive as he is in their glosses, his contribution to the conceptualization of *bal tashḥit* surpasses theirs.

---

139. Ibid., 22.

140. Moshe Sokol, "What Are the Ethical Implications of Jewish Theological Conceptions of the Natural World?," in *Judaism and Ecology: Created World and Revealed World*, ed. Hava Tirosh-Samuelson (Cambridge, MA: Harvard University Press, 2002), 279.

Hirsch stands out as a harbinger of Jewish environmentalism. Not only was he the only one to offer an implicit connection between Genesis 9:5 and Deuteronomy 20:19–20, he phrased his commentary in language reminiscent of Jewish environmental attitudes. His gloss on Genesis 9:5 talked about human responsibility to protect the rest of creation, while his gloss on Deuteronomy 20:19 discussed a prohibition against the needless destruction of anything and humans' responsibility to not abuse the dominion given to them over the rest of creation. This position is affirmed and significantly reinforced in his profound work *Ḥorev*. There he described *bal tashḥit* as "the first and most general call of God . . . when you realize yourself as master of the earth."[141] Hirsch continued his discussion of *bal tashḥit* in *Ḥorev* as follows: "Regard things as God's property and use them with a sense of responsibility for wise human purposes. Destroy nothing! Waste nothing!"[142] Establishing *bal tashḥit* as an edict tempering the extent of human dominion is precisely the line of argumentation that the Jewish environmental movement took in response to Lynn White Jr.'s criticism that the sources of today's ecological crisis are the Judeo-Christian interpretations of Genesis 1:28.[143] Though most who participated in this dialogue used Genesis 2:15 as their proof-text for a Jewish environmental approach, some used Deuteronomy 20:19–20. The fact that Hirsch had presented a deeply environmental approach to these texts a century before Lynn White Jr.'s accusation establishes him as a founding figure in the field of Jewish environmental thought. What emerges from Hirsch's writings in *Ḥorev,* however, is in fact a symbiosis of Deuteronomy 20:19 and Genesis 9:5. In *Ḥorev*, the prohibition of *bal tashḥit* and the prohibition against self-harm are both found in the section entitled "Statutes" (*Ḥukim*). Hirsch defined statutes as "Laws of righteousness towards those beings which are subordinate to man: towards earth, plant, animal, towards one's own body, mind, spirit, and word."[144] In other words, the concept of *bal tashḥit* and the prohibition against self-harm that are connected implicitly through his Bible commentary are explicitly connected in *Ḥorev*.

---

141. Samson Raphael Hirsch, *Horeb*, 279.

142. Ibid., 282.

143. See Lynn White Jr., "The Historical Roots of Our Ecological Crisis," *Science* 155 (1967): 1203–1207.

144. Samson Raphael Hirsch, *Horeb*, 277.

Samuel Chayen, writing with regard to the environmental thought in Hirsch's writings, summarized Hirsch's environmental approach as follows:

> Hirsch's educational guidelines included the following principles with regard to the environment: Human and environmental health, nature protection, abstention from animal harm and abstention from conspicuous consumption. These principles emerge from Hirsch's understanding of the commandment of "love your neighbour as yourself." In his interpretation of this commandment Hirsch explained that the love of God also necessitates human love for all of God's creations. . . . Hirsch's commentary which viewed the commandment of "love your neighbour as yourself" as a principle relating to the love and concern of humans with all of creation is unique in the orthodox world. This approach, which still requires discussion and development, could act as a blueprint for a Jewish environmental ethic that would be adopted by contemporary Jewish orthodoxy.[145]

The next conclusion is that the vast majority of Bible interpreters based their glosses on the midrash. The midrash itself offered more than one possible interpretation for key aspects of Genesis 9:5 and Deuteronomy 20:19–20. For instance, in Genesis 9:5 the most significant issue that the exegetes contended with is whether the text is a prohibition against murder or suicide. The vast majority of those who commented on the verse fell into one camp or the other. The midrash, however, offered both interpretations. The interpretive style of the midrash allows such conflicting interpretations to occur. The midrash is not concerned with asserting the possibility of only one understanding of the text. Rather, it offers an abundance of different interpretations with no regard for the possible contradictions that emerge as a result. For Leviticus 19:27 the debate that emerged between the commentators concerned whether the use of scissors was prohibited or whether the prohibition against destruction of the beard

145. Samuel Chayen, "Svivah, Ḥevrah VeKhalkalah BeHagutam shel HaRav Shimshon Raphael Hirsch VeDoctor Yitzḥak Breuer," PhD dissertation, Bar-Ilan University (Ramat-Gan, Israel, 2010), 82–83.

only referred to shaving with a razor. Again, both these approaches appeared in the midrash.

In Deuteronomy 20:19–20 the chief interpretive conundrum was understanding the phrase *"ki ha'adam etz hasadeh."* Though some commentators offered varying interpretations of these words, two distinct camps emerged: those who viewed this phrase as a rhetorical question and those who understood it as a statement. These are two vastly different interpretations. If the phrase is a rhetorical question, then these words emerge as meaning that the trees have intrinsic value and should not be destroyed on account of a war between humans. Trees are unable to remove themselves from battle, and it would be unethical to subject them to the repercussions of warfare. This position provides an ethical framework through which fruit trees are protected. The other position views the phrase as a statement equating humans to fruit trees. While it certainly provides a degree of environmental protection for fruit trees, the reasoning is not one that necessarily provides trees with moral standing. Instead, the fruit trees are to be protected because of their instrumental value. They provide humans with an important service. As an environmental ethic this approach is not as beneficial for the fruit trees, even though it may produce the same outcome. The reason that even the outcome is not guaranteed is that once one enters the world of utilitarianism, the status of the trees becomes dynamic, as we saw from the Talmudic discourse regarding the eventual cutting down of even fruit trees.[146]

We might also consider two alternative ways to understand the differences in interpretation. The first, regarding Rashi's gloss, is that it is not the tree that has moral standing, but the human. The warring army does not cut down the fruit trees for the sake of the trees, but for their own moral development. Cutting down trees needlessly works against the inculcation of good character. Such a reading is consistent with the views of scholars such as the author of *Sefer haḤinukh*, who in his rationalization of *bal tashḥit* suggests that the commandment comes to teach us to love what is good. Another possibility to consider is that ibn Ezra's gloss stating that human life is dependent on the fruit of the tree is in fact less utilitarian than at first glance. It is possible to read the verse in a way that offers a message of deep ecological thought; the tree is a microcosm of the environment, and so, too, is the human. Harming the tree harms the human. If we scale

146. See b*Baba Qama* 91b.

this line of thought upward, harming the environment is harmful to humans, because humans are the environment. Yet such a reading is constructivist in its approach, and ibn Ezra's interpretation of the verse was probably much closer to the utilitarian notion already mentioned.

The debate on how to read this verse is well established in the commentaries, with exegetes taking positions on the matter from Saadiah onward. Once again, the midrash offered more than one way to read the verse. This, of course, is not to say that nothing new of interest has emerged over the past 2000 years in the understanding of the verses. Indeed, Rashbam and Alsheikh offer alternatives to the midrash, together with commentators such as Meyuḥas bar Eliyahu, Samson Raphael Hirsch, Samuel David Luzzatto, and others who go beyond the midrashic rubric. Rather, while the general trend in interpretation has not varied greatly, the nuances offered by some of the exegetes become the focus of interest. In other words, what is of interest in the various interpretations of these verses cannot necessarily be found through a superficial reading of the glosses but rather by reading them through a magnifying glass such as we have demonstrated above.

In summary, we have seen the glosses of a very considerable number of exegetes on the relevant verses. Through these commentaries and interpretations we have seen the major and minor trends in the scholarship. None of the three key verses analyzed could be understood in only a single way. The original intention of the verses is beyond anyone's capacity to discern, which is possibly why there is no consensus with regard to their interpretation. This variety, while perhaps frustrating to the purist, is what creates the richness of the Jewish tradition histories.

Amidst all the various interpretations it is possible to hone in on the interpretive trajectory that connects the verses. The majority position was that Genesis 9:5 should be understood as a prohibition against suicide, with a minority position in this group asserting that the prohibition includes all forms of self-harm. Even if it is understood as a prohibition against murder, this does not preclude the interpretation of the prohibition to be against suicide, because suicide is the murder of oneself. Just as harming someone is a step in the direction of murder, self-inflicted harm is a step toward the direction of suicide. Likewise, the majority position on "*ki ha'adam etz hasadeh*" in Deuteronomy 20:19 was that of the plain sense (*peshat*) commentators who view fruit trees as an extension of the self. Human dependency on food makes destroying it a step toward destroying humans, and as the expectation of the verse is that the Israelites will emerge victorious in the war, the fruit trees in question actually belong to them. As such, destroying these trees would be equivalent to harming oneself. In other words, destroying fruit trees would be a transgression of the specific prohibitions of both Deuteronomy 20:19 and Genesis 9:5. Connecting the two specific prohibitions is a common principle: the general prohibition against wastefulness and wanton destruction. It can be argued that the connection between these two verses is facilitated by Leviticus 19:27. Understanding that the prohibition of *lo tashḥit* in Leviticus is in fact a prohibition against self-inflicted harm (as Baḥya bar Asher clearly does) strengthens the argument made above in two ways. First, it provides the prohibition against self-inflicted harm found in Genesis 9:5 with a name or category: *lo/bal tashḥit*. Also, it facilitates the connection between Genesis 9:5 and Deuteronomy 20:19. The *lo tashḥit* of Leviticus and Deuteronomy can be understood as two manifestations of what is in fact the same general prohibition.

In approaching Deuteronomy 20:19–20 after examining its tradition histories of Jewish Bible commentary, it is possible to see *bal tashḥit* as an holistic ethic. Deuteronomy 20:19–20 presents an example of a situation where tangible goods are protected from destruction in the most extreme circumstances, in which the enemies' property might be considered to hold no value whatsoever. By prohibiting suicide or self-harm, Genesis 9:5 prohibits the destruction of the entity of the greatest possible value, one's own life. One deals with things, the other with people. Together, these two extreme scenarios create a complete ethic regarding wastefulness/destruction.

The protected status given to fruit trees offered by the literal reading of Deuteronomy 20:19 is in fact a more realistic form of environmentalism. With all the different forces at play in the real world, it is unlikely that anything but an anthropocentric form of environmentalism can truly work. When it comes to survival, evidence shows that humans would be willing to cut down even the last tree.[147] In other

147. See for example Jared Diamond, "Chapter Two: Twilight at Easter," in *Collapse: How Societies Choose to Fail or Succeed* (New York: Penguin Books), 2011; Partha S. Dasgupta, "Population, Poverty and the Local Environment," *Scientific American* 272, no. 2 (February, 1995): 40–45, and *Seeing the Forest and the Trees: Human-Environment Interactions in Forest Ecosystems*, eds. Emilio F. Moran and Elinor Ostrom (Cambridge, MA: MIT Press, 2005).

words, ecocentrism, while a valuable environmental theory, simply does not work in practice. To work, environmentalism must provide for human needs and moderate human wants.

The interplay of both the ecocentric and anthropocentric approaches is necessary for a real-world setting. The anthropocentric/utilitarian approach allows human societies and cultures to flourish. It allows nature to be exploited, but only to a degree that does not jeopardize the integrity of human existence. Once overexploitation occurs, the sustainability of human life itself is compromised, which contradicts the preservationist notion presented in Deuteronomy 20:19. Confronting consumption and understanding when the transition from exploitation to overexploitation occurs is nigh impossible. Also, adding to this difficulty is the reality of inequality in an age of globalization. Can limits be placed on people in Africa who have not received their fair share of the environment's bounty while others in North America have clearly exceeded theirs? This is where the ecocentric approach acts to balance the scales. As mentioned, ecocentrism can truly only work in a theoretical framework. Nevertheless, certain aspects of ecocentrism can be put into play in the attempt to set and enforce limits on consumption. Humans will always need to exploit nature to some degree. Trees need to be cut down to build homes and mountains need to be mined to secure resources essential to human survival in our time. At the same time, viewing the natural world as having value for humans and having intrinsic value instills in humans an appreciation for the environment. This appreciation can be a considerable force in moderating human desire to consume. Ecocentrism can create a buffer zone that prevents a strictly anthropocentric approach from exceeding reasonable limits and thereby reaching the point of overexploitation, to the detriment of both humans and the environment. Both ecocentrism and anthropocentrism can be found in Hirsch's writings. He did not advocate non-use, simply wise use. These approaches are included within theocentrism; all creation is imbued with Divine value. Only God has true ownership. Thus, even nonhuman creation cannot be wantonly wasted or destroyed.

The remaining biblical texts, together with the rabbinic and legal texts found throughout this book, all have their place in the intellectual history of the prohibition against wastefulness. Moreover, it is not just the interpretations I highlighted that contribute to building *bal tashḥit* as a concept, but also the entire range of other interpretations. Together, they all contribute to the evolving intellectual history of the concept. One must also take into consideration the wide variety of other verses that are beyond the scope of this work but at the same time have surely made their mark on the evolution of the concept of *bal tashḥit*. Among these biblical texts one could include texts such as Isaiah 44:23 and 55:12, Psalms 96:12 and 148:7–12, and 1 Chronicles 16:31–33, which present trees together with other animate and inanimate creations as sentient beings that can rejoice and offer praise to God.

Chapter 3

Codes and Their Cognates

The next stage in charting the evolution of the prohibition against wastefulness/destruction is to look at how it developed throughout history in the various codes of Jewish law. Unfortunately, there is not enough extant material from the *geonim* of Babylonia to chart their contributions to the evolution of the prohibition in the centuries after the redaction of the Babylonian Talmud. Since the positions of the *geonim* are not mentioned with regard to *bal tashḥit* in the scholarship that succeeded them, it is possible that they did not play a significant role in the conceptualization of the prohibition and the ethic that flows from it. Despite this lack, other codes of Jewish law had a considerable and lasting impact on the development of *bal tashḥit.*

We must ask, Where do the codes fit relative to the material discussed thus far? Outwardly, the Talmud appears to have a topical arrangement. Even from the small number of examples presented earlier, however, we can see that the rabbis often went off on tangents, making the material confusing and giving it a disorderly appearance. The goal of the authors of the codes was to present Jewish law in a more direct, topical, effective, and accessible manner than the Talmud. For instance, Maimonides stated that his *Mishneh Torah* would be the only book anyone would need to access knowledge of Jewish law.[1] His approach has been both criticized and lauded throughout history, for many reasons. In his code he presented only the law without the Talmudic discussion. This is particularly important for the development of the concept of *bal tashḥit.* As we will see with

1. Moshe ben Maimon, *Mishneh Torah: Hu HaYad HaḤazaqah LeRabbeinu Moshe ben Maimon, Haqdamat HaRambam, Sefer HaMada,* Vol. 2, ed. Mordekhai Dov Rabinovitz (Jerusalem: Mossad HaRav Kook, 1958), 15.

regard to *bal tashḥit*, the aspects of the tannaitic and amoraic deliberations that Maimonides chose to mute or highlight had an enduring impact. Due to Maimonides's stature, his presentation of any given law influenced its subsequent reception. As Isadore (Yitzḥak) Twersky writes, "Their [Maimonides's writings'] influence, direct as well as indirect, reflected through many works in various genres by a host of authors, was global."[2]

Not all the codes had the same approach as Maimonides in their presentation of *halakhah*. While their goal was similar to Maimonides's insofar as their quest was for a simplified version of Jewish law, unlike him not all of them limited themselves to merely stating the law. To varying degrees, they presented some of the deliberations found in the traditional sources with regard to these laws. This procedure allowed for an understanding of the process through which they reached their conclusions and illustrated that there is not always consensus on a particular legal decision.

The goal of this chapter is to illustrate how the various codes developed the prohibition against wastefulness and wanton destruction. Specifically, this chapter highlights the aspects of *bal tashḥit* retained from the rabbinic sages by the authors of the major codes and how their conceptualization of the prohibition contributed to its evolution. Only the most influential codes, those with the greatest impact on the Jewish tradition, are presented here, together with their cognates and their commentaries.[3] These codes include Maimonides's (1138–1204, Spain, Morocco, Land of Israel, and Egypt) *Mishneh Torah*, Yaakov bar Asher's (c. 1270–1343, Germany and Spain) *Arba'ah Turim* (*Tur*), and Yosef Karo's (1488–1575, Spain, Portugal, Turkey, Bulgaria, and Land of Israel) *Shulḥan Arukh*. Maimonides's preamble to his code, *Sefer HaMitzvot*, and a cognate of his code, *Sefer HaḤinukh* (thirteenth century, Spain) of anonymous authorship, often attributed to Aharon HaLevi of Barcelona, but decisively proved to be authored by his brother Pinḥas HaLevi,[4] are also included in this chapter.

2. Isadore Twersky, *Introduction to the Code of Maimonides (Mishneh Torah)* (New Haven, CT: Yale University Press, 1980), 1.

3. It was decided not to include Saadiah Gaon's (*Rasag*) (882–942, Egypt and Babylonia) *Sefer HaMitzvot LaRasag*, Shimon Qayyara's (*Bahag*) (8th century Babylonia) *Sefer Halakhot Gedolot*, and Yitzḥak Alfasi's (*Rif*) (1013–1103, North Africa and Spain) *Sefer HaHalakhot* due to a lack of relevant material. Moses ben Yaakov of Coucy's (thirteenth century, France and Spain) *Sefer Mitzvot Gadol* is presented only where relevant.

4. Israel Ta-Shma, *"Meḥabro HaAmiti shel Sefer 'HaḤinukh,'" Kiryat Sefer* 55 (1980): 787–90.

Part of the evolution of *bal tashḥit* as a concept occurs through its extended use in the codes and their commentaries. It would be too lengthy a process to deal with every single instance in this body of literature that deals with wastefulness/destruction, yet does not use the term *bal tashḥit*. The sages of the Talmud turned *bal tashḥit* into a concept, and as the codes come historically much later, it is likely that further conceptualization of *bal tashḥit* will be done using the term itself.[5] But such an endeavor is unnecessary to demonstrate the trends that are important in the conceptualization of *bal tashḥit*. Instead, this chapter focuses on collecting and analyzing the material that demonstrates either continuity or change from the understanding of the prohibition against wastefulness found in earlier material. To help readers chart their way through the material, this chapter is organized typologically (as is the following chapter on responsa), and diachronically within each topic. A number of the subjects dealt with in this chapter were not discussed in the rabbinic chapter. This is generally because the earlier rabbinic texts did not use the terminology of *bal tashḥit*.

Fruit Trees and Wastefulness/Destruction in General

Maimonides, *Sefer HaMitzvot LaRambam* (Book of Commandments)

> ***Mitzvat Lo Ta'aseh* 57**. The 57th commandment is that when laying siege upon a city we were warned not to destroy the fruit trees for the purpose of harming its inhabitants and tormenting their hearts.[6] God commanded (Deuteronomy 20:19): "You must not destroy its trees . . . you may eat of them, but you must not cut them down." And so too is all wastefulness included in this commandment, such as burning a garment for no purpose or breaking a utensil for no reason; these too are transgressions of "do not destroy" (*lo tashḥit*) and the transgressor is liable. In b*Makkot* 22a it

5. This, of course, is not exclusively the case, as can be seen from the important contributions made by biblical commentators highlighted in the previous chapter.

6. The comments in rabbinic literature until now did not mention destruction for the sake of "harming its inhabitants and tormenting their hearts." Previously the issue seemed connected to trees as an obstruction to the besieging army or as a hiding place for the inhabitants of the city.

> is clarified that anyone who cuts down good trees is liable, the forewarning being (Deuteronomy 20:19): "for you may eat of them, but you must not cut them down." The clarification of this commandment has already been included in the discussion in chapter 2 of b*Baba Batra* (26a).[7]

Following the rabbinic precedent, Maimonides expanded the specific commandment of not cutting down fruit trees during wartime to a general prohibition against wastefulness and wanton destruction. Special attention needs to be paid to the language used by Maimonides in the expansion of the prohibition from fruit trees to all things. He defined wastefulness as an act that is done for no purpose, in other words, wantonly. This suggests the possibility that an act of wastefulness or destruction is permitted if it has a purpose. In his *Mishneh Torah,* Laws of Kings, this purposeless destruction is conceptualized through a term coined by Maimonides, *derekh hashḥatah* (a destructive manner), and is elaborated on below.

Maimonides, Mishneh Torah, Laws of Kings and Their Wars (*Hilkhot Melakhim UMilḥamoteihem*)

> **6:8**. Fruit-bearing trees outside of the [besieged] city are not to be cut down and they must not be deprived of their water source in order that they dry out, as it is written (Deuteronomy 20:19), "You must not destroy its trees," and anyone who cuts down such trees is liable. This is applicable not only during siege, but in any place where a person cuts down a fruit tree in a destructive manner (*derekh hashḥatah*) the person is liable. It is, however, permissible to cut down a fruit tree if it is damaging other fruit trees, or it is damaging someone else's field, or if it has greater value cut down; the Torah only prohibited cutting down such trees in a destructive manner (*derekh hashḥatah*).
>
> **6:9.** Any non-fruit-bearing tree may be cut down even for no purpose, as may a fruit-bearing tree that has aged and

7. Moshe ben Maimon, *Sefer HaMitzwot: Book of Commandments*, Vol. 1, ed. Mordekhai Yehudah Leib Zaqash, trans.Yosef Kapaḥ (Jerusalem: Mossad HaRav Kook, 1958). My translation from the Hebrew.

produces such a small quantity of fruit that it is not worth the effort that it requires to tend to it. How much must an olive tree produce so that it is not cut down? Such a tree must produce [at least] a quarter *qab* of olives, while a palm tree that produces [at least] a *qab* of dates must not be cut down.

6:10 And not only are fruit-bearing trees included in this prohibition, but so too anyone who breaks utensils, tears garments, destroys a building, blocks a spring of water, and wastes food in a destructive manner (*derekh hashḥatah*) transgresses "do not destroy [*lo tashḥit*], but is only liable for lashes for transgressing a rabbinic edict [and not a biblical commandment]."[8, 9]

This is the central Maimonidean text dealing with the prohibition against wastefulness and wanton destruction. As demonstrated in the introduction, it is often cited in environmental writings discussing *bal tashḥit*, and it is one of the main texts of reference in the responsa literature. This is based on Maimonides's stature as one of the greatest Jewish scholars of all time. Another significant reason for Maimonides's predominance is the simplicity and clarity of his presentation. We are concerned with the intellectual history of the ethic of *bal tashḥit*, so it is important not only to demonstrate what Maimonides contributed to advance the concept, but to illustrate how he changed the concept from its manifestation in the Talmud. To accomplish this goal, each of the three *halakhot* from the Laws of Kings is analyzed, illustrating how they are similar to the rabbinic understanding of the prohibition, and the manner in which the prohibition evolved into what might be called the Maimonidean trajectory.

In Laws of Kings 6:8, we observe a number of important elements. First, Maimonides expanded the prohibition against cutting down fruit trees through his exegesis of Deuteronomy 20:19. He removed the prohibition from its wartime context and expanded it to include

8. The distinction between a biblical commandment and a rabbinic edict is made because there is no explicit commandment in the Torah prohibiting wastefulness, whereas there is an explicit commandment prohibiting the cutting down of fruit trees.

9. Moshe ben Maimon, *Mishneh Torah: Hu HaYad HaḤazaqah LeRabbeinu Moshe ben Maimon, Sefer Shofetim*, Vol. 17 (Jerusalem: Mossad HaRav Kook, 1959).

fruit trees in all places. From our analysis of the prohibition as it appeared in rabbinic texts, it is clear that the prohibition was already understood to apply to contexts beyond warfare. Even though this is clearly implied in the tannaitic and amoraic literature, nowhere is it explicitly mentioned. The examples brought by Maimonides all appear in the Talmud: fruit trees may be cut down if they are damaging other fruit trees (b*Baba Batra* 26a and b*Baba Qama* 92a), if they are damaging someone else's field (b*Baba Batra* 26a), or if they are more valuable cut down than as trees (b*Baba Qama* 91b). Thus, through his assertion that "This is applicable not only during siege, but in any place where a person cuts down a fruit tree in a destructive manner he is liable," we see that Maimonides expanded the parameters of the prohibition in an explicit manner. Nowhere prior to Maimonides do we see this idea explicitly articulated. Through this assertion, however, he created new parameters for the prohibition that do not appear in the Talmud even implicitly, namely that *bal tashḥit* only applies in situations where the act is done in a destructive manner (*derekh hashḥatah*). Maimonides implied that such acts are committed with the intent to destroy.

A number of indicators support the claim that Maimonides was referring to acts that are deliberately wasteful/destructive. First and foremost, a person is only liable for capital or corporal punishment for intentionally committed transgressions. All unintentional transgressions either go unpunished or are liable for fines or various offerings at the Temple.[10] For example, in Laws Concerning Unintentional Transgressions (*Hilkhot Shegagot*) 1:1, Maimonides asserted that all unintentional transgressions of prohibitions for which one is liable for "untimely death by heaven" (*karet*) one must sacrifice a sin offering in lieu of punishment. Thus, because Maimonides clarified that a person is liable for corporal punishment for acts committed in a destructive manner (*derekh hashḥatah*), he must have been referring to acts that were deliberately destructive (either the act itself or the direct consequences of the act).

The notion that an action can be punished on the basis of intent is reinforced in Maimonides's Laws Concerning the Sabbath (*Hilkhot Shabbat*) 1:17. In this law, Maimonides asserted that a person who ruins/destroys (*meqalqel*) items on the Sabbath is exempt from punish-

10. For a fuller description of the parameters of unintentional transgressions, see Moshe ben Maimon, *Mishneh Torah—Hilkhot Shegagot* (Laws Concerning Unintentional Transgressions).

ment for desecrating the Sabbath (but is still liable for transgressing the prohibition against wastefulness/destruction). In his conclusion to this commandment, Maimonides added the words "because his intent was to destroy" (*ho'il vekavanato leqalqel*), affirming that there is only a transgression when there is intent. The person either had to deliberately desecrate the Sabbath, or deliberately commit a destructive act. If a person is not deliberately engaged in destruction, but rather is intending to desecrate the Sabbath, the person would be liable for desecrating the Sabbath (even though his action was also unintentionally destructive). If, however, a person is intending neither to desecrate the Sabbath nor to intentionally be destructive, that person would not be liable at all. Maimonides's statement "because his intent was to destroy" demonstrates not only that Maimonides was clearly concerned with the intent of the individual committing the act, but was specifically concerned with the motive of wastefulness/destruction. With regard to *bal tashḥit*, if a person's intention was not to be destructive/wasteful (*derekh hashḥatah*), the person is not liable. Finally, understanding Maimonides's *derekh hashḥatah* as destructive intent is supported by four different translations of the *Mishneh Torah* into English. All these translations translate the term *derekh hashḥatah* as either "destructive intent" or "deliberate destruction."[11]

Maimonides took the various examples in the Talmud that discussed the prohibition against cutting down trees and added to them the parameter of destructive intent. While it can be argued that this is implied in the Talmud, the generalization suggested by Maimonides appears to expand the exceptions to the prohibition. The generalization offered in the Talmud by Ravina (b*Baba Qama* 91b), who claimed that as long as a fruit tree is worth more cut down than rooted in the earth it is permissible to remove it, is still limited to economic parameters.

---

11. See Moshe ben Maimon, *The Code of Maimonides*,Book 14: *The Book of Judges*, trans. Abraham M. Hershman (New Haven, CT: Yale University Press, 1949); Moshe ben Maimon, *Kings, Their Wars and the Messiah: From the Mishneh Torah of Maimonides*, trans. H. M. Russell and J. Weinberg (Edinburgh: Royal College of Physicians of Edinburgh, Publication No. 61, 1987); Moshe ben Maimon, *Maimonides, Mishneh Torah: Hilchot Melachim U'Milchamoteihem—The Laws of Kings and Their Wars*, trans. Eliyahu Touger (New York: Maznaim Publishing Corporation, 1987). Moses Hyamson did not translate this part of the *Mishneh Torah*, but in his translation of Maimonides's *Hilkhot Yesodei HaTorah* 6:7, he translates the term *derekh hashḥatah* as "destructive intent." Moshe ben Maimon, *Mishneh Torah: The Book of Knowledge*, ed. and trans. Moses Hyamson (Jerusalem: Boys Town Publishers, 1965).

The parameters of destructive intent offered by Maimonides include the economic variable, but go significantly further in providing allowances for cutting down fruit trees. One can easily imagine a scenario where cutting down a fruit tree results in an economic loss but the act is not done with destructive intent.[12] Thus, the Maimonidean creation of the concept of "destructive intent" (*derekh hashḥatah*) resulted in a more lax system than the one found in the Talmud insofar as fruit trees are concerned.

Halakhah 9 also shows a strong deviation from the prohibition against wastefulness as found in the classic rabbinic tradition. Maimonides asserted that a non-fruit-bearing tree may be cut down under any circumstance, even needlessly. The only way to understand such an extreme position in reference to non-fruit-bearing trees is to go back to the verses in Deuteronomy. The prohibition in Deuteronomy 20:19 with regard to fruit trees is juxtaposed in the very next verse with a directive to cut down non-fruit-bearing trees in their stead. Contextually, the verse indicates that non-fruit-bearing trees are to be cut down for the purpose of building siege-works, but removed from its context the verse can be taken to mean that it is permitted to destroy non-fruit-bearing trees without reason, that is, wantonly. It is difficult to understand his approach to non-fruit-bearing trees in any other way, especially in light of the very next clause.

Halakhah 10 is an extension of *bal tashḥit* to include other forms of wastefulness and wanton destruction. Even though Maimonides does not specifically state in the *Mishneh Torah* that the prohibition includes all things, his position on the general applicability of *bal tashḥit* is clear from what he wrote in *Sefer HaMitzvot*, cited above. The specific examples presented as included under *bal tashḥit* appear to be a collection from earlier sources, including Scripture: breaking utensils (t*Baba Qama* 9:31), tearing garments (t*Baba Qama* 9:31 and b*Qiddushin* 32a), and blocking a spring (2 Kings 3:19), while the waste of food appears in multiple places in b*Berakhot*.[13]

12. For instance, to take a modern example, a fruit tree might be blocking a window but providing shade at the same time. Cutting it down would unblock the window, but also raise the electricity bills due to increased air conditioning.

13. The examples of wastefulness in b*Berakhot* do not mention the specific prohibition of *bal tashḥit* even though it is implied. These examples have not been presented and are beyond the scope of this work.

Sefer HaḤinukh (The Book of Moral Education)

The main goal of the *Sefer HaḤinukh* is to offer morally based rationalizations of the commandments as listed by Maimonides in his *Sefer HaMitzvot*. Although *Sefer HaḤinukh* is anonymous, many have attributed it to Aharon HaLevi of Barcelona. As mentioned above, Israel Ta-Shma convincingly claimed that the work belonged to his older brother, Pinḥas HaLevi. Though not much is known about HaLevi the elder, Aharon HaLevi was one of Yonah of Gerona's students. As we saw in the rabbinic chapter, Yonah of Gerona was one of the few voices in a fragmented line of transmission keeping the connection between wastefulness and self-harm alive. HaLevi (cited below) views the prohibition against wastefulness as an issue of human morality. His approach, however, does not connect the prohibition against wastefulness to the prohibition against self-harm.

Law 529. The author claimed that we learn from Deuteronomy 20:19 not only about the prohibition against cutting down fruit trees during wartime, but that all forms of wastefulness and destruction are included under the umbrella of this prohibition. He asserted that the purpose of this commandment was to instruct our inner selves to embrace goodness and usefulness. The love of goodness distances one from evil and destruction. Most importantly he claimed that "this is the way of the righteous and people of deeds who love peace and delight in the goodness of human beings and draw them near to the Torah; they do not waste even a grain of mustard in this world. Their instinct when encountering wastefulness and destruction is to try to prevent it with all their strength."[14] *Sefer HaḤinukh* is one of the only sources to discuss the rationale behind the prohibition against wastefulness/destruction. As can be seen, his rationalization could be construed as being in step with an environmental ethic. Those who pursue goodness and peace avoid even the smallest degree of wastefulness. Even the most minute wastefulness conceivable, described here as "a grain of mustard," is seen as an extension of the extent to which one should aspire to observe this commandment. *Sefer HaḤinukh* understood *bal tashḥit* to be a theoretical ideal, perhaps never fully achievable, but

14. Pinḥas HaLevi (?), *Sefer HaḤinukh*, ed. Ḥaim Dov Chavel (Jerusalem: Mossad HaRav Kook, 1952).

certainly something to aspire toward. According to the author, those who attempt to uphold this ethic are pursuers of goodness, while those who transgress it have an evil inclination. To reinforce this point he presented the *baraita*,[15] which states that those who engage in destructive behavior also have the propensity to worship idols.

He built on the theory of the prohibition with practical guidelines based on those established by the rabbis of the Talmud. These guidelines outline the application of the prohibition in the real world, at least in part. Using Maimonides's terminology, *Sefer HaḤinukh* asserted that the prohibition only applied to cutting down fruit trees in a destructive manner (*derekh hashḥatah*). When there are utilitarian reasons for cutting down a fruit tree, it is permissible. Thus, in a practical sense, the prohibition was understood only to apply to the intent of the individual, and not only with regard to fruit trees, but to all things. One can assume, of course, that the author understood the utilitarian exceptions through which one is permitted to engage in wastefulness/destruction to be under the moral sway of the theory on which they are based and actively limited by it.

Interestingly, like Maimonides, *Sefer HaḤinukh* held the position that the only things that can be destroyed, even wantonly, are non-fruit-producing trees. Again, this exception can really only be understood in light of Deuteronomy 20:20, in which permission is granted to destroy non-fruit-bearing trees. The Torah granted permission "to destroy" (*lehashḥit*) the non-fruit-bearing trees, which appears to have been incorporated into *halakhah* and stands out as an exception to the rule. Samson Raphael Hirsch addressed this issue, as has been shown in the Bible chapter. Hirsch was clearly aware of the problematic that arose from the wording of the text, and its subsequent appearance in Maimonides's code. Hence he asserted that non-fruit-bearing trees cannot be wantonly destroyed. This assertion would not have been necessary if Maimonides, and subsequently *Sefer HaḤinukh*, had not specifically listed non-fruit-bearing trees as an exception to the prohibition.

Self-Harm

In the rabbinic chapter we observed an amoraic splitting of the prohibition against self-harm from the tannaitic understanding of the

15. See t*Baba Qama* 9:31 and b*Shabbat* 105b found in the rabbinic chapter.

prohibition against wastefulness. In that chapter we also noted that there was a small but qualitatively important group of tradents who understood the prohibition against self-harm to be a subcategory of *bal tashḥit*. Due to the severing of this connection by the *amoraim*, it is not obvious how subsequent generations of scholars would relate to these prohibitions. This section offers an analysis of the various passages found in the legal codes and the commentaries and compositions on these works in order to see the manner in which they understood the prohibition against self-harm. In particular I examine whether any connections were made between the prohibition against self-harm and *bal tashḥit*, or if the earlier muting of this relationship was upheld.

Below are the laws in the various codes that deal explicitly with the prohibition against self-harm. It is worth noting that nowhere in the codes are these laws connected to fruit trees or to wastefulness in general.

Maimonides, *Mishneh Torah*, Laws Regarding Those Who Cause Injury to People or Property (*Hilkhot Ḥovel UMeiziq*)

> **5:1**. A person is not allowed to harm himself or others . . .[16]

Yaakov bar Asher, *Tur*, *Ḥoshen Mishpat*, Laws Regarding Those Who Cause Injury to People (*Hilkhot Ḥovel BaḤavero*)

> **420.** A person who harms himself, even though he is not permitted [he is not liable for punishment], others who harm him are liable. Meir HaLevi Abulafia (*Ramah*) wrote that this is not the *halakhah*. Rather, a person is permitted to harm himself.[17]

---

16. Moshe ben Maimon, *Mishneh Torah: Hu HaYad HaḤazaqah LeRabbeinu Moshe ben Maimon, Sefer Neziqin*, Vol. 14, ed. Moshe Reich (Jerusalem: Mossad HaRav Kook, 1959). Moshe bar Yaakov of Coucy had a very similar approach to that of Maimonides (*Sefer Mitzvot Gadol, Aseh* 70)—Moses of Coucy, *Sefer Mitzvot Gadol*, Vol. 2, *Aseh* (Jerusalem: Offset Brody-Katz, 1973).

17. Yaakov bar Asher, *Tur: Ḥoshen Mishpat*, Vol. 2 (Jerusalem: Makhon Ḥatam Sofer, 1972).

Yosef Karo, *Shulḥan Arukh*, *Ḥoshen Mishpat*, Laws Regarding Those Who Cause Injury to People (*Hilkhot Ḥovel BaḤavero*)

> **420:31**. A person who harms himself, even though he is not permitted [he is not liable for punishment], others who harm him are liable.[18]

All three authors of the major codes were of the opinion that self-harm is forbidden. Even though Yaakov bar Asher himself asserted that a person is not allowed to engage in self-harm, he presented Abulafia's opinion showing that there is no consensus on the matter. Yosef Karo, in his *Beit Yosef, Ḥoshen Mishpat* 420:21, discussed Yaakov bar Asher's mention of Abulafia's rejection of the claim that there is a prohibition against harming oneself.[19] Even though we just observed that Yosef Karo accepted the position that one is prohibited from engaging in self-harm, he justified Abulafia's position by stating that nowhere do we find Rabbi Eleazar HaQappar's approach with regard to Nazirites abstaining from wine as *halakhah* (b*Baba Qama* 91b). Yoel Sirkis (1561–1640, Poland) in his *Bayit Ḥadash*, Laws Regarding those Who Cause Injury to People 420:21, also discussed Abulafia's assertion that it is permitted to engage in self-harm by claiming that Rabbi Eleazar HaQappar's opinion is his alone, that it goes against the majority, and the majority opinion rules.[20] These statements are of particular importance because they reinforce the approach that not everyone accepted the amoraic conclusion that the prohibition against self-harm is derived from Rabbi Eleazar HaQappar's midrash.

Those contributing the most to the tradition connecting the prohibition against self-harm to the prohibition against wastefulness are Shneiur Zalman of Liadi (1745–1813, Russia) and Shlomo Gantzfried (1802–1884, Hungary). Most telling is the framework in which Shneiur Zalman brought up the prohibition against wastefulness.

---

18. Yosef Karo, *Shulḥan Arukh: Ḥoshen Mishpat*, Vol. 2 (New York: Grossman's Publishing House, 1954).

19. Yosef Karo, *Beit Yosef: Ḥoshen Mishpat*, in Yaakov bar Asher, *Tur: Ḥoshen Mishpat*, Vol. 2 (Jerusalem: Makhon Ḥatam Sofer, 1972).

20. Yoel Sirkis, *Bayit Ḥadash: Ḥoshen Mishpat*, in Yaakov bar Asher, *Tur: Ḥoshen Mishpat*, Vol. 2 (Jerusalem: Makhon Ḥatam Sofer, 1972).

Shulḥan Arukh HaRav, *Ḥoshen Mishpat*, Laws of Protecting the Body (*Hilkhot Shemirat HaGuf*)

> **14.** Just as he must be careful with his body so that he does not destroy it, ruin it, or harm it, so too must he be careful with his property so that he does not destroy it, ruin it or harm it. Any person who breaks utensils, or tears clothing, or destroys a building, or blocks up a spring, or wastes food or drink, or renders them unfit for consumption (or throws money away), and anyone who ruins anything from which people can derive benefit/enjoyment transgresses a negative commandment, as it was said (Deuteronomy 20:19): "Do not destroy its trees . . ." (and if the Torah issued a warning with regard to [the possessions] of Gentiles with whom they are warring, this applies *a fortiori* to the possessions of Jews or even ownerless items). This applies even if his purpose is to demonstrate anger and wrath and to project his fear/awe on insubordinate household members.[21]

Shlomo Gantzfried, *Qitzur Shulḥan Arukh*

> **190:3**. Just as a person must be careful with his body so that he does not destroy, ruin or harm it, as it was said (Deuteronomy 4:9): "But take utmost care and watch yourselves scrupulously," so too must a person be careful with his possessions not to destroy, ruin or harm them. Any person who breaks utensils, or tears clothing, or wastes food or drink, or renders them unfit for consumption, or throws money away, and anyone who ruins anything from which people can derive benefit/enjoyment transgresses a negative commandment, as it was said (Deuteronomy 20:19): "Do not destroy its trees . . ."[22]

21. Shneiur Zalman, *Shulḥan Arukh HaRav*, Part 6, *Ḥoshen Mishpat* (Jerusalem: Even Yisroel Publishing, 2011).

22. Shlomo Gantzfried, *Qitzur Shulḥan Arukh*, Vol. 2, ed. Elyaqim Shlanger (Bnei Braq, Israel: Seminar Be'er Yaakov, 1978).

Both these works are cognates of the *Shulḥan Arukh*. The most obvious difference between these two works and the *Shulḥan Arukh* is that they describe *bal tashḥit* as a general ethic, and not just as one that applies to specific circumstances. In this aspect they resemble much more closely Maimonides's description of *bal tashḥit*, especially in their lists of behavior to which *bal tashḥit* applies. They differ from Maimonides in two key aspects. The first is that they both viewed the prohibition against wastefulness as being intrinsically connected to the prohibition against self-harm while Maimonides made no connection between the two, save implicitly in Laws of Ethical Behavior (*Hilkhot De'ot*). In fact, the language that they use to link self-harm with general wastefulness is "just as . . . so too." This formulation is used very frequently throughout rabbinic literature and is indicative of an analogous relationship between two categories. The second is through their generalization of the prohibition. After listing the specific behavior that would result in a transgression of *bal tashḥit*, they generalized the prohibition by stating that the transgressor includes "anyone who ruins anything from which a person can derive benefit/enjoyment." This is a qualitatively different assertion from that of Maimonides who in his generalization of the prohibition stated "And so too is all wastefulness included in this commandment."[23]

Even though Maimonides did not include a human parameter in his description of *bal tashḥit* found in *Sefer HaMitzvot*, he defined the prohibition in his *Mishneh Torah* as applying only in situations when the act is done in a destructive manner (*derekh hashḥatah*). In other words, while Maimonides at first appears to be more inclusive in his definition of the prohibition, by adding the parameter of destructive intent, he becomes much more lenient in his definition of what behavior is included in the prohibition of *bal tashḥit*. In light of this, when compared to Shneiur Zalman and Gantzfried, it can be understood that Maimonides may allow the destruction of something from which an individual can derive benefit/enjoyment as long as the act is not performed in a destructive manner. Alternatively, Shneiur Zalman and Gantzfried may theoretically allow something from which humans do not derive benefit/enjoyment to be destroyed in a destructive manner. This, however, would be unlikely, as Shneiur Zalman understood even ownerless items to be under the prohibition of *bal tashḥit*.

While on its surface Shneiur Zalman and Gantzfried appear to have similar approaches to the relationship between the prohibition

23. Maimonides, *Sefer HaMitzvot LaRambam—Mitzvat Lo Ta'aseh* 57.

against self-harm and the prohibition against wastefulness, there is one significant difference. Gantzfried attributed the prohibition against self-harm to a specific verse in Scripture (Deuteronomy 4:9: "take utmost care"),[24] while Shneiur Zalman did not provide a reference. This is noteworthy insofar as this is yet another verse from which the prohibition against self-harm is thought to be derived (even though contextually the verse is a warning against idolatry). From the various verses suggested, this perhaps is the most obvious one insofar as it is the verse that requires the least exegesis to derive this prohibition. The variety of verses associated with the prohibition against self-harm poses no difficulties for the theory of the connection of this prohibition to the prohibition against wastefulness. The environmental ethic resulting from the association of these two prohibitions does not depend on which verses they are derived from, but rather on the fact that they are conceptually connected, as they are in the writings of Shneiur Zalman and Gantzfried. What makes these scholars stand out in particular is that this association does not exist in the major codes, most notably in the *Shulḥan Arukh* on which they are based.

The notion that *bal tashḥit* applies only to things from which humans derive benefit/enjoyment is a continuation of the utilitarian approach found in the Talmud and seen in the rabbinic chapter, but it is not connected to self-harm. It is a conceptualization that enables *bal tashḥit* to work in real-world situations. After all, there are times when destroying is a necessary part of the creative process. Defining the prohibition in strictly human parameters ("anything from which a person can derive benefit/enjoyment"), however, limits the effectiveness of *bal tashḥit* as an environmental ethic by not considering the intrinsic value of the nonhuman material world. Perhaps, however, this is not as detrimental to the environmental cause as it may seem at first glance. Subjectively, it is easy to imagine certain things that one does not derive benefit/enjoyment from and could theoretically be destroyed or wasted without further consideration and with no fear of transgressing *bal tashḥit*. Objectively, however, both Shneiur Zalman and Shlomo Gantzfried iterate that the person deriving benefit/enjoyment is not a specific person, but people in general. In other words, just because I do not derive benefit/enjoyment from a particular tree, or animal, or food, or any part of nature for that matter, does not mean

24. In his gloss to Deuteronomy 4:15 that uses very similar language "be most careful," Naḥmanides writes that this is a warning to not cut down the plantings, creating another strong link between the notion of being careful and *bal tashḥit*.

that there are no people who derive benefit, thereby revoking my license to wantonly destroy/waste that particular thing. While this still phrases the ethic in anthropocentric terms and does not take into consideration the intrinsic value of the nonhuman world, by defining the parameters of the prohibition in objective terms, the end result could still offer the nonhuman world significant protection.

Other connections made in this genre of literature form less explicit links between self-harm and wastefulness. For instance, Pinḥas HaLevi, whose goal was to rationalize the commandments, discussed the prohibition against self-harm in the context of the commandment of "you shall not gash [mutilate] yourselves" (*lo titgodedu*) (*Sefer HaḤinukh*, 467).[25] This prohibition arises in Deuteronomy 14:1 in the context of forbidden mourning practices. Pinḥas HaLevi explained that this act is prohibited because it emulates idolatrous practices. In his discussion he took the act of self-harm outside of the context of mourning practice and made the general statement that "destroying our bodies and ruining ourselves is not good for us and is not the way of the wise and intelligent." Although he did not explicitly connect the prohibition against self-harm to *bal tashḥit*, there are implicit connections. For instance, he mentioned that Naḥmanides, in his Bible commentary, claimed that "you shall not gash yourselves" is what the sages meant when they stated that one is not to mourn too much (*yoter midai*) over the dead. The notion of excessiveness while mourning is connected in more than one source to *bal tashḥit*. As we observed in b*Baba Qama* 91b, Rabbi Eleazar claimed that he heard that anyone rending their clothing excessively (*yoter midai*) as a sign of mourning was transgressing the prohibition of *bal tashḥit*. In *Semaḥot* 9:23 it is asserted that anyone who buries the dead with an excessive amount (*yoter midai*) of material goods transgresses the prohibition of *bal tashḥit*. Thus, there is a conceptual connection between self-harm and wastefulness through the idea of excessive behaviors. This fits precisely within the framework discussed below in Maimonides's ethic of moderation found in Laws of Ethical Behavior 3:1 and expounded on by Abraham de Boton.

Maimonides, *Mishneh Torah*, Laws of Ethical Behavior (*Hilkhot De'ot*)

> **1:1**. Every human being is characterised by numerous moral dispositions which differ from each other and are

25. Pinḥas HaLevi (?), *Sefer HaḤinukh*, 427.

exceedingly divergent. One man is choleric, always irascible; another sedate, never angry; or, if he should become angry, is only slightly and very rarely so. One man is haughty to excess; another humble in the extreme. One is a sensualist whose lusts are never sufficiently gratified; another is so pure in soul that he does not even long for the few things that our physical nature needs. One is so greedy that all the money in the world would not satisfy him, as it is said, "He who loveth silver shall not be satisfied with silver" (Ecclesiastes 5:9). Another so curbs his desires that he is contented with very little, even with that which is insufficient, and does not bestir himself to obtain that which he really needs. One will suffer extreme hunger for the sake of saving, and does not spend the smallest coin without a pang, while another deliberately and wantonly squanders all his property. In the same way, men differ in other traits. There are, for example, the hilarious and the melancholy, the stingy and the generous, the cruel and the merciful, the timid and the stout-hearted, and so forth.[26]

3:1.[27] If a person states that "due to the fact that lust and honor and their like set one on a path of evil and remove the individual from the world, I will separate myself from these desires as much as possible and distance myself from them," until that person does not eat meat or drink wine, does not marry a woman, does not dwell in a nice abode, and does not wear fine clothing but rather wears rags and coarse wool and their like as do the priests of Edom [Christian priests], this too is a bad path and it is prohibited to follow it. The person following this path is called a sinner, as it is written with regard to the Nazirite (Numbers 6:11): "and make expiation on his behalf for the guilt that he incurred through the corpse." The sages stated that if a Nazirite who did nothing but abstain from wine requires a sin offering, how much more so does any-

26. Moshe ben Maimon, *The Book of Knowledge,* ed. and trans. Moses Hyamson (Jerusalem: Boys Town Jerusalem Publishers, 1965).

27. Some emendations to the standard Hebrew text were made based on the MS. Huntingdon 80.

> one who denies themselves anything. In light of this the sages commanded that a person should abstain only from the things that the Torah prohibited, but not prohibit for themselves through oaths and vows that which is permitted. Thus sages declared: "Are the prohibitions of the Torah insufficient that you deny yourself other things?" Similarly, those who habitually afflict themselves are not on a good path. The sages prohibited individuals from being ascetics through fasting. And with regard to all these things and their like, Solomon commanded (Ecclesiastes 7:16): "So do not overdo goodness and do not act the wise man to excess, or you may be dumbfounded."[28]

In these passages Maimonides advocated the path of moderation. In Law 1:1 he listed a large number of different excessive tendencies that characterize all people. In Law 1:3 he asserted that should people find themselves drifting toward one of the excesses, they should rectify their behavior and return to the "straight path." This law sets limits on excessive behavior, implying that one should always take the middle path and shy away from extremes. The idea of the "Golden Mean" can also be seen much earlier in Aristotelian thought (Nicomachean Ethics, Book II), which greatly influenced Maimonides. Even though Maimonides separated the prohibition against self-harm and the prohibition against wastefulness in general, in Laws of Ethical Behavior the two prohibitions once again emerge together. Excess can be found in waste of material just as it can be found in ascetic or other self-harming behaviors. According to Maimonides, the reason we are to avoid excesses is for the purpose of emulating God, which in turn he understood as walking "the straight path" (Laws of Ethical Behavior 1:5).

In Laws of Ethical Behavior 3:1, he asserted that one should avoid extremism in the form of asceticism. This *halakhah* quashes the notion that one should adopt an extreme lifestyle in the form of asceticism to avoid the temptation of sin. As such, asceticism is in itself sinful. The example presented by Maimonides of a person engaging in an ascetic lifestyle and inflicting self-harm through their asceticism is the Nazirite. As we have already observed, Rabbi Eleazar HaQappar's exegesis of Numbers 6:11 concerning the sinning Nazirite is the proof-text used by the sages to demonstrate that it is prohibited to engage in self-harm.

---

28. Moshe ben Maimon, *Sefer HaMada*.

Abraham de Boton (c.1560–c.1605, Greece and Land of Israel), in his commentary on Maimonides's *Mishneh Torah*, *Leḥem Mishneh*, Laws of Ethical Behavior 3:1, understood the prohibition against self-harm to derive from different origins.[29] He asserted that the prohibition against self-harm originates either from the prohibition of *bal tashḥit* or from Genesis 9:5 (and not from Rabbi Eleazar HaQappar's midrash). De Boton considered both to be equally appropriate. This is of great importance and has already been discussed in the rabbinic chapter, but here it serves yet another purpose. De Boton offered another way of understanding the ethic of moderation than that of Maimonides. It can be argued that for de Boton, the excesses on either side of moderation are one and the same. In other words, both asceticism (self-harm) and overindulgence (wastefulness) lead to the same place: waste/destruction of the self. This view appears to be consistent with the tannaitic approach found in t*Baba Qama* 9:31.

Even though some assumptions must be made for the above statements to be validated, a number of things are clear. First, we observe the fact that Maimonides accepted the amoraic conclusion that the prohibition against self-harm is derived from the sinning Nazirite. This is reinforced by commentaries on the *Mishneh Torah* such as Moshe ben Yosef di Trani (1505–1585, Greece and Land of Israel) (*Qiryat Sefer*, Laws Regarding Those Who Cause Injury to People or Property 5)[30] and Masoud Ḥai Roqeaḥ (1690–1768, Turkey, Land of Israel, and Libya). The latter in his *Ma'aseh Roqe'aḥ*, Laws Regarding Those Who Cause Injury to People or Property 5:1 asserted that the source of the prohibition may be either the midrashic interpretation of the Nazirite abstaining from wine or the commandment of "be most careful" (Deuteronomy 4:15).[31] Moreover, this prohibition is separate and exclusive from the prohibition against wastefulness. This specific *halakhah* is the only place where a conceptual connection is made between these prohibitions, even though, as mentioned above, discerning this connection requires a certain amount of exegesis. Another noteworthy matter is that once again, the connection to idolatry/foreign cultural practices is highlighted, as Maimonides specified that

29. Abraham de Boton, "*Leḥem Mishneh*," in *Mishneh Torah hu HaYad HaḤazaqah: Sefer HaMada* (Warsaw: Kalinberg and Partners, 1881).

30. Moshe ben Yosef di Trani, *Qiryat Sefer* (Venice: 1551).

31. Masoud Ḥai Roqeaḥ, *Sefer Ma'aseh Roqe'aḥ*, Part 4 (Bnei Braq, Israel: Samuel Akiva Schlesinger, 1964).

the reason behind this *halakhah* is distancing oneself from emulating the practices of Christian priests.

Idolatry

In the rabbinic chapter we saw an abundance of conceptual links between idolatry and wastefulness. This passage in *Sefer HaMitzvot* is connected to the argument in that chapter regarding the inherent relationship between the prohibition against wastefulness and idolatry. The exception made to the prohibition is specifically with regard to idol worship; one is prohibited to engage in destructive/wasteful behavior, save with regard to idolatry.[32]

Maimonides, *Sefer HaMitzvot LaRambam* (Book of Commandments)

Positive Commandment (*Mitzvat Aseh*) 185.

> The 185th commandment is that we have been commanded to eliminate all forms of idol worship and its houses in all manners of elimination and destruction: breaking, burning, ruining, and cutting down; each type should be destroyed by the method that suits it best. Meaning, whatever method is most expeditious in eliciting its destruction. The intention is that we should not leave any trace of them. And He, may He be praised, said [Deuteronomy 12:2] "Utterly destroy all the places in which idols are worshiped . . ." God also commanded [Deuteronomy 7:5]: "Break down their altars . . ." and [Deuteronomy 12:3]: "Break down their altars . . ." Since the phrase "a positive commandment" is mentioned in the Talmud concerning idolatry, a question is posed in b*Sanhedrin* [90a]: What possible positive commandment is there concerning idol worship? The answer was given by Rav Ḥisda, that one is commanded in the Torah "Break down their altars . . ." The *Sifre* (*Re'eh*) stated, "How do we know that if an Asherah tree is cut down and replanted even ten

32. There are, of course, other exceptions, but they are the products of the conceptualization of *bal tashḥit* and not explicit directives in Scripture.

> times it is still obligatory to cut it down? From what was written [Deuteronomy 12:2]: 'Utterly destroy.'" It is also stated there [Deuteronomy 12:3]: "And you shall wipe out their names from that place." In the Land of Israel you are commanded to pursue them, but you are not commanded to pursue them outside of the land [of Israel].[33]

The vehemence with which Maimonides describes the obligation to eradicate idol worship from the Land of Israel ("breaking, burning, ruining, and cutting down; each type should be destroyed by the method that suits it best.") is not his own, but can already be found in Scripture (Deuteronomy 7:5): "This is what you are to do to them: break down their altars, smash their sacred stones, cut down their Asherah groves, and burn their idols in the fire."Interestingly, Yosef Karo understood the Asherah to be a fruit tree,[34] which would make the cutting down of these sacred groves an almost direct transgression of Deuteronomy 20:19 (and simultaneously a fulfillment of Deuteronomy 7:5).[35] The command to utterly destroy idols stands as an exception to *bal tashḥit*. It is interesting to point out that Yaakov bar Asher in *Tur, Yoreh De'ah,* Laws Concerning Idolatry, and Yosef Karo in the *Shulḥan Arukh, Yoreh De'ah,* Laws Concerning Idolatry, asserted that it is prohibited to derive enjoyment from things associated with idol worship, but did not go as far as Maimonides with regard to the obligation to utterly destroy such accoutrements. Yaakov bar Asher did mention that if wood from an Asherah tree is used in an oven, the oven needs to be destroyed,[36] but he remained silent on the tree itself.

Maimonides, *Mishneh Torah*, Laws Concerning Idolatry (*Hilkhot Avodat Kokhavim VeḤukot Ovdeihah*)

The premise for this law is that benefit may not be derived from the tools of idolatry.

> **7:19**. If a knife that has been used for idol worship is used [by a Jew] for slaughter, [the meat] is permitted because

33. Moshe ben Maimon, *Sefer HaMitzwot*. My translation from the Hebrew.
34. See *Shulḥan Arukh, Yoreh De'ah, Hilkhot Avodat Kokhavim* 142:12.
35. For it to be considered a direct transgression the context would have to be wartime.
36. See *Tur, Yoreh De'ah, Hilkhot Avodat Kokhavim,* 142.

> the act [of killing an animal] is destructive. But if the animal slaughtered was sickly, it is prohibited, because [the act of killing the animal] is an improvement derived from the effects of idolaters. And so, too, is it prohibited to cut meat with the knife because the act [of cutting the meat] is beneficial. And if he cut the meat in a wasteful and destructive manner (*derekh hefsed vehashhatah*) [the meat] is permitted.[37, 38]

If benefit is derived from the knife, a transgression occurs and the transgressor is liable for punishment. Maimonides, and later Yosef Karo, had almost identical approaches to a knife used for idol worship. Both clarified that there are exceptions to this rule. They indicated that if an animal is slaughtered using the knife of an idol worshiper, the meat of the animal is still permitted for consumption, because the issue surrounding the knife stems from the prohibition of benefiting from the effects of idol worship. In this case, the knife is used for a detrimental activity (that is, the killing of an animal), even though the meat can be consumed, which would be considered a benefit. The act of using the knife for this purpose, therefore, does not render the flesh of the animal unsuitable for consumption. Preparing the meat of the animal by cutting it with such a knife, however, is prohibited because the act is beneficial. This is discussed in the Talmud (b*Ḥullin* 8a–b) and at considerable length in some of the commentaries on the *Mishneh Torah*. These discussions are beyond the scope of this work, but what is important for our purposes is that both Maimonides and Karo agreed that if the meat is prepared in a wasteful/destructive manner (*derekh hashḥatah*), it is permissible to benefit from it. This addendum is not found in the Talmud, though perhaps it can be argued that it is implied. Maimonides, and later Karo, shifted the discussion surrounding a specific prohibition regarding the use of a knife belonging to an idolater to a discussion of waste versus benefit.[39] Understood in the context of *bal tashḥit*, the implication is that one can engage in illicit activities and not be punished for them as long as there is waste and destruction involved in the process. One can

37. Moshe ben Maimon, *Sefer HaMada*.

38. Yosef Karo has an almost identical description listed in *Shulḥan Arukh, Yoreh De'ah, Hilkhot Avodat Kokhavim* (Laws Concerning Idolatry) 142:2 (Yosef Karo, *Shulḥan Arukh: Yoreh De'ah, with All Commentaries*, Vol. 2 [New York: Grossman's Publishing House, 1954]).

39. Yaakov bar Asher did not include this parameter in the *Tur*.

assume, however, that they would still be liable for the transgression of *bal tashḥit*. This shift is indicative of the expanded understanding of *bal tashḥit* promulgated by Maimonides.

These laws are a direct contrast with the treatment required for Jewish holy items.

Maimonides, *Mishneh Torah*, Laws Concerning the Foundation of the Torah (*Hilkhot Yesodot HaTorah*)

> **6:7**. Anyone who tears down even one stone from the tabernacle, Temple or Temple Court in a destructive manner is liable, as it is said with regard to idol worship [Deuteronomy 7:5]: "Break down their altars," and it is written [Deuteronomy 12:4]: "You shall not do thus unto the Lord your God." And so, too, one who burns consecrated wood in a destructive manner [*derekh hashḥatah*] is liable, as it is stated [Deuteronomy 12:3]: "Burn with fire their Asherah groves," and it is written [Deuteronomy 12:4]: "You shall not do thus unto the Lord your God."[40]

Just as preventing idolatrous practices is seen by some as a valid exception to the prohibition against wastefulness, so too is behavior associated with glorifying Judaism. For instance, Yehudah ben Shmuel HeḤasid (1140–1217, Germany) (*Sefer Ḥasidim*, 884)[41] claimed that if a person writes a book (presumably a Torah scroll) and one of the pages is of inferior quality, it is permitted to replace it with a better one. He specifically stated that such an act is not a transgression of *bal tashḥit*.[42] Avraham bar Yeḥiel Mikhel Danziger (1748–1820, Poland, Bohemia, and Lithuania) (*Ḥayei Adam*, Laws of *Tzitzit* 11:32) and Yisrael Meir HaCohen (1839–1933, Poland) (*Mishnah Berurah*, Laws of *Tzitzit* 15:3) permitted the removal of kosher fringes from a prayer shawl (*tallit*) to replace them with nicer ones, specifically claiming that such a practice was not a transgression of *bal tashḥit* because the act is not performed in a destructive manner (*derekh hashḥatah*).[43] Danziger used Herod's

---

40. Moshe ben Maimon, *Sefer HaMada*.

41. In some editions, 883.

42. Yehudah ben Shmuel HeḤasid, *Sefer Ḥasidim* (Bologna: 1538).

43. Avraham bar Yeḥiel Mikhel Danziger, *Ḥayei Adam* (Vilnius: Menaḥem Mann and Simḥah Zimel publishers [sic 1799] 1829), and Yisrael Meir HaCohen, *Sefer Mishnah Berurah, Oraḥ Ḥaim*, Vol. 1 (Jerusalem: Va'ad HaYeshivot BeEretz Yisrael, 1972).

renovation and improvements of the Temple described in b*Baba Batra* 4a as a proof that in all instances when holy or religious articles are being upgraded, even though they were already fully functional, the act is permitted, and not considered a transgression of *bal tashḥit*. These exceptions appear only to extend to religious contexts and not beyond.

Mourning

As we have already observed in the rabbinic chapter, mourning is one of the times when *bal tashḥit* becomes a major issue. The rabbis were concerned with preventing Jews from emulating the foreign cultural practices of their neighbors. We have already seen that wastefulness and destruction, including self-harm, were practices that the rabbis wanted to deter. Many of these laws add little to our knowledge of the prohibition of *bal tashḥit*. What is of particular interest, however, is that in some instances the laws that were only implicitly connected to *bal tashḥit* by the sages are explicitly presented in such terms within this new framework.

Maimonides, *Mishneh Torah*, Laws of Mourning (*Hilkhot Evel*)

> **4:2**. It is prohibited to bury a person in shrouds of silk and clothing embroidered in gold, even if they are a leader of Israel. Such conduct is considered to be loutish and wasteful (*hashḥatah*) and the act of idolaters.[44]
>
> **14:24**. A person should be taught not to be destructive (*ḥablan*) and not to destroy (*lo yafsid*) utensils or discard them in a wasteful manner. It is better to give them to the poor than to send them to rot and worms. And anyone who buries the dead with many effects transgresses the prohibition against wastefulness (*lo tashḥit*).[45]

These two commandments were taken by Maimonides directly from Tractate *Semaḥot, Baraitot meEvel Rabbati* 4:11, and *Semaḥot* 9:23, respectively. The first of these two laws is discussed in b*Mo'ed Qatan*

44. Moshe ben Maimon, *Sefer Shofetim*.

45. Ibid. Yaakov bar Asher (*Tur, Yoreh De'ah, Hilkhot Aveilut* 349) and Yosef Karo (*Shulḥan Arukh, Yoreh De'ah, Hilkhot Aveilut* 349:4) also mention *bal tashḥit* with regard to mourning practices.

27a. In the Talmud, burying the dead in costly garments is prohibited due to the shame that it causes to those who cannot afford to lavish such riches on their dead. Already in *Semaḥot* there is a shift from the Talmudic premise of embarrassment to that of wastefulness and idolatry as the reasons to avoid such practices. It is very difficult to analyze the reasons for this shift. *Semaḥot* is a post-Talmudic compilation, though it contains earlier tannaitic material. There is the possibility that around the time *Semaḥot* was being compiled, there was also an expanding conceptualization of *bal tashḥit*, increasing the range of circumstances in which the concept is brought to bear. With regard to Laws of Mourning 14:24, there is also no significant Maimonidean development of the prohibition against wastefulness. The one nuance that Maimonides added to this commandment was a dose of rationalization: "It is better to give them to the poor than to send them to rot and worms." In *Semaḥot* 9:23 the sages mention that burying the dead with too many effects is "disgraceful" and "invites more worms," but there is no mention of giving these items to the poor. Yitzhak Twersky argues that adding an ethical dimension to the commandments even when there is no pressing need is a characteristically Maimonidean attribute.[46]

In the following two laws Maimonides dealt with ways in which kings or rulers are to be mourned.

Maimonides, *Mishneh Torah*, Laws of Mourning (*Hilkhot Evel*)

> **14:25**. [They] castrate a horse which had been ridden on by a king who dies. [He] removes the hooves of the calf [heifer] which had pulled the cart in which he sat from the knee downwards in a manner that does not render it unfit for consumption . . .[47]

> **14:26.** They burn the bed and all the effects of a king or leader who dies, and doing so is not an emulation of the Amorites, and is not considered wasteful, as it is stated [Jeremiah 34:5]: "Thou shalt die in peace; and with the burnings of thy fathers, [the former kings] that were before thee, so shall they make a burning for thee."[48]

---

46. Yitzhak Twersky, "On Law and Ethics in the Mishneh Torah: A Case Study of Hilkhot Megillah II:17," *Tradition: A Journal of Orthodox Thought* 24, no. 2 (1989): 138.

47. Moshe ben Maimon, *Sefer Shofetim*.

48. Ibid.

On its surface, the first of these two laws appears to be a violation of the prohibition against causing animals to suffer needlessly (*tza'ar ba'alei ḥayim*). It appears that an exception is made to this law because honoring the king is of greater import. Though this certainly raises ethical questions with significant environmental ramifications, it remains beyond the scope of this book. What is relevant to our discussion, however, is the discourse surrounding the difference in treatment of the king's horse and his calf [heifer]. This issue is discussed already in b*Avodah Zarah* 11a. A horse is considered an unclean animal, but a calf in theory can be eaten if ritually slaughtered. Rashi explained that while it is prohibited to render a clean animal unclean, cutting the calf below the knee does not make it unfit for consumption. Even though this particular calf is prohibited for consumption because it belonged to the king, it is still not permissible to render it unfit. Yosef Karo, in his commentary on Maimonides's *Mishneh Torah, Kesef Mishneh,* Laws of Mourning 14:25 explained that the prohibition in question is in fact *bal tashḥit*:

> [They] castrated a horse which had been ridden on by a king who dies, etc.: And what was written [with regard to removing the hooves of the calf] in a manner that does not render it unfit for consumption is so that the prohibition against wastefulness is not transgressed (*bal tashḥit*).[49]

The *Tosafot* (b*Avodah Zarah* 11a), taking a different approach, claimed that in the case of kings, an exception is made to the prohibition of *bal tashḥit* in deference to their stature.

Barzilai Yaabetz (d. 1760, Turkey), in his commentary on Maimonides's *Mishneh Torah, Leshon Arumim,* Laws of Mourning 14:25, had a very lengthy discussion of this practice contradicting the prohibition against wastefulness and the prohibition against causing animals to suffer needlessly. In part, he reconciled the matter by explaining, as clarified by Maimonides in Laws of Kings 6:10, that *bal tashḥit* with regard to all things other than fruit trees is considered only to be a rabbinic prohibition. To honor the king, one is permitted to "transgress" rabbinic edicts but not scriptural ones. Yaabetz then circumvented the

49. Yosef Karo, *Kesef Mishneh: Sefer Shofetim,* in Moshe ben Maimon, *Mishneh Torah: Hu HaYad HaḤazaqah LeRabbeinu Moshe bar Maimon Zal, Sefer Shofetim,* Vol. 12, ed. Shabse Frankel (New York: Congregation Bnei Yosef, 1998).

problem in its entirety by stating that since the prohibition is only understood to be transgressed through acts that Maimonides described as being performed in a destructive manner (*derekh hashḥatah*), and since honoring kings is not a destructive act, *bal tashḥit* is not truly transgressed.[50] For his part, Raphael Ashkenazi (d. 1825, Turkey), in his commentary on Maimonides's *Mishneh Torah, Mareh HaNogah*, Laws of Mourning 14:25, attempted to reconcile Rashi with *Tosafot*. He claimed that even though it is permitted to destroy to honor the king, once this has been done sufficiently, anything superfluous is in fact a transgression of *bal tashḥit*. As such, mutilating a clean animal to the extent that it becomes unclean no longer honors the king and enters the domain of wanton destruction.[51]

Yaakov bar Asher did not add much that was novel to what Maimonides had already written regarding the prohibition against wastefulness and mourning practices.[52] He did, however, make explicit in section 348 that while it is permissible to burn valuable items to honor kings and leaders, doing so to honor a simple person is considered haughty and wasteful. This is perhaps implied by Maimonides, but not explicitly mentioned. Burning the personal effects of the dead is discussed as early as t*Shabbat* 7:18, yet conceptualizing these mourning practices through the lens of the prohibition against wastefulness is novel and not found in the *Tosefta*.

Yosef Karo, *Shulḥan Arukh*, Yoreh De'ah, Laws of Mourning (*Hilkhot Aveilut*)

> **348:1**. The bed and effects of the king are burned, but this is prohibited for the simple person.[53]

Karo's terseness is surprising, especially considering that both Maimonides and Yaakov bar Asher framed this practice in terms of *bal tashḥit*. This void is filled in part by the commentaries and compositions on the *Shulḥan Arukh*. For instance, Mordechai Yaffe (1530–1612, Poland),

50. Barzilai Yaabetz, *Leshon Arumim*, Friedberg ed. (Jerusalem: 2006).

51. Raphael Ashkenazi, *Sefer Mareh HaNogah* (Salonika, Greece: Sa'adi HaLevi Ashkenazi, 1840).

52. Yaakov bar Asher, *Tur: Yoreh De'ah, Hilkhot Aveilut* 348–49 and 352, Vol. 2.

53. Yosef Karo, *Shulḥan Arukh: Yoreh De'ah*, Vol. 3.

in his *Levush, Yoreh De'ah* 348:1,[54] Shabbetai bar Meir Cohen (1621–1662, Lithuania and Bohemia), in his *Siftei Cohen* (*Shakh*), *Yoreh De'ah,* Laws of Mourning, 348:1,[55] and Avraham bar Yeḥiel Mikhel Danziger (1748–1820, Poland and Lithuania), in his *Ḥokhmat Adam, Sha'ar HaSimḥah,* Laws of Mourning 155:27,[56] clarified that burning the items of kings is not an emulation of Amorite practices and is not considered a transgression of *bal tashḥit*. They, together with Ḥaim Yosef David Azulai (*Ḥida*) (1724–1806, Land of Israel, but traveled extensively), in his *Birkei Yosef, Yoreh De'ah,* Laws of Mourning 348:2,[57] and Yeḥiel Mikhel bar Aharon HaLevi Epstein (1829–1908, Russia), in his *Arukh HaShulḥan, Yoreh De'ah,* Laws of Mourning 348:1,[58] also asserted that it is prohibited to do the same to honor a simple person because doing so would be haughty and wasteful. In other words they were simply repeating what they probably read in the *Mishneh Torah* and the *Tur*. Epstein also added that this is where we learn that it is prohibited to be excessive with regard to burying clothing with the dead. Only what is necessary is permitted.

Tearing clothing over the dead is another part of the mourning process in which the issue of wastefulness arises. This practice is documented already in Genesis, where Jacob tears his clothes on hearing of Joseph's "death" (Genesis 37:34). The connection between this practice and the prohibition against wastefulness was seen in the rabbinic chapter and is found in the *baraita* in b*Baba Qama* 91b, where a statement is made in the name of Rabbi Eleazar that he heard that anyone who rends their clothing over the dead too much transgresses the prohibition of *bal tashḥit*. Interestingly, although they discuss the parameters of tearing clothing as mourning for the dead,[59] Maimonides, Yaakov bar Asher, and Yosef Karo did not discuss this act with regard to the prohibition against wastefulness. Many of the commentaries on the *Tur* and *Shulḥan Arukh*, however, did raise the issue of *bal tashḥit* in the context of tearing clothing as mourning for the dead. For instance,

54. Mordechai Yaffe, *Sefer Levush Malkhut*, Part 3, *Levush Ateret Zahav*, ed. A. H. A. P. P. (Israel: 2000).

55. Shabbetai Cohen, *Sefer Siftei Cohen: Yoreh De'ah* (Krakow: Menaḥem Naḥum Maizlish, 1646).

56. Avraham Danziger, *Sefer Ḥokhmat Adam*, Part 2 (Jerusalem: A. Bloom Books, 1992).

57. Ḥaim Yosef David Azulai, *Sefer Birkei Yosef* (Livorno: Vincenzo Falorni, 1776).

58. Yeḥiel Mikhel Epstein, *Sefer Arukh HaShulḥan: Yoreh De'ah*, Vol. 2.

59. Maimonides (*Mishneh Torah, Hilkhot Evel* 9–10), Yaakov bar Asher (*Tur, Yoreh De'ah, Hilkhot Qeriah* 340), and Yosef Karo (*Shulḥan Arukh, Yoreh De'ah, Hilkhot Qeriah* 340).

Yosef Karo (*Beit Yosef, Yoreh De'ah,* Laws of Tearing (over the Dead) 340:7),[60, 61] and Yoel Sirkis (*Bayit Ḥadash, Yoreh De'ah,* Laws of Tearing 340:17),[62] commentators on the *Tur,* discussed *bal tashḥit* with regard to tearing clothing for a person for whom tearing is not required, and tearing for the wrong person accidentally.

The commentaries on and compositions around the *Shulḥan Arukh* also discussed *bal tashḥit* with regard to tearing over the dead in a wide variety of contexts. For instance, Ḥaim Yosef David Azulai in his *Birkei Yosef* (*Yoreh De'ah* 340:13)[63] and Avraham Tzvi Hirsch Eisenstadt (1813–1868, Lithuania) in his *Pitḥei Teshuvah* (*Yoreh De'ah,* Laws of Mourning 340:1)[64] discussed the prohibition of excessive tearing. Mordechai Yaffe in his *Levush* (*Yoreh De'ah* 402:4)[65] and Yeḥiel Mikhel bar Aharon HaLevi Epstein in his *Arukh HaShulḥan* (*Yoreh De'ah, Hilkhot Aveilut* 402:3)[66] brought up *bal tashḥit* in reference to those who tear over individuals for whom they are not obligated to tear. Shlomo Gantzfried (1802–1884, Hungary) in his *Qitzur Shulḥan Arukh* 195:3[67] discussed the degree to which it is permissible to tear before the tearing becomes a transgression of *bal tashḥit,* the extent one can tear depending on who died, tearing on hearing about the death of a relative or a great scholar, and the time frame after the death when it is still permissible to tear clothing on hearing of it.

Ritual Slaughter

The economic parameter is also the decisive factor in other legal deliberations. For instance, for a legally kosher slaughtering, the

60. It is interesting to note that Yosef Karo in his commentary on the *Tur* did bring up *bal tashḥit,* but in his own code, the *Shulḥan Arukh,* he did not.

61. Yosef Karo, *Beit Yosef: Yoreh De'ah,* in Yaakov bar Asher, *Tur: Yoreh De'ah,* Vol. 2 (Jerusalem: Makhon Ḥatam Sofer, 1972).

62. Yoel Sirkis, *Bayit Ḥadash: Yoreh De'ah,* in Yaakov bar Asher, *Tur: Yoreh De'ah,* Vol. 2 (Jerusalem: Makhon Ḥatam Sofer, 1972).

63. Ḥaim Yosef David Azulai, *Birkei Yosef.*

64. Avraham Tzvi Hirsch Eisenstadt, *Pitḥei Teshuvah,* in *Shulḥan Arukh: Yoreh De'ah,* Vol. 3 (New York: Grossman's Publishing House, 1954).

65. Mordechai Yaffe, *Sefer Levush Malkhut.*

66. Yeḥiel Mikhel Epstein, *Sefer Arukh HaShulḥan: Yoreh De'ah,* Vol. 2 (Jerusalem: 1973).

67. Shlomo Gantzfried, *Qitzur Shulḥan Arukh,* Vol. 2, ed. Elyaqim Shlanger (Bnei Braq, Israel: Seminar Be'er Yaakov, 1978).

blood of certain categories of slaughtered animals must be ceremoniously covered. Yosef Karo in his *Shulḥan Arukh, Yoreh De'ah,* Laws of Slaughter 28:21, asserted that if one does not have earth with which to perform this ceremony, it is forbidden to slaughter the animal.[68] This issue becomes a reality in situations when one wants to eat meat in places where no earth is available, such as aboard a ship or in a desert or rocky mountains. Karo in his *Beit Yosef,* Laws of Slaughter 28:36, dealt with *bal tashḥit* in the context of slaughtering animals while on a journey.[69] He claimed that one can rip a piece of cloth off of their garment (*tallit*), or even burn a coin to create ash (which in this context is considered to be earth) to use in the ceremonial covering. This is permissible as long as the value of the slaughtered animal has a greater value than the object being burned. Otherwise, the destruction and waste by burning would be considered a transgression of *bal tashḥit.* Karo did not justify his position regarding why it is permissible to waste up to the value of the chicken, but not beyond it.[70] Karo disagreed with what was considered the authoritative position given by Mordekhai ben Hillel (1250–1298, Germany)[71] and others on the issue, which stated that instead of using earth or creating ash, a person can soak up the blood with his clothing, and when they reach a place with earth, they can rinse the blood out of the clothes and cover it. Karo took issue with this position because if indeed one could soak up the clothing and defer the ceremonial covering to a more convenient time and place, then how could the burning of a garment or coin be permissible? With an alternative solution available, such burning would be considered a transgression of *bal tashḥit.*

Yoel Sirkis in his *Bayit Ḥadash, Yoreh De'ah,* Laws of Slaughter 28:18, however, claimed that Karo's concerns were unfounded, because there is still a clear preference for an immediate ceremonial burial with earth or ash, which supersedes the prohibition of *bal tashḥit*

68. Yosef Karo, *Shulḥan Arukh: Yoreh De'ah, with All Commentaries,* Vol. 1 (New York: Grossman's Publishing House, 1954).

69. Yosef Karo, *Beit Yosef: Yoreh De'ah,* in Yaakov bar Asher, *Tur: Yoreh De'ah,* Vol. 1 (Jerusalem: Makhon Ḥatam Sofer, 1972).

70. It is possible that he based his approach on the position of Rabbi Ḥisma, who claimed that agricultural laborers should not eat more than the value of the work for which they were hired (m*Baba Metzia* 7:5).

71. Mordekhai ben Hillel, *Sefer Rav Mordekhai, Masekhet Ḥullin, Pereq Kisui HaDam* (Riva di Trento, Italy: 1559), 1053 (654 in the Vilna ed.).

when the economics work out in terms of the relative value of all items involved.[72]

Education and Moralistic Issues

The Talmud in b*Qiddushin* 32a discusses *bal tashḥit* in the context of the commandment to honor one's parents. In the Talmudic narrative Rav Huna tested his son to see if he would observe the commandment even in extreme circumstances. Rav Huna tore an expensive garment in the presence of his son Rabbah to observe what his reaction would be. The anonymous narrator of the Talmud (*stam*) asserted that such behavior is a transgression of *bal tashḥit,* but then retorted that Rav Huna tore the garment along the seam in a manner that is easy to repair. As such, Rav Huna cannot be considered to have transgressed the prohibition against wastefulness. Interestingly, this example and others are used as proof-texts that it is permissible to engage in wastefulness/destruction for educational purposes, and more specifically for the sake of establishing decorum in one's household. For example, Eliezer ben Samuel of Metz (d. 1175, France) asserted that wastefulness is permitted in such circumstances, because the value gained in having a peaceful household is greater than the expense of the destruction.[73] Shneiur Zalman of Liadi, however, held that the prohibition applies even in circumstances where the "purpose is to demonstrate anger and wrath and to project his fear on insubordinate household members."[74] Eliezer of Metz's position, however, appears to be the more commonly accepted one.

For example, when describing the tradition of the ceremony marking the transition from the holy Sabbath to the mundane week (*havdalah*), Moshe ben Yisrael Isserles (1520–1572, Poland) stated that "a home in which wine has not been spilled like water is not blessed."[75]

72. Yoel Sirkis, *Bayit Ḥadash: Yoreh De'ah,* in Yaakov bar Asher, *Tur: Yoreh De'ah,* Vol. 1 (Jerusalem: Makhon Ḥatam Sofer, 1972).

73. Eliezer ben Samuel of Metz, *Sefer Yere'im HaShalem,* Vol. 2 (Jerusalem: Makhon Ḥatam Sofer, 1973), 382.

74. Shneiur Zalman, *Shulḥan Arukh HaRav,* Part 6, *Ḥoshen Mishpat, Hilkhot Shemirat HaGuf* (Jerusalem: Even Yisroel Publishing, 2011), 14.

75. Moshe Isserles, *Rama al HaShulḥan Arukh,* in *Shulḥan Arukh: Oraḥ Ḥaim,* Vol. 1 (New York: Grossman's Publishing House, 1954), *Hilkhot Shabbat,* 296:1.

David HaLevi Segal (1586–1667, Poland and elsewhere) indicated that this tradition is not to outright spill the wine after the blessing, which would be disgraceful, but rather to allow the cup to overflow.[76] Spilling wine is outright wasteful, but allowing the cup to overflow signifies the blessing of abundance. Segal went one step further in explaining the tradition by mentioning that spilled wine is usually a reason for anger and anger disrupts the tranquility of a household. As such, intentionally spilling the wine preemptively prevents the anger from occurring. In other words, the outcome of wasting the wine is considered to be of greater value than the cost of the wine itself.

This is not the only instance where we see a legal ruling in favor of maintaining peace. Yeḥiel Mikhel Epstein ruled that when dividing property, one can divide it even if the total value of the property decreases due to the division.[77] He asserted that the decrease in value is not considered a transgression of *bal tashḥit* if those involved believe they will be happy with the outcome.

To be sure, there are other instances where *bal tashḥit* arises, yet not all of them can be presented. As a final example in this section, we turn to one of the most universally known Jewish traditions, that of the breaking of a glass under the wedding canopy. The ceremony is performed to remember Jerusalem and its destruction. The codes themselves do not raise the issue of wastefulness in this context, yet a number of the commentaries and cognates do, especially on the *Shulḥan Arukh*. Yosef bar Meir Teomim (1727–1792, Poland and Germany),[78] Pinḥas bar Tzvi Hirsch HaLevi Horowitz (1730–1805, Poland and Germany),[79] Yisrael Meir HaCohen (1839–1933, Poland),[80] and others declared that such practice was not included under the prohibition of *bal tashḥit* due to its symbolism and educational nature.

---

76. David HaLevi Segal, *Turei Zahav*, in *Shulḥan Arukh: Oraḥ Ḥaim*, Vol. 1 (New York: Grossman's Publishing House, 1954), *Hilkhot Shabbat*, 296:1.

77. Yeḥiel Mikhel HaLevi Epstein, *Sefer Arukh HaShulḥan: Ḥoshen Mishpat, Hilkhot Ḥaluqat Shutafut*, Vol. 1 (Jerusalem: 1973), 171:8.

78. Yosef bar Meir Teomim, *Sefer Pri Megadim, Mishbetzot Zahav, Oraḥ Ḥaim* (Frankfurt an der Oder, Prussia: Defus Almanat Grila, 1787).

79. Pinḥas bar Tzvi Hirsch HaLevi Horowitz, *Sefer HaMaqneh* (Offenbach, Germany: Tzvi Hirsch Spitz, 1824).

80. Yisrael Meir HaCohen, *Sefer Mishnah Berurah, Oraḥ Ḥaim, Hilkhot Tishah BeAv VeSha'ar Ta'aniyot*, Vol. 6 (Jerusalem: Va'ad HaYeshivot BeEretz Yisrael, 1973), 560:2:9.

Conclusion

This chapter was divided into a number of categories that highlight the directions in which the concept was taken in the Jewish codes of law and their cognates. These categories include *bal tashḥit* as a general prohibition against wastefulness/destruction, idolatry and religious practices, mourning, and self-harm. Other categories that emerged through the discussion of these issues were ritual slaughter and educational/moralistic issues. While the Talmud first introduced us to the prohibition against wastefulness and destruction as "*bal tashḥit*" and greatly expanded the parameters of the prohibition, the conceptualization of the prohibition in the codes is yet one order of magnitude greater. The single greatest advance in the conceptualization of *bal tashḥit* is the fact that it is explicitly expanded into a general concept. The array of circumstances in which the term is used in the Talmud indicates that it was perceived as a general prohibition, but nowhere in the corpus of classic rabbinic scholarship is it defined as such. Maimonides changed this in his *Sefer HaMitzvot*. As far as we know, he was the first to define *bal tashḥit* in an explicit manner. Possibly because he was the first, and perhaps because of his stature as one of the greatest Jewish legists of all time, but certainly because of the two together, his influence on the legal decisions that succeeded him was considerable. As such, his generalization of the prohibition had an important impact on the trajectory of the concept, as did, perhaps more importantly, the manner in which he defined that generalization.

In his definition, Maimonides coined the term *derekh hashḥatah* (destructive manner), asserting that one only transgresses the prohibition of *bal tashḥit* if one does things in a destructive manner. The importance of this cannot be overstated. *Bal tashḥit* emerged from the Talmud largely as an economic concept; "wastefulness" was permitted insofar as the end result was something of greater value than the original product. Even though the Talmudic discussion revolved around fruit trees, Maimonides clearly understood the economic parameters as part of a general rule applying to wastefulness in all its forms. The idea of destructive intent, however, made the prohibition largely subjective. According to Maimonides's novel approach, people only transgress *bal tashḥit* if their intention is to be wasteful/destructive. With one hand Maimonides broadened the circumstances in which the prohibition applies, and with the other he weakened the possibility of transgressing it by requiring that wasteful/destructive intent accompany wasteful/destructive actions. This may be consistent with his desire that we lead a life of moderation as expressed in Laws of Ethical Behavior.

The issue of intent calls into question the applicability of the economic parameter. If someone's actions result in a decrease in value of something, but at the same time the action is not done in a destructive manner, is this a transgression of *bal tashḥit* according to Maimonides? It seems clear that any action that is done with foreknowledge that it will decrease the value of an object means that it was undertaken with the intent to be wasteful/destructive. There are those who followed Maimonides's approach who found exceptional circumstances in which a particular action was performed knowing that the end result would be a decrease in value, but that action was not considered a violation of the prohibition.[81]

The relationship between the prohibition against self-harm and the prohibition against wastefulness/destruction was severed by Maimonides by virtue of the fact that he listed these as completely separate commandments, without so much as hinting that there is a connection between them. The separation of the prohibition against self-harm from the prohibition against wastefulness is further reinforced by the fact that the codifiers do not address the amoraic concept that "the prohibition of the destruction of the body takes precedence [over nonhuman objects]" (*bal tashḥit degufa adif*). Barukh Epstein (1860–1941, Belarus), in his comments on Deuteronomy 20:19, expressed considerable surprise that Maimonides did not relate to this dimension of *bal tashḥit* whatsoever.[82]

One of the most surprising elements found in this body of literature is the scant attention given to *bal tashḥit* by Yaakov bar Asher and Yosef Karo. It is possible that since Karo's *Shulḥan Arukh* is based in part on Yaakov bar Asher's *Tur*, and that since Yaakov bar Asher did not deal with this particular prohibition extensively, neither did Karo. This lacuna did not go unnoticed by later scholars. For instance, David

81. Examples of this can be found above. For instance, see Epstein on the division of property and Segal on wine (both on p. 210). For Reischer this issue arises in his responsum on fruit trees (Yaakov Reicher, *Sefer She'elot UTeshuvot Shevut Yaakov*, Part 1 (Jerusalem: Luḥot Frank, 2004), 1:159).

82. Barukh HaLevi Epstein, *Ḥamishah Ḥumshei Torah im Ḥamesh Megilot, Torah Temimah: Sefer Devarim* (New York: Avraham Yitzḥak Friedman, 1962).

HaLevi Segal[83] and Barukh Epstein[84] expressed surprise that earlier codes did not address the prohibition of *bal tashḥit*. As can be seen above, Yaakov bar Asher and Yosef Karo clearly did mention *bal tashḥit* occasionally, yet the limited scope of their coverage of the prohibition is somewhat surprising. Unlike Maimonides, they did not include *bal tashḥit* as a separate prohibition in its own right. Rather, they used *bal tashḥit* in a manner reminiscent of the Talmud. Instead of explaining that *bal tashḥit* is a general prohibition against wastefulness, they used the term to indicate that certain behaviors were prohibited. More specifically, these behaviors are the excessive burial of material effects with the dead and the spilling of wine left over from someone's cup. They claimed that these actions would violate *bal tashḥit*, but nowhere did they explain what *bal tashḥit* actually entails. In other words, as in the Talmud, their use of the term implies that *bal tashḥit* is a broad prohibition, but they themselves only use the expression narrowly with specific examples. As codifiers of Jewish law the expectation is that the laws they list are elucidated. Why bring scattered examples of how a particular law is applied instead of explaining the law in its own right in an organized manner? Because they did mention *bal tashḥit* in the above circumstances, it is impossible to claim that they simply forgot about this law in its entirety. While I have no good explanation for this lack in the two most significant legal codes after Maimonides, it resulted in strengthening Maimonides's influence with regard to this specific prohibition and reinforcing his approach.

Maimonides generalized the prohibition against wastefulness, confirmed its economic parameters, asserted that its extended application was only rabbinic and not directly from the Torah, divorced *bal tashḥit* from the prohibition against self-harm, and added the parameter of intent through coining the term "in a destructive manner" (*derekh hashḥatah*). Most subsequent scholars addressed the prohibition within this Maimonidean framework. What this means is that the economic dimension of the prohibition is almost exclusively the angle from which *bal tashḥit* is analyzed, at the cost of a weakened environmental approach. The term *derekh hashḥatah* is now commonplace in the

83. David HaLevi Segal, *Turei Zahav: Yoreh De'ah—Hilkhot Ma'akhalei Avodat Kokhavim*, in *Shulḥan Arukh: Yoreh De'ah*, Vol. 5, ed. Yosef Karo (Jerusalem: Mifal Shulḥan Arukh HaShalem, 2010), 116:6.

84. Barukh HaLevi Epstein, *Sefer Devarim*.

literature, and from Maimonides to the present almost no one made an association between self-harm and wastefulness. The exceptions in this corpus of literature are Shneiur Zalman of Liadi and Shlomo Gantzfried. Even though the vast majority of literature had guided scholars away from making this particular association, they nonetheless made it in a matter-of-fact manner. To them this connection was so obvious that it required no special explanation, even though its appearance in the literature that preceded them was exceedingly rare. They stand out as those in this particular genre of Jewish scholarship who understood there to be a relationship between *bal tashḥit* and self-harm, and kept this association alive in their writings.

Chapter 4

Responsa

Scripture and classic rabbinic literature did not, and could not, always sufficiently cover every legal situation that arose. Throughout history, specific contexts not mentioned in the existing scholarship and new circumstances brought about by cultural changes and technological advances at times left Jewish communities and individuals uncertain about how to behave. In addition, the legal structure is largely theoretical. The transition from theory into practice is not always straightforward. Real-world contexts are often quite different than pure legal assumptions. We saw this manifest itself in the Talmud, where the theory of never cutting down a fruit tree was first developed and then revisited. There are times when one simply must cut down a fruit tree, for a variety of reasons. For example, a fruit tree might be old, diseased, unproductive, or taking up space needed for a different purpose. If the legal system, however, asserts that cutting down a fruit tree is prohibited, how does one go about cutting it down without transgressing the law? The Talmud went through a number of different stages discussing the degree of productivity for a fruit tree to still be considered viable before Ravina, a late *amora*, asserted that it was simply a question of economics. If the fruit tree is more valuable cut down than planted, it is permissible to cut it down. In other words, to aid the transition from theory into practice with regard to fruit trees, Ravina created a new legal tool meant to simplify the deliberations.

Not every observant Jew, however, was able to understand or access the vast Talmudic corpus. Moreover, even though sages like Ravina attempted to ease the transition from theory into practice, it was impossible to cover all possible scenarios, especially in a continuously evolving and developing world. As such, the genre of responsa emerged in which a question was posed to a Jewish legist and an answer was issued. This process is described by Menachem Elon: "Questions submitted to a respondent arose in the factual context of the time, and the responsum had to resolve the issues in a manner consonant with the contemporaneous circumstances. The subjects of the questions generally related to social, economic, technological, and moral conditions, which differed from period to period and from place to place."[1] These answers set legal precedents and were often quoted by legists in succeeding generations when faced with similar yet slightly nuanced questions.

The major evolutionary shifts in the prohibition against wastefulness occurred in the classic rabbinic era and in the codes. While this responsa literature is not highlighted by major changes in the understanding of *bal tashḥit,* it does illustrate how the existing understanding of the prohibition is applied to new circumstances. As seen in the previous chapter, Maimonides had the greatest impact on the conceptualization of *bal tashḥit*. This chapter will demonstrate that the Maimonidean approach to *bal tashḥit* became dominant. Maimonides took Ravina's economic theory with regard to fruit trees and applied it to the general prohibition against wastefulness.

The three most recent traditional legal publications on *bal tashḥit* mentioned in the literature review do an excellent job of covering this genre of scholarship.[2] This chapter does not aim to recreate the fruit of their labors. Writing in 1990, Haym Soloveitchik stated that there are over 8,000 volumes of responsa.[3] It would be too great a task to tackle the entire genre, or even every legist who dealt with matters concerning wastefulness. Instead, a select number of responsa are discussed to

---

1. Menachem Elon, *Jewish Law: History, Sources, Principles*, Vol. 3, *The Literary Sources of Jewish Law*, trans. Bernard Auerbach and Melvin J. Sykes (Philadelphia: Jewish Publication Society, 1994), 1461.

2. See Siman Tov David, *Sefer al Pakkim Qetanim: Hilkhot Bal Tashḥit* (Jaffa, Israel: S. M. Publishers, 2000); Yitzḥak Eliyahu Shtasman, *Sefer Etz HaSadeh: BeDinei Bal Tashḥit, Qetzitzat Ilanot UVizui Okhalin* (Jerusalem: Foundation for the Advancement of Torah Study, 1999); and Moshe Yitzḥak Vorhand, *Sefer Birkat HaShem: Leqet Dinei Issur Qetzitzat Ilanei Ma'akhal, Bal Tashḥit BiShe'ar Devarim, VeIssur Hefsed UVizui Okhalim* (Jerusalem: private printing, 2000).

3. Haym Soloveitchik, *The Use of Responsa as Historical Source: A Methodological Introduction* (Jerusalem: Zalman Shazar Center, 1990), 12.

illustrate the breadth of issues the scholarship has dealt with regarding practical applications of *bal tashḥit*. Some of the topics presented here are very modern issues such as plastic surgery and smoking. Such topics could not have been dealt with historically because scientific and medical advances had to occur before they became a reality that needed to be addressed legally. Most significantly, this chapter highlights questions and answers that use the terminology and ideas of Maimonides (destructive intent—*derekh hashḥatah*), Meyuḥas bar Eliyahu (need—*tzorekh*), the *Midrash Aggadah* (benefit/enjoyment—*hana'ah*), Baḥya bar Asher (utility—*to'elet*), and *Sefer HaḤinukh* (utility—*to'elet* and morality) to demonstrate the lasting influence of their ideas on the conceptualization of *bal tashḥit*.

It was difficult to divide the responsa in this chapter into categories. Due to their relatively late historical time frame, many of the responsa reference multiple topics. It was ultimately decided to present the material under the following categories: fruit trees, inculcation of moral dispositions, self-harm, specialized terminology (destructive intent, need, benefit/enjoyment, and utility), and contemporary writings. As such, the division is not always perfect, though in my estimation, it is entirely adequate for our purposes. It should also be noted that in the synthesis of these responsa, some of the details were left out to provide a coherent section for the reader. This method of presentation does not diminish their capacity to be understood, nor does it alter their overall meaning.

Fruit Trees

Teshuvot HaRambam, 112[4]

Maimonides was asked whether it is permissible to cut down a problematic palm tree. In this specific circumstance the tree was at the edge of a garden belonging to a Jew, adjacent to a fence separating the garden from publicly owned land. On the other side of the public property was a mosque and a garden belonging to Muslims. It was feared that during stormy weather the tree would be toppled

4. Moshe ben Maimon, *Teshuvot HaRambam*, ed. and trans. Yehoshua Blau (Jerusalem: Mekitzei Nirdamim Publishers, 1958).

and destroy adjacent property. Moreover, when harvesting the fruit, people would throw stones at the tree to try and knock down the fruit, littering the garden and even causing bodily harm to people.

Maimonides responded that indeed the tree could be cut down to prevent the types of damage already delineated in the query. In his response, Maimonides went beyond the question at hand and asserted that it is permissible to cut down a fruit tree if one wants to benefit from the area in which the tree is planted (for other reasons), or from the value of the tree (presumably as lumber). According to him, the Torah only prohibits the cutting down of fruit trees in a destructive or wasteful manner (*derekh hashḥatah*).

Tzemaḥ Tzedeq (HaQadmon) 41[5]

In this responsum Menaḥem Mendel bar Avraham Krokhmal (1600–1661, Poland and Moravia) was asked whether it is permissible to cut down an unwanted nut tree that was harming a vineyard. Krokhmal first mentioned two reasons why such a tree would not be cut down: it produces more than the minimum amount under which it would be permissible to cut it down (b*Baba Qama* 91b), and cutting down a tree before its time is a life-endangering act, as can be seen from Rav Ḥisda's son Shiveḥat (b*Baba Qama* 91b). Krokhmal argued, however, that in this particular case a number of factors make cutting down the nut tree permissible. First, the tree was harming the vines and decreasing their value. To this end he presented the example of Shmuel (b*Baba Qama* 92a), who on touring his land holdings, seeing palm trees and vines planted in close proximity to each other and tasting the flavor of the grapes in the dates, decreed that the palm trees should be uprooted. This was because he perceived them as diminishing the value of the grapes, which were of far greater value, by impairing their flavor. His only hesitation was that perhaps the example presented by Shmuel was limited to situations where the flavor of the grapes was definitively affected and did not just have the potential to have an effect. In other words, the damage had to be discernible, not just potential. Second, it is permissible to cut down a fruit tree if the space is needed for something else. Krokhmal did not grant outright permission to cut down the nut tree, instead claiming

5. Menaḥem Mendel Krokhmal, *She'elot UTeshuvot Tzemaḥ Tzedeq* (Jerusalem: Alter Shmuel Stefansky, 2008).

that in a situation where the nut tree was being replaced by more vines, it was certainly permissible to cut it down.

Ḥavot Yair 195[6]

Yair Ḥaim ben Moshe Shimshon Bakhrakh (1638–1702, Moravia and Germany) was asked whether a peach tree that grew without it having been planted but was blocking a window could be cut down. He responded that it was certainly permitted to cut it down, because the prohibition against cutting down fruit trees only applies if it is done in a wanton destructive manner (*derekh hashḥatah beli tzorekh*). Bakhrakh added that if he were able to prune the branches of the tree to rectify the situation without cutting down the tree that would be preferable.

Divrei Ḥaim, Yoreh De'ah 2:57[7]

Ḥaim bar Aryeh Leib Halbershtam (1793–1876, Poland and Galicia) was asked by the residents of a town whether they were allowed to cut down fruit trees to build a ritual bath (*mikveh*). He opened his responsum by stating that the issue had already been covered by David HaLevi Segal, who stated that it is permissible to cut down fruit trees when the space where they are planted is needed.[8] He nevertheless went into a lengthy discussion of the matter. As part of his justification he mentioned that in this particular context cutting down the trees is undoubtedly permissible and there is no danger[9] because the act provides a necessary public service. In fact, in the tradition of Maimonides's Laws of Kings 6:10, he asserted that *bal tashḥit* only truly encompasses actions undertaken in a deliberately wasteful/destructive manner (*derekh hashḥatah*). In this particular context, Halbershtam argued that there is an additional justification because not only will it not be done in a destructive/wasteful manner, but the trees would also be cut down for the sake of a mitzvah.

6. Yair Ḥaim Bakhrakh, *Sefer She'elot UTeshuvot Ḥavot Yair*, ed. Shimon ben-Tzion HaCohen Kots (Ramat-Gan, Israel: Makhon Akad Sefarim, 1997).

7. Ḥaim bar Aryeh Leib Halbershtam, *Sefer She'elot UTeshuvot Divrei Ḥaim: Yoreh De'ah*, Part 2 (New York: Mosdot Babov, 2002).

8. See David HaLevi Segal, *Turei Zahav, Yoreh De'ah* 116:6.

9. The issue of danger arises in reference to the son of Rabbi Ḥanina, Shikheḥat, from b*Baba Batra* 26a, or alternatively Shiveḥat from b*Baba Qama* 91b.

Interestingly, Halbershtam concluded his responsum by addressing an issue we saw in the previous chapter regarding kosher slaughtering of an animal when no earth is available to ceremonially cover the blood (*kisui hadam*). He cited Alexander Sender Schorr (1673–1737, Poland), who stated that it is permissible to burn a gold coin to use the ash created for the purposes of a ceremonial covering of the blood, as a subjective measure, that is, if the person values the meat more than he values the gold. This approach is a deviation from Yosef Karo's ruling seen in the previous chapter in which one is permitted to create ash in this manner only if the chicken being slaughtered is of higher value than the item destroyed to create the ash.

Shevut Yaakov 1:159[10]

Yaakov ben Yosef Reischer (c. 1670–1733, Prague, Bavaria, Germany, and France) was asked whether it is permissible to cut down fruit trees that were planted and came to block the neighbor's window. He began by stating that it was indeed permissible to cut down the trees. He then cited the Talmud from b*Baba Qama* 91b–92a and Yaakov bar Asher, who stated that if the location of the tree is needed for other purposes, it is permissible to cut it down. He continued his justification that the prohibition is transgressed when there is wastefulness/destruction, but in this case the cutting down of the trees is in fact the righting of a wrong and not an act of destruction. Among other sources, he also cited Maimonides's Laws of Kings, which claim that cutting down a fruit tree is only prohibited if done in a destructive manner (*derekh hashḥatah*). He concluded by stating that if it is possible to resolve the issue by pruning a number of the trees' branches so that sunlight still reaches the neighbor's window, this would be the preferable solution.

Binyan Tzion 61[11]

Jacob Ettlinger (1798–1871, Germany) also dealt with the question of cutting down fruit trees. He was told that for an individual to get

10. Yaakov Reischer, *Sefer She'elot UTeshuvot Shevut Yaakov*, Part 1 (Jerusalem: Luḥot Frank, 2003).

11. Jacob Ettlinger, *Binyan Tzion HaShalem*, Vol. 1, ed. Yehudah Aharon Horowitz (Jerusalem: Devar Yerushalayim Publishers, 2002).

married he needed to buy land and build a house, but the only plot available had a number of old fruit trees that would need to be cut down. He was asked whether under such circumstances it would be permissible to cut down these trees. He cited a number of different legal positions dealing with the nuances of cutting down fruit trees and concluded that the Torah only prohibits cutting down fruit trees in a destructive manner (*derekh hashḥatah*). He asserted that the prohibition does not hold when the act of cutting down the fruit tree has utility (*to'elet*), either through the lumber or through the land use. He suggested that the best practice would be to uproot the trees and replant them elsewhere, as previously suggested by Moshe Sofer (1762–1839, Germany). In this particular case, Ettlinger assumed that this would be unnecessary since the trees were already old. He also suggested that the trees be cut down by Gentiles. He then stated that the best option would be to have the Gentiles uproot the trees and replant them prior to the Jew buying the land. He concluded, however, that because the end result of cutting down the trees and building a house would possibly be marriage, it would be permissible even for a Jew to cut down these trees.

Mashiv Davar 2:56[12]

Though the exact question was not included in his writings, Naftali Tzvi Yehudah Berlin (1817–1893, Russia and Poland) was asked whether it is permissible to cut down fruit trees to use the space for other purposes (presumably to build a house). He suggested that the questioner rely on David HaLevi Segal's ruling (*Turei Zahav, Yoreh De'ah* 116) that it is permissible to cut down fruit trees to build a house. Berlin, however, also suggested that he proceed with extreme caution and only cut down the trees if the product is of greater value than the fruit. If the benefit (*hana'ah*) is not greater through their destruction, it would be prohibited under *bal tashḥit*. As a proof-text he referenced b*Shabbat* 129a, claiming that if not for the concept of "the prohibition against destroying the body is more dear" (*bal tashḥit degufa adif*), it would be prohibited to destroy anything for the benefit (*hana'ah*) of the body. Berlin claimed that cutting down fruit trees is particularly severe, because there is an inherent danger in destroying them (presumably he

12. Naftali Tzvi Yehudah Berlin, *Shu"t Mashiv Davar*, Parts 1 and 2 (Jerusalem: private printing, 1968).

was referring to the case of Rabbi Ḥanina's son Shiveḥat/Shikheḥat). Moreover, according to Maimonides, the Torah treats the cutting down of trees more stringently than the waste/destruction of other material, because there were differences in punishment (transgressing a Torah law vs. a rabbinic edict [*malkot* vs. *makat mardut*]).

He claimed that the quantities of fruit that the Talmud stipulated as giving a tree protected status are so miniscule that they speak to the severity of the prohibition, so much so that virtually any other benefit (*hana'ah*) or purpose (*tzorekh*) for the fruit tree would be of greater value than the fruit. Nevertheless, Berlin asserted that the prohibition stands, not because of issues of value, but because of the severity of the prohibition; only the cases delineated by Maimonides are considered reasonable exceptions to the rule. Cutting down a fruit tree for any other reason is prohibited. In fact, Berlin claimed that according to Maimonides, Ravina's assertion that a fruit tree may be cut down if the lumber is of greater value than the fruit (b*Baba Qama* 91b) holds only in cases where there is benefit from the lumber itself. If the tree is cut down for any other benefits (*hana'ot*), it is considered a transgression of *bal tashḥit*. Berlin did acknowledge that Asher ben Yeḥiel permitted the cutting down of fruit trees if the space were needed for other purposes. This position is very similar to that of David HaLevi Segal, and Berlin opened his responsum by saying that Segal's ruling should be accepted. Nevertheless, he qualified this approach with his final statement. In it, he evoked rabbinic sources (b*Megillah* 26b and m*Kilayim* 2), which indicate that one should first perform a constructive act before a destructive act. Since circumstances are wont to change, if the destructive act is performed first, it is possible that the constructive act will simply never occur, leaving only the destruction.

Har Tzvi, Oraḥ Ḥaim, Part Two, 102[13]

Tzvi Pesaḥ Frank (1873–1960, Lithuania and Land of Israel) was asked whether it is permitted to cut down a fruit tree in its first three years (when consumption of the fruit it bears is forbidden) when the space is needed to build a sukkah.[14] Frank replied that there are two issues with cutting down a fruit tree. First, Deuteronomy 20:19 prohibits cutting down fruit trees. Second, the case of Rabbi Ḥanina in b*Baba*

---

13. Tzvi Pesaḥ Frank, *Sefer Har Tzvi: Oraḥ Ḥaim*, Part 2 (Jerusalem: 1973).

14. A sukkah is a temporary structure that is built for the Festival of Booths (*Sukkot*).

Qama 91b demonstrates that there is considerable danger in cutting down fruit trees. He then cited Maimonides (Laws of Kings 6:8), where the prohibition is said to include only the cutting down of fruit trees in a destructive manner (*derekh hashḥatah*). He also presented the opinion of Asher ben Yeḥiel (*Rosh al* b*Baba Qama* 8:15), who claimed that if the space occupied by the fruit tree is needed to build a house, then it is permissible to cut it down. He then brought the opinion of David HaLevi Segal, who claimed that it is permissible to cut down a fruit tree if the space is needed to build a house. Yaakov Emden, however, qualified this position by stating that the house must be of greater value than the fruit tree. As such, Frank determined that the same must hold for the sukkah, which is problematic, because as a temporary structure the sukkah has very little value. He reasoned, however, that building a sukkah is an actual commandment (as opposed to building a house), and *bal tashḥit* does not apply under such circumstances. Basing his opinion on the *Tosafot*, he asserted that as a negative commandment *bal tashḥit* is only superseded by positive commandments.[15] This only holds, however, in cases where it is not possible to carry out the positive commandment in a non-transgressive manner. Yehudah HeḤasid, however, held the position that a negative commandment can be superseded even for the sake of enhancing a positive commandment. In the case of *bal tashḥit*, the action undertaken to glorify the positive commandment would not even be considered destructive/wasteful. After continuing his deliberations somewhat further, he concluded that while in this particular case the act is permitted (i.e., cutting down the young fruit tree to use the space to build a sukkah), one should still proceed with caution because of the danger involved (i.e., premature death). As such, he recommended that the cutting down be done by a Gentile, but even the request to the Gentile should be phrased to explicitly state that the act is carried out exclusively by the Gentile and not under the volition of the owner.

Analysis

As can be seen relative to the material in the previous chapters, the questions posed were by and large nuanced situations in which it was

15. Negative commandments prohibit certain actions, whereas positive commandments require certain actions to be carried out.

not always clear how the context fit under the established *halakhah*. How does one judge a situation in which a fruit tree causes damage or potential damage? How does a person's well-being or convenience compare with the importance of not cutting down a fruit tree? Does a fruit tree whose fruits are forbidden for consumption fall under the prohibition of *bal tashḥit*? Is it permissible to cut down fruit trees for the purpose of building something in their place? What if the building has a religious function? Having read the earlier chapters, you might find that some responses to such questions could be anticipated. Nevertheless, these issues were of great enough concern to the questioners that they made the effort to seek a legal solution.

The first major noticeable element in the responsa that deal with fruit trees is that Maimonides applied his concept of destructive intent when questioned with regard to a nuanced situation regarding a fruit tree. Maimonides's innovation moved from the realm of theory in his *Mishneh Torah* to the sphere of practice in his responsa. He was, of course, not the only one to use this term when dealing with the issue of cutting down fruit trees; Ḥaim bar Aryeh Leib Halbershtam, Jacob Ettlinger, Yaakov Reischer, and Tzvi Pesaḥ Frank, among others not presented in this chapter, also applied the idea of destructive intent in their responsa.

Destructive intent was not the only major concept that had been adopted from previous scholars and was now being applied to new contexts concerning *bal tashḥit*. Jacob Ettlinger used the term "utility" (*to'elet*) when claiming that any time there is utility in cutting down a fruit tree it is permissible. This essentially took Ravina's statement from b*Baba Qama* 91b and reframed it. Naftali Tzvi Yehudah Berlin did not agree with this interpretation of Ravina's statement. He limited what appears to be a very general statement and determined that it applies only to actual lumber and not to other uses, though this position does not appear to be widely accepted. Berlin used the term "benefit/enjoyment" (*hana'ah*) when claiming that the only reason we are permitted to destroy/waste anything for the benefit of the body is because of the concept of "the prohibition against destroying the body is more dear" (*bal tashḥit degufa adif*).

Some of the legists were more stringent than others. This is a theme emphasized by Meir Ayali in his study of responsa on the cutting down of fruit trees. He suggested that later legal authorities were hesitant to permit the cutting down of fruit trees because of the hortatory Talmudic tale relating to Shiveḥat/Shikheḥat's untimely death.[16] Ultimately, however, almost all authorities gave permission for the trees in question to be cut down. In a number of cases, suggestions were offered that the questioners take action to prevent the cutting down of the trees, but in the end permission was granted (at least in the cases we have presented here). When a tree is blocking a window, the branches should be trimmed (Bakhrakh and Reischer). When a tree needs to be cut down, a Gentile should be the one who performs the action (Frank). When a tree is harming other trees, it can be cut down if it is being replaced with plantings that are not harmful (Krokhmal and Ettlinger).

While the above responsa show significant elements of continuity, Halbershtam's responsa presents some novelty. In essence, his approach suggests that the entire notion of what is wasteful or destructive is subjective. This is arguably an extreme example of how far Maimonides's destructive intent can be taken if the concept of wastefulness is relegated to subjectivity. There is nothing in Maimonides's writings, however, that suggests that subjectivity embraces irrationality. Schorr (and Halbershtam through his citation of Schorr's position) removed the prohibition of destruction/wastefulness from the realm of rationality and opened the door to subjectivity in the application of the law. According to this approach (which is clearly not widely accepted), individuals can determine for themselves which actions constitute wastefulness and are prohibited and which do not and are permissible.

Self-Harm

Shevut Yaakov 3:71[17]

Yaakov Reicher (1670–1733, Bohemia, Bavaria, Germany, and France) was asked whether it is permissible to test medicines on animals

16. Meir Ayali, "*HaḤaradah Bifnei Keritat Etz-Ma'akhal BeSafrut HaShu"t*," in *Tura: Studies in Jewish Thought, Simon Greenberg Jubilee Volume* (Tel-Aviv: Hakibbutz Hameuchad Publishing House, 1989), 135–40.

17. Yaakov Reischer, *Sefer She'elot UTeshuvot Shevut Yaakov*, Part 3 (Jerusalem: Luḥot Frank, 2003).

that are impure (i.e., not kosher even if ritually slaughtered) prior to administering them to a human. Reicher replied that it has already been established by Binyamin Aharon Solnick (1550–1620, Poland), David HaLevi Segal (1586–1667, Poland and elsewhere), Gershon Ashkenazi (c. 1620–1693, Poland, Moravia, Austria, and France), and Yaakov ben Shmuel (seventeenth century, Poland) that anything that is done to fulfill a need (*tzorekh*) or that is done for the sake of health or for material advantage (*hana'at mamon*) is not considered a transgression of *bal tashḥit*. Based on these authorities, he further asserted that it is permissible to kill an animal for medicinal purposes, even if the medicinal benefit is only in potential. This, he claimed, is because "the prohibition against destroying the body is more dear" (*bal tashḥit degufa adif*). He did, however, express surprise that none of the authorities cited the case from b*Ḥullin* 7b, where the prohibition against causing animals to suffer needlessly and the prohibition against wastefulness were used as excuses by Rabbi Pinḥas to not eat at the house of Rabbi. Rabbi Pinḥas refused to eat in Rabbi's home because of the presence of two white mules on his property. The mules were considered to be supernaturally pernicious. Rabbi, wanting the company of Rabbi Pinḥas, offered to maim them (thus removing their dangerous nature); Rabbi Pinḥas responded that this would transgress the prohibition against causing animals to suffer needlessly (*tza'ar ba'alei ḥayim*). Rabbi then offered to kill them, to which Rabbi Pinḥas replied that this would be a transgression of *bal tashḥit*. This would seem to indicate that it is not permissible to transgress these commandments for the sake of human benefit or utility. Reicher concluded, however, that Rabbi Pinḥas just evoked these prohibitions for other reasons because he did not want to eat at Rabbi's house, as he had already invited danger into his home by having the white mules. Ultimately, Reicher concluded that this type of animal experimentation was permissible, and it would not be a transgression of any prohibition; indeed anything that has human utility and benefit casts these prohibitions aside.

Yaakov Reicher based himself on a long line of earlier authorities who asserted that any case necessitating waste/destruction for the purposes of human health, need (*tzorekh*), or benefit (*hana'ah*) is not considered a transgression of *bal tashḥit*. His innovation was that "the prohibition against destroying the body is more dear" can be applied in circumstances where the benefit is uncertain, such as in the case of animal experimentation.

Yabia Omer 8, Ḥoshen Mishpat 12:1[18]

Ovadiah Yosef (1920–2013, Iraq, Egypt, and Israel) was asked whether a woman can undergo plastic surgery to beautify herself or whether doing so transgresses the prohibition against self-harm. He started by presenting the Talmudic discourse on the prohibition (b*Baba Qama* 91a) and then brought in the codes and a large number of legal authorities on whether it is indeed prohibited to engage in self-harm. One of the sources he brought in, which fell on the side of self-harm being permissible, was Bezalel Ashkenazi (c. 1524–c. 1594, Egypt and Land of Israel), who brought the opinion of Meir Abulafia (c. 1170–1244, Spain), who stated that the position that Rav Ḥisda took, that of lifting his garments so that the thorns scratched his legs instead of his clothing, was authoritative because his opinion came later. Ovadiah Yosef then presented the opinions of Maimonides and Yosef Karo, who prohibit self-harm. He himself claimed that one must distinguish between various types of harm, and that in the case of the woman in question, it would be permissible to undergo the operation, because it is done with anesthetics and the benefit is long term. This, he claimed, is reinforced in a case where a woman is so ashamed of her appearance that her embarrassment is continuous. He then cited Maimonides, who claimed that self-harm is only prohibited when done in a quarrelsome and shameful manner (*derekh nitzayon* and *bizayon*). Finally, Ovadiah Yosef compared Maimonides's ideas of "shameful manner" (*derekh bizayon*) and "destructive manner" (*derekh hashḥatah*), asserting that just as wastefulness is only prohibited when done in a destructive manner, so too, self-harm is only prohibited when done in a shameful manner. Because the self-harm the woman is undergoing is for the exact opposite reason, Ovadiah Yosef ruled that it is indeed permissible.

In dealing with the question of whether plastic surgery is permitted for aesthetic reasons, Ovadiah Yosef made an important comparison with regard to Maimonidean terminology. He justified the surgery in this case because, just as *bal tashḥit* is only prohibited when done in a destructive manner, so too is self-harm only prohibited when done in a quarrelsome and shameful manner. In

18. Ovadiah Yosef, *Yabia Omer*, Vol. 8, *Ḥoshen Mishpat* (Jerusalem: 1995).

other words, if someone engages in self-harm and their intention is neither to be quarrelsome nor to cause themselves shame, the act is permissible.

Mishneh Halakhot 12:23[19]

Menasheh Klein (1923–2011, Ukraine, USA, and Israel) was asked if a son is permitted to buy his father tobacco products under the obligation of "honoring one's parents," or whether such a request should be treated in the same manner as a parent who asks his son to transgress the commandments of the Torah. Klein responded that each case must be treated in its own right. According to him, a person who does not already smoke is certainly prohibited from starting for the following reasons: it causes self-harm, it is a waste of time, it transgresses *bal tashḥit*, and it habituates people to lusts and cravings. If, however, a person is already addicted to smoking and cannot quit, smoking should then be treated as a bodily necessity. Klein then addressed the issue of whether giving the father a cigarette or lighting a cigarette for him is a transgression of "not putting a stumbling block before the blind." This, too, he claimed is dependent on the specific case. For a healthy person, opium is a deadly drug, but for the ill person it can be medicinal. Similarly, sugar can be deadly for diabetics, but in certain cases, even for the diabetic, sugar intake is essential. He then claimed that smoking is no worse than any other thing that a son could give his father that causes bodily harm. Finally, he presented Maimonides's opinion (Laws of Ethical Behavior 4:9) that many foods should be considered deadly and be avoided, but consuming them is still not prohibited outright. As such, he concluded that the matter is not straightforward and there are conflicting opinions.

Menasheh Klein dealt with the issue of smoking, and while not prohibiting smoking for those already addicted, he did prohibit encouraging one to develop the habit. He considered smoking to be harmful to a person's health, as well as a waste of time and money. Neither Reicher in his responsum nor Klein explicitly stated that the prohibition against self-harm comes as part of *bal tashḥit*, but in their specific cases they list both as reasons to either permit or prohibit their respective issues.

---

19. Menasheh Klein, *Sefer Mishneh Halakhot—Mahadurah Tinyana*, Part 12 (New York: Makhon Mishneh Halakhot Gedolot, 2000).

Ḥashuqei Ḥemed, bBaba Qama 90b[20]

Yitzḥak Zilberstein (b. 1934, Poland and Israel) asked (or was asked) whether a person who has a tooth causing pain can have it pulled out if that person cannot financially manage the cost of treatment to repair the diseased tooth. He presented the *baraita* of Rabbi Eleazar, who claimed that tearing too much clothing over the dead is a transgression of *bal tashḥit* and the Talmud's rejection of this through the example of Rav Ḥisda's protection of his garments while walking through thorns. Since tearing a garment too much as an act of mourning is considered a transgression of *bal tashḥit*, Zilberstein claimed that an act of self-harm is prohibited even when it has utility (*to'elet*). In other words, because we learn *a fortiori* from material about the body, and because it is prohibited to tear too much over the dead even though there is utility in the act (the utility being the psychological assuagement that contributes to the healing process), so too is it prohibited to engage in self-harm, even when the act has utility. He then asserted that the passage (*sugya*) in the Talmud teaches us that it is permitted to engage in self-harm that is reversible, but it is prohibited to engage in self-harm that causes permanent damage under the prohibition of *bal tashḥit*. The *a fortiori* reasoning of prohibiting self-harm that emerges from the prohibition to destroy material stands when the damage is permanent. Thus, pulling out a tooth (causing permanent damage) would be a transgression of *bal tashḥit*. Zilberstein added, however, that in cases in which there is a great need (*tzorekh*), it is permissible to engage in wastefulness. For Zilberstein, an example of great need includes someone who would be mentally unable to endure the healing process. He did not consider poverty to be such a cause and even gave suggestions on how a person could finance treatment. He claimed that the dentist was prohibited from pulling out the patient's tooth even if requested, because a person's body does not actually belong to him but to God. In his concluding line, however, he claimed that when there is the need (*tzorekh*) to pull a tooth for the sake of the health of the body it is permissible to do so, because *bal tashḥit* does not apply in cases where there is utility (*to'elet*).[21]

20. Yitzḥak Zilberstein, *Ḥashuqei Ḥemed al Masekhet Baba Qama* (Jerusalem: 2009).

21. Zilberstein's conclusions appear to be somewhat contradictory. He first claimed that self-harm is prohibited even when the act has utility and then asserted that self-harm is included under *bal tashḥit*. He then concluded that *bal tashḥit* does not apply in circumstances that have utility. The cases, however, should not be understood as contradictory, because the second case is qualified as being a *tzorekh gadol* (a great need), making it permissible.

Through his responsum, Yitzḥak Zilberstein offered a nuanced explanation of the Talmud's rejection of Rabbi Eleazar's *baraita*; Rav Ḥisda's position only holds in cases where the damage is reversible. Thus, the prohibition against irreversible harm is still learned from the prohibition against the waste/destruction of material. This allowed him to hold that pulling out the tooth is prohibited unless there is great need. Through his use of the terms "need" and "utility" (*tzorekh* and *to'elet*), Zilberstein demonstrates the continued use of the contributions to the conceptualization of *bal tashḥit* offered by Meyuḥas bar Eliyahu, Baḥya bar Asher, and the *Sefer HaḤinukh* to the present day.

Derekh Hashḥatah, Tzorekh, Hana'ah

Shu"t Maharashda"m, Yoreh De'ah 51[22]

Samuel de Medina (1506–1589, Greece) dealt with whether a Jew slaughtering an animal for a Gentile can do so with an imperfect knife, which would result in a non-kosher slaughtering, and concluded that prima facie, it is permissible. Although the question itself is not presented by de Medina, it appears that the questioner suggested that one reason for the prohibition could be *bal tashḥit*. In response, de Medina referenced b*Ḥullin* 2a, which discusses the prohibition forbidding deaf-mutes, simpletons, and youngsters from slaughtering animals. The Talmud did not explain why this is the case, leaving open the possibility that the prohibition emerges from *bal tashḥit*. De Medina asserted that the reasoning behind the prohibition to eat an animal slaughtered by this group was correctly argued by Rabbeinu Tam in the *Tosafot*; it was prohibited because it was possible that a Jew would inadvertently eat the animal they slaughtered. He rejected the possibility that their slaughtering would be a transgression of the prohibition of *bal tashḥit*, because *bal tashḥit* is only transgressed when an action is done in a destructive or wasteful manner (*derekh hashḥatah*). In other words, de Medina rejected the view that a deaf-mute, a simpleton, or a youngster cannot slaughter animals because of *bal tashḥit*. He did, however, suggest that the use of an imperfect knife

22. Samuel de Medina, *She'elot UTeshuvot Maharashda"m: Oraḥ Ḥaim, Yoreh De'ah*, ed. David Avitan (Jerusalem: Zikhron Aharon, 2009).

could still relate to the issue of *bal tashḥit* because, as a result of the slaughtering, the animal would certainly be prohibited for consumption by Jews. This would be similar to the prohibition against spilling out well water while others are in need of water (b*Yevamot* 44a).

Tzemaḥ Tzedeq (Lubavitch), Oraḥ Ḥaim 20[23]

Menaḥem Mendel Schneerson's (1789–1866, Russia) responsum deals with whether it is permissible to knock down the wall of a synagogue to expand the women's sanctuary. The question rests on the issue of whether it is permissible to destroy in order to create something useful. He stated that b*Baba Qama* 91b indicates that it is permissible to destroy something as long as the final product is of greater value than the original item destroyed. He concluded that as long as it is not done in a destructive manner (*derekh hashḥatah*), it is permissible. One of the main issues was that to gain the added space the wall would lose its thickness and its strength would be diminished. This he justified by claiming that such an act was not a complete ruining of the wall, which would remain thick enough, and at any rate the health of the women was endangered from overcrowding.

Divrei Ḥaim, Oraḥ Ḥaim 2:13[24]

Like Schneerson, Ḥaim bar Aryeh Leib Halbershtam (1793–1876, Poland and Galicia) dealt with the question of whether one is allowed to destroy a synagogue wall to increase the size of the women's section. In other words, he was asked whether it is permissible to destroy something holy to improve it. He problematized the issue by referencing Maimonides's discussion from the Laws Concerning the Foundation of the Torah (6:7), which concerns the prohibition against damaging even one stone from the tabernacle in a destructive manner (*derekh hashḥatah*). He also presented Yosef Karo's position (*Shulḥan Arukh, Yoreh De'ah,* Laws of Slaughtering 28:21) regarding the ceremonial covering of blood for an animal that is slaughtered in a circumstance

---

23. Menaḥem Mendel Schneerson, *Sefer Tzemaḥ Tzedeq: She'elot UTeshuvot MiShulḥan Arukh Oraḥ Ḥaim* (New York: Otzar HaḤasidim, 1994).

24. Ḥaim bar Aryeh Leib Halbershtam, *Sefer She'elot UTeshuvot Divrei Ḥaim: Oraḥ Ḥaim,* Part 2 (New York: Mosdot Babov, 2002).

where there is no earth available to cover the blood. As has been seen, burning gold to create ash for the sake of ceremonial blood covering is permitted when the value of the gold is less than that of the animal. Halbershtam then drew an analogy between the waste/destruction of the gold and the destruction of the tabernacle, which is priceless. If it is prohibited to burn the gold when it is of greater value than the animal, how much greater is the prohibition of destroying even one stone of the tabernacle, which is priceless?[25] The main difference between the two cases is, of course, that the tabernacle is holy, while gold is not. The question then remains—how is it possible to destroy something holy like the synagogue wall during renovation? Halbershtam based his conclusion on David HaLevi Segal (*Taz*) who ruled that such an action is permitted, because it is not done in a destructive manner (*derekh hashḥatah*) and because the end result is an improved product once the renovation is completed. Due to the controversial nature of destroying something imbued with holiness, Halbershtam suggested that the wall be sold to a Gentile prior to its renovation.

Both Menaḥem Mendel Schneerson and Ḥaim bar Aryeh Leib Halbershtam used the term "destructive intent" (*derekh hashḥatah*) to justify tearing down part of a synagogue to expand the women's sanctuary. The end result was constructive, so the destructive means were legitimate.

Torah LiShmah 76[26]

Yosef Ḥaim ben Eliyahu (1834–1909, Iraq) was asked whether it is permissible to put extra oil in the Sabbath lamps so that they would burn for the entire Sabbath. Basing his responsum on b*Shabbat* 67b, he concluded that doing so would be a transgression of *bal tashḥit* because the candle is only of use when it is dark. Burning the lamp during the day is of no benefit (*hana'ah*) and is wasteful. The only context in which it would be permissible according to ben Eliyahu would be in the synagogue, out of respect of place.

25. Above (p. 220) it appears that Halbershtam accepted Alexander Sender Schorr's position on the subjective nature of *bal tashḥit*, while here it appears he accepted Yosef Karo's contradictory ruling on the same issue. One possible way to reconcile this is by considering the qualitatively different scenarios. Above, Halbershtam was dealing with the cutting down of fruit trees and could take a more lenient position. Here, however, the scenario involves destroying something imbued with holiness, which would require a more stringent approach.

26. Yosef Ḥaim ben Eliyahu, *Sefer Torah LiShmah*.

In a case similar to the hypothetical situation found in the Talmud, Yosef Ḥaim ben Eliyahu contended with the question of whether prior to the Sabbath an oil lamp could be set up with enough fuel to burn for the entire duration of the day (approximately twenty-five hours). He compared the burning of the lamp unnecessarily during the day to the case in the Talmud that prohibits the inefficient burning of an oil lamp under the prohibition of *bal tashḥit*. He used the terminology of the *Midrash Aggadah* by claiming that there is no benefit (*hana'ah*) to burning the lamp during the day, and doing so would transgress the prohibition against wastefulness.

Melamed LeHo'il, Part Two, Yoreh De'ah 148[27]

David Tzvi Hoffmann (1843–1921, Slovakia, Austria, and Germany) was asked whether an old well with water unsuitable for drinking could be closed off. Hoffmann claimed that the only source that would potentially disallow such an action is b*Yevamot* 44b, where it states that a person should not spill out (waste) the water of their well while another person is in need of water. Hoffmann argued that this only applies to water that is suitable for use. He then claimed that all the Jewish legists follow the opinion of Maimonides, who in the Laws of Kings 6:8–10 ruled that if an action is not performed in a destructive manner (*derekh hashḥatah*), then it is not prohibited under the law of *bal tashḥit*.

Hoffmann related to the specific prohibition of not wasting water while other people are in need of it. The water in question was fetid, and the very fact that someone would ask about it shows the seriousness with which the questioner was following the law. After all, the Talmud already stipulates other people's need as the determining factor, and it seems clear that such water does not have extensive utility, especially in the time the question was posed. Hoffmann concluded that since the act would not be performed in a destructive manner (*derekh hashḥatah*) it is permissible.

Shu"t HaRaba"z, Part Three, Ḥoshen Mishpat 88[28]

Ḥanokh Henikh Safran (1887–1959, Romania and Israel) was asked to clarify a difficulty in b*Ta'anit* 31a. In the Talmud it states that the axes

27. David Tzvi Hoffmann, *Shu"t Melamed LeHo'il*, Part 2, *Yoreh De'ah* (Jerusalem: David Tzvi Hoffmann, 2010).

28. Bezalel Ze'ev Safran, *Sefer She'elot UTeshuvot HaRaba"z*, ed. Ḥanokh Henikh Safran (Bnei Braq, Israel: private printing, 1979). This particular responsum belongs to Bezalel Ze'ev Safran's son, Ḥanokh Henikh Safran.

used to cut down trees for the altar were broken after the fifteenth of the month of Av. This appeared to be a clear transgression of *bal tashḥit*. Why destroy the axes? Specifically, the difficulty was phrased in the following manner: "Why did they break the axe with which they cut down trees for the altar, thereby scornfully transgressing *bal tashḥit*, which commands us to not destroy anything which is needed by humans (*yesh bo tzorekh*), for the sages have said, 'Anyone who destroys utensils with destructive intent (*derekh hashḥatah*) transgresses the prohibition of *bal tashḥit*.'" It is unclear whether Safran was directly quoting the person who posed the question or whether he was paraphrasing. Ultimately, Safran asserted that breaking these axes was not a transgression of *bal tashḥit* because it was used for items that were consecrated; it would be improper to use the same axes for anything profane. This is based on the logic from b*Avodah Zarah* 11a: the utensils of the sovereign must be burned so that others could not use them, and this is not a transgression of *bal tashḥit*.

While Schneerson and Halbershtam discussed cases where sanctified items cannot be destroyed (even though they both end up justifying it in their particular cases), Safran dealt with a sanctified item that must be destroyed due to its status. He based his answer on the directive that necessitates the destruction of a deceased sovereign's effects so that they are not used by anyone else. In his responsum he used both Meyuḥas bar Eliyahu's term, "need" (*tzorekh*), claiming that *bal tashḥit* only applies to things that fill human needs, and Maimonides's term, *derekh hashḥatah*, claiming that even when an item that is needed is wasted/destroyed, for there to be a transgression the act must be done in a destructive manner.

Mishneh Halakhot 12:432[29]

Menasheh Klein was asked whether it is permissible to fish for pleasure (in this particular case it appears that Klein assumed that the fish would not be consumed). Klein claimed that such sport is forbidden for two reasons; the first, because it transgresses the prohibition against causing animals to suffer needlessly (*tza'ar ba'alei ḥayim*) and this unnecessarily harms the fish, and the second because it transgresses the prohibition of *bal tashḥit*. He elaborated that it is prohibited to waste/destroy anything, and this is so *a fortiori* in the case of a living

29. Menasheh Klein, *Sefer Mishneh Halakhot*, Part 12.

animal. He also argued that fish were given to humanity to consume and not to needlessly destroy. With regard to harming animals, he asked rhetorically, when a fish is caught unnecessarily (*lo letzorekh*), how can there be benefit/enjoyment in it (*hana'ah*)? He then brought up the question of whether *bal tashḥit* applies to ownerless items. He concluded that it did, referencing the interaction between Rabbi and Rabbi Pinḥas from b*Ḥullin* 7b (presented earlier). Klein claimed that if it were permissible to destroy ownerless items, then Rabbi would have disowned the mules and then killed them. That he did not do so proves, according to Klein, that *bal tashḥit* still applies to ownerless items.

Menasheh Klein's rejection of fishing for pleasure highlights both Meyuḥas bar Eliyahu and Baḥya bar Asher's innovations. Any action that functionally serves no need and has no benefit is prohibited because of *bal tashḥit*. Klein, of course, was making his own judgment call about what defines benefit, rejecting the possibility that the pleasure gained from the fishing could offset the prohibition. Without his having explicitly said so, it seems clear that Klein would define benefit within economic parameters. He then shifted his response to discuss ownerless items (in this case the fish), making the claim that destroying/wasting them would be a transgression of *bal tashḥit*.[30]

Inculcation of Moral Dispositions

Shu"t Ḥakham Tzvi 26[31]

Tzvi Hirsch ben Yaakov Ashkenazi (1660–1718, Moravia, but traveled throughout Europe) offered his opinion on a legal dispute Shlomo ben Yeḥiel Luria (1510–1574, Poland) had with Maimonides. Maimonides held that Jews are accountable for their actions toward Gentiles, just as they are toward Jews. Luria, however, contended that the Torah was only given to Israel and the laws within it are only applicable to Jews in relation to other Jews (unless otherwise stated). Ashkenazi rejected

30. This is an important voice countering Yeḥezkel Landau and Avraham Tzvi Hirsch Eisenstadt's claim seen below that hunting could not be prohibited on the grounds of *bal tashḥit*, because the prohibition does not apply to ownerless items.

31. Tzvi Hirsch Ashkenazi, *Sefer She'elot UTeshuvot Ḥakham Tzvi HaShalem* (Tel-Aviv: Leon Publishing, 1963).

Luria's position, by explaining that even though Gentiles may rob and mistreat Jews, it would be inappropriate to reciprocate. He based this approach in part on Maimonides's Laws of Kings (6:7–8), which states that when one is besieging a city one side should be left open to allow those who want to escape with their lives to do so. To this he added examples of the prohibitions against cutting down trees and harming animals and concluded that leaving these unharmed is not for the sake of plant and animal life, but for the sake of the individual—"for ourselves, so that we instill in our souls true opinions and good and honest qualities for our merit in order to better ourselves."

In discussing relations between Jews and Gentiles, Tzvi Hirsch Ashkenazi claimed that even if mistreated, Jews should not reciprocate. He compared this law to the prohibitions against wastefulness and causing animals to suffer needlessly, justifying his approach on moral grounds. He asserted that though trees and animals have no intrinsic value, abstaining from harming them instills good qualities in human beings. Though *Sefer HaḤinukh* is not mentioned in the responsum by name, its author was the first (after the Talmudic account of Rabbi Ḥanina and his son Shiveḥat) to apply the aspect of morality and human betterment through humane treatment of the nonhuman world to the rationalization of *bal tashḥit*.

Torah LiShmah 400[32]

Yosef Ḥaim ben Eliyahu (1834–1909, Iraq) was asked whether it is permissible for a husband to destroy his wife's immodest clothes. The background to the question was that a man bought some expensive silk at the market and gave it to his wife for her to have a dress made from the material. The problem was that the silk was so fine that it was sheer, and due to its fine quality it attracted attention. The man pleaded with his wife that she not wear the garment for reasons of modesty, but on occasion she would defy his request. The questioner asked whether it would be permissible to secretly burn the garment in a way that would not be noticed, or would doing so be a transgression of the prohibition against wastefulness? Yosef Ḥaim ben Eliyahu claimed that doing so would not be a transgression of *bal tashḥit*. He based his reply on b*Berakhot* 31a, in which certain expensive items were

32. Yosef Ḥaim ben Eliyahu, *Sefer Torah LiShmah* (Jerusalem: Offset Re'em, 1976).

destroyed to temper the joy of the sages.[33] He reasoned that if their actions were not a transgression of *bal tashḥit*, then destroying things for the sake of fulfilling a commandment is permissible. He suggested that the man act in a discreet manner to avoid bringing strife into his marriage. He then presented a number of other examples where it is considered permissible to act in a wasteful/destructive manner to perform commandments or even to do so in an exalted manner. The examples included the burning of expensive clothing to honor Rabbi Shimon bar Yoḥai on the festival of *Lag BaOmer*, and keeping candles lit during the day in the synagogue when their light is unnecessary. Basing himself on Maimonides (Laws of Kings 6:8–10), he concluded that *bal tashḥit* is only a transgression of biblical law with regard to destroying fruit trees; all extensions of *bal tashḥit* beyond this are rabbinic law.

Another approach to moral issues concerning *bal tashḥit* can be found in the responsum of Yosef Ḥaim ben Eliyahu. He had to balance a number of factors in the case presented to him—modesty, peace and harmony in the home, and the prohibition against wastefulness. He presented modesty as a moral issue and by weighting the various parameters he created a hierarchy of values. Issues of modesty together with the stress caused to the marriage as a result justified for ben Eliyahu the destruction of an expensive garment

Mishneh Halakhot 17:170[34]

Menasheh Klein was asked whether it is prohibited to treat nonsentient material such as plants or nonliving material disgracefully, or whether the prohibition only applies to sentient animals. Klein answered that the *halakhah* states that anyone who embarrasses their fellow in public does not merit the world to come. There are, however, exceptions to the rule. In particular, it does not apply to a person who shames someone who feels no shame, such as a fool (b*Baba Qama* 86b). Such a case might indicate that it is indeed permitted to disgrace nonsentient material. However, he then mentioned the connection made in *BeMidbar Rabbah* 17 of the Israelite spies who spoke poorly of the land of Canaan and as a result the Israelites ended up wandering

---

33. The sages asserted that all joy in the world should be tempered so long as the Temple is destroyed.

34. Menasheh Klein, *Sefer Mishneh Halakhot*, Part 17 (New York: Machon Mishneh Halachos, 2009).

the desert for forty years. Klein also presented another midrash from b*Berakhot* 62b in which Rabbi Yose bar Ḥanina stated that David could not keep warm in his old age (1 Kings 1) because he had cut off part of Saul's garment (1 Samuel 24). In other words, because he disrespected the garment by cutting it, garments no longer provided him with warmth.[35] These midrashic narratives indicate that it is prohibited to disrespect nonsentient material. To reinforce this position he claimed that the interpretation of m*Avot* 4:3[36] is that the entire created world has value and should not be disgraced. He presented the work of Yonah of Gerona, who claimed that a righteous person is aware of the purpose (*tzorekh*) of all things in the world; there is nothing superfluous in the world as it is all the fruit of God's creation. Finally, Klein concluded that in books of ethics the sources discuss someone who needlessly (*lelo tzorekh*) tears the leaf off a tree, calling such an action a transgression of the prohibition against wastefulness. These sources assert that everything in God's world was created for a purpose (*tzorekh*). As such, there is no difference between a person or nonsentient material; defiling either is transgressive.

Menasheh Klein took a very different approach to the issue of morality with respect to *bal tashḥit*. He brought examples from the midrash of instances where those who, whether by actions or by words, treated the nonsentient world disgracefully were punished measure for measure. The reason for the legal standing of the nonsentient world was not to inculcate humans with good character, but because of their intrinsic value. In other words, the prohibition comes not to imbue humans with moral qualities, but the righteous who already have such qualities are inherently aware that these things are imbued with divine purpose (*tzorekh*).

Hunting

Noda BiYehudah, Mahadurah Tinyana, Yoreh De'ah 10[37]

Yeḥezkel ben Yehudah Landau (1713–1793, Poland and Bohemia) was asked whether hunting animals is permissible. Landau approached

35. This is an example of *middah keneged middah* (measure for measure).

36. m*Avot* 4:3: He [Ben Azzai] used to say: Despise not any man, and discriminate not against any thing, for there is no man who has not his hour, and there is no thing that has not its place.

37. Yeḥezkel Landau, *Sefer Noda BiYehudah, Mahadurah Tinyana, Yoreh De'ah* 10, Part 1, ed. David Aharon Freundlich (Jerusalem: Makhon Yerushalayim, 2004).

the query by discussing whether hunting falls under the prohibition against causing animals to suffer needlessly (*tza'ar ba'alei ḥayim*) or *bal tashḥit*. He concluded that since the animal is not being made to suffer, this could not be a reason for prohibiting hunting, and since, in his opinion (and contrary to Shneiur Zalman's), *bal tashḥit* does not apply to ownerless things, it would not be a transgression of *bal tashḥit* to engage in such activities. He also asserted that since there is value in the hide of the animal, killing is not considered a violation of *bal tashḥit*. He did, however, have difficulty with permitting hunting, due to the cruelty of hunting as a sport and the danger the hunter puts himself in by hunting dangerous animals. He concluded by permitting it for those who hunt for a living, but not for sport. From a strictly legal perspective he could find no problematic issue with hunting, but when taking into account other considerations such as morality and inherent danger he was able to prohibit it.

While not part of the responsa literature, Avraham Tzvi Hirsch Eisenstadt (1813–1868, Russia and Lithuania) in his work on the *Shulḥan Arukh, Pitḥei Teshuvah, Yoreh De'ah*, Laws of Slaughter 28:10, summarized Landau's position.[38] In his explanation of why killing an animal through hunting is not *bal tashḥit*, Eisenstadt claimed that the prohibition only applies to the destruction of things that have value, and animals have value only insofar as humans can derive benefit/enjoyment from them. He claimed that while alive, the wild animal has no value to humans, but when dead, the animal's hide and flesh have value. In other words, Eisenstadt qualified benefit/enjoyment solely in monetary terms.

While both Landau and Eisenstadt assert that it is permissible to wantonly destroy things from which humans do not derive benefit, they are both careful to add that in this particular case value is accrued through the death of the animal.[39] By adding this they are doing two important things. First, they are assuming that the hunter will use the hide and/or flesh of the dead animal. Second, part of their justification for permitting an act that they consider abhorrent is that the hunter is doing a service by creating value out of something which, in their eyes, has none. In other words, the hunter is transformed from being unethical to making a positive contribution to human welfare.

---

38. Avraham Tzvi Hirsch Eisenstadt, *Pitḥei Teshuvah*, in *Shulḥan Arukh: Yoreh De'ah*, Vol. 1 (New York: Grossman's Publishing House, 1954).

39. Also, see the previous chapter regarding the discussion of slaughtering a sickly animal with a knife used for idolatry.

Contemporary

There are, perhaps surprisingly, very few examples of contemporary rabbis writing on wastefulness. This section covers three rabbis who weighed in on wastefulness from a legal perspective. The following discourses do not necessarily carry the weight of legal rulings and as such cannot really be defined as responsa. Nevertheless, this type of legal essay has become commonplace among contemporary scholars of *halakhah*. Moshe Yitzhak Vorhand (UK and Israel) and Yosef Gavriel Bechhofer (USA) wrote in the form of legal essays that are meant to inform their readers, yet do not carry the weight of actual responsa. The weight of Avraham Dov Auerbach's (Israel) position is somewhat less clear because Yitzhak Eliyahu Shtasman presents it as "I heard from my teacher and father-in-law [Auerbach] . . ."

Electricity

Avraham Dov Auerbach is the son of one of the greatest legal authorities of the twentieth century, Shlomo Zalman Auerbach, and a legal authority in his own right as the Chief Rabbi of Tiberias. He claimed that while it is prohibited to burn a candle or an oil lamp inefficiently under the prohibition of *bal tashhit* (the prohibition against wastefulness), this does not apply to the use of electricity.[40] He argues that whereas the candle or the oil lamp are composed of materials that have a value that is diminished when burned, the same does not apply to electricity. Presumably, he based his claim on the fact that there is just as much light in the room every time the switch is flipped. Thus, he claimed that the only issue at hand is whether the additional cost of the electricity transgresses the prohibition against wastefulness; he asserted that it does not, because the money is not lost but rather it is acquired by another person (the utility company).

Disposable Utensils

Moshe Yitzhak Vorhand claimed that discarding items such as disposable dishes, even though in theory they could be washed and used again, would not be a transgression of *bal tashḥit*. His reasoning was

---

40. Yitzḥak Eliyahu Shtasman, *Sefer Etz HaSadeh: BeDinei Bal Tashḥit, Qetzitzat Ilanot UVizui Okhalin* (Jerusalem: Foundation for the Advancement of Torah Study, 1999), 7:11:33.

that the very function of disposable dishes is one-time use. As such, using the dishes once and discarding them is in fact a fulfillment of their purpose, and no special effort needs to be made in trying to salvage them for additional use.[41] Though Vorhand frames the issue as a legal statement, it could easily have been posed as a question/answer (responsa) form: Is it necessary to reuse disposable dishes to avoid transgressing *bal tashḥit*?

Recycling

Yosef Gavriel Bechhofer sought to understand whether recycling is mandated by *halakhah*.[42] After providing a brief but thorough background to the *bal tashḥit* he narrowed down the issue to whether wastefulness caused by inaction (in this case failure to recycle) is in fact a transgression. He claimed that recycling would be a fulfillment of the commandments to love your neighbor and to perform acts of loving-kindness. He then claimed that the issue of wastefulness with regard to recycling is only relevant in circumstances where the value of recycled product exceeds the cost of the process. Due to the fact that some legal authorities hold that preventing gain (and not just causing loss) is a transgression, not recycling, especially in cases where it is not difficult to do so, is a transgression of *bal tashḥit*.

Analysis

All three of these contemporary scholars deal with various issues that touch on the prohibition against wastefulness. None, however, frame their discourse as environmental issues. The conclusions reached by Auerbach and Vorhand are indicative of this lack. Auerbach justifies unlimited use of electricity and Vorhand allows for the disposing of disposables. Auerbach's position also appears completely ignorant of the process of electricity production in general and specifically in Israel, where approximately 97 percent of electricity comes from nonrenewable resources.[43] Vorhand's question is also indicative of a

41. Moshe Yitzḥak Vorhand, *Sefer Birkat HaShem: Leqet Dinei Issur Qetzitzat Ilanei Ma'akhal, Bal Tashḥit BiShe'ar Devarim, VeIssur Hefsed UVizui Okhalim* (Jerusalem: private printing, 2000), 2:22, 153–54.

42. Yosef Gavriel Bechhofer, "*HaMiḥzur BaHalakhah*," *Teḥumin* 16 (1996): 296–302.

43. http://www.sviva.gov.il/English/env_topics/climatechange/renewable-energy/Pages/Renewable-Energy-Implementation-in-Israel.aspx, accessed May 28, 2018.

very different frame of reference than that of environmentalists. An environmentalist would ask whether the use of disposable dishes to begin with is a transgression of *bal tashḥit*. Of the three, Bechhofer is the only one to conclude as we might expect an environmentalist to conclude—that not recycling would be a transgression of *bal tashḥit*. Yet Bechhofer, too, had to rely on more vague commandments (loving your neighbor and performing acts of loving-kindness) to justify his overall approach. The prohibition against wastefulness was limited in its use to the parameter of monetary value.

Conclusion

Bal tashḥit continues to prove itself to be a highly nuanced concept. For instance, as we observed, there is a debate in the traditional scholarship as to whether the prohibition against wastefulness applies to ownerless items. In the responsa literature, Menasheh Klein argued that it does, whereas Yeḥezkel Landau argued that it does not. Clearly, from an environmental perspective, Landau's approach appears to undermine the understanding of *bal tashḥit* as an environmental ethic. His position completely rejects the notion of nonhuman material having any intrinsic value. Even so, as we have already seen, understanding the nonhuman world as having intrinsic value is unnecessary for offering the environment a modicum of protection. Nevertheless, his position is certainly not the dominant one, and even those who do reject the idea of nonhuman material having value independent of their utility to humans might hold that such acts are to be avoided due to their corruption of human morality. The prime advocate for *bal tashḥit* as a measure for human morality was the author of *Sefer HaḤinukh*. His approach clearly left a legacy, as can be seen in the responsa dealing with moral aspects of the prohibition against wastefulness.

The very different approaches to how morality is read into the prohibition against wastefulness is reminiscent of the earlier debate encountered in the Bible chapter regarding the competing readings of Deuteronomy 20:19. Rashi's gloss is echoed in Menasheh Klein's responsum regarding the inherent value in all of God's creations. Similarly, ibn Ezra's reading of the verse resonates in Tzvi Hirsch Ashkenazi's responsum, which ascribes value based on human utility.

The legacy that Maimonides left on the conceptualization of *bal tashḥit* is perhaps apparent in no place more than in the responsa literature. The concept of destructive intent (*derekh hashḥatah*) was applied well beyond the realm of fruit trees. The use of the term is commonplace throughout the responsa dealing with *bal tashḥit*, and it is often used without any reference to its progenitor. Of particular note is David Tzvi Hoffmann's claim that the idea of destructive intent is universally accepted. Whether or not this is the case (and there is no reason to believe it is not), Hoffmann clearly understood it as such. Almost all the responsa presented in this chapter eventually give the questioner the green light to engage in whatever action they had doubts about, confirming that such behavior would not be a transgression of *bal tashḥit*. The permissive nature of the majority of the responsa can be attributed to the concept of "destructive intent." As demonstrated in the previous chapter, to do something in a destructive manner requires intent. Intent is an essential component of culpability for transgressions. A person who takes the time to write to a legal authority and wait for a response is unlikely to have any destructive intent. Subsequently, it is not surprising that most of the behaviors in question were permitted.

Of great significance are the legacies left by Meyuḥas bar Eliyahu, Baḥya bar Asher, the *Midrash Aggadah*, and *Sefer HaḤinukh*. The expressions of need (*tzorekh*), benefit/enjoyment (*hana'ah*), and utility (*to'elet*) have been widely adopted in the responsa scholarship concerning *bal tashḥit*. Interestingly, save for *Sefer HaḤinukh*, these individuals are simply not mentioned in the discourse on the prohibition against wastefulness. While it could be argued that such expressions are necessary to deal with the aspects of the prohibition and therefore there is nothing special about their use, such an approach is not compelling. After all, *bal tashḥit* as a concept required a significant degree of conceptualization before it became so economically focused. Nevertheless, the mere fact that the prohibition is evoked in such a variety of circumstances, including economics, moral issues, and self-harm, among others, shows definitively that *bal tashḥit* is not a mere prohibition but a broadly applied concept.

Also important was Klein's statement regarding the transgressive nature of treating the nonsentient world disgracefully. He asserted that there was no difference between defiling humans and materials. This is reminiscent of the early tannaitic stages of the conceptualization of *bal tashḥit*, in which the prohibition against wasting/destroying materials emerges analogously from the prohibition to harm oneself (t*Baba Qama* 9:31), and the prohibition against self-harm emerges *a fortiori* from the prohibition to waste/destroy material (b*Baba Qama* 91b). At this stage, a firm hierarchy that placed the body over material had not yet been established, allowing each prohibition to be learned from its counterpart. The fact that Klein can claim that there is no difference between humans and material in this case does not imply a rejection of the manner in which the prohibition was conceptualized by the *amoraim* and later authorities. Rather, it demonstrates that not every idea that is cast aside by one generation of thinkers is also cast aside by subsequent ones.

The responsa dealing with the relation between self-harm and wastefulness are varied. Yaakov Reicher evoked the concept of "the prohibition against destroying the body is more dear" (*bal tashḥit degufa adif*) to justify animal experimentation for medicinal purposes. This amoraic concept that confirms a hierarchy between the human body and material is used as a license to justify wastefulness and not prevent it. Ovadiah Yosef justified cosmetic surgery on the grounds of Maimonides's destructive manner and quarrelsome and shameful manner (*derekh hashḥatah* and *derekh nitzayon uvizayon*). In other words, both these legists used various conceptualizations of *bal tashḥit* to permit certain behaviors.

Yitzḥak Zilberstein is the most recent legist to hold that *bal tashḥit* encompasses both the prohibition against wastefulness/destruction and the prohibition against self-harm. To the best of my knowledge, he is also the only individual who explicitly differentiated permanent and temporary injuries with regard to the amoraic exemplum of Rav Ḥisda. His position demonstrates the continuity of the approach from the tannaitic era that *bal tashḥit* as an umbrella prohibition includes within it the prohibition against self-harm.

Finally, it is important to highlight that among contemporary scholars, individuals who have probably been exposed to environmental discourse to at least some extent, there is very little acknowledgement of *bal tashḥit* as a prohibition concerning the environment. Bechhofer discusses *bal tashḥit* in the context of recycling, one of the behaviors most closely associated with environmentalism, but does not mention the environment even once. Auerbach's apparent lack of understanding of how fossil fuels work is unlikely to be representative of the majority of the ultra-Orthodox. Yet the fact that Shtasman inserts Auerbach's position in his book without any critical analysis puts this assertion into question. At the very least, it demonstrates the gap between environmental and legal approaches to wastefulness that need to be bridged. Vorhand's position on disposables is also indicative of this gap. The different frame of reference Vorhand has as a legist as opposed to an environmentalist is eye-opening. Even when discussing disposables and wastefulness, Vorhand does not suggest that disposable dishes might be inherently wasteful.

Conclusions

This book charts the evolution of *bal tashḥit* ("waste not") as a prohibition over the course of its intellectual history, from Scripture to the classic rabbinical era through the Bible commentaries, codes, responsa, and finally, the environmental era in which we find ourselves. This book has been concerned with understanding the evolving nature of the concept, its compatibility with environmental values throughout its intellectual history, and through these, its utility as a contemporary environmental ethic.

I see three major phases in the postbiblical evolution of *bal tashḥit*. The first is the classic rabbinic period. The earliest and most important contributors to the conceptualization of *bal tashḥit* were Rabbi Eleazar ben Azariah and his student Rabbi Akiva (first and second centuries CE, Land of Israel) and an anonymous teaching from the Tosefta.[1, 2] As mentioned in the rabbinic chapter, at least a rudimentary version of the prohibition against wastefulness existed as early as the Jesus narratives in the New Testament, and probably prior to that as well. The latest contributor in this era to the discourse on *bal tashḥit* was Ravina (d. 421), who is considered to be one of those who began the process of compiling the Talmud. It is possible and even likely, however, that the arrangement of the narrative in which Ravina appears to have the final word was done by the later *savoraim* (c. 550–c. 630).

A number of rabbis throughout the Mishnah, Tosefta, and Babylonian Talmud contributed to the collection of teachings and narratives on

1. It is problematic to assert that a particular teaching originated with a particular sage even if the teaching is attributed to one and no competing traditions suggest an alternative. Entering this debate is beyond the scope of this book.

2. According to the Talmudic tradition, any anonymous statement made in the Tosefta belongs to Rabbi Neḥemiah (c. 150 CE). See b*Sanhedrin* 86a.

the cutting down of trees, self-harm, and other forms of wastefulness. Rabbi Eleazar taught, "I heard that he who rends [his garments] too much for a dead person transgresses the command, 'Thou shalt not destroy (*bal tashḥit*),' and it seems that this should be the more so in the case of injuring his own body" (b*Baba Qama* 91b). Rabbi Eleazar was the earliest known rabbi to use (or have attributed to him) the term *bal tashḥit* with regard to wasteful/destructive behavior. His *a fortiori* statement claimed that we learn about the prohibition against self-harm from the prohibition against wastefulness. While he linked the prohibitions to each other, he also established a hierarchy between humans and nonhuman creation. Although the link between the prohibitions is maintained by Rabbi Akiva and the Tosefta, the hierarchy established by Rabbi Eleazar is absent in their teachings.

In his defense of a woman who had been publically embarrassed, Rabbi Akiva taught, "[W]here one injures oneself though forbidden, he is exempt, yet, were others to injure him, they would be liable. So also he who cuts down his own plants, though not acting lawfully, is exempt, yet were others to [do it], they would be liable" (m*Baba Qama* 8:6). Rabbi Akiva made an analogy between the prohibition against self-harm and the prohibition against cutting down one's own trees. Rabbi Akiva did not attribute the prohibition against self-harm to any specific verse, but his parallel teaching regarding the prohibition to cut down plantings is implicitly derived from Deuteronomy 20:19. The Tosefta attributed the prohibition against self-harm to Genesis 9:5 and applied it to a general prohibition against wastefulness. The Tosefta did not specifically mention *bal tashḥit* by name, but was clearly referring to the prohibition against wastefulness, and made an analogy between self-harm and wanton destruction. According to the Tosefta, if physical and emotional self-harm is prohibited, then so too must the harm of one's material possessions be forbidden. The second part of the Tosefta, which connects acts of wanton destruction to idolatry, is attributed to Rabbi Yoḥanan ben Nuri (late first and early second centuries), who was a friend and colleague of Rabbi Akiva (d. 135 CE), and there is certainly the possibility of a shared ideology on this matter. In summary, the earliest conceptualizations of *bal tashḥit* associated the prohibition against self-harm with the prohibition against wastefulness.

Over the course of a few hundred years and through the amoraic era, the conceptualization of *bal tashḥit* underwent a significant evolution. The teachings of the later sages of this era indicate just how radical the shift in understanding the prohibition was. Ravina took *bal tashḥit* in its rawest manifestation, the prohibition against cutting down fruit trees, and turned it into a utilitarian idea. Instead of prohibiting the cutting down of all fruit trees, now fruit trees could always be cut down as long as it could be justified economically. If the fruit tree could be worth more cut down than alive and growing, it became permissible to cut it down. At least in theory this created an avenue to cut down the last tree in the world. From this point forward, almost all considerations of *bal tashḥit* are economically oriented.

The relationship between self-harm and wastefulness was also addressed by the rabbis of the Talmud. The passage in b*Shabbat* 129a presented a list of rabbis who had expensive furniture broken and turned into firewood to create a source of heat after bloodletting. The list began with Samuel (c. 165–257, Babylonia), continued with his student Rav Yehudah bar Yeḥezkel (c. 220–299 CE, Babylonia), and ended with Rabbah bar Naḥmani (c. 270–c. 330 CE, Babylonia). Rabbah's nephew and student Abaye asked whether such an action was a transgression of *bal tashḥit*, to which Rabbah replied, "*bal tashḥit degufai adif li*," meaning "the prohibition against destroying my body is more dear to me." In other words, when faced with the problem of wasting a fine piece of furniture or potentially harming his body, he chose his body as being of greater concern. It is possible that such an approach comes to counter the teaching found in b*Sanhedrin* 74a stated in the name of Rabbi Eliezer (possibly ben Hyrcanus [c. first and second centuries CE, Land of Israel]) that the possessions of the righteous are more dear to them than their own bodies. This view was embodied by Rav Ḥisda in b*Baba Qama* 91b, who preferred to let his legs be scratched by thorns than to let the thorns tear his clothes.

The subjective element of Rabbah's statement is important. As far as we know, Rabbah was not relying on an earlier teaching, but rather was stating his own perspective on the matter. For him, the health of his body was more important than a piece of furniture, but for others, such as Rav Ḥisda, perhaps that was not the case. Shortly after Rabbah's generation this approach became the standard. In response to Rav Ḥisda and Rav Papa's statements in b*Shabbat* 140a that one should eat barley (bread) instead of wheat (bread) and drink beer instead of wine, the anonymous narrator of the Talmud (the *stam*), declared that these positions did not hold because of the overriding concept of "*bal tashḥit degufa adif*" or "the prohibition against destroying the body is more dear." The subjective element added by Rabbah was removed; his position had already become authoritative.

To summarize, over the course of a few hundred years, *bal tashḥit* evolved from a scriptural verse dealing with an anti-scorched-earth policy to a general prohibition against wastefulness. This transition was unspoken. Nowhere in the classic rabbinic sources do we find anything articulating the shift; it simply happened. Catherine Hezser argues that such a phenomenon is not surprising, because the rabbinic authors were not interested in creating general rules or principles, but dealt with each issue on a case-by-case basis.[3] That the Talmud offers examples of when *bal tashḥit* applies but does not discuss it as a concept is not exclusive to *bal tashḥit*. Nevertheless, just because the rabbis never discussed the conceptualization process does not mean that they were not intimately involved in it. Though they never use the term *bal tashḥit*, the Tosefta and Rabbi Akiva present the idea behind the prohibition against wastefulness and the prohibition against self-harm to be one and the same. A few hundred years later, the anonymous voice of the Talmud reframed the relationship between wastefulness and self-harm: the well-being of the body takes precedence over other forms of wastefulness. In other words, it became permissible to cause waste and destruction if there were competing bodily interests. In fact, "the prohibition against destroying the body is more dear" (*bal tashḥit degufa adif*) is only ever used to permit the destruction of material. The prohibition evolved in the tannaitic era into what might be today considered a powerful environmental concept, and due to Ravina's establishment of an economic framework through which to enact *bal tashḥit*, left the amoraic era environmentally weakened and with a strong economic focus.

The rabbis themselves certainly did not view *bal tashḥit* as an environmental ethic. Environmental awareness such as we have today is a very recent phenomenon. The rabbis, however, would have been aware of their local environment, and occasionally understood that their actions did have an impact on it. This distinction is a prelude to the position that the understanding reached by the rabbis toward the end of the amoraic era regarding the prohibition against wastefulness was not through any conscious antienvironmental trend whatsoever. Instead, the continued evolution of *bal tashḥit* was a conscious effort by the rabbis to find a balance between the limits on human behavior

3. Catherine Hezser, "Roman Law and Rabbinic Legal Composition," *The Cambridge Companion to the Talmud and Rabbinic Literature*, eds. Charlotte Elisheva Fonrobert and Martin S. Jaffee (Cambridge, UK: Cambridge University Press, 2007), 145.

caused by the prohibition and the creation of allowances for human needs. As such, it rapidly became a thoroughly anthropocentric concept.

As far as we know, no significant changes to the understanding of *bal tashḥit* manifested themselves in the geonic era. The next major stage in the evolution of the prohibition came in twelfth-century Egypt, advanced by one of the greatest Jewish thinkers of all time, Moses Maimonides. Maimonides made order of the Talmud, whose great wealth of material proved inaccessible to the uninitiated layperson simply looking for guidance on how to live life as a Jew. Maimonides collected the laws scattered throughout the Talmud and presented them as general principles in his *Sefer HaMitzvot* and his code of law, the *Mishneh Torah*. As such, he was the first person to articulate *bal tashḥit* as a general prohibition against wastefulness, even though it is clear that the sages of the classic rabbinic era also understood it in a similar light. Of great importance is not just the novel framework in which he showcased the prohibition against wastefulness, but also the nuanced manner in which he articulated it.

While Maimonides very much kept the economic aspect of the prohibition against wastefulness alive, he created a new framework for the prohibition based on subjectivity and intent. He asserted that an action had to be done in a destructive manner (*derekh hashḥatah*) to be considered a transgression of *bal tashḥit*.[4] The magnitude of Maimonides's impact on the conceptualization of *bal tashḥit* can be seen through the vast number of times the term is used in subsequent scholarship. How does one properly define what doing something in a destructive manner entails? What is it that Maimonides meant when he decreed that unless something is done in a destructive manner, there is no transgression? *Halakhah* tends to reflect what is permitted and what is prohibited, and not necessarily communal values. It is possible that Maimonides had in mind a notion that, based on the communal Jewish values of his day, would be an objective understanding of "destructive intent." This, however, is not reflected in his writing, which in effect implies that just as actions are carried out by individuals, so too are they the judges of their own actions. If one does not consider or intend one's actions to be wasteful or destructive, then they are not. This is supported by the fact that Maimonides asserted that the punishment for actions done in a destructive manner is lashes. Intent makes a

4. Laws of Kings 6:8, 10.

world of difference in *halakhah*. One is only ever liable for capital or corporal punishments for intentionally committed transgressions. All unintentional transgressions either go unpunished, or are liable to fines or various offerings at the Temple.

The idea of subjectivity is reflected in later sources as well, giving credence to this position. One such example is the case mentioned in earlier chapters of the individual aboard a ship who wants to eat a chicken, but has no earth with which to ceremonially cover the blood. Various authorities decreed that the individual is permitted to create ash for this purpose by burning a gold coin. According to Yosef Karo (1488–1575, Spain, Portugal, Turkey, Bulgaria, and Land of Israel), such an act would only be permissible so long as the chicken is worth more than the coin.[5] Karo's position understood the necessary calculations made with regard to *bal tashḥit* as being strictly economic. If the chicken is worth more than the gold coin, there is no transgression, and if it is not then there is a transgression, if the act is carried out.[6] There is no consensus, however, with regard to Karo's position, and there are contradicting legal rulings basing themselves on *bal tashḥit* as a subjective principle. For instance, Alexander Sender Schorr (c. 1673–1737, Poland) asserted that the issue is entirely based on subjectivity.[7] A rich person might have no qualms about wasting/destroying something if the end product is of greater importance for that person than the item destroyed to achieve it. Schorr claimed that even if the gold is worth more than the chicken, the act could still be permissible. For him, the only calculation necessary is whether one values eating the chicken more than one values the gold. If one were to extrapolate, for a particularly wealthy person, this could be taken to an extreme; a small fortune could be burned so long as the individual values the meal more than the money. While not a majority opinion, his ruling demonstrates the extremes to which a subjective understanding of the parameters of *bal tashḥit* can be taken.

Another important stage in the conceptualization of *bal tashḥit* is the assertion that the prohibition applies only to things for which humans have need (*tzorekh*). This innovation belonged to Meyuḥas

5. Yosef Karo, *Shulḥan Arukh, Yoreh De'ah, Hilkhot Sheḥitah* 28:21.

6. Again, there is no indication as to why "wasting" up to the value of the chicken is permissible while anything beyond that is transgressive.

7. Alexander Sender Schorr, *Sefer Simlah Ḥadashah, Tevu'ot Shor, Bekhor Shor* (Jerusalem: Levin-Epstein Publishing, 1966), 28:36.

bar Eliyahu (1150–1200, Byzantium). Other similar conceptualizations of the parameters of *bal tashḥit* emerged over the course of the next century or two. Solomon Buber's critical edition of *Midrash Aggadah* (twelfth or thirteenth century) to Deuteronomy 20:19 states that the prohibition against cutting down fruit trees extends beyond its context to prohibit the waste/destruction of anything from which one can derive benefit/enjoyment (*hana'ah*). This idea can also be seen in Baḥya bar Asher's (1255–1340, Spain) gloss on the same verse, in which he asserted that the prohibition is based on the understanding that a wise and intelligent person would not waste/destroy something needlessly but would rather derive utility (*to'elet*) from it. This is addressed by Pinḥas HaLevi, the author of *Sefer HaḤinukh* (thirteenth century, Spain), from a slightly different angle. He claimed that it is, of course, permissible to cut down a tree if one would derive utility (*to'elet*) from such an action. In other words, the prohibition is not absolute, the one exception being the ability to derive benefit from the destroyed item. It would be very difficult to make an accurate argument regarding the progenitor of this idea. Nevertheless, it is likely that this conceptualization of *bal tashḥit* emerged during this time period and was widely adopted in later sources dealing with the prohibition. This is profoundly significant, because it further weakened the claim of intrinsic value within the nonhuman parts of the created world, and with it the efficacy of *bal tashḥit* as an environmental ethic. Most notable in this regard is Yeḥezkel Landau's (1713–1793, Poland and Bohemia) responsum discussed in the responsa chapter, in which he asserted that a wild animal (and ownerless items in general) has no value unless it is killed and its pelt becomes a commodity.

After *Sefer HaḤinukh* in the thirteenth century and until today, Samson Raphael Hirsch (1808–1888, Germany and Moravia) is without doubt the person who made the most significant impact on the conceptualization of *bal tashḥit*. Hirsch expanded the moral dimension of *bal tashḥit* and described the prohibition as the most fundamental aspect of human interaction with God. He called *bal tashḥit* "the first and most general call of God."[8] The profundity of such a statement cannot be overstated. As a commandment not mentioned explicitly in the Decalogue or in the Torah and only in passing in codes such as the *Tur* and *Shulḥan Arukh*, this is an incredibly bold statement.

8. Samson Raphael Hirsch, *Horeb: A Philosophy of Jewish Laws and Observances*, 2nd ed., Vol. 2, trans. I. Grunfeld (London: Soncino Press, 1968), 279.

Through such statements and others noted above in the Bible chapter, he connected the prohibition against wastefulness with the human responsibility for stewardship (Deuteronomy 20:19), and the prohibition against self-harm with human responsibility toward the rest of creation (Genesis 9:5). He establishes himself as one of the most fundamental thinkers of Jewish environmental wisdom. As such, Hirsch must be considered one of the founding figures of the field of Judaism and environment.

Today there has been a proliferation of the use of the term *bal tashḥit* as a Jewish environmental ethic. A simple internet search shows just how many environmentally leaning organizations and communities use the term as part of their activist, religious, or educational agendas. Over the past few years alone, scores if not hundreds of new groups have evoked the concept from an environmental perspective.

As the conclusions demonstrate, this study does not come to undermine the environmental understanding of *bal tashḥit,* but to reinforce it. By using established methodological tools, it charts the evolution of *bal tashḥit* as a concept anchored firmly in Jewish tradition (as opposed to a largely "foreign" environmental concept). Such an approach accomplishes two things. First, it provides a solid foundation on which scholars and activists can build. This document acts as an accessible resource that can be understood by religious practitioners, environmental scholars, activists, and others. The presentation of the material strives to be as nuanced and as objective as possible, enabling readers to formulate their own opinions on the subject. Second, by presenting the intellectual history of *bal tashḥit,* it is assumed that the conclusions reached may be more palatable to religious practitioners. Demonstrating that the religious and environmental approaches are not in conflict with one another, but rather that on this subject they can complement each other, should help advance the joint discourse.

Morality and Rationality

As can be seen throughout this book, the prohibition against wastefulness encompasses a considerable number of daily life circumstances. The prohibition sets behavior parameters that define how it expects humans to interact with the material world. *Bal tashḥit* is not merely a prohibition with a fixed set of parameters to which a Jew is expected to adhere. Rather, due to the scope of the circumstances to which the prohibition applies, particularly with regard to people's daily routine, it is, at least in theory, a way of life. The fact that this is a prohibition one must keep in mind almost constantly led people to attempt to rationalize its purpose and imbue it with ethical meaning. These rationalizations can be seen throughout the various genres of literature covered in the different chapters. As such, in the conclusion to this work it is useful to summarize these rationalizations.

Though rationalizations of the prohibition can be found throughout the various genres of literature, the sources for the most part focus on the practical dimensions of the prohibition. This makes considerable sense, since people have generally been concerned with defining the legal parameters of *bal tashḥit* in light of its being first and foremost a prohibition. In other words, the prohibition has been seen as a guide to direct people's behavior, but understanding the purpose of the prohibition has not been a primary concern. This is not to say that people have not written about the rationale behind the prohibition, as indeed many have. Rather, those who have explicitly written in detail about the ethical dimensions of *bal tashḥit* are limited in number.

Two main approaches can be found in the literature. One views the prohibition as coming to protect human interests and the other to protect nonhuman interests. The second approach distances itself from a human-centered outlook and sees value in all of God's creations such that they should not be needlessly wasted or destroyed. If one were to define these approaches using technical environmental jargon, the terms "ecocentric" and "anthropocentric" would be appropriate. Both are also theocentric, as the prohibition itself is a divine directive and ultimately, the offence in transgressing the prohibition is against God.

These different rationalizations for *bal tashḥit* are in part reflected in the scriptural interpretations of Deuteronomy 20:19. One need only look at the number of Bible commentators who weighed in on the meaning of the phrase "*ki ha'adam etz hasadeh*" from Deuteronomy 20:19 to see that the issue has received considerable attention. The two dominant approaches found in the Bible commentaries are those of Rashi and Abraham ibn Ezra. Their positions have been analyzed in depth in the Bible chapter. If we were to extrapolate a broader approach from Rashi's comments we might conclude that he understood the prohibition against wastefulness to be concerned with the intrinsic value of the nonhuman world. Why should the nonhuman world suffer on account of unrelated human affairs? This approach comes with a number of problems and has already been critiqued, so I will not repeat it here. This is one way in which Rashi could be read. As we have seen, the idea of attributing intrinsic value to the nonhuman world is not uniquely his own, so Rashi would not be unique in this regard. This is important because if he were the only one advancing such an idea, it would be significantly more difficult to argue that this is what he meant.

Ibn Ezra understood the verse in a significantly different, much more human-oriented light. Fruit trees should not be cut down because they are a future food source from which benefit can be derived. Ultimately, the fruit trees themselves are not what matter; rather, the benefit they provide to humans is what is important. A broader ethic can be extrapolated from ibn Ezra's gloss, which is in fact the dominant force behind most legal rulings on *bal tashḥit*, namely that anything from which humans can benefit should not be wasted. As we have seen, the flip side of this approach is that anything that a person does for human benefit is not considered wasteful. Both Rashi and ibn Ezra's opinions can be found elsewhere, with ibn Ezra's approach being much more widely applied. This, of course, should come as no surprise considering that it is based on an idea that is much more readily translated into practice.

These medieval giants are not the first to express these ideas. Both of their approaches can be found in the midrash—*Sifre Devarim* and *Midrash Tannaim leSefer Devarim*. Among Bible commentators, however, they are certainly the ones who popularized them. Ibn Ezra's approach appears to be more pragmatic, while Rashi's is morally inclined. The conclusions from the chapter on Bible interpretation indicate that while the commentaries offered explanations as to what the above phrase meant, it was almost always exclusively in the context of why one should not cut down fruit trees. Only very rarely did any of the exegetes explicitly extend their glosses to include the general prohibition against wastefulness. Thus, it takes a certain degree of deduction to apply these glosses more widely than the context of the verse. Other sources, however, do rationalize the prohibition against wastefulness in much more explicit terms.

Ecocentrism

In many instances in Scripture and elsewhere, the intrinsic value of nonhuman creation is assumed. Some examples from Scripture include

Psalms 114, in which inanimate entities such as rivers and mountains become animated, or Psalms 104, which describes God sustaining all of creation independent of human involvement. Another source, *Pereq Shirah*, has a long list of nonhuman creations singing praises of God by quoting verses from Scripture (mainly Psalms).[9] The same is true for the Sabbath and festival liturgies, which recite the prayer *Nishmat Kol Ḥai* (the soul of all living things). Moreover, in Grace after Meals (*Birkat HaMazon*) the opening paragraph relates to God's providing sustenance for all of creation. Moses Maimonides himself was a strong proponent of seeing intrinsic value within the created world: "I consider therefore the following opinion as most correct according to the teaching of the Bible, and best in accordance with the results of philosophy; namely, that the Universe does not exist for man's sake, but that each being exists for its own sake, and not because of some other thing."[10]

Another example can be found in Genesis *Rabbah* (aggadic midrash from the fifth or sixth centuries): "Rabbi Simon said: There is no grass or greenery that does not have a sign (*mazal*) in heaven that strikes it and tells it: grow!"[11] Naḥmanides (1194–1270, Spain and Land of Israel) used this midrash as a rationale for the prohibition against hybrid species (*kilayim*), adding that "whosoever fixes hybrids or plants [seeds] in a way such that they feed off of each other nullifies the laws of heaven."[12] More recently, a biography on Aryeh Levine (1885–1969, Lithuania and Israel) discussed Avraham Yitzḥak Kook's (1865–1935, Latvia and Israel) understanding of this midrash as a reason not to engage in wastefulness and wanton destruction.[13] These examples illustrate an established tradition attributing intrinsic value to the nonhuman world, making it more readily acceptable that this position could exist also with regard to *bal tashḥit*. This may be reflected in the strong antihunting tradition in Judaism, which is also

9. *Pereq Shirah* is a pseudoepigraphical writing whose authorship has been attributed to King David and King Solomon, but it is more likely to be a medieval text.

10. Moses Maimonides, *The Guide for the Perplexed*, 2nd ed., trans. M. Friedlander (London: Routledge and Kegan Paul, 1904), 3:8, 274.

11. *Bereishit Rabbah* (Albeck ed.), *Parashat Bereishit* 10.

12. Naḥmanides, Leviticus 19:19.

13. Simḥah Raz, *Ish Tzadik Hayah: Masekhet Ḥayav shel Rabbi Aryeh Levine* (Jerusalem: Zak and Partners Publishing, 1982), 74.

evident in the many Passover *haggadot* that identify the prototypical evil son (*rasha*) as a hunter.[14]

While illustrating the intrinsic value of the nonhuman world is an important backdrop to an ethical understanding of *bal tashḥit*, the point strikes home through examples that demonstrate such an understanding vis-à-vis human behavior. This approach can be found in Psalms 145:9: "The Lord is good to all, and His mercy is upon all His works." The verse itself is a continuation of the theme of intrinsic value but is connected by David Qimḥi (1160–1235, Provence) to wastefulness and wanton destruction in his gloss: "The Lord is good to all: He is even kind and compassionate to the animals, beasts and fowl. Thus, it is worthy for humans to walk in [good and compassionate] paths and avoid damaging or destroying life, other than when it is necessary."[15]

Another example can be found in Moshe Alsheikh's (1507–c. 1600, Turkey, Land of Israel, and elsewhere) gloss to Deuteronomy 20:19. Among other things he stated, "Behold and see how great the mercy of the Blessed One is; not only does He have mercy on humans, but also on every fruit tree in the place which you conquer." Not only do humans have value, but so do the fruit trees in their own right. Alsheikh derived from this statement that if God has compassion on lesser creations such as fruit trees then *a fortiori* God has compassion on humans. While Alsheikh's bottom line focuses on humans, he clearly held the position that God has compassion even on the nonhuman world, indicating that all of God's creations have intrinsic value.

A final example (though undoubtedly there are others) relating specifically to the cutting down of fruit trees and thus to the core of Deuteronomy 20:19 is the midrash from *Pirqei deRabbi Eliezer* 33 (Higger edition). This midrash stated that there are six things that evoke a cry that can be heard from one end of the world to the other. One of the six on the list is the fruit-bearing tree that is cut down. The animation of the fruit tree not only imbues it with intrinsic value, it illustrates the transgressive nature of such behavior.

Anthropocentrism: Morality

The anthropocentric approach can be broken down into two groups united by a focus on the human dimension of the prohibition. The

14. As I have observed in dozens of *haggadot*.

15. David Qimḥi, Psalms 145:9.

first group views the rationale for the prohibition as instilling good moral values in humans. The other group rationalizes the prohibition through economic considerations; wastefulness and wanton destruction have a harmful economic impact on humans and consequently should be avoided. It is possible to imagine that Rashi falls into the first anthropocentric group, rather than seeing him as thinking fruit trees have intrinsic value.

Phrasing the prohibition as a moral issue is best represented by the thirteenth-century work of *Sefer HaḤinukh* quoted above in the codes chapter:

> [Observing the prohibition against wastefulness] is the way of the righteous and people of deeds who love peace and delight in the goodness of humanity/creation and draw them near to the Torah; they do not waste even a grain of mustard in this world. Their instinct when encountering wastefulness and destruction is to try to prevent it with all their strength.[16]

This view does not broach the topic of whether the nonhuman created world has value beyond what it has to offer the human world. *Sefer HaḤinukh* asserted that the prohibition comes to instill humans with good values, something that might be described as moral education. Presumably, the assumption is that if humans are concerned even with the most minor things, how much more should they be concerned with the most significant aspects of life, such as God, Torah, and fellow humans? The focus of the prohibition for him, however, is grounded in human morality. There is no indication that *Sefer HaḤinukh* attributes any value to the nonhuman creations and the world beyond what they have to offer humans on a moral level. The view that the nonhuman world is only valuable insofar as it can offer something to humanity, however, would not be uniquely his. This approach appears very similar to the one found in Ecclesiastes *Rabbah*:[17]

> Behold God's creation, for who could fix it if it was marred? At the time when God created the first man he took him to

16. Pinḥas HaLevi (?), *Sefer HaḤinukh*, ed. Ḥaim Dov Chavel (Jerusalem: Mossad HaRav Kook, 1952), 529.

17. This midrash is found in many contemporary writings in the field of Judaism and environment.

> review each and every tree in the Garden of Eden and told him: "Behold my creations how pleasant and praiseworthy they are. All that I created, I created for you. Pay heed that you do not ruin and destroy My world. For if you ruin it, there is no one after you who will fix it."[18]

The concern both in Ecclesiastes *Rabbah* and in *Sefer HaḤinukh* is first and foremost with preventing wastefulness and wanton destruction. There are two key elements in the midrash, however, that shape how the prohibition is viewed. The first is "All that I have created, I created for you." All nonhuman creations were created for the sake of humans and for their utility. The second is that that the midrash emphasizes that while all of God's creations were made explicitly for humans, they still belong to God ("My world"). God is the ultimate owner, implying that use is permitted, but wastefulness and wanton destruction are not. Even though the midrash and *Sefer HaḤinukh* do not explicitly reject the idea that the nonhuman world has value of its own accord, they do nothing to suggest that this is the case.

A somewhat different angle, but along the same line of moral approaches to *bal tashḥit*, is the concept of *hakarat hatov* or awareness of [God's] beneficence. This is a well-known idea in classic Jewish literature that also happens to arise in the context of the prohibition against wastefulness. To illustrate the connection, a few examples are helpful. The first is a question posed by Rava (c. 280–c. 352 CE, Babylonia) to his teacher Rabbah bar Mari (approximately the same time period) found in b*Baba Qama* 92b:

> Rava said to Rabbah bar Mari: "From whence is the popular saying: 'A well that you have drunk from you should not throw dirt into?'" He said to him "As it is written in the Torah (Deuteronomy 23:8): 'You shall not abhor an Edomite, for he is your brother; you shall not abhor an Egyptian, because you were a stranger in his land.'"

This adage offers a nuanced approach to *bal tashḥit*. As can be seen by Rabbah bar Mari's response, the answer is not simply because of the prohibition against wastefulness. It is not merely another example of

18. *Qohelet Rabbah* (Vilna ed.), 7:13.

a specific application of *bal tashḥit*. Rather, the prohibition applies to a situation in which someone benefited from something and as a result of that benefit that something acquires a protected status. The *Midrash Tanḥuma* (fourth to fifth centuries CE, Land of Israel) drew a more overt connection in this regard by bringing the very same adage to explain why Moses did not want to be personally involved in the war against the Midianites: "Due to the fact that he grew up in Midian he said: 'It is unjust that I harass them in light of the good they did unto me.' "[19] Samuel David Luzzatto (1800–1865, Italy) applied this wisdom to his gloss on Deuteronomy 20:19. There he claimed that the prohibition against cutting down fruit trees comes in order to distance Israelites from ungratefulness and teach them to love the things from which they derive benefit. A food source from which benefit was derived should not then be destroyed. By mentioning ungratefulness, Luzzatto explicitly connected the idea of "awareness of [God's] beneficence" to *bal tashḥit*. As we saw, Ecclesiastes *Rabbah* asserted that all nonhuman creation was created for the benefit of humans. Thus, understood in a meta sense, by virtue of this relationship, all nonhuman creation is under this protected status.

Another *midrash* dealing with similar ideas is based on the well-known narrative of Jacob's wrestling with the angel (Genesis 32:25). The *baraita/midrash* (b*Ḥullin* 91a) explains that the reason Jacob returned to his previous campsite was to see if he forgot "*pakkim qetanim*," defined by Markus Jastrow as "small flasks."[20] Returning to the campsite was a dangerous endeavor, so for Jacob to put himself in such danger for almost worthless items is confounding. The midrash capitalizes on this by stating that the righteous are more concerned with their belongings than their welfare. To illustrate our point, the midrash is best explained by Samson Raphael Hirsch in his gloss to this verse:

> According to the sages "he returned for small flasks" (b*Ḥullin* 91a). After crossing the stream with all his possessions he returned to see that he had not forgotten anything. "From here we see that the righteous are more concerned with their possessions than their bodies. And why is this so? Because

19. *Midrash Tanḥuma al Ḥamishah Ḥumshei Torah*, Vol. 2, ed. Shlomo Buber (Jerusalem: Ortsel, 1964), *Matot* 5.

20. Markus Jastrow, *Dictionary of the Targumim, the Talmud Babli and Yerushalmi and Midrashic Literature*, Peabody, MA: Hendricks Publishers, 2006), s.v. פך.

> they do not extend their hands to robbery." Property that was acquired honestly by a righteous person, even if it has no value whatsoever, is considered holy in his eyes. He will not waste it or wantonly destroy it and is responsible for its efficient use. Thousands of *zuzim*[21] are in his eyes as a shoestring when they are being spent for a worthy cause, while the value of a shoestring is worth thousands of *zuzim* when it is being wantonly wasted. Whosoever "does not extend his hand to robbery," and calls his own only what he succeeding in acquiring through his honest efforts, will experience supervising grace over all items which he acquires. Whether a thread or a shoestring, it all comes to him through the honest sweat of his brow, is divinely blessed and is of inestimable value.[22]

While Hirsch describes the ultimate righteous person as someone who is concerned with even the smallest of items, this concern stems not from the intrinsic value of the item, but rather from the relationship of the individual to God. Part of the way this relationship manifests itself is through the material world, and the respect shown to material is in fact a respect for God and not the material itself.

Anthropocentrism: Economics

The other side of the anthropocentric approach is economic. Having a human-centered approach often requires viewing issues and ideas from an economic perspective. The prohibition against wastefulness and wanton destruction is no exception to this. The vast majority of sources dealing with *bal tashḥit* had an economically oriented approach to the prohibition. This approach is based on Ravina's assertion in the Talmud seen above. Even though Maimonides's greatest impact on the conceptualization of *bal tashḥit* is through its generalization and the coining of the term "in a destructive manner" (*derekh hashḥatah*), the very fact that he affirmed the economic dimension of the prohibition undoubtedly had a significant impact on its perseverance and pre-

21. A monetary unit.

22. Samson Raphael Hirsch, *Ḥamishah Ḥumshei Torah im Peirush Rashar Hirsch: Sefer Bereishit*, 4th ed., ed. and trans. Mordekhai Breuer (Jerusalem: Mossad Yitzḥak Breuer, 1989).

dominance in the discourse. Adding to this the nuanced approaches of Meyuḥas bar Eliyahu (need—*tzorekh*), Buber's *Midrash Aggadah* (benefit/enjoyment—*hana'ah*), and *Sefer HaḤinukh* and Baḥya bar Asher (utility—*to'elet*) mentioned above, one can see the development of the utilitarian manner in which *bal tashḥit* manifests itself.

This makes a great deal of sense. Translating *bal tashḥit* from theory into practice necessitates a certain degree of compromise. Sometimes trees need to be cut down, food thrown out, and clothes retired. When building urban infrastructure, safety measures are a standard part of the design process. Roads, bridges, tunnels, and buildings are often built to withstand the forces of nature to a certain extent. History tells us that severe weather events come once every certain number of years. For instance, we might have one severe storm every 10 years, one very severe storm every 50 years and one extremely severe storm every 100 years. The financial cost of building safety measures goes up in a commensurate manner for every increase in the magnitude of storm severity. Naturally, the more severe the weather event, the greater the economic damage and potential for loss of life. How does one proceed in such a circumstance? Do you plan for the 50-year storm? The 100-year storm? The 1,000-year storm? Clearly, at some point a cost/benefit analysis and assessment must be made, even when it is known that such decisions quantify, to some extent, the value of human life. Giving a monetary value to human life is standard practice for insurance companies. In other words, to not waste money, compromises are even made with regard to human life.

There are no cookie-cutter solutions with regard to protecting the environment. Wastefulness and wanton destruction can be prevented, whether out of concern for human morality, because of the intrinsic value of the nonhuman world, or even by considering long-term economics. If indeed waste is prevented, then the outcome is the same regardless of the underlying ideological motivators. The ideological premise for behaving a certain way does, however, become an issue when translated into practice. Such claims are best illustrated with examples. Imagine a situation in which you are scheduled to host a feast. The plan is to serve beef and for this very purpose you purchase a cow from your neighbor's farm. You know that you will only require half of the cow for your feast and are planning to freeze the remainder for future consumption. Prior to the arrival of the butcher, the local power generator blows a fuse and you are told that it will be days before power returns. You can still host your feast by candlelight and cook your food on gas burners. Freezing the unused beef, however, is no longer an option, and you are certain that it will spoil. You have enough food to feed your guests without the beef, but as a result the meal would not be quite as festive. Do you still go ahead with slaughtering the cow, keeping in mind that you are concerned with the prohibition against wastefulness? If your ethical reasoning behind the prohibition is that the cow has intrinsic value, and wasting a significant portion of it would disregard that value, then you might decide against slaughtering it. If, however, you are primarily concerned with making sure your feast is still a feast and you are willing to accept the economic loss, then perhaps you might still slaughter the cow. This is by no means a perfect example, nor does it occur in a vacuum, because there are clearly other factors that would influence your decision. Nevertheless, this example demonstrates the possibility of different outcomes based on one's moral understanding of *bal tashḥit*.

Until now, we have framed these as separate and perhaps even competing moral approaches to the prohibition against wastefulness. This, however, is not necessarily the case. It is possible to subscribe to more than one approach, because they are not necessarily in competition with each other. One can be concerned with the intrinsic value of the nonhuman world while simultaneously caring about instilling humans with good morals and still being mindful of the economic factors at play. The midrash itself presented both approaches as possible interpretations of Deuteronomy 20:19. Though it is not uncommon for midrash to have conflicting approaches to an issue on the same page, a second possible interpretation does not necessarily mean an opposing idea. Perhaps the fact that it is simpler for an individual approach to be directed by a single governing premise as opposed to multiple ones, especially if they can come into conflict with each other, led to an inherent narrowing of the application of *bal tashḥit*.

Religious vs. Environmental Approaches

One of the best examples illustrating the different approaches of religious thinkers and environmentalists can be found in Moshe Yitzḥak Vorhand's legal statement regarding the use of disposable dishes, which you saw in the responsa chapter (he issued a disclaimer in the introduction to his book that all of his own legal statements should be taken merely as suggestions and not as practical *halakhah* (*halakhah lema'aseh*).[23] He claimed that discarding items such as disposable dishes, even though in theory they could be washed and used again, would not be a transgression of *bal tashḥit*. His reasoning was that the very function of disposable dishes is one-time use. As such, using the dishes once and discarding them is in fact a fulfillment of their purpose, and no special effort needs to be made to try to salvage them for additional use.[24] Though Vorhand frames the issue as a legal statement, it could easily have been posed as a question/answer (responsa) form: Is it necessary to reuse disposable dishes to avoid transgressing *bal tashḥit*? Such a question indicates a very different frame of reference than that of environmentalists. An environmentalist would ask whether the use of disposable dishes to begin with is a transgression of *bal tashḥit*. With this example in mind, the gap between the theory and practice of the prohibition against wastefulness becomes a little clearer. This example is relatively straightforward because disposable dishes and plastic waste in general are issues that receive considerable attention in environmental discourse.

Other examples are somewhat more obscure, but still serve as clear ways to illustrate the difference between environmental and religious approaches. For instance, Siman Tov David stated that a (Jewish) woman who has become religious can throw out her immodest clothing without transgressing *bal tashḥit*.[25] Vorhand and Yitzḥak Eliyahu Shtasman dealt with the same issue from a somewhat different approach but with the same conclusion: a man is permitted to destroy his wife's immodest clothing and does not transgress *bal tashḥit* in doing so.[26] As we have seen, these rulings can be found in the works of earlier legal authorities, but David, Vorhand, and Shtasman have compiled the various sources dealing with this issue. A final example is the question of whether it is permissible to cause oneself to vomit

23. Moshe Yitzḥak Vorhand, *Sefer Birkat HaShem: Leqet Dinei Issur Qetzitzat Ilanei Ma'akhal, Bal Tashḥit BiShe'ar Devarim, VeIssur Hefsed UVizui Okhalim* (Jerusalem: private printing, 2000), 11.

24. Ibid., 153–54.

25. Siman Tov David, *Sefer al Pakkim Qetanim: Hilkhot Bal Tashḥit* (Jaffa, Israel: S. M. Publishers, 2000), 75.

26. Vorhand, *Sefer Birkat HaShem*, 159, and Yitzḥak Eliyahu Shtasman, *Sefer Etz HaSadeh: BeDinei Bal Tashḥit, Qetzitzat Ilanot UVizui Okhalin* (Jerusalem: Foundation for the Advancement of Torah Study, 1999), 151–52.

in order to eat a mandatory meal (such as matzah during Passover or one of the three Sabbath meals) or simply to feel better, or would such an action be a transgression of *bal tashḥit*?[27] These sources discuss the instances when induced vomiting would be permissible and when not.

On the one hand, these examples and others illustrate the wide variety of circumstances to which *bal tashḥit* has been applied. On the other hand, each of these circumstances is very narrowly focused and makes little effort to view the issue of wastefulness as part of a broader issue. In other words, much like how *bal tashḥit* is presented in the Talmud, the concern tends to be whether or how to apply the prohibition to a particular case, instead of understanding the case as part of a greater paradigm. The prohibition has been used mostly to address the issue of directly causing waste, but indirect waste has not yet found its place in legal discourse regarding *bal tashḥit*. This distinction is important. Direct waste is the more obvious of the two. If I have an object and I discard it, I have caused that object to be wasted. Yet legists have barely addressed unintentional waste or the waste that occurs through overconsumption and inefficient use of resources. Moreover, the act of discarding an item does not mean that it ceases to exist. It still exists as material, and that material, perhaps now in a different form, continues to have an impact on the environment. This, too, is an area neglected by legal decisors. This narrow frame through which the prohibition has been and is still being viewed has caused the prohibition to focus on issues such as the waste of food, but at the same time has neglected to extend that concern to the disposable dish on which the food might rest.

The "hidden" costs of wastefulness have not been considered in legal discourse. This issue is not unique to *halakhah*. Only the most forward-thinking societies have been able to advance far-reaching environmental legislation, such as the principle that the "polluter pays." The cost of pollution extends well beyond an individual product. Until recently, environmental costs were not (and in most cases are still not) part of the cost/benefit analysis of products and services. The environmental cost of the full life cycle of products, including extraction, transportation, manufacturing, use, and disposal, in terms of emissions, effluents, land use, and energy use, are not fully taken into account, if they are addressed at all. Yet "waste" in this form

27. See David, *Sefer al Pakkim Qetanim*, 64; Shtasman, *Sefer Etz HaSadeh*, 236–37; and Vorhand, *Sefer Birkat HaShem*, 287–91.

has significant environmental consequences and detrimental health effects that come at great economic cost. For instance, an increase in air pollution causes an increase in respiratory illnesses, and polluted water needs to be purified at great expense before it can be used, to say nothing about the almost unimaginable cost of mitigating and adapting to anthropogenic climate change. It is extremely difficult, however, to quantify these external costs. How can cause and effect be accurately measured? Life does not occur in a vacuum. Sometimes the answer is simple, but in many if not most cases, it is very difficult to attribute diseases such as cancer to a specific source. Understanding that it is necessary to take all stages in the life cycle of a product into consideration is a relatively recent breakthrough. Thus, just as it is difficult to create appropriate policy and legislative measures to deal with environmental issues, so too is it difficult to create a legal framework for them. The problem, however, is that *halakhah* in the area of *bal tashḥit* is as yet a few steps behind the scientific communities. To create up-to-date legal rulings that are in line with the current scientific knowledge, "hidden" environmental costs and the need to incorporate a full life cycle assessment of products must be acknowledged and addressed.

Those advancing the legal sphere of *bal tashḥit* tend not to be avid environmentalists, and environmentalists tend not to be legal experts and authorities. It is possible that reemphasizing the connection between wastefulness and self-harm (and harm of others) and bringing it back into mainstream discourse will create a bridge between the worlds of *halakhah* and environmentalism. The global community has embraced environmentalism not because of its concern with this or that particular plant or animal species. Rather, environmental concern arises first and foremost through a concern for humans, their health and well-being. These are also among the prime concerns of *halakhah*. It is no accident that "the prohibition against destroying the body is more dear" (*bal tashḥit de gufa adif*) came into existence. In Judaism, humans sit atop the hierarchy of the created world. Thus, when a decision needs to be made between human and nonhuman well-being, human interests take precedence. After defining the relationship between the human and nonhuman as hierarchical, the idea that human well-being is dependent on the integrity of the nonhuman world was marginalized. As emphasized throughout this book, however, this idea was nonetheless kept alive through the writings of a small number of Jewish thinkers over the course of history. To sages such as Rabbi Akiva and scholars such as Yonah of Gerona (d. 1263, Spain), Menaḥem HaMeiri (1249–1315, Provence), Shlomo Luria (1510–1574, Poland), Abraham de Boton (c. 1560–c. 1605, Greece and Land of Israel), Shneiur Zalman of Liadi (1745–1813, Russia), Israel Lipschutz (1782–1860, Germany), Jacob Ettlinger (1798–1871, Germany), Shlomo Gantzfried (1802–1884, Hungary), Barukh Epstein (1860–1941, Belarus), and Yitzḥak Zilberstein (b. 1934, Poland and Israel), the connection of *bal tashḥit* to self-harm was obvious, just as it is fundamental to environmental wisdom today.

Now more than at any time in history, it is essential to reemphasize the Jewish noetic connection between humans and the environment. Humans depend on the environment, and harming the environment is commensurate to harming oneself or humankind as a whole, whether directly or indirectly. This value is at the core of *bal tashḥit*. Sometimes harm manifests itself over the short term, but often the time scale is longer and harm is more difficult to discern and directly attribute to human behavior. Through scientific progress these connections have gradually been elucidated and become more widely established. Perhaps amazingly, Judaism does not need to be reinvented to align itself with such progress. If it did, the ethos would probably meet resistance. Yet as it stands, it has the potential to be universally accepted. Highlighting the existing age-old tradition and demonstrating that on this fundamental principle, Jewish thought and environmental thought share similar concerns makes it possible to bridge these worlds in order to motivate religious communities to create positive environmental change.

Further Research

The intention of this research is not to be the final word on the topic of wastefulness in the Jewish tradition. This research could be expanded in many ways mentioned in this book. For instance, the use of the words *bizbuz* (wastefulness), *heres* (destruction), and *hefsed* (loss) (among others) were not included in this study. They could benefit from an analysis similar to the one I conducted in this book for the term *bal tashḥit*. There is also need for further research on the waste of food. Another significant step forward would be to conduct similar research in the other great "Abrahamic" traditions. Concern regarding wastefulness can be found in Christianity and Islam and offers a common point of reference. As such, *bal tashḥit* has potential for interfaith research and dialogue. It is my hope that the historic basis I have demonstrated, the perseverance of the connection between self-harm and wastefulness despite marginalization, and its remarkable similarity to mainstream environmentalism (i.e., concern for the environment for self-serving purposes) make it a probable focal point for future environmental discourse. Environmentalism has not yet made a significant inroad into religious praxis. This is due in part to the challenge of finding a common language between environmentalists and religious communities. The religious prohibition against wastefulness, however, merits being termed an environmental ethic. As such, its environmental dimensions need to be brought into the mainstream discourse on the environment we all share. By creating documents that can be understood by both religious practitioners and environmentalists, the present study hopes to make progress toward activating this latent environmental potential.

Appendix

To acknowledge that their writings have been considered, this appendix lists Bible interpreters who were analyzed but found not to have made comments on the relevant verses.

Deuteronomy

Aḥai Gaon (c. 680–c. 752, Babylonia)[1]
Shmuel ben Ḥofni Gaon (c. 10th–11th centuries, Babylonia)[2]
Ḥananel bar Ḥushiel (c. 980–c. 1057, southern Italy and Kairouan [North Africa])[3]
Shlomo ibn Gevirol (1021–c. 1050, Spain)[4]
Samuel of Rossano (11th–12th centuries, southern Italy)[5]
Yehudah HaLevi (*Kuzari*) (1075–12th century, Spain, Egypt, and possibly Land of Israel)[6]

1. Aḥai Gaon, *Sheiltot DeRav Aḥai Gaon*, Vol. 5: *BeMidbar, Devarim*, ed. Shmuel Kalman Mirski (Jerusalem: Sura Institute for Research and Publication and Yeshiva University, 1977).

2. Shmuel ben Ḥofni Gaon, *Peirush HaTorah LeRav Shmuel ben Ḥofni Gaon*, ed. and trans. Aaron Greenbaum (Jerusalem: Mossad HaRav Kook, 1979).

3. Ḥananel bar Ḥushiel, *Peirushei Rabbeinu Ḥananel al HaTorah*, ed. Ḥaim Dov Chavel (Jerusalem: Mossad HaRav Kook, 1972).

4. Shlomo ben Gevirol, "*Peirush al HaTorah LeRabbeinu Shlomo ben Gevirol Zal*," in *Peirush Menahem Meiri al HaTorah*, ed. Yosef Gad (London: Hachinuch, 1957).

5. Samuel of Rossano, *Sefer Rushaina: Peirush al Sefer BeMidbar—Devarim LeRabbeinu Shmuel MiRussiah*, ed. Moshe Weiss (Jerusalem: Mossad HaRav Kook, 1996).

6. Yehudah HaLevi, "*Peirush Qitzur MiSefer HaKuzari al HaTorah*," in *Peirush Rabbeinu Yosef Bekhor Shor*, Part 2, ed. Joseph Gad (London: HaMadfis, 1960).

Yosef Bekhor Shor (12th century, France)[7]
Yehudah HeḤasid (12th century–1217, Italy and Germany)[8]
David Qimḥi (*Radaq*) (1160–1235, southern France)[9]
Elazar of Worms (1160–1237, Germany)[10]
Yonah Gerondi (early 13th century–1263, Spain and France)[11]
Shlomo ben Aderet (*Rashba*) (1235–1310, Spain)[12]
Menaḥem Meiri (1249–c. 1310, France and Spain)[13]
Yeshayah DiTrani (*Rid HaZaqen*) (13th century, Italy)[14]
Nissim ben Reuven Gerondi (*Ran*) (early 14th century–1380, Spain)[15]
Yosef ibn Ḥabib (14th–15th centuries, Spain)[16]
Talmid HaRan (an anonymous student of Nissim ben Reuven Gerondi)[17]
Yitzḥak Arama (*Aqedat Yitzḥak*) (1420–1494, Spain and Italy)[18]

---

7. Joseph Bechor Shor, *Commentary on the Pentateuch* (Jerusalem: Makor Publishing, 1978).

8. Yehudah HeḤasid, *Peirushei HaTorah LeRabbi Yehudah HeḤasid*, ed. Isaak Shimshon Lange (Jerusalem: Daf Ḥen, 1975).

9. David Qimḥi, *Peirushei Rabbi David Qimḥi al HaTorah*, 2nd ed., ed. Moshe Kamlher (Jerusalem: Mossad HaRav Kook, 1975).

10. Elazar of Worms, *Peirush Rabbeinu Elazar MiGermaiza Zal Ba'al Sefer HaRoqe'aḥ al HaTorah ve'al Megilat Ester*, ed. Yosef Gad (London: private printing, 1959).

11. Yonah of Gerona, *Derashot UPheirushei Rabbeinu Yonah Gerondi LeḤamishah Ḥumshei Torah*, ed. Shmuel Yerushalmi (Jerusalem: Ḥ. Vagshel, 1980).

12. Shlomo ben Aderet, *Peirushei Shlomo ben Aderet VeRabbeinu David bar Yosef Qimḥi al Ḥamishah Ḥumshei Torah*, ed. Joseph Gad (London: L. Honig and Sons, 1962).

13. Menaḥem Meiri, *Peirush Menaḥem Meiri al HaTorah*, ed. Yosef Gad (London: Hachinuch, 1957).

14. Yeshayah di Trani HaZaqen, *Peirush Rabbeinu Yeshayah di Trani HaZaqen al HaTorah ve'al Nach*, ed. Joseph Gad. London: L. Honig and Sons, 1957).

15. Nissim ben Reuven Gerondi, *Rabbeinu Nissim ben Reuven Gerondi (HaRan): Peirush al HaTorah*, ed. Leon Aryeh Feldman (Jerusalem: Makhon Shalem, 1968).

16. Yosef ben David, *Peirush al HaTorah LeRabbeinu Yosef ben David MeSaragossa*, ed. Leon Aryeh Feldman (Jerusalem: Makhon Shalem, 1973).

17. Talmid HaRan, *Peirush al HaTorah Meyuḥas LeTalmid Rabbeinu Nissim bar Reuven (HaRan)*, ed. Leon Aryeh Feldman (Jerusalem: Makhon Shalem, 1970).

18. Yitzḥak Arama, *Sefer Aqeidat Yitzḥak*, Vol. 5, ed. Avigdor Katz (Jerusalem: Independent Publishing, 1961).

Yoḥanan bar Aharon Luria (*Meshivat Nefesh*) (c. 1440–c. 1514, France and Germany)[19]

Yitzḥak bar Yosef Caro (*Toledot Yitzḥak*) (1458–1535, Spain, Turkey, and Land of Israel)[20]

Shlomo ben Moshe HaLevi Alqabetz (c. 1505–c. 1584, Land of Israel)[21]

Moshe ben Yisrael Isserlis (c. 1525–1572, Poland)[22]

Shlomo Ephraim of Luntshitz (*Keli Yaqar*) (1540–1619, Poland and Prague)[23]

Abraham Joshua Heschel (*Ḥanukat HaTorah*) (c. 1595–1663, Poland)[24]

Ḥaim bar Moshe ibn Atar (*Or HaḤaim*) (1696–1743, Morocco, Algeria, and Land of Israel)[25]

Yosef bar Meir Teomim (*Teivat Gomeh*) (1727–1792, Poland and Germany)[26]

Moses Schreiber (*Ḥatam Sofer*) (1762–1839, Germany and Austria)[27]

Yosef Dov Ber HaLevi Soloveitchik (*Beit HaLevi*) (1820–1892, Lithuania)[28]

---

19. Yoḥanan Luria, *Sefer Meshivat Nefesh: Be'urim al HaTorah Me'Et Rabbeinu Yoḥanan Luria Zatzal*, ed. Yaakov Hoffmann (Jerusalem: Mifal Torat Ḥakhmei Ashkenaz, Makhon Yerushalayim, 1993).

20. Isaac Caro, *Toledot Yizhak* (Jerusalem: Makor Publishing, 1978).

21. Shlomo ben Moshe HaLevi Alqabetz, "*Peirush Rabbeinu Shlomo Alqabetz HaLevi*," in *Peirush Rabbeinu Yeshayah di Trani HaZaqen al HaTorah ve'al Nakh*, ed. Joseph Gad (London: L. Honig and Sons, 1957).

22. Moshe ben Yisrael Isserlis, "*Peirush Rabbeinu HaRama al HaTorah*," in *Peirush Rabbeinu Yeshayah di Trani HaZaqen al HaTorah ve'al Nakh*, ed. Joseph Gad (London: L. Honig and Sons, 1957).

23. Shlomo Ephraim of Lunshitz, *Sefer Keli Yaqar HaShalem*, Part 2: *VaYiqra, BeMidbar, Devarim* (Jerusalem: Orot Ḥaim Publishing, 2001).

24. Abraham Joshua Heschel, *Sefer Ḥanukat HaTorah*, ed. Ḥanokh Henikh Erzahan (Jerusalem: private printing, 2008).

25. Ḥaim bar Moshe ibn Atar, *Ḥamishah Ḥumshei Torah im Peirush Or HaḤaim: Sefer Devarim*, ed. Yisrael Yosef Friedman (Jerusalem: Mossad HaRav Kook, 2008).

26. Yosef Teomim, *Sefer Teivat Gomeh*, ed. Shmuel Einstein (Bnei Braq: private printing, 1998).

27. Moses Schreiber, *Sefer Ḥatam Sofer al HaTorah: Devarim*, ed. Yosef Naphtali Stern (Jerusalem: Makhon Ḥatam Sofer, 1978).

28. Yosef Dov Ber HaLevi Soloveitchik, *Sefer MiShulḥano shel Beit HaLevi*, ed. Y. Hershkovitz (Jerusalem: private printing, 2004).

Meir Simḥah bar Shimshon Qelonimus HaCohen (*Meshekh Ḥokhmah*) (1843–1926, Lithuania)[29]

Genesis

Aḥai Gaon (c. 680–c. 752, Babylonia)[30]
Shmuel ben Ḥofni Gaon (c. 10th–11th centuries, Babylonia)[31]
Ḥananel bar Ḥushiel (c. 980–c. 1057, southern Italy and Kairouan [North Africa])[32]
Samuel of Rossano (11th–12th centuries, southern Italy)[33]
Yehudah HaLevi (*Kuzari*) (1075–12th century, Spain, Egypt, and possibly Land of Israel)[34]
Samuel ben Meir (*Rashbam*) (c. 1080–1174, northern France)[35]
Menaḥem bar Shlomo (*Sekhel Tov*) (written in 1139, most likely in Italy)[36]
Yehudah HeḤasid (12th century–1217, Italy and Germany)[37]
Avraham ben HaRambam (1186–1237, Egypt)[38]
Ephraim bar Shimshon (c. late 12th–13th centuries, France)[39]

---

29. Meir Simḥah HaCohen, *Meshekh Ḥokhmah*, ed. Yehudah Cooperman (Jerusalem: 2002).

30. Aḥai Gaon, *Sheiltot DeRav Aḥai Gaon*, Vol. 1, *Bereishit*, ed. Shmuel Kalman Mirski (Jerusalem: Sura Institute for Research and Publication, Yeshiva University and Mossad HaRav Kook, 1960).

31. Shmuel ben Ḥofni Gaon, *Peirush HaTorah*.

32. Ḥananel bar Ḥushiel, *Peirushei Rabbeinu Ḥananel*.

33. Samuel of Rossano, *Sefer Rushaina: Peirush al Sefer Bereishit LeRabbeinu Shmuel MiRussiah*, ed. Moshe Weiss (Jerusalem: Mossad HaRav Kook, 1977).

34. Yehudah HaLevi, "*Peirush Qitzur MiSefer HaKuzari*."

35. Samuel ben Meir, *Peirush HaTorah LeRabbeinu Shmuel ben Meir*, Vol. 1, *Bereishit, Shemot*, ed. Martin I. Lockshin (Jerusalem: Chorev Publishing House, 2009).

36. Menaḥem bar Shlomo, *Midrash Sekhel Tov al Sefer Bereishit VeShemot*, ed. Shlomo Buber (Berlin: 1900).

37. Yehudah HeḤasid, *Peirushei HaTorah*.

38. Avraham ben HaRambam, *Peirush Rabbeinu Avraham ben HaRambam Zal al Bereishit VeShemot*, ed. Saliman D. Sassoon (London: L. Honig and Sons, 1958).

39. Ephraim bar Shimshon, *Peirush Rabbeinu Ephraim bar Shimshon UGedolei Ashkenaz HaQadmonim al HaTorah*, Part 1, *Bereishit—Shemot*, ed. Tzvi Yehoshua Leitner and Ezra Koraḥ (Jerusalem: Orthodox Publications Co., 1992).

Yonah Gerondi (early 13th century–1263, Spain and France)[40]
Shlomo ben Aderet (*Rashba*) (1235–1310, Spain)[41]
Menaḥem Meiri (1249–c. 1310, France and Spain)[42]
Menaḥem Recanati (c. 1250–c. 1310, Italy)[43]
Asher ben Yeḥiel (*Rosh*) (1250 or 1259–1327, Germany, France, and Spain)[44]
Yeshayah DiTrani (*Rid HaZaqen*) (13th century, Italy)[45]
Nissim ben Moshe of Marseille (13th–14th centuries, southern France)[46]
Moshav Zeqenim (c. 13th–14th centuries, anonymous[47])[48]
Yosef ibn Ḥabib (14th–15th centuries, Spain)[49]
Talmid HaRan (an anonymous student of Nissim ben Reuven Gerondi)[50]
Yitzḥak Arama (1420–1494, Spain and Italy)[51]
Yoḥanan bar Aharon Luria (*Meshivat Nefesh*) (c. 1440–c. 1514, France and Germany)[52]
Yitzḥak bar Yosef Caro (*Toledot Yitzḥak*) (1458–1535, Spain, Turkey, and Land of Israel)[53]

40. Yonah of Gerona, *Derashot LeḤamishah Ḥumshei Torah.*

41. Shlomo ben Aderet, *Peirushei Shlomo ben Aderet.*

42. Menaḥem Meiri, *Peirush Menaḥem Meiri.*

43. Menaḥem Recanati, *Sefer Levushei Or Yaqar*, ed. Ḥaim Yaakov HaCohen (Jerusalem: private printing, 1960).

44. Ba'alei HaTosafot, *Sefer Hadar Zeqenim: Tosafot VeHaRosh al HaTorah*, ed. Avraham Forianti (Jerusalem: Herbert Zarkin Offset Institute, 1963).

45. Yeshayah di Trani HaZaqen, *Peirush Rabbeinu Yeshayah di Trani.*

46. Nissim ben Moshe, *Ma'aseh Nissim: Peirush LaTorah LeRabbi Nissim ben Rabbi Moshe MiMarseille*, ed. Howard Kriesel (Jerusalem: Mekitzei Nirdamim, 2000).

47. This is a compilation made up mainly of *Tosafist* commentaries. The compiler is considered to have lived around the time of Asher ben Yeḥiel.

48. *Sefer Moshav Zeqenim al HaTorah*, ed. Saliman D. Sassoon (London: L. Honig and Sons, 1959).

49. Yosef ben David, *Peirush al HaTorah.*

50. Talmid HaRan, *Peirush al HaTorah.*

51. Yitzḥak Arama, *Sefer Aqeidat Yitzḥak*, Vol. 1, ed. Avigdor Katz (Jerusalem: private printing, 1961).

52. Yoḥanan Luria, *Sefer Meshivat Nefesh.*

53. Isaac Caro, *Toledot Yizhak.*

Shlomo ben Moshe HaLevi Alqabetz (c. 1505–c. 1584, Land of Israel)[54]
Moshe ben Yisrael Isserlis (c. 1525–1572, Poland)[55]
Shlomo Ephraim of Luntshitz (*Keli Yaqar*) (1540–1619, Poland and Prague)[56]
Abraham Joshua Heschel (*Ḥanukat HaTorah*) (c. 1595–1663, Poland)[57]
Ḥaim bar Moshe ibn Atar (*Or HaḤaim*) (1696–1743, Morocco, Algeria, and Land of Israel)[58]
Eliyahu ben Shlomo Zalman (*Gra*) (1720–1797, Lithuania)[59]
Yosef bar Meir Teomim (*Teivat Gomeh*) (1727–1792, Poland and Germany)[60]
Pinḥas bar Tzvi Hirsch HaLevi Horowitz (*Panim Yafot*) (1730–1805, Poland)[61]
Moses Schreiber (*Ḥatam Sofer*) (1762–1839, Germany and Austria)[62]
Yosef Dov Ber HaLevi Soloveitchik (*Beit HaLevi*) (1820–1892, Lithuania)[63]
Meir Simḥah bar Shimshon Qelonimus HaCohen (*Meshekh Ḥokhmah*) (1843–1926, Lithuania)[64]

54. Shlomo ben Moshe HaLevi Alqabetz, "*Peirush Rabbeinu Shlomo Alqabetz.*"

55. Moshe ben Yisrael Isserlis, "*Peirush Rabbeinu HaRama.*"

56. Shlomo Ephraim of Lunshitz, *Sefer Keli Yaqar HaShalem*, Part 1, *Bereishit, Shemot* (Jerusalem: Orot Ḥaim Publishing, 2001).

57. Abraham Joshua Heschel, *Sefer Ḥanukat HaTorah.*

58. Ḥaim bar Moshe ibn Atar, *Ḥamishah Ḥumshei Torah im Peirush Or HaḤaim: Sefer Bereishit, Bereishit—Ḥayei Sarah*, ed. Yisrael Yosef Friedman (Jerusalem: Mossad HaRav Kook, 2008).

59. Eliyahu (Kremer?), *Ḥumash HaGra: Bereishit*, Weinreb ed., ed. Dov Eliakh (Jerusalem: Makhon Moreshet HaYeshivot, 2004).

60. Yosef Teomim, *Sefer Teivat Gomeh.*

61. Pinḥas HaLevi Horowitz, *Sefer Panim Yafot HaShalem al HaTorah*, Part 1, *Sefer Bereishit* (Jerusalem: private printing, 1998).

62. Moses Schreiber, *Sefer Ḥatam Sofer al HaTorah: Bereishit*, ed. Yosef Naphtali Stern (Jerusalem: Makhon Ḥatam Sofer, 1978).

63. Yosef Dov Ber HaLevi Soloveitchik, *Beit HaLevi.*

64. Meir Simḥah HaCohen, *Meshekh Ḥokhmah.*

Bibliography

Environmental Literature

Bechhofer, Yosef Gavriel. "*HaMiḥzur BaHalakhah.*" *Teḥumin* 16 (1996): 296–302.

Benstein, Jeremy. *The Way Into Judaism and the Environment.* Woodstock, VT: Jewish Lights Publishing, 2006.

Bernstein, Ellen, and Dan Fink. "Bal Tashchit." In *This Sacred Earth: Religion, Nature, Environment,* edited by Roger S. Gottlieb, 451–68. New York: Routledge, 1996.

Cain, Clifford Chalmers. *An Ecological Theology: Reunderstanding Our Relation to Nature.* Toronto Studies in Theology. Vol. 98. Lewiston, NY: Edwin Mellon Press, 2009.

Callicott, J. Baird. "Environmental Ethics: An Overview." www.fore.yale.edu/disciplines/ethics/, 2000.

Chayen, Samuel. "Sevivah, Ḥevrah VeKhalkalah BeHagutam shel HaRav Shimshon Raphael Hirsch VeDoctor Yitzḥak Breuer." PhD dissertation, Bar-Ilan University, Ramat-Gan, Israel, 2010.

Cohen, Jeremy. *Be Fertile and Increase, Fill the Earth and Master It: The Ancient and Medieval Career of a Biblical Text.* Ithaca, NY: Cornell University Press, 1989.

Cohn, Ellen. "Growing an Environmental Ethic: The Conceptual Roots of *Bal Tashchit.*" In *Compendium of Sources in Halacha and the Environment,* edited by Ora Sheinson and Shai Spetgang, 38–44. Jerusalem: Canfei Nesharim Publication, 2005.

Dasgupta, Partha S. "Population, Poverty and the Local Environment." *Scientific American* 272, no. 2 (February, 1995): 40–45.

Diamond, Eliezer. "Jewish Perspectives on Limiting Consumption." In *Ecology and the Jewish Spirit: Where Nature and the Sacred Meet,* edited by Ellen Bernstein, 80–87. Woodstock, VT: Jewish Lights Publishing, 1998.

Diamond, Jared. *Collapse: How Societies Choose to Fail or Succeed.* New York: Penguin Books, 2011.

Fink, Daniel B. "The Environment in *Halakhah*." In *Judaism and Ecology*, 34–47. New York: Hadassah, The Women's Zionist Organization of America, and Shomrei Adamah, 1993.

The Forum on Religion and Ecology at Yale. http://fore.research.yale.edu.

Gerstenfeld, Manfred. *Judaism, Environmentalism and the Environment: Mapping and Analysis*. Jerusalem: Jerusalem Institute for Israel Studies, Rubin Mass, 1998.

———. *The Environment in the Jewish Tradition: A Sustainable World*. Jerusalem: Jerusalem Institute for Israel Studies, Center for Environmental Policy, 2002.

Gotteib, Roger. *A Greener Faith: Religious Environmentalism and Our Planet's Future*. New York: Oxford University Press, 2006.

———. "Introduction: Religion and Ecology—What Is the Connection and Why Does It Matter?" In *The Oxford Handbook of Religion and Ecology*, edited by Roger S. Gottleib, 3–21. New York: Oxford University Press, 2006.

———. "Introduction: Religion in an Age of Environmental Crisis." *This Sacred Earth: Religion, Nature, Environment*. 2nd ed., edited by Roger Gottleib, 1–15. New York: Routledge, 2004.

Hardin, Garrett. "The Tragedy of the Commons." *Science* 162, no. 3859 (1968): 1243–48.

Harrison, Peter. "Subduing the Earth: Genesis 1, Early Modern Science, and the Exploitation of Nature." *Journal of Religion* 79, no. 1 (1999): 86–109.

Hay, Peter. *Main Currents in Western Environmental Thought*. Bloomington: Indiana University Press, 2002.

Isaacs, Ronald H. *The Jewish Sourcebook on the Environment and Ecology*. New Jersey: Jason Aronson, 1998.

Jacob, Walter. "Eco-Judaism: Does It Exist? 'The Earth Is the Lord's' versus 'Everything Is Given into Your Hand.'" In *The Environment in Jewish Law: Essays and Responsa*, edited by Walter Jacob and Moshe Zemer, 1–23. New York: Berghahn Books, 2003.

Jenkins, Willis. "After Lynn White: Religious Ethics and Environmental Problems." *Journal of Religious Ethics* 37, no. 2 (2009): 283–309.

Lamm, Norman. "Ecology in Jewish Law and Theology." In *Torah of the Earth: Exploring 4,000 Years of Ecology in Jewish Thought*. Vol. 1: *Biblical Israel: One Land, One People*, edited by Arthur Waskow, 103–26. Woodstock, VT: Jewish Lights Publishing, 2000.

Loevinger, N. J. "(Mis)reading Genesis: A Response to Environmentalist Critiques of Judaism." In *Ecology and the Jewish Spirit: Where Nature and the Sacred Meet*, edited by Ellen Bernstein, 32–40. Woodstock, VT: Jewish Lights Publishing, 1998.

McDaniel, Jay. "Ecotheology and World Religions." In *Ecospirit: Religions and Philosophies for the Earth*, edited by Laurel Kearns and Catherine Keller, 22–44. New York: Fordham University Press, 2007.

Mikva, Rachel S. "When Values Collide: Economics, Health and the Environment." In *The Environment in Jewish Law: Essays and Responsa,* edited by Walter Jacob and Moshe Zemer, 34–44. New York: Berghahn Books, 2003.

The Ministry for Environmental Protection, Israel. http://www.sviva.gov.il/English/env_topics/climatechange/renewable-energy/Pages/Renewable-Energy-Implementation-in-Israel.aspx, accessed May 28, 2018.

Moran, Emilio F., and Elinor Ostrom, eds. *Seeing the Forest and the Trees: Human-Environment Interactions in Forest Ecosystems.* Cambridge, MA: MIT Press, 2005.

Nir, David. "A Critical Examination of the Jewish Environmental Law of *Bal Tashchit.*" *Georgetown International Environmental Law Review* 18, no. 2 (Winter 2006): 335–53.

Norton, Bryan. *Toward Unity Among Environmentalists.* New York: Oxford University Press, 1994.

Rakover, Nahum. *Eikhut HaSvivah: Heibetim Ra'ayoniyim UMishpatiyim BaMeqorot HaYehudiyim.* Jerusalem: Moreshet HaMishpat BeYisrael, 1993.

———. *Environmental Protection: A Jewish Perspective,* Policy Study No. 4. Jerusalem: Institute of the World Jewish Congress, 1996.

Rasmussen, Larry L. *Earth-Honoring Faith: Religious Ethics in a New Key.* New York: Oxford University Press, 2013.

Rolston III, Holmes. *Environmental Ethics: Duties and Values in the Natural World.* Philadelphia: Temple University Press, 1988.

———. "Value of Nature and the Nature of Value." In *Philosophy and the Natural Environment,* edited by Robin Attfield and Andrew Belsey, 13–30. Cambridge, UK: Cambridge University Press, 1994.

Rozenson, Israel. *VeHinei Tov Me'od.* Jerusalem: Yeshivat Beit Orot, 2001.

Salomon, David, Yaakov Weinberger, Meir Batiste, Meir Zikhel, Menaḥem Slae, and Tzvi Ilani. *Eikhut HaSvivah (Ecologia) BiMeqorot HaYahadut,* edited by Meir Zikhel, 11–36. Ramat-Gan Israel: Bar-Ilan Responsa Project, 1990.

Schwartz, Eilon. "*Bal Tashchit*: A Jewish Environmental Precept." In *Judaism and Environmental Ethics: A Reader,* edited by Martin D. Yaffe, 230–49. New York: Lexington Books, 2001.

———. "Judaism and Nature: Theological and Moral Issues to Consider While Renegotiating a Jewish Relationship to the Natural World." In *Judaism and Environmental Ethics: A Reader,* edited by Martin Yaffe, 297–308. New York: Lexington Books, 2001.

Seidenberg, David Mevorach. *Kabbalah and Ecology: God's Image in a More-Than-Human World.* New York: Cambridge University Press, 2015.

Sokol, Moshe. "What Are the Ethical Implications of Jewish Theological Conceptions of the Natural World?" In *Judaism and Ecology: Created World and Revealed World,* edited by Hava Tirosh-Samuelson, 261–75. Cambridge, MA: Harvard University Press, 2002.

Stern, Paul C. "New Environmental Theories: Toward a Coherent Theory of Environmentally Significant Behavior." *Journal of Social Issues* 56, no. 3 (2000): 407–24.

Strasser, Susan. *Waste and Want: A Social History of Trash*. New York: Henry Holt and Company, 1999.

Sulomm Stein, David E. "*Halakhah*: The Law of *Bal Tashchit* (Do Not Destroy)." In *Torah of the Earth: Exploring 4,000 Years of Ecology in Jewish Thought*, edited by Arthur Waskow, 96–102. Woodstock, VT: Jewish Lights Publishing, 2000.

Taylor, Bron. "Critical Perspectives on 'Religions of the World and Ecology.'" In *The Encyclopedia of Religion, Nature and Culture*, edited by Bron Taylor, 1375–76. New York: Continuum Books, 2008.

Tirosh-Samuelson, Hava. "Nature in the Sources of Judaism." *Daedalus* 130, no. 4 (2001): 99–124.

Vogel, David. "How Green Is Judaism? Exploring Jewish Environmental Ethics." *Business Ethics Quarterly* 11, no. 2 (April, 2001): 349–63.

Waskow, Arthur. "Introduction." *Torah of the Earth: Exploring 4,000 Years of Ecology in Jewish Thought*, edited by Arthur Waskow, vii–xiv. Woodstock, VT: Jewish Lights Publishing, 2000.

———. "Jewish Environmental Ethics: Intertwining *Adam* with *Adamah*." In *The Oxford Handbook of Jewish Ethics and Morality*, edited by Elliot N. Dorff and Jonathan K. Crane, 401–18. New York: Oxford University Press, 2013.

White, Lynn, Jr. "The Historical Roots of Our Ecologic Crisis." *Science* 155, no. 3767 (1967): 1203–7.

Wolff, Akiva. "A Closer Examination of Deuteronomy 20:19–20." *Jewish Bible Quarterly* 39, no. 3 (2011): 143–52.

———. "Bal Tashchit: The Jewish Prohibition Against Needless Destruction," PhD dissertation, Leiden University, 2009.

Wybrow, R. C. J. *The Bible, Baconianism, and Mastery over Nature: The Old Testament and Its Modern Misreading*. New York: Peter Lang Publishing, 1991.

Yoreh, Tanhum. "Environmental Embarrassment: Genesis 1:26–28 vs. Genesis 2:15." In *Vixens Disturbing Vineyards: Embarrassment and Embracement of Scriptures*, edited by Tzemah Yoreh, Aubrey Glazer, Justin Jaron Lewis, and Miryam Segal, 558–91. Boston: Academic Studies Press, 2010.

———. "Involuntary Simplicity: A Case Study of Haredi Consumption Patterns in Canada and Israel." In *From Antiquity to the Post-Modern World: Contemporary Jewish Studies in Canada*, edited by Daniel Maoz and Andrea Gondos, 232–49. Newcastle upon Tyne, UK: Cambridge Scholars Publishing, 2011.

———. "Rethinking Jewish Approaches to Wastefulness." *Review of Rabbinic Judaism* 22, no. 1 (2019): 31–45.

———. "Ultra-Orthodox Recycling Narratives: Implications for Planning and Policy." *Journal of Enterprising Communities: People and Places in the Global Economy* 4, no. 4 (2010): 323–45.

Zemer, Moshe. "Ecology as a Mitzvah." In *The Environment in Jewish Law: Essays and Responsa*, edited by Walter Jacob and Moshe Zemer, 24–33. New York: Berghahn Books, 2003.

Zipperstein, Edward. "Waste in Judaic Tradition." In *Essays in Jewish Thought*, 58–98. Los Angeles: privately printed, 1989.

General Bibliography

Ayali, Meir. "*HaḤaradah Bifnei Keritat Etz-Ma'akhal BeSafrut HaShu"t.*" In *Tura: Studies in Jewish Thought, Simon Greenberg Jubilee Volume*, 135–40. Tel-Aviv: Hakibbutz Hameuchad Publishing House, 1989.

Bazak, Yaakov. "*Ma'asei Vandalism VeIssur 'Bal Tashḥit.'*" *Teḥumin* 1 (1980): 329–39.

Bernard, J. H. *The International Critical Commentary: A Critical and Exegetical Commentary on the Gospel According to St. John*. Vol. 2, edited by A. H. McNeile. Edinburgh: T & T Clark, 1942.

Bransdorfer, Meir. "*BeInyan Qetzitzat Ilanei Peirot.*" *Or Yisrael* 18 (2000): 58–64.

Breuer, Edward. "Jewish Study of the Bible Before and During the Jewish Enlightenment." In *Hebrew Bible/Old Testament: The History of Its Interpretation*. Vol. II: *From Renaissance to the Enlightenment*, edited by Magne Saebo, 1006–23. Gottingen, Germany: Vandenhoeck & Ruprecht, 2008.

Breuer, Edward, and Chanan Gafni. "Jewish Biblical Scholarship Between Tradition and Innovation." In *Hebrew Bible/Old Testament: The History of Its Interpretation*. Vol. 3: *From Modernism to Post-Modernism (The Nineteenth and Twentieth Centuries)*. Part I: *The Nineteenth Century—A Century of Modernism and Historicism*, edited by Magne Saebo, 262–306. Gottingen, Germany: Vandenhoeck & Ruprecht, 2013.

Brody, Robert. "The Geonim of Babylonia as Biblical Exegetes." In *Hebrew Bible/Old Testament: The History of Its Interpretation*. Vol. 1: *From the Beginnings to the Middle Ages (Until 1300)*. Part 2: *The Middle Ages*, edited by Magne Saebo, 74–88. Gottingen, Germany: Vandenhoeck & Ruprecht, 2000.

Cohen, She'ar Yashuv. "*Keritat Ilanot BiShe'at Milḥamah UViShe'at Shalom.*" *Teḥumin* 4 (1983): 44–53.

Eidelberg, Shlomo. "Ettlinger, Jacob." *Encyclopaedia Judaica*. 2nd ed. Vol. 6, edited by Michael Berenbaum and Fred Skolnik, 546. Detroit: Macmillan Reference USA, 2007. Gale Virtual Reference Library.

Elbaum, Jacob. "Yalkut Shimoni." *Encyclopedia Judaica*. 2nd ed. Vol. 21, edited by Michael Berenbaum and Fred Skolnik, 275–76. Detroit: Macmillan Reference USA, 2007. Gale Virtual Reference Library.

Elman, Yaakov. "Moses ben Nahman / Nahmanides (Ramban)." In *Hebrew Bible/Old Testament: The History of Its Interpretation*. Vol. 1: *From the Beginnings to the Middle Ages (Until 1300)*. Part 2: *The Middle Ages*, edited by Magne Saebo, 416–32. Gottingen, Germany: Vandenhoeck & Ruprecht, 2000.

Elon, Menachem. *Jewish Law: History, Sources, Principles*. Vol. 3: *The Literary Sources of Jewish Law*. Translated by Bernard Auerbach and Melvin J. Sykes. Philadelphia: Jewish Publication Society, 1994.

Fisch, Menahem. *Rational Rabbis: Science and Talmudic Culture*. Bloomington: Indiana University Press, 1997.

Fishbane, Michael. "Introduction." In *The Midrashic Imagination*, edited by Michael Fishbane, 1–4. Albany: State University of New York Press, 1993.

Frank, Yitzḥak. *The Practical Talmud Dictionary*. Jerusalem: Ariel, United Israel Institutes, 1991.

Fox, Harry. "The Embarrassment of Embarrassment." In *Vixens Disturbing Vineyards: Embarrassment and Embracement of Scriptures*, edited by Tzemah Yoreh, Aubrey Glazer, Justin Jaron Lewis, and Miryam Segal, 5–18. Boston: Academic Studies Press, 2010.

Gartenberg, Moshe, and Shmuel Gluck. "Destruction of Fruit-Bearing Trees." *Journal of Halacha and Contemporary Society* 38 (Fall 1999): 86–99.

Goldberg, Avraham Hillel. "*Aqirat Etz Pri*." *Noam* 13 (1972): 203–21.

Grajetski, Wolfram. *Burial Customs in Ancient Egypt: Life in Death for Rich and Poor*. London: Gerald Duckworth and Co., 2003.

Grossman, Avraham. "Rabbi Ovadiah Sforno." In *Jewish Bible Exegesis: An Introduction*. 2nd ed., edited by Moshe Greenberg, 98–100. Jerusalem: Bialik Institute, 1992.

HaLevi, Yosef bar Aharon Amar. *Masekhet Baba Qama, Talmud Bavli: Menuqad al pi Masoret Yehudei Teiman*, edited by Yosef bar Aharon Amar HaLevi. Jerusalem: HaMenaqed Publishing, 1980.

Hezser, Catherine. "Roman Law and Rabbinic Legal Composition." *The Cambridge Companion to the Talmud and Rabbinic Literature*, edited by Charlotte Elisheva Fonrobert and Martin S. Jaffee, 144–64. Cambridge, UK: Cambridge University Press, 2007.

Hirsch, Samson Raphael. "Do Not Destroy!" In *Judaism and Human Rights*, edited by Milton R. Konvitz, 259–74. New York: Norton, 1972.

Idel, Moshe. "Between Authority and Indeterminacy: Some Reflections of Kabbalistic Hermeneutics." In *Death, Ecstasy, and Other Worldly Journeys*, edited by John J. Collins and Michael Fishbane, 245–64. Albany: State University of New York Press, 1995.

Jacobs, Louis. *Religion and the Individual: A Jewish Perspective*. Cambridge, UK: Cambridge University Press, 1992.

Jastrow, Markus. *Dictionary of the Targumim, the Talmud Babli and Yerushalmi and Midrashic Literature*. s.v. פך. Peabody, MA: Hendrickson Publishers, 2006.

Kalmin, Richard. "Patterns and Developments in Rabbinic Midrash of Late Antiquity." In *Hebrew Bible/Old Testament: The History of Its Interpretation*. Vol. 1: *From the Beginnings to the Middle Ages (Until 1300)*. Part 1: *Antiquity*, edited by Magne Saebo, 285–302. Gottingen, Germany: Vandenhoeck & Ruprecht, 1996.

Katz, Yeḥiel Mikhel. "Introduction." In *Peirush Rabbeinu Meyuḥas al Sefer Devarim*, edited by Yeḥiel Mikhel Katz, 9–23. Jerusalem: Mossad HaRav Kook, 1968.

Lau, Yisrael Meir. "*Issur Bal Tashḥit BiMeqom Mitzvah*." *Teḥumin* 22 (2002): 293–300.

Melamed, Ezra Tzion. *Talmud Bavli: Masekhet Baba Qama*, translated by Ezra Tzion Melamed. Jerusalem: Dvir and Mesada Publishing, 1952.

Naiman, Abba Zvi. *The Schottenstein Edition Talmud Bavli: Tractate Bava Kamma*. Vol. 3, edited by Yisroel Simcha Schorr. New York: Mesorah Publications, 2001.

Neusner, Jacob. *The Tosefta: Translated from the Hebrew, Fourth Division—Neziqin (The Order of Damages)*. New York: Ktav Publishing House, 1981.

Raz, Simḥah. *Ish Tzadik Hayah: Masekhet Ḥayav shel Rabbi Aryeh Levine*. Jerusalem: Zak and Partners Publishing, 1982.

Rohde, Erwin. *Psyche: The Cult of Souls and Belief in Immortality Among the Greeks*, translated by W. B. Hillis. New York: Books for Libraries Press, 1972.

Shapira, Amnon. "'Human Dignity' [K'vod HaAdam] in the Hebrew Bible." *Mo'ed: Annual for Jewish Studies* 19 (2009): 1–22.

Soloveitchik, Haym. *The Use of Responsa as Historical Source: A Methodological Introduction*. Jerusalem: Zalman Shazar Center, 1990.

Strack, H. L., and G. Stemberger. *Introduction to the Talmud and Midrash*, translated by Markus Bockmuehl. Minneapolis, MN: Fortress Press, 1992.

Stroumsa, Sarah. "Saadya and Jewish *Kalam*." In *The Cambridge Companion to Medieval Jewish Philosophy*, edited by Daniel H. Frank and Oliver Leaman, 71–90. Cambridge, UK: Cambridge University Press, 2003.

Ta-Shma, Israel. "*Meḥabro HaAmiti shel Sefer 'HaḤinukh*.'" *Qiryat Sefer* 55 (1980): 787–90.

Ta-Shma, Israel Moses, and David Derovan. "Meiri, Menaḥem ben Solomon." *Encyclopaedia Judaica*. 2nd ed. Vol. 13, edited by Michael Berenbaum and Fred Skolnik, 785–88. Detroit: Macmillan Reference USA, 2007. Gale Virtual Reference Library.

Twersky, Isadore. *Introduction to the Code of Maimonides (Mishneh Torah)*. New Haven, CT: Yale University Press, 1980.

Twersky, Yitzhak. "On Law and Ethics in the Mishneh Torah: A Case Study of Hilkhot Megillah II:17." *Tradition: A Journal of Orthodox Thought* 24, no. 2 (1989): 138–49.

Wazana, Nili. "Are Trees of the Field Human? A Biblical War Law (Deuteronomy 20: 19–20) and Neo-Assyrian Propaganda." In *Treasures on Camels' Humps: Historical and Literary Studies from the Ancient Near East Presented to Israel Eph'al*, edited by Mordechai Cogan and Dan'el Kahn, 274–95. Jerusalem: Hebrew University Magnes Press, 2008.

Wright, Jacob L. "Warfare and Wanton Destruction: A Reexamination of Deuteronomy 20:19–20 in Relation to Ancient Siegecraft." *Journal of Biblical Literature* 27, no. 3 (2008): 423–58.

Zevin, Shlomo Yosef, ed. *Encyclopedia Talmudit LeInyanei Halakhah*. Vol. 3. s.v. בל תשחית, 335–37. Jerusalem: Hotza'at Encyclopedia Talmudit, 1951.

Zlotnick, Dov, trans. *The Tractate "Mourning" (Semaḥot)*. Yale Judaica Series. Vol. 17. New Haven, CT: Yale University Press, 1966.

Rabbinic and Other Jewish Literature

Because the majority of scholars appearing in this section do not have surnames, they have been listed in alphabetical order using their first names.

Abraham de Boton. "*Leḥem Mishneh*." In Moshe ben Maimon, *Mishneh Torah, Hu HaYad HaḤazaqah: Sefer HaMada*. Warsaw: Kalinberg and Partners, 1881.

Abraham ibn Ezra. *Peirushei HaTorah LeRabbeinu Avraham ibn Ezra*. Vol. 1. 2nd ed., edited by Asher Weiser. Jerusalem: Mossad HaRav Kook, 1977.

———. *Peirushei HaTorah LeRabbeinu Avraham ibn Ezra*. Vol. 2. 2nd ed., edited by Asher Weiser. Jerusalem: Mossad HaRav Kook, 1977.

———. *Peirushei HaTorah LeRabbeinu Avraham ibn Ezra*. Vol. 3. 2nd ed., edited by Asher Weiser. Jerusalem: Mossad HaRav Kook, 1977.

Abraham Joshua Heschel. *Sefer Ḥanukat HaTorah*, edited by Ḥanokh Henikh Erzahan. Jerusalem: private printing, 2008.

Aḥai Gaon. *She'iltot DeRav Aḥai Gaon*. Vol. 1: *Bereishit*, edited by Shmuel Kalman Mirski. Jerusalem: Sura Institute for Research and Publication, Yeshiva University and Mossad HaRav Kook, 1960.

———. *She'iltot DeRav Aḥai Gaon*. Vol. 5: *BeMidbar, Devarim*, edited by Shmuel Kalman Mirski. Jerusalem: Sura Institute for Research and Publication and Yeshiva University, 1977.

Aharon ben Yosef. *Mivḥar Yesharim*, edited by Avraham ben Shmuel. Yevpatoria, Crimea, 1835.

Alexander Sender Schorr. *Sefer Simlah Ḥadashah, Tevu'ot Shor, Bekhor Shor*. Jerusalem: Levin-Epstein Publishing, 1966.

Avraham bar Yaakov Saba. *Sefer Tzeror HaMor al Ḥamishah Ḥumshei Torah*. Tel-Aviv: Offset Brody-Katz, 1975.

Avraham ben HaRambam. *Peirush Rabbeinu Avraham ben HaRambam Zal al Bereishit VeShemot*, edited by Saliman D. Sassoon. London: L. Honig and Sons, 1958.

Avraham bar Yeḥiel Mikhel Danziger. *Ḥayei Adam*. Vilnius: Menaḥem Mann and Simḥah Zimel, publishers (sic 1799), 1829.

———. *Sefer Ḥokhmat Adam*, Part 2. Jerusalem: A. Bloom Books, 1992.

Avraham Tzvi Hirsch Eisenstadt. *Pitḥei Teshuvah* in *Shulḥan Arukh: Yoreh De'ah*. Vol. 1. New York: Grossman's Publishing House, 1954.

———. *Pitḥei Teshuvah* in *Shulḥan Arukh: Yoreh De'ah*. Vol. 3. New York: Grossman's Publishing House, 1954.

Ba'alei HaTosafot. *Da'at Zeqenim MiBa'alei HaTosafot*. Jerusalem: HaMeir LeYisrael, 2008.

———. *Sefer Hadar Zeqenim al HaTorah*, edited by Avraham Forianti. Jerusalem: Herbert Zarkin Offset Institute, 1963.

———. *Sefer Moshav Zeqenim al HaTorah*, edited by Saliman D. Sassoon. London: L. Honig and Sons, 1959.

———. *Sefer Tosafot HaShalem: Otzar Peirushei Ba'alei HaTosafot*. Part1: *Bereishit—Noaḥ*, edited by Yaakov Gliss. Jerusalem: Mifal Tosafot HaShalem, 1982.

Baḥya bar Asher. *Rabbeinu Baḥya: Be'ur al HaTorah*. Vol. 1: *Bereishit*, edited by Ḥaim Dov Chavel. Jerusalem: Mossad HaRav Kook, 1974.

———. *Rabbeinu Baḥya: Be'ur al HaTorah*. Vol. 2: *Shemot, VaYiqra*, edited by Ḥaim Dov Chavel. Jerusalem: Mossad HaRav Kook, 1974.

———. *Rabbeinu Baḥya: Be'ur al HaTorah*. Vol. 3: *BeMidbar, Devarim*, edited by Ḥaim Dov Chavel. Jerusalem: Mossad HaRav Kook, 1974.

Baḥya ibn Paquda. *The Book of Direction to the Duties of the Heart*, translated by Menaḥem Mansoor. London: Routledge and Kegan Paul, 1973.

Barukh HaLevi Epstein. *Ḥamishah Ḥumshei Torah im Ḥamesh Megilot, Torah Temimah: Sefer Bereishit*. New York: Avraham Yitzḥak Friedman, 1962.

———. *Ḥamishah Ḥumshei Torah im Ḥamesh Megilot, Torah Temimah: Sefer Devarim*. New York: Avraham Yitzḥak Friedman, 1962.

Barzilai Yaabetz. *Leshon Arumim*. Friedberg edition. Jerusalem, 2006.

Bereishit Rabbah. Vilna edition, 1878. Reprinted in Jerusalem.

Bernard J. Bamberger. *The Torah: A Modern Commentary*, edited by Gunther Plaut. New York: Union of American Hebrew Congregations, 1981.

Bezalel Ze'ev Safran. *Sefer She'elot UTeshuvot HaRaba"z*, edited by Ḥanokh Henikh Safran. Bnei Braq, Israel: private printing, 1979.

David HaLevi Segal. "*Turei Zahav*." In *Shulḥan Arukh: Oraḥ Ḥaim*. Vol. 1. New York: Grossman's Publishing House, 1954.

———. *Turei Zahav: Yoreh De'ah—Hilkhot Ma'akhalei Avodat Kokhavim*, in Yosef Karo, *Shulḥan Arukh: Yoreh De'ah*. Vol. 5. Jerusalem: Mifal Shulḥan Arukh HaShalem, 2010.

David Kimḥi. *Nevi'im UKhetuvim HaMefo'ar Miqraot Gedolot: Melakhim*. Vol. 3. Jerusalem: HaḤumash HaMefo'ar, 1996.

———. *Peirushei Rabbi David Qimḥi al HaTorah*. 2nd ed., edited by Moshe Kamlher. Jerusalem: Mossad HaRav Kook, 1975.

David Tzvi Hoffmann. *Sefer Bereishit*. Tel-Aviv: Netzaḥ Publishing, 1969.

———. *Sefer Devarim*. Tel-Aviv: Netzaḥ Publishing, 1961.

———. *Shu"t Melamed LeHo'il*. Part 2: *Yoreh De'ah*. Jerusalem: David Tzvi Hoffmann, 2010.

Elazar of Worms. *Peirush Rabbeinu Elazar MiGermaiza Zal Ba'al Sefer HaRoqe'aḥ al HaTorah ve'al Megilat Ester*, edited by Yosef Gad. London: private printing, 1959.

Eliezer ben Samuel of Metz. *Sefer Yere'im HaShalem*. Vol. 2. Jerusalem: Makhon Ḥatam Sofer, 1973.

Eliyahu Mizraḥi. *Ḥumash HaRe'em: Sefer Bereishit*, edited by Moshe Filip. Petaḥ Tiqva, Israel: private printing, 1992.

———. *Ḥumash HaRe'em: Sefer Devarim*, edited by Moshe Filip. Petaḥ Tiqva, Israel: private printing, 1992.

Ephraim bar Shimshon. *Peirush Rabbeinu Ephraim bar Shimshon UGedolei Ashkenaz HaQadmonim al HaTorah*. Part 1: *Bereishit—Shemot*, edited by Tzvi Yehoshua Leitner and Ezra Koraḥ. Jerusalem: Orthodox Publications Co., 1992.

———. *Peirush Rabbeinu Ephraim bar Shimshon UGedolei Ashkenaz HaQadmonim al HaTorah*. Part 2: *VaYiqra—BeMidbar—Devarim*, edited by Tzvi Yehoshua Leitner and Ezra Koraḥ. Jerusalem: Orthodox Publications Co., 1992.

Gunther Plaut. *The Torah: A Modern Commentary*, edited by Gunther Plaut. New York: Union of American Hebrew Congregations, 1981.

Ḥaim bar Aryeh Leib Halbershtam. *Sefer She'elot UTeshuvot Divrei Ḥaim: Oraḥ Ḥaim*. Part 2. New York: Mosdot Babov, 2002.

———. *Sefer She'elot UTeshuvot Divrei Ḥaim: Yoreh De'ah*. Part 2. New York: Mosdot Babov, 2002.

Ḥaim bar Moshe ibn Atar. *Ḥamishah Ḥumshei Torah im Peirush Or HaḤaim: Sefer Bereishit, Bereishit—Ḥayei Sarah*, edited by Yisrael Yosef Friedman. Jerusalem: Mossad HaRav Kook, 2008.

———. *Ḥamishah Ḥumshei Torah im Peirush Or HaḤaim: Sefer Devarim*, edited by Yisrael Yosef Friedman. Jerusalem: Mossad HaRav Kook, 2008.

Ḥaim Paltiel. *Peirushei HaTorah LeRabbeinu Ḥaim Paltiel*, edited by Isaak Shimshon Lange. Jerusalem: private printing, 1981.

Ḥaim Yosef David Azulai. *Birkei Yosef*. Livorno, Italy: Vincenzo Falorni, 1776.

———. *Sefer Birkei Yosef al Shulḥan Arukh*. Vol. 2: *Yoreh De'ah*, edited by David Avitan. Jerusalem, 2006.

Ḥananel bar Ḥushiel. *Perushei Rabbeinu Ḥananel bar Ḥushiel LaTalmud*, edited by Yosef Mordekhai Dubowik. Jerusalem: Makhon Lev Sameaḥ Publishing, 2011.

———. *Peirushei Rabbeinu Ḥananel al HaTorah*, edited by Ḥaim Dov Chavel. Jerusalem: Mossad HaRav Kook, 1972.

Herz Homberg. *Sefer Netivot HaShalom: Sefer Devarim*. Jerusalem, 1974.

Ḥizqiyah bar Manoaḥ. *Ḥizquni: Peirushei HaTorah LeRabbeinu Ḥizqiyah bar Manoaḥ*, edited by Ḥaim Dov Chavel. Jerusalem: Mossad HaRav Kook, 1981.

Isaac Abarbanel. *Peirush al HaTorah—Bereishit*. Jerusalem: Bnei Arbael Publishing, 1964.

———. *Peirush al HaTorah—BeMidbar, Devarim*. Jerusalem: Bnei Arbael Publishing, 1964.

———. *Peirush al Nevi'im Rishonim*. Jerusalem: Torah VeDa'at, 1976.

Israel Lipschutz. *Mishnayot Tiferet Yisrael, Yakhin VeBoaz*. New York: Pardes, 1953.

Jacob Ettlinger. *Binyan Tzion HaShalem*. Vol. 1, edited by Yehudah Aharon Horowitz. Jerusalem: Devar Yerushalayim Publishers, 2002.

———. *Sefer Binyan Tzion*. Altona, Germany: Gebruder Bonn, 1867.

Joseph Bechor Shor. *Commentary on the Pentateuch*. Jerusalem: Makor Publishing, 1978.

Judah Loew ben Bezalel. *Ḥumash Gur Aryeh HaShalem*. Vol. 1: *Bereishit—Ḥayei Sarah*, edited by Yehoshua David Hartman. Jerusalem: Makhon Yerushalayim, 1989.

———. *Ḥumash Gur Aryeh HaShalem*. Vol. 8: *Devarim—Zot HaBerakha*, edited by Yehoshua David Hartman. Jerusalem: Makhon Yerushalayim, 1989.

Levi ben Gershom. *Nevi'im UKhetuvim HaMefo'ar Miqraot Gedolot: Melakhim*. Vol. 3. Jerusalem: HaḤumash HaMefo'ar, 1996.

———. *Peirushei HaTorah LeRabbeinu Levi ben Gershom (Ralbag)*. Vol. 1: *Bereishit*, edited by Yaakov Leib Levi. Jerusalem: Mossad HaRav Kook, 1992.

———. *Peirushei HaTorah LeRabbeinu Levi ben Gershom (Ralbag)*. Vol. 3: *VaYiqra*, edited by Yaakov Leib Levi. Jerusalem: Mossad HaRav Kook, 1997.

———. *Peirushei HaTorah LeRabbeinu Levi ben Gershom (Ralbag)*. Vol. 5: *Devarim*, edited by Yaakov Leib Levi. Jerusalem: Mossad HaRav Kook, 2000.

Masoud Ḥai Rokeaḥ. *Sefer Ma'aseh Roqe'aḥ*. Part 4. Bnei Braq, Israel: Samuel Akiva Schlesinger, 1964.

Meir Leibush Weiser. *Otzar HaPeirushim al Tanakh, Miqraot Gedolot, Sidra 1, HaTorah VeHaMitzvah*. Tel-Aviv: Mefarshei HaTanakh, n.d.

———. *Otzar HaPeirushim al Tanakh, Miqraot Gedolot, Sidra 2, HaTorah VeHaMitzvah*. Tel-Aviv: Mefarshei HaTanakh, n.d.

Meir Simḥah HaCohen. *Meshekh Ḥokhmah*, edited by Yehudah Cooperman. Jerusalem, 2002.

Menaḥem bar Shlomo. *Midrash Sekhel Tov al Sefer Bereishit VeShemot*, edited by Shlomo Buber. Berlin, 1900.

Menaḥem HaMeiri. *Beth HaBehira on the Talmudical Treatise Baba Kamma*. 2nd rev.ed., edited by Kalman Schlesinger. Jerusalem: private printing, 1961.

———. *Peirush Menaḥem Meiri al HaTorah*, edited by Yosef Gad. London: Hachinuch, 1957.

Menaḥem Mendel Kasher. *Ḥumash Torah Shlemah*. Vol. 2. Jerusalem: Levin-Epstein Bros and Partners Press, 1936.

Menaḥem Mendel Krokhmal. *She'elot UTeshuvot Tzemaḥ Tzedeq*. Jerusalem: Alter Shmuel Stefansky, 2008.

Menaḥem Mendel Schneerson. *Sefer Tzemaḥ Tzedeq: She'elot UTeshuvot MiShulḥan Arukh Oraḥ Ḥaim*. New York: Otzar HaḤasidim, 1994.

Menaḥem Recanati. *Sefer Levushei Or Yaqar*, edited by Ḥaim Yaakov HaCohen. Jerusalem: private printing, 1960.

Menasheh Klein. *Sefer Mishneh Halakhot—Mahadurah Tinyana*. Part 12. New York: Makhon Mishneh Halakhot Gedolot, 2000.

———. *Sefer Mishneh Halakhot*. Part 17. New York: Machon Mishneh Halachos, 2009.

Meyuḥas bar Eliyahu. *Peirush Rabbeinu Meyuḥas al Sefer VaYiqra*, edited by Yitzḥak Yaakov Har Shoshanim Weinberg. Bnei Braq, Israel: private printing, 2005.

———. *Peirush Rabbi Meyuḥas al Bereishit*, edited by A. W. Greenup and C. H. Titterton. Jerusalem: private printing, 1967.

———. *Peirush al Sefer Devarim*, edited by Yeḥiel Mikhel Katz. Jerusalem: Mossad HaRav Kook, 1968.

Midrash Bereishit Rabbah, edited by J. Theodor and Ch. Albeck. Jerusalem: Wahrmann Books, 1965.

Midrash Tanḥuma al Ḥamishah Ḥumshei Torah. Vol. 2, edited by Shlomo Buber. Jerusalem: Ortsel, 1964.

Midrash Tannaim al Sefer Devarim, edited by David Tzvi Hoffmann. Tel-Aviv: Offset Israel-America, 1963.

Mordechai Yaffe. *Sefer Levush Malkhut*. Part 3. *Levush Ateret Zahav*, edited by A. H. A. P. P. Israel, 2000.

Mordekhai ben Hillel. *Sefer Rav Mordekhai, Masekhet Ḥullin, Pereq Kisui HaDam*. Riva di Trento, Italy, 1559.

Moses of Coucy. *Sefer Mitzvot Gadol*. Vol. 1. *Lo Ta'aseh*. Jerusalem: Offset Brody-Katz, 1973.

———. *Sefer Mitzvot Gadol*. Vol. 2. *Aseh*. Jerusalem: Offset Brody-Katz, 1973.

Moses Schreiber. *Sefer Ḥatam Sofer al HaTorah: Bereishit*, edited by Yosef Naphtali Stern, Jerusalem: Makhon Ḥatam Sofer, 1978.

———. *Sefer Ḥatam Sofer al HaTorah: Devarim*, edited by Yosef Naphtali Stern. Jerusalem: Makhon Ḥatam Sofer, 1978.

Moshe Alsheikh. *Torat Moshe: Derushim, Peirushim UVe'urim LeḤamishah Ḥumshei Torah—Sefer Bereishit*, edited by Makhon Lev Sameaḥ. Jerusalem: H. Vagshel, 1990.

———. *Torat Moshe: Derushim, Peirushim UVe'urim LeḤamishah Ḥumshei Torah—Sefer VaYiqra*, edited by Makhon Lev Sameaḥ. Jerusalem: H. Vagshel, 1990.

———. *Torat Moshe: Derushim, Peirushim UVe'urim LeḤamishah Ḥumshei Torah—Sefer Devarim*, edited by Makhon Lev Sameaḥ. Jerusalem: H. Vagshel, 1990.

Moshe ben Maimon. *The Code of Maimonides*. Book 14. *The Book of Judges*, translated by Abraham M. Hershman. New Haven, CT: Yale University Press, 1949.

———. *The Guide for the Perplexed*. 2nd ed., translated by M. Friedlander. London: Routledge and Kegan Paul, 1904.

———. *Kings, Their Wars and the Messiah: From the Mishneh Torah of Maimonides*, translated by H. M. Russell and J. Weinberg. Edinburgh: Royal College of Physicians of Edinburgh, Publication No. 61, 1987.

———. *Maimonides, Mishneh Torah: Hilchot Melachim U'Milchamoteihem—The Laws of Kings and Their Wars*, translated by Eliyahu Touger. New York: Maznaim Publishing Corporation, 1987.

———. *Mishneh Torah: Hu HaYad HaḤazaqah LeRabbeinu Moshe ben Maimon. Haqdamat HaRambam. Sefer HaMada*. Vol. 2, edited by Mordekhai Dov Rabinovitz. Jerusalem: Mossad HaRav Kook, 1958.

———. *Mishneh Torah: Hu HaYad HaḤazaqah LeRabbeinu Moshe ben Maimon. Sefer Neziqin*. Vol. 14, edited by Moshe Reich. Jerusalem: Mossad HaRav Kook, 1959.

———. *Mishneh Torah: Hu HaYad HaḤazaqah LeRabbeinu Moshe ben Maimon. Sefer Shofetim*. Vol. 17. Jerusalem: Mossad HaRav Kook, 1959.

———. *Mishneh Torah: The Book of Knowledge*, edited and translated by Moses Hyamson. Jerusalem: Boys Town Publishers, 1965.

———. *Sefer HaMitzwot: Book of Commandments*. Vol. 1, edited by Mordekhai Yehudah Leib Zaqash, translated by Yosef Kapaḥ. Jerusalem: Mossad HaRav Kook, 1958.

———. *Teshuvot HaRambam*, edited and translated by Yehoshua Blau. Jerusalem: Mekitzei Nirdamim Publishers, 1958.

Moshe ben Naḥman. "*Hasagot HaRamban LeSefer HaMitzvot LaRambam*." In Moshe ben Maimon, *Sefer HaMitzvot*, edited by Yitzḥak Simḥah Horowitz. Jerusalem, 1927 (*Shikheḥat HeAsin, Mitzvah Vav*).

———. *Peirushei HaTorah LeRabbeinu Moshe ben Naḥman (Ramban)*. Vol. 1. *Bereishit Shemot*, edited by Ḥaim Dov Chavel. Jerusalem: Mossad HaRav Kook, 1959.

———. *Peirushei HaTorah LeMoshe ben Naḥman*. 9th ed., edited by Ḥaim Dov Chavel. Jerusalem: Mossad HaRav Kook, 1976.

Moshe ben Yisrael Isserles. "*Peirush Rabbeinu HaRama al HaTorah*." In *Peirush Rabbeinu Yeshayah di Trani HaZaqen al HaTorah ve'al Nakh*, edited by Joseph Gad. London: L. Honig and Sons, 1957.

Moshe ben Yosef di Trani. *Qiryat Sefer*. Venice, 1551.

Moshe HaDarshan. *BeMidbar Rabbah*. Vilna edition, 1878. Reprinted in Jerusalem.

Moshe Isserles. *Rama al HaShulḥan Arukh*. In *Shulḥan Arukh: Oraḥ Ḥaim*. Vol. 1. New York: Grossman's Publishing House, 1954.

Moshe Yitzḥak Vorhand, *Sefer Birkat HaShem: Leqet Dinei Issur Qetzitzat Ilanei Ma'akhal, Bal Tashḥit BiShe'ar Devarim, VeIssur Hefsed UVizui Okhalim*. Jerusalem: private printing, 2000.

Naftali Tzvi Yehudah Berlin. *Shu"t Mashiv Davar*. Parts1 and 2. Jerusalem: private printing, 1968.

Nissim ben Moshe. *Ma'aseh Nissim: Peirush LaTorah LeRabbi Nissim ben Rabbi Moshe MiMarseille*, edited by Howard Kriesel. Jerusalem: Mekitzei Nirdamim, 2000.

Nissim ben Reuven Gerondi. *Rabbeinu Nissim ben Reuven Gerondi (HaRan): Peirush al HaTorah*, edited by Leon Aryeh Feldman. Jerusalem: Makhon Shalem, 1968.

Ovadiah Seforno. *Be'ur al HaTorah LeRabbi Ovadiah Seforno*, edited by Ze'ev Gottleib. Jerusalem: Mossad HaRav Kook, 1980.

Ovadiah Yosef. *Yabia Omer*. Vol. 8. *Ḥoshen Mishpat*. Jerusalem, 1995.

Pinḥas HaLevi (?). *Sefer HaḤinukh*, edited by Ḥaim Dov Chavel. Jerusalem: Mossad HaRav Kook, 1952.

Pinḥas HaLevi Horowitz. *Sefer HaMaqneh*. Offenbach, Germany: Tzvi Hirsch Spitz, 1824.

———. *Sefer Panim Yafot HaShalem al HaTorah*. Part 1: *Sefer Bereishit*. Jerusalem: private printing, 1998.

Pirqei deRabbi Eliezer. Higger edition. New York: Chorev, 1948.

Qohelet Rabbah. Vilna edition, 1893. Reprinted in Jerusalem.

Raphael Ashkenazi. *Sefer Mareh HaNogah*. Salonika, Greece: Sa'adi HaLevi Ashkenazi, 1840.

Saadiah Gaon. *Peirushei Rav Saadiah Gaon LiVereishit*, edited by Moshe Tzuker. New York: Beit HaMidrash LeRabanim BeAmerica, 1984.

———. *Rabbi Saadiah Gaon's Commentary on the Book of Creation*, edited and translated by Michael Linetzky. Northvale, NJ: Jason Aronson, 2002.

———. *Sefer Mitzvot LaRasag*, edited by Yehudah Yeruḥam Fishel Perale. Jerusalem: *Hotza'at Qeset*, 1973.

———. "*Targum HaTafsir shel Rav Saadiah Gaon.*" In *Torat Ḥaim—Devarim*, edited by Yosef Kapaḥ. Jerusalem: Mossad HaRav Kook, 1993.

Samson Raphael Hirsch. *Ḥamishah Ḥumshei Torah im Peirush Rashar Hirsch: Sefer Bereishit*. 4th ed., edited and translated by Mordekhai Breuer. Jerusalem: Mossad Yitzḥak Breuer, 1989.

———. *Ḥamishah Ḥumshei Torah im Peirush Rashar Hirsch: Sefer Devarim*. 4th ed., edited and translated by Mordekhai Breuer. Jerusalem: Mossad Yitzḥak Breuer, 1989.

———. *Horeb: A Philosophy of Jewish Laws and Observances*.Vol. 2. 2nd ed., translated by I. Grunfeld. London: Soncino Press, 1968.

Samuel ben Meir. *Peirush HaTorah LeRabbeinu Shmuel ben Meir*. Vol. 1. *Bereishit, Shemot*, edited by Martin I. Lockshin. Jerusalem: Chorev Publishing House, 2009.

———. *Peirush HaTorah LeRabbeinu Shmuel ben Meir*. Vol. 2. *VaYiqra, BeMidbar, Devarim*, edited by Martin I. Lockshin. Jerusalem: Chorev Publishing House, 2009.

———. *Rashbam's Commentary on Deuteronomy: An Annotated Translation*, edited and translated by Martin Lockshin. Providence, RI: Brown Judaic Studies, 2004.

Samuel David Luzzatto. *Peirush Shadal—Rabbi Shmuel David Luzzatto al Ḥamishah Ḥumshei Torah*. Tel-Aviv: Dvir Publishing, 1971.

Samuel de Medina. *She'elot UTeshuvot Maharashda"m: Oraḥ Ḥaim, Yoreh De'ah*, edited by David Avitan. Jerusalem: Zikhron Aharon, 2009.

Samuel of Rossano. *Sefer Rushaina: Peirush al Sefer Bereishit LeRabbeinu Shmuel MiRussiah*, edited by Moshe Weiss. Jerusalem: Mossad HaRav Kook, 1977.

———. *Sefer Rushaina: Peirush al Sefer BeMidbar—Devarim LeRabbeinu Shmuel MiRussiah*, edited by Moshe Weiss. Jerusalem: Mossad HaRav Kook, 1996.

The Schottenstein Edition Interlinear Chumash: Genesis, edited by Menachem Davis. New York: Mesorah Publications, 2006.

The Schottenstein Edition Interlinear Chumash: Leviticus, edited by Menachem Davis. New York: Mesorah Publications, 2008.

The Schottenstein Edition Interlinear Chumash: Deuteronomy, edited by Menachem Davis. New York: Mesorah Publications, 2009.

Sefer Midrash Aggadah al Ḥamishah Ḥumshei Torah, edited by Solomon Buber. Jerusalem: M. D. Bloom, 1961.

Shabbetai Cohen. *Sefer Siftei Cohen: Yoreh De'ah*. Krakow: Menaḥem Naḥum Maizlish, 1646.

Shimon HaDarshan. *Midrash Yalqut Shimoni: VaYiqra*, edited by Daniel Bitton. Jerusalem: HaMaor Institute, 2001.

———. *Yalqut Shimoni LeRabbeinu Shimon HaDarshan: Sefer Devarim*. Vol. 1: *Devarim—Shofetim*, edited by Aharon Heiman and Yitzhak Shiloni. Jerusalem: Mossad HaRav Kook, 1991.

Shimon Qayyara, *Sefer Halakhot Gedolot*. Jerusalem: Makhon Or HaMizraḥ and Makhon Yerushalayim, 1992.

Shlomo ben Aderet. *Peirushei Shlomo ben Aderet VeRabbeinu David bar Yosef Qimḥi al Ḥamishah Ḥumshei Torah*, edited by Joseph Gad. London: L. Honig and Sons Ltd., 1962.

Shlomo ben Gevirol. *"Peirush al HaTorah LeRabbeinu Shlomo ben Gevirol Zal."* In *Peirush Menaḥem Meiri al HaTorah*, edited by Yosef Gad. London: Hachinuch, 1957.

Shlomo ben Moshe HaLevi Alqabetz. *"Peirush Rabbeinu Shlomo Alqabetz HaLevi."* In *Peirush Rabbeinu Yeshayah di Trani HaZaqen al HaTorah ve'al Nakh*, edited by Joseph Gad. London: L. Honig and Sons, 1957.

Shlomo Ephraim of Lunshitz. *Sefer Keli Yaqar HaShalem*. Part1: *Bereishit, Shemot*. Jerusalem: Orot Ḥaim Publishing, 2001.

———. *Sefer Keli Yaqar HaShalem*. Part 2: *VaYiqra, BeMidbar, Devarim*. Jerusalem: Orot Ḥaim Publishing, 2001.

Shlomo Gantzfried. *Qitzur Shulḥan Arukh*. Vol. 2, edited by Elyaqim Shlanger. Bnei Braq, Israel: Seminar Be'er Yaakov, 1978.

Shlomo Luria. *Sefer Yam shel Shlomo al Masekhet Baba Qama*. Prague: 1616–1618.

Shlomo Yitzḥaki. *Nevi'im UKhetuvim HaMefo'ar Miqraot Gedolot: Melakhim*. Vol. 3. Jerusalem: HaḤumash HaMefo'ar, 1996.

———. *Peirushei Rashi al HaTorah*, edited by Ḥaim Dov Chavel, Jerusalem: Mossad HaRav Kook, 1982.

Shmuel ben Ḥofni Gaon. *Peirush HaTorah LeRav Shmuel ben Ḥofni Gaon*, edited and translated by Aaron Greenbaum. Jerusalem: Mossad HaRav Kook, 1979.

Shneiur Zalman. *Shulḥan Arukh HaRav*. Part 6: *Ḥoshen Mishpat*. Jerusalem: Even Yisroel Publishing, 2011.

Sifra, edited by I. Weiss. Vienna: Jacob Schlosberg Publishing, 1862.

Sifre DeVei Rav, Sifrei Zuta, edited by Ḥaim Shaul Horowitz. Jerusalem: Wahrmann, 1966.

Sifre Devarim, edited by L. Finkelstein. New York: Beit HaMidrash LeRabanim BeAmerica, 1969.

Sifre im Peirush Toledot Adam: Sefer BeMidbar, edited by Moshe David Avraham Troyes Ashkenazi. Jerusalem: Mossad HaRav Kook, 1972.

Siman Tov David. *Sefer al Pakkim Qetanim: Hilkhot Bal Tashḥit*. Jaffa, Israel: S. M. Publishers, 2000.

Solomon Dubno. *Sefer Netivot HaShalom: Sefer Bereishit*. Jerusalem, 1974.

Talmid HaRan. *Peirush al HaTorah Meyuhas LeTalmid Rabbeinu Nissim bar Reuven (HaRan)*, edited by Leon Aryeh Feldman. Jerusalem: Makhon Shalem, 1970.

Targum Yonatan, edited by S. Wertheimer. Jerusalem, 1997.

Tuvia bar Eliezer. *Midrash Leqaḥ Tov HaMekhuneh Pesiqta Zutarta al Ḥamishah Ḥumshei Torah—Bereishit*. Vol. 1, edited by Shlomo Buber. Israel: Books Export Enterprises, 1960.

———. *Midrash Leqaḥ Tov HaMekhuneh Pesiqta Zutarta al Ḥamishah Ḥumshei Torah—VaYiqra*. Vol. 2, edited by Shlomo Buber. Israel: Books Export Enterprises, 1960.

———. *Midrash Leqaḥ Tov HaMekhuneh Pesiqta Zutarta al Ḥamishah Ḥumshei Torah—Devarim*. Vol. 2, edited by Shlomo Buber. Israel: Books Export Enterprises, 1960.

Tzvi Hirsch Ashkenazi. *Sefer She'elot UTeshuvot Ḥakham Tzvi HaShalem*. Tel-Aviv: Leon Publishing, 1963.

Tzvi Pesaḥ Frank. *Sefer Har Tzvi: Oraḥ Ḥaim*, Part 2. Jerusalem, 1973.

Yaakov bar Asher. *Peirush HaTur al HaTorah LeHaRabbi Yaakov ben HaRosh*. Vol. 1: *Bereishit—Shemot*, edited by Yaakov Kapel Reinitz. Jerusalem: Feldheim Publishers, 2006.

———. *Peirush HaTur al HaTorah LeHaRabbi Yaakov ben HaRosh*. Vol. 2: *VaYiqra—Devarim*, edited by Yaakov Kapel Reinitz. Jerusalem: Feldheim Publishers, 2006.

———. *Tur: Ḥoshen Mishpat*. Vol. 2. Jerusalem: Makhon Ḥatam Sofer, 1972.

———. *Tur: Yoreh De'ah*. Vol. 2. Jerusalem: Makhon Ḥatam Sofer, 1972.

Yaakov Reischer. *Sefer She'elot UTeshuvot Shevut Yaakov*. Part 1. Jerusalem: Luḥot Frank, 2003.

———. *Sefer She'elot UTeshuvot Shevut Yaakov*. Part 3. Jerusalem: Luḥot Frank, 2003.

Yair Ḥaim Bakhrakh. *Sefer She'elot UTeshuvot Ḥavot Yair*, edited by Shimon ben-Tzion HaCohen Kots. Ramat-Gan, Israel: Makhon Akad Sefarim, 1997.

Yeḥezkel Landau. *Sefer Noda BiYehudah, Mahadurah Tinyana, Yoreh De'ah*. Part 1, 10, edited by David Aharon Freundlich. Jerusalem: Makhon Yerushalayim, 2004.

Yeḥiel Mikhel HaLevi Epstein. *Sefer Arukh HaShulḥan: Ḥoshen Mishpat, Hilkhot Ḥalukat Shutafut*. Vol. 1. Jerusalem, 1973.

———. *Sefer Arukh HaShulḥan: Yoreh De'ah*. Vol. 2. Jerusalem, 1973.

Yehudah HaLevi. "*Peirush Qitzur MiSefer HaKuzari al HaTorah*." In *Peirush Rabbeinu Yosef Bekhor Shor*. Part 2, edited by Joseph Gad. London: HaMadfis, 1960.

Yehudah ben Shmuel HeḤasid. *Sefer Ḥasidim*. Bologna, 1538.

Yehudah HeḤasid. *Peirushei HaTorah LeRabbi Yehudah HeḤasid*, edited by Isaak Shimshon Lange. Jerusalem: Daf Ḥen Ltd., 1975.

Yeshayah di Trani HaZaqen. *Peirush Rabbeinu Yeshayah di Trani HaZaqen al HaTorah ve'al Nakh*, edited by Joseph Gad. London: L. Honig and Sons, 1957.

Yisrael Meir HaCohen. *Sefer Mishnah Berurah, Oraḥ Ḥaim*. Vol. 1. Jerusalem: Va'ad HaYeshivot BeEretz Yisrael, 1972.

———. *Sefer Mishnah Berurah, Oraḥ Ḥaim, Hilkhot Tishah BeAv VeSha'ar Ta'aniyot*. Vol. 6. Jerusalem: Va'ad HaYeshivot BeEretz Yisrael, 1973.

Yitzḥak Arama. *Sefer Aqeidat Yitzḥak*. Vol. 1, edited by Avigdor Katz. Jerusalem, 1961.

———. *Sefer Aqeidat Yitzḥak*. Vol. 1, edited by Avigdor Katz. Jerusalem, 1961.

Yitzḥak Caro. *Toledot Yitzḥak*. Jerusalem: Makor Publishing, 1978.

Yitzhak Eliyahu Shtasman. *Sefer Etz HaSadeh: BeDinei Bal Tashḥit, Qetzitzat Ilanot UVizui Okhalin*. Jerusalem: Foundation for the Advancement of Torah Study, 1999.

Yitzḥak Zilberstein. *Ḥashuqei Ḥemed al Masekhet Baba Qama*. Jerusalem, 2009.

Yoel Sirkis. "*Bayit Ḥadash: Yoreh De'ah*." In *Tur: Ḥoshen Mishpat*. Vol. 1. Jerusalem: Makhon Ḥatam Sofer, 1972.

———. "*Bayit Ḥadash: Yoreh De'ah*." In *Tur: Yoreh De'ah*. Vol. 1. Jerusalem: Makhon Ḥatam Sofer, 1972.

Yoḥanan Luria. *Sefer Meshivat Nefesh: Be'urim al HaTorah Me'Et Rabbeinu Yoḥanan Luria Zatzal*, edited by Yaakov Hoffmann. Jerusalem: Mifal Torat Ḥakhmei Ashkenaz, Makhon Yerushalayim, 1993.

Yonah of Gerona. *Derashot UPheirushei Rabbeinu Yonah Gerondi LeḤamishah Ḥumshei Torah*, edited by Shmuel Yerushalmi. Jerusalem: Ḥ. Vagshel, 1980.

———. *Sha'arei Teshuvah*. Venice, 1544.

Yosef ben David. *Peirush al HaTorah LeRabbeinu Yosef ben David MeSaragossa*, edited by Leon Aryeh Feldman. Jerusalem: Makhon Shalem, 1973.

Yosef Dov Ber HaLevi Soloveitchik. *Sefer MiShulḥano shel Beit HaLevi*, edited by Y. Hershkovitz. Jerusalem: private printing, 2004.

Yosef Ḥaim ben Eliyahu. *Sefer Torah LiShmah*. Jerusalem: Offset Re'em, 1976.

Yosef Karo. "*Beit Yosef: Ḥoshen Mishpat*." In *Tur: Ḥoshen Mishpat*. Vol. 1. Jerusalem: Makhon Ḥatam Sofer, 1972.

———. "*Beit Yosef: Ḥoshen Mishpat*." In *Tur: Yoreh De'ah*. Vol. 2. Jerusalem: Makhon Ḥatam Sofer, 1972.

———. "*Kesef Mishneh: Sefer Shofetim*." In *Mishneh Torah: Hu HaYad HaḤazaqah LeRabbeinu Moshe bar Maimon Zal. Sefer Shofetim*. Vol. 12, edited by Shabse Frankel. New York: Congregation Bnei Yosef, 1998.

———. *Shulḥan Arukh: Ḥoshen Mishpat, with All Commentaries*. Vol. 2. New York: Grossman's Publishing House, 1954.

———. *Shulḥan Arukh: Yoreh De'ah, with All Commentaries*. Vol. 1. New York: Grossman's Publishing House, 1954.

———. *Shulḥan Arukh: Yoreh De'ah, with All Commentaries*. Vol. 2. New York: Grossman's Publishing House, 1954.

———. *Shulḥan Arukh: Yoreh De'ah, with All Commentaries*. Vol. 3. New York: Grossman's Publishing House, 1954.

Yosef Teomim. *Sefer Pri Megadim, Mishbetzot Zahav, Oraḥ Ḥaim*. Frankfurt an der Oder, Prussia: Defus Almanat Grila, 1787.

———. *Sefer Teivat Gomeh,* edited by Shmuel Einstein. Bnei Braq, Israel: private printing, 1998.

Concept Index

Abrahamic, 2, 256
Amorite, 64, 88, 149, 191, 194. *See also* Foreign cultural practices; Idol worship
Antediluvian, 132, 134n75
  postdiluvian, 134, 137
Anthropocentrism, 46–47, 130, 164–165, 182, 239, 243, 246–252
  weak anthropocentrism, 47
Asherah, 186–187, 189
Asmakhta, 141

Bal tashḥit degufa adif, 19, 40, 79–81, 83, 97–98, 125–126, 200, 209, 212, 214, 232, 237–238
  Bal tashḥit degufai adif, 80, 237
Beard. *See* facial hair
Benefit, 7, 9, 11, 16, 18, 26, 32, 36–37, 46, 48, 62, 81, 84, 98, 107, 114–116, 118–121, 130, 150, 159, 179–180, 182, 187–188, 205–206, 209–210, 212, 214–215, 220–221, 223, 227, 231, 241, 244, 249, 251, 254, 256
Benevolence, 124

Capital punishment, 136, 172, 240
Carbon storage, 130
Chain of transmission. *See* tradent
Climate change, xi, 14, 255
Commandment
  negative, 43–44, 121–122, 179, 211
  positive, 43–44, 186, 211
Commons, 40, 83–87
Compassion, 43, 118–120, 131, 159, 246
Consumption, xii, 21, 24, 26, 30, 57, 71, 82–84, 132–134, 136–138, 161, 165, 179, 188, 191–192, 210, 212, 219, 251
  Overconsumption, xii, 14, 254
Corporal punishment, 172, 240

Deep ecology, 19, 47, 162
Deluge, 131, 134
Derekh bizayon, 215, 232
Derekh hashḥatah, 16, 18, 170–174, 176, 180, 188–189, 193, 199, 201, 205–209, 211, 215, 218–222, 231–232, 239, 250
Derekh nitzayon. See *Derekh bizayon*
Destructive intent, Destructive manner. See *Derekh hashḥatah*
Diḥui be'alma, 79, 140
Disposable/s, 228–230, 233, 252–254
Dominion, 2, 7–11, 122–123, 126, 160. *See also* Gen 1:28, Gen 2:15

Ecocentrism, 165, 243–246
EcoJudaism, 6, 26

Ecotheology, xi, 5–7
ecotheologian, xi, 4, 27
Ecofeminists, 47
Ein ra'u'i, 117–118, 131
Electricity, xii, 174n12, 228–229
Embarrassment, 59, 74, 155, 191, 215
Enjoyment, 16, 18, 36, 107, 114, 118, 150, 159, 179–181, 187, 205, 212, 223, 227, 231, 241, 251. See also *Hana'ah*
Environmental ethic, xii, 13–14, 19–23, 25–26, 28, 31, 37, 39, 57–58, 87, 95, 130–131, 139, 150, 161–162, 175, 181, 230, 235, 238, 241–242, 257
Environmental ethics, 6, 12, 24, 26–27, 29, 45–46, 128, 150
Environmental protection, 28, 36, 46–47, 86, 162
Environmental responsibility, 8
Environmentalism, 1, 4, 7, 12, 20–21, 23–24, 33, 100, 160, 164–165, 232, 255, 257
Environmentalists, xi–xii, 1, 3, 7, 10, 13, 20–21, 27, 29, 33–34, 84, 105n6, 131, 230, 233, 252–253, 255, 257
Excessive, 26, 75, 182, 184, 194–195, 201. See also *Yoter Midai*
excessiveness, 182
Exploit. *See* Exploitation
Exploitation, 2–3, 27, 47, 165
overexploitation, 84, 165

Facial hair, 16, 73, 75, 145–148, 150–151, 157, 161
Five senses, 147, 150
Food source, 26, 113, 119–120, 123, 128, 130, 244, 249
Food waste. *See* Waste of food
Foreign cultural practices, 40, 87–89, 185, 190. *See also* Idol worship

General prohibition against wastefulness, 12, 15, 17, 20, 34–35, 48, 55, 75–76, 79, 95, 102, 108, 114, 116, 122, 126–127, 130–131, 143, 149–150, 157–159, 164, 170, 177, 180, 184, 199, 201, 204, 236, 238–239, 244
General wastefulness. *See* General prohibition against wastefulness
Gentile, 132, 140, 146–147, 149, 179, 209, 211, 213, 218, 220, 223–224
God's image, 138
God's representatives, 138–139
Goring ox, 133, 136, 142

Hana'ah, 16, 114, 116, 118, 150, 159, 205, 209–210, 212, 214, 218, 220–221, 223, 231, 241, 251
yesh alav hana'ah, 18, 107
Harm
direct, 97
indirect, 37, 62, 97–98
Hierarchical. *See* Hierarchy
Hierarchy, 4, 17, 19, 32, 40, 43–47, 97, 113, 124, 225, 232, 236, 255
Human welfare, 81, 83, 125–126, 227
Humiliation, 72–74
Hunting, 9, 85, 223n30, 226–227, 245

Idol worship, 40, 65, 73, 76, 87–89, 106, 144, 149, 153, 176, 181–182, 185–191, 199, 227n39, 236. *See also* Pagan; Foreign cultural practices; Amorite
Idolatrous, Idolatry. *See* Idol worship
Imitatio Dei, 159
Inculcate (good character), 46n10, 121, 162, 205, 223–226
Indirect nature, 48
Intellectual history/ies. *See* Tradition history/ies

Ki ha'adam etz hasadeh (Deuteronomy 20:19), 41–44, 46, 53, 107, 109–111, 113, 115–120, 123, 125–129, 162–163, 243
Kilayim, 147, 245

Luxury, 71, 81

Maimonidean, 16, 99, 171, 174, 191, 201, 204, 215
Mastery. *See* Dominion
Midrash Aggadah, 16, 18, 103, 107, 114, 116, 150, 157, 159, 205, 221, 231, 241, 251
Morally culpable, 135
Mourning, 64–65, 182, 190–195, 199, 217
Murder, 16, 63, 115, 131–144, 152, 161, 163

Nature, 2–3, 5–7, 11n38, 14, 25, 27–28, 36–37, 47–48, 64, 87, 161, 165, 181, 251
Nonsentient, 131, 225–226, 231
Nonsubstantive casting aside; Nonsubstantive rejection. See *Diḥui be'alma*

Ownerless, 32, 40, 85–86, 179–180, 223, 227, 230, 241
Ownership, 84, 86–87, 144, 165
Ox that gores. *See* Goring ox

Pagan, 2, 87, 146, 148. *See also* Idol worship
Peace, 12, 53, 106, 123, 130, 153–154, 156, 175, 191, 197–198, 225, 247
Peaceful. *See* Peace
Peshat, 103–104, 133, 156, 158, 163
Plastic surgery, 205, 215
Potential, xi, 12, 24, 26, 98, 151, 206, 212, 214, 221, 237, 251, 256–257
Pro-environmental behavior, 130

Pyrrhic victory, 128

Recycling, 24, 34, 229–230, 232
Reimagining religion, 5–7
Religion and environment, 1–4, 21, 46, 105
Religious environmentalism, 4, 7
environmentalists, 3
Ritual slaughter, 84, 195–197, 199

Scorched-earth, 114, 116, 118, 126, 153, 156, 238
Scriptural support. See *Asmakhta*
Sefer HaḤinukh, 16, 18, 32, 127, 162, 168, 175–176, 182, 205, 218, 224, 230–231, 241, 247–248, 251
Self-interest, 40, 84
Siege, 12, 22, 41–44, 72, 106–107, 109–120, 122–123, 126, 130, 153–154, 156, 169–170, 172, 174
Sinful, 71, 184
Splendor, 146–147, 150
Smoking, 205, 216
Steward. *See* Stewardship
Stewardship, xii, 4, 7–9, 11, 25, 84, 242
Suicide, 16, 19, 53, 63–64, 77n55, 79, 131–144, 150, 161, 163–164
Sustainability, 4, 14, 28, 46–47, 98, 165
Sustenance, 46, 109, 111–112, 115–116, 119–120, 122, 124, 128, 130, 245

Theocentrism, 144, 165, 243
To'elet, 16, 18, 115–116, 118, 120, 150, 159, 205, 209, 212, 217–218, 231, 241, 251. *See also* Utility
Tradent, 41, 69–70, 75, 140, 177
Tradition history/ies, 1, 4, 7, 10–11, 15–16, 20–21, 28, 32, 65, 93, 107, 128–129, 145, 163–165, 171, 235, 242

Tree
fig tree, 49, 51, 53, 115
good tree, 120, 153–154, 156, 170
last tree, 96, 164, 237
non-fruit-bearing tree, 40, 43–46, 49, 51, 54, 107, 110, 113–114, 117–119, 122, 124–125, 130, 154, 156, 170, 174, 176
Tza'ar ba'alei ḥayim, 86, 192, 214, 222, 227
Tzorekh, 16, 18, 113, 131, 150, 159, 205, 207, 210, 214, 217–218, 222–223, 226, 231, 240, 251

Usefulness. *See* Utility
Utility, 16, 26, 31, 37, 46, 57, 113, 115–116, 118, 120, 126, 130–131, 150, 159, 175, 205, 209, 212, 214, 217–218, 221, 230–231, 235, 241, 248, 251. See also *To'elet*

Value
inherent, 30, 46–47, 51, 130, 230
instrumental, 46–47, 64, 96, 162
intrinsic, 46, 51, 57, 96–97, 130, 150, 162, 165, 181–182, 224, 226, 230, 241, 243–247, 250–252
Vegetarian, 134n75, 136

Wartime, 12, 16, 26, 45, 53, 129–130, 156, 170–171, 175, 187n35
Waste of food, 93, 113, 174, 254, 256
Wastefulness in general. *See* General prohibition against wastefulness
Well-being, 57, 70, 79–80, 154, 212, 238, 255
Wise use, 122, 165
Worldview, 28, 30, 46

Yoter Midai, 182

Name Index

Alsheikh, Moshe, 118–119, 137–138, 143, 149, 163, 246

bar Asher, Baḥya, 16, 18, 114–116, 122, 135–136, 142–143, 147, 150–151, 157, 159, 164, 205, 218, 223, 231, 241, 251
bar Eliyahu, Meyuḥas, 16, 32, 110, 113–114, 131, 134–135, 142–143, 149–150, 157–159, 163, 205, 218, 222–223, 231, 240–241, 251
bar Naḥmani, Rabbah, 17, 60, 80, 82–83, 237
Bechhofer, Yosef Gavriel, 34, 228–230, 232
ben Azariah, Eleazar, 17, 19, 62–70, 75–76, 78–79, 95–96, 140, 152n125, 182, 194, 217–218, 235–236
ben Naḥman, Moshe, 9, 78, 110–112, 114, 117, 123, 129, 135–136, 143, 181–182, 245
ben Maimon, Moshe, 16–17, 19, 22, 32, 77, 113, 122–126, 167–177, 180, 182, 184–194, 199–202, 204–208, 210–213, 215–216, 219, 221–225, 230, 232, 239, 245, 250
ben Yeḥiel Luria, Shlomo, 19, 76–77, 99, 223–224, 256
ben Yosef, Akiva, 17, 19, 58–62, 67, 70, 74–77, 235–236, 238, 255
ben Yosef, Saadiah, 8–9, 15, 102–103, 105, 108–109, 132, 163, 168n3
Benstein, Jeremy, 22, 86

Callicott, J. Baird, 19
Cohen, Jeremy, 7, 15, 104–105

David, Siman Tov, 35, 253
de Boton, Abraham, 19, 77–78, 99, 182, 185, 256

Epstein, Barukh HaLevi, 19–20, 64, 79, 99, 114, 116, 125–126, 140–141, 143, 157–158, 200–201, 256
Ettlinger, Jacob, 19, 78–79, 99–100, 208–209, 212–213, 256

Gantzfried, Shlomo, 19, 178–181, 195, 202, 256
Gottleib, Roger, 1–2, 4, 19

HaLevi, Pinḥas. See *Sefer HaḤinukh*
HaMeiri, Menaḥem ben Shlomo, 19, 76, 99, 256
Hardin, Garrett, 83, 98
Hirsch, Samson (Shimshon) Raphael, 18, 32, 99–100, 112, 114, 116, 121–123, 126, 130, 138–139, 142–143, 152, 157–158, 160–161, 163, 165, 176, 241–242, 249–250

Ibn Ezra, Abraham, 111–115, 119–121, 125, 128, 133, 142, 146–147, 149–150, 162–163, 230, 243–244

Jacobs, Louis, 66
Jenkins, Willis, 3–4
Jesus, 89–94, 235

Karo, Yosef, 16, 168, 178, 187–188, 190, 192–196, 200–201, 208, 215, 219–220, 240

Lipschutz, Israel 19, 78, 99, 256
Luzzatto, Samuel David, 119–121, 125, 138, 142–143, 155n135, 163, 249

Maimonides. *See* ben Maimon, Moshe

Naḥmanides. *See* ben Naḥman, Moshe
Neḥemiah, Rabbi, 17, 74–75, 235n2
Nir, David, 23, 29–31, 37
Norton, Bryan, 47

Rakover, Nahum, 36–37
Rambam. *See* ben Maimon, Moshe
Ramban. *See* ben Naḥman, Moshe
Rashi. *See* Yitzḥaki, Shlomo
Ravina, 17, 49–50, 96, 173, 203–204, 210, 212, 235–236, 238, 250
Rolston, Holmes, III, 47, 150n122

Saadiah Gaon. *See* ben Yosef, Saadiah
Schorr, Alexander Sender, 82, 208, 213, 220n25, 240
Schwartz, Eilon, 23, 29–30, 37, 87, 129–130
Seidenberg, David Mevorach, 6–7, 11n38
Shikheḥat, 53, 207n9, 210, 213
Shiveḥat, 49, 206–207, 210, 213, 224
Shtasman, Yitzḥak Eliyahu, 35, 54n23, 204n2, 228, 232, 253–254
Sokol, Moshe, 159

Taylor, Bron, 2–3
Tucker, Mary Evelyn and John Grim, 3, 5

Vorhand, Moshe Yitzḥak, 35, 204n2, 228–229, 233, 252–254

Waskow, Arthur, 6, 23, 27–28
Wazana, Nili, 129
White, Lynn, Jr., 2–4, 7–8, 12, 160
Wright, Jacob L., 50

Yitzḥaki, Shlomo, 71, 109, 113, 115, 117–121, 128–129, 133, 154, 156, 162, 192–193, 230, 243–244, 247
Yonah of Gerona, 19, 75–76, 99, 175, 226, 256

Zalman, Shneiur, of Liadi, 19, 86, 178–181, 197, 202, 227, 256
Zilberstein, Yitzḥak, 20, 70n46, 217–218, 232, 256

Source Index

Bible
Genesis
1:28, 2, 7–10, 13, 27, 123, 126, 139, 160
2:15, 7, 10–13, 84, 139, 160
9:4, 132, 134
9:5, 16, 18, 20, 40, 54, 62–64, 73–79, 96–97, 100, 131–144, 148, 150, 157, 160–161, 163–164, 185, 236, 242, 262–264
9:6, 132, 141, 144
32:25, 249
37:34, 194
Exodus
20:12, 144
21:12, 144
21:28, 133, 136
34:13, 87
Leviticus
5:4, 61
10:6–7, 45
19:14, 85
19:27, 16, 75, 104, 144–152, 157, 161, 164
19:37, 145
21:5, 146
Numbers
6:11, 71, 78, 183–184
Deuteronomy
4:9, 179, 181
4:15, 181n24, 185
5:16, 144
6:5, 67
7:5, 87, 186–187, 189
12:2, 186–187
12:3, 186–187, 189
12:4, 189
14:1, 182
20:16, 106n9
20:19, 12, 15–16, 18, 20, 22, 24–26, 29, 41–42, 44–45, 50, 53–54, 75, 95, 102, 104, 106–131, 143, 145, 148, 150–151, 153–165, 169–171, 174, 179, 187, 200, 210, 230, 236, 242–243, 246, 249, 252, 259–262
20:20, 12, 15, 20, 22, 24–26, 29, 41–42, 44, 49, 54, 102, 104, 106–131, 148, 153, 156–158, 160–162, 164, 176, 259–262
ch. 21, 117
23:7, 156
23:8, 248
1 Samuel
ch. 24, 226
31:4–5, 133
2 Samuel
1:6–9, 133
21:6, 133
1 Kings
ch. 1, 226
2 Kings
3:19, 16, 56, 104, 123, 126, 152–156, 174
3:25, 16, 104, 123, 152–156

Isaiah
44:23 166
50:6 72–73
55:12 166
Jeremiah
34:5 191
Micah
4:14 72–73
Psalms
3:8, 72–73
96:12, 166
ch. 104, 245
ch. 114, 245
145:9, 246
148:7–12, 166
Proverbs
23:6–7, 85
Job
38:14, 89
Ecclesiastes
5:9, 183
7:16, 184
1 Chronicles
16:31–33, 166

Mishnah
Avot
4:3, 226
Baba Metzia
7:5, 196n70
Baba Qama
8:6, 17, 57–59, 236
Kilayim
ch. 2, 210
Shevi'it
4:10, 49n17

Tosefta
Baba Qama
ch. 9, 113
9:31, 17, 72–73, 96, 139, 141, 174, 176n15, 185, 231
Shabbat
7:18, 193

Babylonian Talmud
Avodah Zarah
11a, 192, 222
23b, 88
Baba Batra
4a, 190
26a, 49n18, 51–53, 170, 172, 207n9
Baba Qama
50b, 86
86b, 225
90b, 57–59, 217
91a, 60–72, 125, 141, 215
91b, 17, 39, 43, 48, 60–72, 74–76, 78, 88, 95, 96, 115, 122, 124, 140–142, 162n146, 172–173, 178, 182, 194, 206–208, 210–212, 219, 232, 236–237
92a, 43, 48, 172, 206, 208
92b, 118, 120, 148
Berakhot
31a, 224
61b, 67n37
62b, 226
Ḥullin
2a, 218
7b, 39, 74, 84–86, 95, 214, 223
8a–b, 188
Makkot
22a, 169
Megillah
26b, 210
Mo'ed Qatan
27a, 190–191
Niddah
13a, 78
Pesaḥim
25a, 67–68
50b, 55
Qiddushin
32a, 74, 174, 197
Sanhedrin
59b, 134n75
74a, 67n37, 144n101, 237
86a, 74n50, 235n2
90a, 186

Shabbat
67a, 88
67b, 74, 88, 108, 220
105b, 75, 113, 176n15
129a, 17, 74, 79–80, 82–83, 97–98, 209, 237
140b, 80–82, 97–98, 237
Shavu'ot
27a, 62
Sota
12a, 67
Sukkah
52b, 133
Ta'anit
7a, 54, 95
20b, 82
31a, 221
Yevamot
11b–12a, 56–57
44a, 219
44b, 221
Yoma
82a, 67–68

Minor Tractates
Semaḥot
9:23, 39, 74, 88–89, 95, 182, 190–191
Semaḥot, Baraitot meEvel Rabbati
4:11, 88–89, 190

Midrash Halakhah
Sifra (Weiss edition)
Qedoshim 6:4–6, 145n103
Qedoshim 10:6–7, 45, 55
Sifre BeMidbar (Ashkenazi edition)
Naso 30, 71
Sifre Devei Rav (Horowitz edition)
35:27, 63n30, 142
Sifre Devarim (Finkelstein edition)
Shofetim 203–204, 43–45
Midrash Tannaim al Sefer Devarim (Hoffmann edition)
20:19, 44–45

Midrash Aggadah
Bereishit Rabbah (Theodor/Albeck edition)
Bereishit 10, 245
Noaḥ 34, 9:5, 63n30, 77n55, 142
Midrash Tanḥuma (Buber edition)
Pinḥas 5, 153n127
Matot 5, 249
Pirqei DeRabbi Eliezer (Higger edition)
ch. 33, 115, 117, 246
Qohelet Rabbah (Vilna edition)
7:13, 247–249
Bemidbar Rabbah (Vilna edition)
Pinḥas 21:6, 153, 156
Midrash Leqaḥ Tov (Buber edition)
Bereishit – Noaḥ 9:5, 132
Devarim—Shofetim 34a, 110, 128–129
Yalqut Shimoni (Bitton edition)
Qedoshim 19:690, 145–146
Yalqut Shimoni (Heiman/Shiloni edition)
Shofetim 923, 108, 114

Classical Christian Literature
The New Testament
John
6:1–12, 90–91
12:1–8, 91–93
Mark 14:1–9, 91–92
Matthew 14:1–9, 91–92